The Lofts of SoHo

HISTORICAL STUDIES OF URBAN AMERICA

Edited by Lilia Fernández, Timothy J. Gilfoyle, and Amanda I. Seligman
James R. Grossman, Editor Emeritus

RECENT TITLES IN THE SERIES

Nicholas Dagen Bloom, *The Great American Transit Disaster: A Century of Austerity, Auto-Centric Planning, and White Flight*

Sean T. Dempsey, *City of Dignity: Christianity, Liberalism, and the Making of Global Los Angeles*

Claire Dunning, *Nonprofit Neighborhoods: An Urban History of Inequality and the American State*

Tracy E. K'Meyer, *To Live Peaceably Together: The American Friends Service Committee's Campaign for Open Housing*

Mike Amezcua, *Making Mexican Chicago: From Postwar Settlement to the Age of Gentrification*

Arnold R. Hirsch, *Making the Second Ghetto: Race and Housing in Chicago, 1940–1960*, With a New Afterword by N. D. B. Connolly

William Sites, *Sun Ra's Chicago: Afrofuturism and the City*

David Schley, *Steam City: Railroads, Urban Space, and Corporate Capitalism in Nineteenth-Century Baltimore*

Rebecca K. Marchiel, *After Redlining: The Urban Reinvestment Movement in the Era of Financial Deregulation*

Steven T. Moga, *Urban Lowlands: A History of Neighborhoods, Poverty, and Planning*

Andrew S. Baer, *Beyond the Usual Beating: The Jon Burge Police Torture Scandal and Social Movements for Police Accountability in Chicago*

Matthew Vaz, *Running the Numbers: Race, Police, and the History of Urban Gambling*

Ann Durkin Keating, *The World of Juliette Kinzie: Chicago before the Fire*

Jeffrey S. Adler, *Murder in New Orleans: The Creation of Jim Crow Policing*

David A. Gamson, *The Importance of Being Urban: Designing the Progressive School District, 1890–1940*

Kara Murphy Schlichting, *New York Recentered: Building the Metropolis from the Shore*

Mark Wild, *Renewal: Liberal Protestants and the American City after World War II*

Meredith Oda, *The Gateway to the Pacific: Japanese Americans and the Remaking of San Francisco*

Sean Dinces, *Bulls Markets: Chicago's Basketball Business and the New Inequality*

Julia Guarneri, *Newsprint Metropolis: City Papers and the Making of Modern Americans*

Kyle B. Roberts, *Evangelical Gotham: Religion and the Making of New York City, 1783–1860*

Amanda I. Seligman, *Chicago's Block Clubs: How Neighbors Shape the City*

Timothy Neary, *Crossing Parish Boundaries: Race, Sports, and Catholic Youth in Chicago, 1914–1954*

Julia Rabig, *The Fixers: Devolution, Development, and Civil Society in Newark, 1960–1990*

Additional series titles follow index

The Lofts of SoHo

Gentrification, Art, and Industry in New York, 1950–1980

AARON SHKUDA

The University of Chicago Press
Chicago and London

FOR CHRISSY AND MY PARENTS

The University of Chicago Press, Chicago 60637
The University of Chicago Press, Ltd., London
© 2016 by The University of Chicago
All rights reserved. No part of this book may be used or reproduced in any manner whatsoever without written permission, except in the case of brief quotations in critical articles and reviews. For more information, contact the University of Chicago Press, 1427 E. 60th St., Chicago, IL 60637.
Published 2016
Paperback edition 2024

33 32 31 30 29 28 27 26 25 24   1 2 3 4 5

ISBN-13: 978-0-226-33418-9 (cloth)
ISBN-13: 978-0-226-83341-5 (paper)
ISBN-13: 978-0-226-33421-9 (e-book)
DOI: https://doi.org/10.7208/chicago/9780226334219.001.0001

Publication is made possible in part by a grant from the Barr Ferree Foundation Publication Fund, Department of Art and Archaeology, Princeton University.

Library of Congress Cataloging-in-Publication Data

Shkuda, Aaron, author.
    The lofts of SoHo : gentrification, art, and industry in New York, 1950 –1980 / Aaron Shkuda.
       pages cm—(Historical studies of urban america)
    Includes bibliography and index.
    ISBN 978-0-226-33418-9 (cloth : alk. paper)—ISBN 978-0-226-33421-9 (e-book) 1. SoHo (New York, N.Y.)—History—20th century.   2. Artist—Housing—New York (State).   3. Artists—Dwellings—New York (State)—New York.
4. Artist colonies—New York (State)—New York—History—20th century.
5. Gentrification—New York (State)—New York. I. Title.   II. Title: Gentrification art, and industry in New York, 1950 –1980.   III. Series: Historical studies of urban America.
  F128.68.S64S55 2016
  700.974709'04—dc23

2015034612

Contents

Introduction: Art, Artists, and Gentrification 1

1 The Wastelands of New York 12

2 Making the Artist Loft 42

3 Gray Areas and Industrial Slums: The Lower Manhattan Expressway 71

4 Artist Organizations, Political Advocacy, and the Creation of a Residential SoHo 92

5 Moving Art Downtown 107

6 Real Estate and SoHo Politics: Loft Promotion and Historic Preservation in Lower Manhattan 133

7 The Embourgeoisement of SoHo 158

8 The Spread of Loft Living: Real Estate Development and Tenant Conflict in SoHo and Beyond 182

9 Making New York a Loft Living City 209

Conclusion: Contemporary SoHo and the Neighborhood's Significance 230

Acknowledgments 239
Notes 243
Bibliography 273
Index 283

Introduction

Art, Artists, and Gentrification

To find the next hot real estate market, the saying goes, one only needs to "follow the drips of paint" to the latest neighborhood colonized and redeveloped by artists. The power of the arts to reinvigorate moribund urban neighborhoods seems to have no bounds, particularly in New York City. Take, for example, the recent history of Bushwick, Brooklyn, an area closely associated with New York's post–World War II economic and demographic decline, particularly the looting that occurred after the city's 1977 blackout. Musicians, visual artists, and writers began to move into unfinished, unheated Bushwick lofts in the 1990s. By 2002, the opening of a nonprofit arts space in a former industrial building and a coffee shop that quickly became a local hangout brought a critical mass of artists to the neighborhood. In 2004 and 2005, more cafés and artist-affiliated restaurants sprang up, followed by luxury condos and a well-publicized art festival. By 2006, artists were beginning to be displaced by rising housing prices driven by real estate investment and speculation. While the rapid redevelopment of Bushwick might have been startling to some, its evolution from empty lofts to artist community to upper-class neighborhood was familiar—it repeated the "story of SoHo."[1]

SoHo, the New York City neighborhood located south of Houston Street in Lower Manhattan, is frequently presented as the progenitor of a new form of twentieth-century urban development. In the 1960s, artists began to move into lofts in this light industrial neighborhood. Art galleries debuted in the late 1960s and early 1970s. Restaurants and boutiques quickly followed, and upper-income professionals found SoHo an increasingly attractive place to live. By the late 1970s, artists were being priced out and sought homes and studios in other parts of the city.

Since the neighborhood's transformation from industrial area to artist

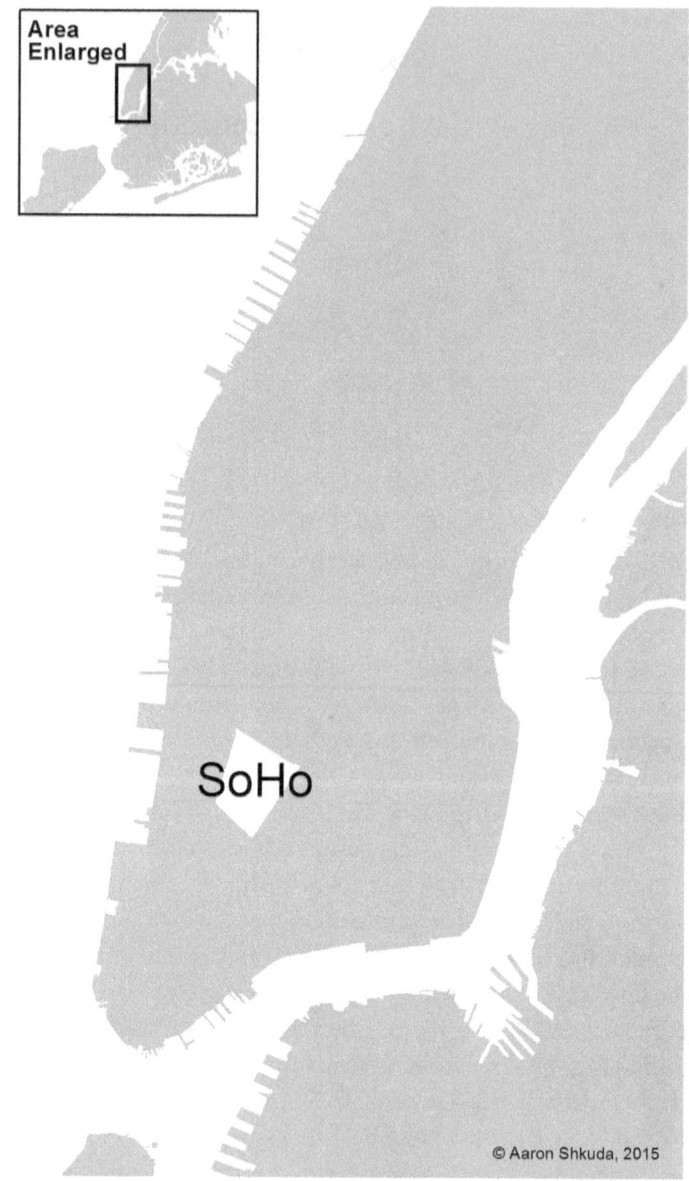

FIGURE 1. Map of SoHo.

enclave to upper-income neighborhood, New Yorkers have been anticipating the "next SoHo." *New York Magazine* observed the "SoHo-ization" of Long Island City, Queens, in 1980. Hoboken, New Jersey, was marked as the next SoHo in 1982. Five years later, debate raged over whether Williamsburg, Brooklyn, would become the next SoHo. By many accounts, it earned the title in the early 1990s. At the end of the century, the Manhattan neighborhood of West Chelsea was the "latest 'next SoHo,'" followed by the nearby Meatpacking District. The opening of the Dia:Beacon art center in a renovated Nabisco box printing factory won the Hudson River mill town of Beacon, New York, the status of the next SoHo in 2004. By 2014, Gowanus, "Brooklyn's Coolest Superfund Site," had assumed the mantle from Bushwick.[2] While these stories often center on New York, the pattern has been repeated in Chicago's Wicker Park, San Francisco's South of Market, and countless other neighborhoods around the world.

Evocations of SoHo obscure our understanding of how artists' actions generated urban change in the second half of the twentieth century. Glibly referring to a neighborhood as "the next SoHo" reduces a complex progression of urban change to a three-step process: industry moves out, artists move in, upper-income professionals push artists out. These references do not constitute analysis; they amount to little more than statements that history is repeating itself once again. Citing SoHo as a model for contemporary urban development obscures the neighborhood's historical transformation. When artists moved into the area south of Houston Street, no one even called it SoHo. The moniker "SoHo" was not coined until a decade after the first artists made their homes in industrial lofts. What, then, explains SoHo without the precedent of SoHo?

The story of artist-led urban development only feels expected because of a confluence of factors that occurred in a New York City neighborhood south of Houston Street from 1960 to 1980. There, completed and proposed urban renewal projects, deindustrialization, artist activism, state and local politics, the development of new methods for transforming vacant industrial space into homes (what urban planners would later call adaptive reuse), novel forms of art making, and changes in the way art was displayed and sold catalyzed the development of SoHo from an industrial area to an artist enclave, and then to an increasingly upper-income neighborhood. Artist-led urban development is not a natural process; it was created in SoHo.

Understanding SoHo's development is critical because the neighborhood is central to historical explanations of gentrification, a contested concept that alternately provokes anger, hope, and confusion. Gentrification is an idea associated with the displacement of low-income residents of color, the revitalization of the central city, artisanal restaurants, and other elements of "hipster" culture. Definitions of gentrification vary, but most focus on the movement of higher-income residents into working-class or low-income areas, resulting in the displacement of previous residents. Gentrification is a physical, social, cultural, and economic phenomenon. It involves the upgrading or renovation of existing housing stock, rising rents and property taxes, changes in local commerce, an altered local political landscape, and a transformed street life. In the United States, race is central to gentrification, which usually entails the movement of whites into previously majority-minority neighborhoods.[3]

Gentrification scholarship falls into three main categories. The "emancipatory city" theory postulates that cities are liberating spaces, particularly for the leftist, countercultural figures who make their homes in urban areas as a reaction against the banality and conformity of the suburbs. The "new middle class" framework, associated with sociologist David Ley, emphasizes the culturally sophisticated residences and lifestyles that these new urban residents created. Finally, other scholars classify gentrification as an example of the revanchist city, an idea associated with geographer Neil Smith. This framework defines gentrification as a "spatialized revenge against the poor and minorities who 'stole' the inner city from the respectable classes."[4] All of these interpretive frameworks identify artists as an important constituency that encourages investment and directs attention to authentic but undervalued urban neighborhoods.[5]

SoHo is central to both popular and scholarly understandings of gentrification. The neighborhood has come to define a distinct variant of this process, one we can call artist-led gentrification. There have been several studies of the area, first among these being Sharon Zukin's 1982 ethnography *Loft Living*. Zukin explores the ways in which artists' living habits became a model for the middle class (how the "aesthetic virtues of loft living turned into bourgeois chic") and the connections between the rise of SoHo and urban deindustrialization and the growth of the service economy in New York.[6] "The SoHo effect" and "gentrification" are often used interchangeably, but citing SoHo as a paradigm of gentrification borders on anachronistic.[7] Though sociologist Ruth Glass coined the term in 1964, no one called SoHo gentrified until the 1980s, two decades after it began to transition from industrial to residential.[8]

There are important questions about SoHo that the social scientific literature on gentrification and ethnographies of the neighborhood do not answer. Analyzing planning documents, papers of artist organizations, art gallery records, city and local periodicals, and oral history interviews with artists, we can begin to answer a series of questions that include the following: How did local politics and industrial conditions encourage and shape artists' efforts to redevelop industrial areas? What inspired art dealers to open galleries near artists' studios? How did the actions of artists help spread the benefits of living like an artist to a broader population? And how is the history of this gentrified neighborhood intertwined with the history of urban renewal and urban crisis in New York City?

The history of SoHo provides an opportunity to reinterpret artist-led gentrification in a way that puts historical actors, local politics, the workings of the art market, and the broader narratives of the post–World War II American city at the forefront. Local politics, in particular the illegality of living in SoHo, led artists to organize politically, promote the neighborhood to outsiders, and develop new arguments about their role in the city that redefined the place of the artist in American society. Artists created attractive homes in former SoHo factories and successfully legalized these residential spaces. It was their actions that convinced both ordinary New Yorkers and policy makers that conversions of industrial lofts into residences represented a viable redevelopment strategy for SoHo, as well as similar neighborhoods across the United States.

Recently, historians have begun to follow the lead of scholars in other disciplines who have investigated gentrification in New York City during the 1960s and '70s. As Suleiman Osman argues, members of a postindustrial middle class found authenticity in the diverse neighborhoods and historic architecture of Brownstone Districts in Brooklyn in the 1960s and '70s. Farther uptown, residents of Harlem pushed for commercial redevelopment through community-based organizations.[9] In response to the vast scholarship on deindustrialization, white flight, suburbanization, and negative effects of highway building and modernist housing projects,[10] there is an emerging historical literature on the resistance to slum clearance urban renewal in postwar American cities. Yet, as Christopher Klemek writes, neighborhood groups that fought these plans were often "incapable of nothing more than resistance and basic self-preservation."[11] In addition to deepening scholarly understanding of the role of artists as urban actors, and of the postwar city in general, an examination of SoHo can help historians better understand how neighborhood political activists not only resisted the old methods of developing cities but also posited new ways forward from the eras of urban crisis and renewal.

The creation and transformation of SoHo began in the late 1950s and early 1960s. During that period, artists moved into the neighborhood's industrial loft buildings, the best-known artist being painter Donald Judd, who owned an entire loft building on Prince Street. Over time, the community of artists living or working in SoHo included several art-world luminaries: painters Chuck Close and Alex Katz, choreographers Yvonne Rainer and Trisha Brown, jazz legend Ornette Coleman, and composer Philip Glass. Yet most SoHo residents were young and college educated but not successful enough at their craft to support themselves on art alone. Some painted or sculpted; others experimented with avant-garde forms of mixed-media art that included performance and video installation.

Their financial constraints and need for large, flexible studios induced these artists to renovate SoHo's lofts into combined living and working spaces. Garment manufacturers, machine shops, and warehousing concerns were abandoning these late-nineteenth-century structures because they were insufficient for their commercial and industrial needs. Others, already working at the margins of the postwar American economy, simply went out of business. Artists found these spaces cheap, available, and well suited for their outsize or mixed-media artworks.

In SoHo, artists used their artistic ingenuity, labor, and financial capital to invent a new type of housing: the residential loft. Artists found SoHo lofts attractive because they allowed for a person of modest means to rent a space that simultaneously served as a home as well as a studio. Residents turned these inexpensive old factory spaces into homes with significant physical labor and financial (and sometimes physical) risk. Plastics warehouses, paper recycling facilities, garment factories, and machine shops became functional and eventually attractive residences. The countercultural ethos of early SoHo residents helped in this regard. Mostly unconcerned with the usual trappings of middle-class success, they were not averse to risking their savings to buy and renovate a loft or to living without creature comforts when transforming the often filthy, dangerous spaces into homes. Loft residents also inadvertently used their artistic abilities to create a new design sensibility that made the former factory interiors look and feel simultaneously homey and chic.

Living in a loft, however, was illegal. Paradoxically, illegality fundamentally shaped the residential development of SoHo, allowing it to evolve into a gentrified neighborhood. Facing the threat of eviction, artists politically organized and defended their right to live in the area. As a result, they created innovative arguments about the role of the arts in society and the place of creativity in the postwar economy. Loft living, many artists argued, should be legalized because it allowed for the growth of communities whose cultural products gave the city a new identity and drove a new urban economy.[12]

City leaders began to take artists' demands to live in lofts seriously, enacting policies that enabled them to legally reside in SoHo. In 1961, a series of fires in loft buildings led to inspections by the New York City Fire Department and the threat of evictions. In response, artists from in and around SoHo formed the Artist Tenants Association (ATA) to advocate for their right to legally inhabit lofts. In 1964, an ATA-led artist strike and march on city hall inspired Mayor Robert Wagner to create the Artist in Residence program, the nation's first policy protecting artists living in lofts from eviction. Although this action was temporary and incomplete, loft residences were here to stay.

As more artists moved to SoHo, artist groups developed a new argument, not only that their presence in a city neighborhood contributed to the city's cultural economy and identity but also that their actions helped revive real estate in previously declining areas of the city. In 1970, a group of artist loft owners organized the SoHo Artists Association (SAA) and rekindled the push for changes that would give living in a loft the sanction of law. Artists' political organizing bore fruit in 1971, when changes to the city's zoning ordinance and the state Multiple Dwelling Law created a special district that allowed certified artists to live in SoHo, provided that they were approved by the Department of Recreation and Cultural Affairs. In 1973, thanks to the efforts of architecture journalist Margot Gayle and her Friends of Cast Iron Architecture, the SoHo Cast-Iron Historic District won designation from the city's Landmarks Commission, preserving the area's built environment and giving it prominence as an architectural gem.

Somewhat paradoxically, artist-led urban development in SoHo would not have taken place without elements of the "urban crisis" of the 1960s and '70s. Throughout this period, older cities in the American Northeast and Midwest, New York among them, experienced a deepening economic and demographic decline. Both industrial and white-collar jobs left for the suburbs, the Sun Belt, or overseas. Residents moved to the suburbs, leaving a segregated, lower-income city behind. Efforts to revitalize the city through large-scale urban renewal projects, which involved declaring large swaths of land "slums," obtaining property through eminent domain, razing existing structures, and replacing them with a single-use development, such as a housing project or highway, often made matters worse.[13]

The real and perceived demographic crises in New York provided SoHo artists with opportunities to forward their cause. Artists found lofts in the neighborhood due to deindustrialization. Although there were profitable businesses and jobs in the area, firms struggled to run twentieth-century companies in spaces built in the last decades of the nineteenth century. Lofts were narrow, held up by brittle cast-iron columns, and arranged over four to six stories, a far cry from the massive horizontally oriented factories of the postwar era. They produced low-end garments, served as warehouses for rags and wastepaper, and held small machine shops. Some of these businesses were moving overseas; many simply closed altogether. Vacancy rates were high, and rising.

Urban renewal also shaped SoHo's residential transition. More specifically, the backlash against urban renewal proved decisive. While artist groups fought to change city and state laws that made loft housing illegal, the Middle Income Cooperators of Greenwich Village (MICOVE) advocated building a housing project that would have replaced all of SoHo. In response, planning professor Chester Rapkin produced a City Planning Commission–sponsored report in 1963 arguing that the neighborhood's small businesses functioned as important industrial incubators that produced needed jobs, particularly for New York's working-class African American and Latino populations. As a result, SoHo was saved from the wrecking ball. Similarly, from 1945 to 1970, plans to construct the Lower Manhattan Expressway through the heart of SoHo remained in place. The threat of the project suppressed local investment and allowed artists to find vacant lofts at cheap rents. Once the specter of the highway was removed, SoHo's redevelopment began in earnest.

By renovating industrial lofts that policy makers viewed as slums, artists produced a new use for underutilized industrial space. In creating the residential loft and lobbying for its regularization, SoHo artist groups posited a new postindustrial future for New York City that did not rely on slum clearance or urban renewal. SoHo artists were not the first people to ever live in former industrial structures, but they were the first to establish this practice on a wide scale, take the risk and put in the labor to turn factories into homes, and fight the political battles necessary to regularize the process. As a result of their actions, industrial lofts, warehouses, and even factories were now considered for the first time as sites for housing, museums, restaurants, and a whole host of other urban amenities.

SoHo's high density of artists also transformed artistic production and residential development. In its early years, SoHo's only residents were artists, making it a place where tenants could interact, collaborate, and support one another's art. Residents heard about gallery shows and performances, found opportunities to collaborate, and created new forms of mixed-media performance art. SoHo's artist community and the unique nature of loft space inspired galleries to move to the area, which then led to the growth of an art-centered retail district. In 1968 the first gallery opened, bringing art sales close to the homes of artists for the first time in New York City history. By 1970, three of the city's leading art dealers had opened at 420 West Broadway in the heart of SoHo. By the end of the decade, the neighborhood had more than one hundred galleries.[14]

Galleries flourishing in SoHo represented a major change in where art was displayed and sold in New York. Whereas galleries had once located near patrons or in commercial districts close to transit, they gravitated to SoHo to have access to artists' studios as well as to take advantage of the neighborhood's large, inexpensive loft spaces. Local art dealers also created showrooms that were more casual and accessible than their more established uptown counterparts. SoHo galleries showed paintings and sculpture but also featured multiple types of artistic performance, including music, dance, theater, and genre-bending performance art. These art forms encouraged galleries to attract visitors, leading to the growth of a popular arts scene. As a result, art lovers treated SoHo like a free museum, browsing in the galleries on Saturday afternoons without any pressure to buy or visiting in-home jazz clubs at night.

From the mid-1970s onward, the actions of artists resulted in loft apartments becoming more upscale commodities. SoHo residents created more fashionable lofts, which the local press began covering more regularly, and it was more common for inhabitants to hire others to renovate their homes. In 1974, *New York Magazine* announced that artists had made SoHo "The Most Exciting Place to Live in the City."[15] As neighborhood industry declined further, new businesses arose that catered to gallery visitors, such as boutiques, restaurants, and other art-related shops. Loft renovation companies became more common, as did stores that artistically used loft space to display their products and interior design firms that sold goods fitting with the loft aesthetic. Emblematic of this trend was the 1977 opening of Dean & DeLuca, the neighborhood's gourmet food emporium.

By the middle of the 1970s, rising demand made residential lofts more valuable than industrial space in SoHo. Building owners, including some artists and industrial landlords, used the ambiguous, illegal status of lofts to push out industrial and artist tenants in favor of higher-paying ones. In response, tenants engaged in rent strikes, took their landlords to court, and brought their cause to the attention of the press and political leaders. Nonartists were moving into SoHo in greater numbers, and illegal loft living spread to areas outside of the neighborhood. As a result, policy makers developed a more formal loft policy. This was a piecemeal process, with multiple city agencies, city and state lawmakers, and the courts all having their say. In 1976, the City Planning Commission made loft housing legal for nonartists for the first time in the adjacent Tribeca neighborhood. The same policy was planned for the area north of Houston Street before pushback from local political groups kept loft housing legal only for artists in the neighborhood that became known as NoHo. New York's first loft law, passed in 1981, curtailed loft living's worst abuses but also opened up much of Lower Manhattan for legal loft conversions. As a result of this policy change, living in a loft had become a housing option for many New Yorkers, and city leaders and developers began to view loft conversions as a redevelopment strategy that could work for the rest of the city. Even this policy did not sanction loft living entirely. To this day, many SoHo lofts have still not been fully legalized.

SoHo artists were thus both victims and agents of gentrification. They instigated many of the changes in SoHo by making lofts upscale, promoting the neighborhood to outsiders, opening galleries and shops, investing in property, and highlighting the fact that their presence improved local real estate values and tax rolls. Though artists still reside in the neighborhood, and some profited from the area's residential transition, many either left or were pushed out of SoHo. The neighborhood has since become an upscale shopping district that contains few traces of its artist or industrial past.

SoHo artists fundamentally changed the way artists are perceived as urban actors. Although communities of artists were important to the histories of cities in Europe and North America in the nineteenth and twentieth centuries, SoHo artists established a new role for artists in the contemporary metropolis: as property developers, urban "pioneers," and small business incubators. Historians have chronicled how, throughout the nineteenth and twentieth centuries, enclaves of artists and bohemians in the United States and Europe have attracted middle-class residents. Parisian bohemians constructed communities of studios, cafés, and salons that inspired members of the bourgeoisie to settle in formerly down-and-out, working-class neighborhoods. In New York's Greenwich Village at the turn of the twentieth century, the neighborhood's community of writers and painters drew members of the middle class to Lower Manhattan and encouraged some to live among the area's artists and bohemians. These enclaves have been most noted for their artistic production and the effect of the bohemian encounter on middle-class culture. Bohemia reflected the contradictions at the center of bourgeois life in eighteenth- and nineteenth-century Paris, while Greenwich Village bohemians pushed class and gender relations in new and modern directions at the turn of the twentieth century.[16] Bohemian locales often contained prominent cafés or bars where the bohemian and middle-class city dweller might interact, but they did not explode as residential and commercial districts in the manner of SoHo.

Through their advocacy, SoHo artists posited a new place for the arts and artists in the city that anticipated later arguments about creative place making and the creative class. Most prominently, Richard Florida has argued that bohemians, including visual artists, actors, dancers, musicians, actors, and directors, help lure the "creative class" to cities, revitalizing neighborhoods and driving urban economies in the process. In 2010, the National Endowment for the Arts began to fund "creative placemaking" projects aimed at rejuvenating urban neighborhoods through cultural activities.[17] Due in part to the influence of this research, scholars have interrogated the categories by which artists or creative workers are defined and have called for studies that examine the specific processes through which artists affect the neighborhoods in which they live.[18] SoHo artist groups argued that they contributed to a vibrant cultural economy that gave the city an identity and generated economic growth at a time when New York struggled to maintain its population and industrial base. Additionally, by looking closely at artists' networks, how and where art was sold, what it took to survive financially as an artist in New York, and how artist communities interacted with the outside world, one can begin to understand how the arts generate urban development.

In SoHo, art and cultural capital were as important as deindustrialization and the flight of the middle class in shaping the area's future. Artists formed their own unique bohemia in SoHo, using a mix of political advocacy, connections with formal cultural institutions, artistic creativity, interior design innovation, work in cooperative organizations, and marketing savvy to create a new type of urban neighborhood that proved attractive to artists, tourists, and the middle class. By making their neighborhood desirable and inviting people in the rest of the city to see it for themselves, artists drew attention to the fact that SoHo, with its mix of housing, shops, restaurants, galleries, and industry, was an exciting place to live. During a time of economic decline in New York, SoHo artists provided a way to generate residential and commercial real estate investment in industrial areas without the economic and social costs of slum clearance urban renewal. Their actions inspired policy makers to view their methods of converting unused industrial space into homes and shops as a viable urban development strategy for the entire city. What happened in SoHo had a worldwide impact: the methods of arts-driven urban development that were established there would catch on nationally and globally in the ensuing decades. Key elements of contemporary urban living—residential lofts, the adaptive reuse of industrial space, gallery-driven commercial districts, the idea of the artist as a central urban actor, and public policies designed to create vibrant neighborhoods through the arts—all had their roots in SoHo.

1

The Wastelands of New York

On January 27, 1966, Manuel Torregrosa was working on the fifth floor of the headquarters of the Weiss & Klau Company at 466–68 Broadway in SoHo when he heard a terrifyingly loud noise. Next, he saw a small portion of floor buckle and then watched with horror as the entire section of the floor slowly collapsed onto the workers below. Soon after, "debris, wooden floors, machinery, and supplies—fell in a cloud of dust," imperiling the two hundred people in the building. Moses Korn, a mechanic, was also on the fifth floor at his bench, just a few feet from where the floor gave out without warning. "I heard a noise," he said, "and then all of the sudden it was dark . . . I couldn't see anything except the windows on Broadway—that was the only light. In a second, there was a cloud of dust. I didn't know what had happened. I thought maybe a machine exploded." One of his coworkers, Augustin Mas, was having a coffee break on the second floor when he heard what sounded like an earthquake. Then, as he described it, "The whole inside of the building toward the rear suddenly fell from the top all the way down to just above where I was. I just ran. I got out somehow."[1]

The aftermath of the collapse was no less terrifying. The *New York Post* reported, "Screams of a man and a woman could be heard in the street." Employees had their arms mangled, legs and necks cut, and heads gashed. Eleven employees were seriously injured, and four were taken to the hospital, including Luz Alvarez, who was pulled unconscious from debris on the fourth floor, and stockroom employee Juan Cadamatori, who was rescued from the rubble after an hour and forty-five minutes. The incident could have been worse. As the *New York Herald Tribune* noted, the collapse occurred shortly before the company's three o'clock coffee break, when many more workers usually congregated around the accident site.[2]

Although there were no fatalities, the collapse of its headquarters quickly led to the death of Weiss & Klau. In this case, it was not the business that was faulty (in fact, the company was quite profitable at the time) but the building in which it was housed. After a monthlong investigation, the New York City Department of Buildings determined that the immediate cause of the collapse was excess stress placed on two bolts attaching the floor of the building to a cast-iron column. The floor was weakened because a light well (a multistory skylight) had once been installed in the loft but subsequently covered over. As a result, the floor could not hold as much weight as it once did. The bolts could hold a maximum of 34,200 to 41,000 pounds per floor, but an investigation found that the load was at least 70,000 pounds. As Buildings Commissioner Charles C. Moerdler reported, there were likely close to one thousand rolls of plastics, each weighing forty to seventy-five pounds, applying pressure on the floor. As a result, "Wood beams a foot thick were snapped like matchsticks. A steel floorbeam under the third floor was bent at right angles, putting a 90-degree twist into the cross beam to which it was fastened. Bolts of plastic, beams, and machinery plunged into the chasm."[3]

One does not have to read that far between the lines to determine that the buildings department did not think that Weiss & Klau should have been operating in its loft. The structure was overcrowded, overburdened, and obsolete for its needs. The building had been built in 1880, and the company had been operating in the loft space since 1948.[4] The nation had fought two world wars, had moved from the industrial age into the space age, and Weiss & Klau and its employees were still making products, coordinating a sales force, and warehousing merchandise in the same building.

Loft buildings such as 466–68 Broadway, the struggles of the businesses that operated in them, and the attempts to upgrade these structures through urban renewal shaped SoHo's redevelopment into a residential neighborhood. Though its demise was more dramatic than most, Weiss & Klau and the hundreds of SoHo businesses operating in century-old lofts shared similar challenges. SoHo's economy and built environment remained stuck in the late nineteenth century decades after World War II. From the late 1700s to 1860, SoHo[5] evolved from farmland, to an enclave for the wealthy, to a simultaneously upscale and vice-ridden commercial district, to an industrial neighborhood, but there was little new construction from the late nineteenth century through the early 1960s. It was challenging for twentieth-century industrial businesses to function in nineteenth-century lofts, and many local enterprises operated at the margins of the postwar economy.

Because of SoHo's outmoded built environment, politicians and planners sought to upgrade buildings such as Weiss & Klau's Broadway loft through urban renewal. Though much of the urban renewal in New York City, and the great bulk of the scholarship on the subject, has revolved around efforts to upgrade slum housing and downtown commercial districts through modernist residential and retail developments, significant numbers of urban renewal projects in New York and across the country focused on upgrading outdated industrial areas at the center of cities. As historian Joel Schwartz writes, a focus on "Blue-Collar Blight" was an unacknowledged policy in New York City for more than thirty years, as industrial businesses were shoved aside for residential and commercial building projects throughout the city from the 1940s onward. Starting with the 1929 Regional Plan of New York and Its Environs, planners envisioned a metropolis where industry would be removed to the outer boroughs of Brooklyn, Queens, and the Bronx, or out of the city altogether. Of particular interest to planners was pushing industry out of areas near prime real estate, such as the Brooklyn waterfront, the west side of Manhattan north of Fourteenth Street, and the loft district that ran between Chambers and Twenty-third Streets, an area that included SoHo. Major urban renewal projects in New York, including the United Nations building, the Brooklyn Civic Center, Peter Cooper Village, Stuyvesant Town, and Corlears Hook, all overtook industrial businesses with little protest.[6]

Some of this indifference or outright hostility to New York's industrial sector was due to the particular nature of New York City industry. Despite its robust industrial sector (New York was the nation's largest manufacturing center on the eve of World War II), there was relatively little heavy industry in the city, and most local enterprises were small; businesses averaged twenty-five workers, half the national average.[7] No one industry predominated, and the American industries that expanded most rapidly in the first half of twentieth century, including automobiles, petroleum, and rubber, were underrepresented in New York. As labor historian Joshua Freeman observed, New York was in many ways a non-Fordist city well into the mid-twentieth century; its manufacturing district looked more like that of a mid-nineteenth-century city than a major production center such as Pittsburgh or Detroit.[8]

Consequently, industry in New York was an easy target for renewal. Industrial businesses were small and old, and there was no single industry with a symbolic hold on the city, leaving these enterprises with few defenders. Even unions rarely spoke up when industry was threatened by renewal.[9] The city's industrial sector was mostly forgotten, except when it stood in the way of someone's plans for New York's future.

By all logic, SoHo should have been the next industrial neighborhood renewed in New York. The neighborhood's buildings were old, its businesses were not flashy, and the skyscrapers of both Midtown and Lower Manhattan beckoned only a few short blocks away. In the 1950s and early 1960s, the loft districts in and around SoHo were the targets of several urban renewal projects aimed at upgrading what their proponents called industrial or commercial slums. Civic organizations, advocacy groups, and political actors, including Robert Moses, New York University (NYU), the City Club of New York, and the United Hatters, Cap and Millinery Workers' Union, argued that these buildings were, at best, obsolete for modern industry and, at worst, dangerous to their inhabitants and neighbors. They dubbed the area "The Wastelands of New York" and noted the high number of vacancies in lofts, the marginal nature of businesses located within, and the unsuitability of vertically oriented nineteenth-century buildings, held up by fragile cast-iron columns and located on cramped streets, for the rigors of modern industrial production. Some of these projects, including the NYU-sponsored and Moses-backed Washington Square Southeast development, were built, replacing hundreds of loft buildings in the process.

Yet much of SoHo was saved from renewal. Both the overall weariness with such projects and specific arguments in favor of SoHo industry saved much of the neighborhood from demolition. Specifically, in the early 1960s, urban planner Chester Rapkin made a successful argument that industrial loft districts such as SoHo were economically vibrant employment incubators and providers of jobs for the city's low-income minority populations. Thanks in large part to Rapkin's research, Mayor Robert Wagner tabled plans for a middle-income housing project sponsored by the Middle-Income Co-operators of Greenwich Village (MICOVE) that would have replaced much of SoHo.[10]

One of the great ironies of the history of SoHo is that if it were not for the value placed on industry, artists might not have had the chance to live there. If the MICOVE project had been built, it would have replaced much of what today is known as SoHo and would have prevented or at least delayed the advent of adaptive reuse of industrial space as an urban development strategy.

Rapkin was an important voice in what Christopher Klemek has called the transatlantic collapse of urban renewal. Much like heralded antirenewal advocate Jane Jacobs, who was instrumental in stopping new housing developments in the nearby West Village and the removal of the roadway through Washington Square Park immediately to the north of SoHo, Rapkin questioned the rationale and efficacy of urban renewal in Lower Manhattan.[11] SoHo experienced a particular variant of the backlash against renewal: the defense of industrial neighborhoods against urban renewal efforts that would cost the city jobs, particularly for low-income workers of color.[12] The history of SoHo in the 1960s also adds an important layer to the story of renewal's downfall. The value placed on local industry spared SoHo the wrecking ball and played an important role in the process of urban development that followed the rejection of urban renewal in New York.

Yet one cannot forget the genuine challenges of operating industrial businesses in lofts. Efforts at renewal in SoHo cannot be chalked up to out-of-touch renewal advocates targeting well-functioning but unsightly neighborhoods. Operating a machine shop or a garment manufacturing business in a nineteenth-century building was nearly always inefficient and often quite dangerous. There were real questions as to whether there was an industrial future in the neighborhood. Despite the successful resistance to renewal in SoHo, no one developed a plan to help industry survive in New York.

Because of the successful resistance to urban renewal in SoHo, the neighborhood's industrial and commercial architecture remained mostly intact. What was left was an industrial neighborhood of manufacturing firms, garment makers, warehouses, waste recyclers, and printers making do, and often struggling, in nineteenth-century loft space. It was this mix of functioning commerce and obsolescence in the shadow of urban renewal that would shape the neighborhood's future development.

SoHo's Early History: From Rural to Commercial

The development of SoHo started slowly. The neighborhood's major thoroughfare and eastern boundary, Broadway, began as a path used by the Weckquasgeek Indians to travel up and down Manhattan. The land in and around SoHo also likely housed the first settlement of free blacks on the island.[13] The area south of Houston Street was a home to Dutch colonists and their descendants throughout the late seventeenth and eighteenth centuries, during which time Augustine Herrman, Nicholas Bayard, and their ancestors owned much of the land. The Revolutionary War forced Nicholas Bayard's grandson to sell off his property to pay creditors in 1781, which split the land south of Houston Street into smaller lots, allowing for further development.[14]

It was an early form of urban renewal, coming in the form of manipulations of the natural environment, that allowed SoHo's development to begin in earnest. In the eighteenth century, the topography of Lower Manhattan was an impediment to growth. Collect Pond, the stream that fed it, Smith's Hill, Bayard's Hill, and Lispenard Meadows stood between the area and the developed part of Lower Manhattan close to the Battery. While the territory was once a rural oasis in the midst of the fast-growing metropolis, by the late eighteenth century Collect Pond was filled with garbage and dead animals, and Lispenard Meadows had become a mosquito-filled bog that regularly claimed livestock. After years of petitions, the Common Council ordered that Bayard's Hill and other rises in elevation nearby be cut down and used to fill in Collect Pond and the surrounding marshy land. As a result, SoHo became joined to the developed part of Manhattan by flat, dry land, making the neighborhood suitable for development.[15]

With the natural impediments out of the way, the residential and commercial development of the area began. In 1809, Broadway was paved and sidewalks were constructed from Canal Street to Astor Place, bringing the city's major thoroughfare above Houston Street. In 1806, shoemaker Conrad Brooks built the earliest structure still standing in SoHo, a frame house with a brick front, at 107 Spring Street.[16] Though it was farmland only decades before, the stretch of Broadway that ran through SoHo soon became New York's most fashionable address. By the 1820s, the street was filled with redbrick row houses, slate sidewalks, and poplar trees. Some of the city's wealthiest families lived on Broadway (including John Jacob Astor and Samuel F. B. Morse), and the neighborhood was among the city's most densely populated.[17]

Yet SoHo did not remain fashionable for long, as the neighborhood became part of the dynamic of constant change that shaped Lower Manhattan during this period. The process began when the wealthy moved northward along Broadway to escape congestion. Soon after, the middle class and the city's less prosperous citizens followed, and soon their residences encroached on the homes of the rich. As population density increased, a formerly residential enclave became an attractive location for business and industry, uses that attracted higher rents. As residents, businesses, and manufacturers pushed farther north, the wealthy migrated outward, starting the process all over again.

It was fitting, then, that even as fashionable row houses spread upward through SoHo, commerce and trade encroached on the area. By the 1830s and '40s, dry goods shops had made their way north as real estate space for warehouses fetched a premium along the lower portion of Broadway. In 1840, the southern section of Broadway (near Bowling Green) was lined with banks and counting houses, while shopping areas and hotels clustered in the middle, around city hall to Canal Street. Upscale residences filled the northernmost developed portion of Broadway, from Canal Street to Union Square. Ten years later, this had all changed, as commercial enterprises populated Canal Street. Shops and hotels popped up between Canal Street and Union Square, and residences entirely disappeared from the portion of the street below Union Square.[18]

By the middle of the nineteenth century, the area north of Canal Street was known for two seemingly contradictory identities: as the home of the city's most notable hotels and department stores and as New York's red-light district. During the mid-nineteenth century, Broadway was filled with wholesale firms, expensive hotels, and upscale shops housed in buildings made of marble, brownstone, and cast iron. On the side streets, however, casinos, theaters, music halls, and brothels predominated.[19]

In the 1850s SoHo developed into an upscale commercial district. Department stores such as Lord & Taylor (opening on the corner of Grand and Broadway in 1859), Tiffany & Co. (opening at 550 Broadway in 1852), and E. V. Haughwout (opening at 488–92 Broadway in 1857) began to dominate Broadway. Major hotels, including the Union Hotel, City Hotel, Prescott House, Metropolitan Hotel, and St. Nicholas Hotel (considered to be the finest in the city), joined them. The side streets featured famous music halls and theaters, as well as P. T. Barnum's American Museum of curiosities, making SoHo one of the entertainment centers of the city.[20]

At the same time, SoHo functioned as the city's red-light district. In the 1820s, Broadway from City Hall Park to Houston Street was an open-air market for commercialized sex, and there were also a number of brothels and bawdy houses between Canal and Houston Streets. In the middle of the nineteenth century, as historian Timothy Gilfoyle has shown, the city's vice district coalesced in SoHo. Entrepreneurs in the sex trades took advantage of a customer base already used to traveling to the neighborhood to patronize its upscale department stores, restaurants, hotels, theaters, and saloons. While the neighborhood was respectable during the day, at night the well-to-do rubbed elbows with visitors attracted to a growing commercial sex district. Nearly all the hotels, saloons, and restaurants along Broadway accommodated prostitutes, earning the reputation of "Gotham's golden mile of whoredom." From 1850 to 1870, the streets off Broadway accommodated more than 40 percent of the city's prostitution. The neighborhood attracted this activity due to municipal tolerance and the fact that landlords did little to discourage it, as they knew houses of prostitution would pay the highest rents.[21]

Industrial SoHo and the Cast-Iron Loft

In the mid-nineteenth century, the same forces that drove SoHo's transition from residential to commercial initiated the growth of the neighborhood's industrial sector. With commercial and manufacturing interests migrating north up Broadway, landowners found that they could extract higher ground rents from the properties by transitioning them to industrial use. As SoHo real estate increased in value (from $18 million in assessed valuations in 1865 to $26 million in 1868), renting to a hotel, brothel, theater, or resident was no longer a profitable venture. As a result, theaters moved farther uptown, prostitution migrated to both tenement and upscale districts throughout the city, and more than a quarter of the population left the Eighth Ward. In its place, a diverse industrial base developed during the 1850s and 60s. Firms dealing in dry goods, china, glass, silks, satin, lace, ribbons, furs, tobacco, and lumber settled in the neighborhood, along with companies making cabinets, pianos, chairs, and tables.[22]

From the years after the panic of 1873 through the 1890s, large factories and stores were built along the streets parallel to Broadway. The area quickly became a center for the mercantile and dry goods trades and included the headquarters for some of the most important textile firms in the country. As these businesses moved into SoHo, the noted commercial establishments that had dominated the area in the 1850s soon left. Tiffany & Co. and Lord & Taylor both moved uptown in 1870, followed by all the area's upscale hotels. Industrial buildings replaced the few older brick ones that remained along Broadway, and a number of warehouses rose west of Broadway from Canal to Houston Streets in the late 1870s and 1880s.[23]

SoHo's era of rapid industrial growth left one of its most prominent legacies: the cast-iron loft building. After 1865, four- to six-story brick structures with cast-iron facades dominated the area's built environment. In typical lofts, the first floors were designed as lobbies or retail spaces, while the upper floors were built as large, unpartitioned, high-ceilinged spaces to be used for warehousing or manufacturing.[24]

The cast-iron loft was a product of both the economic climate and the architectural styles of the Gilded Age. The end of the nineteenth century was a time when the newly successful were not embarrassed to flaunt their wealth. Cast iron allowed for building owners and architects with a limited budget to imitate the opulent design elements popular at the time, many of which aimed to capture elements of French Renaissance or Italianate styles. The neoclassicism popularized by the World's Columbian Exposition of 1893 in Chicago, as well as the heavy arches, stonework, and decorative flourishes of Boston Architect Henry Hobson Richardson, also influenced this local style.[25]

Simultaneously, advances in building technology spurred the popularity of cast iron in SoHo. Compared with a masonry building, a cast-iron structure was easy, inexpensive, and quick to design and build. These structures were an early form of prefabrication, as they were cast in foundries in multiple pieces that could be easily combined and assembled in a variety of ways. This led to a cost savings in materials and also in design; if a client ordered a cast-iron building from a foundry, the client often did not need to pay for the services of an architect. Cast-iron buildings were also easy to maintain and

FIGURE 2. SoHo cast-iron building, 98 Greene Street (1881).

renovate. To give a building a fresh look, all that was needed was a new coat of paint, and if a cast-iron piece became warped or broken, it could easily be replaced by a stock piece or by recasting the piece in the same foundry from the original mold. The invention of the elevator safety brake by Elisha Grave Otis in 1854, which made buildings of this height practical, also spurred the construction of lofts.[26]

The popularity of cast-iron buildings lasted until the 1890s. They fell out of favor in part because it was technically difficult to apply cast-iron facades to the taller steel-frame buildings being erected at that time. There were also questions about the effectiveness of cast iron as a fireproof material. Simultaneously, new terra-cotta manufacturing techniques were developed that allowed for some of the same ornamentation that cast iron provided, but with greater fireproofing. Moreover, by the beginning of the twentieth century, the type of heavily decorated classicism popular in SoHo was being superseded by a new emphasis on lightness and more open design.[27]

The buildings that would shape SoHo's rise as an artist colony trace their roots to the period between 1860 and about 1900. The future home of the Paula Cooper Gallery, 96 Prince Street, was a cast-iron building constructed from 1881 to 1882 to serve as a store. The building stands on a block developed largely in the 1880s, alongside some buildings from the 1850s, 1860s, and early 1900s. The restaurant Food would one day open at 127 Prince Street in a seven-story loft building with a brick, terra-cotta, and iron facade built by Buchman & Deisler architects from 1893 to 1894, with iron from George Jackson Iron Works. The building stands on a block comprising structures built in the 1890s for mostly industrial purposes. A.I.R. Gallery would open at 97 Wooster Street, a seven-story brick, stone, and terra-cotta building erected in 1896 to serve as an industrial loft.[28]

FIGURE 3. SoHo cast-iron building detail, 98 Greene Street (1881).

Weiss & Klau and Local Business Conditions

By the end of the nineteenth century, SoHo's built environment evolved into the form it would take for the next eighty or so years. Similarly, the types of industries that located in the neighborhood, including light industrial enterprises, garment manufacturers, waste recyclers, and warehousing concerns, and even some of the area's firms, would remain consistent throughout from the early twentieth century through the 1960s. These decades were a time of decline for SoHo industry. Some companies found success, but none was at the vanguard of the American economy, and many struggled to run twentieth-century businesses in nineteenth-century buildings.

At the turn of the twentieth century, SoHo was located at the center of two overlapping manufacturing districts: one for the wholesale fur trade and another for women's and children's garments.[29] But starting in 1900, businesses left SoHo in greater numbers. Some of this deterioration can be traced to restructuring in the garment industry. In the early years of the 1900s, a single firm would often control every aspect of garment production, from design to cutting, sewing, finishing, and sales. Yet, after World War I, manufacturers started to divide much of this work among various subcontractors. The cutting shops and showrooms where patterns were made and finished products were displayed congregated in what is currently Manhattan's Garment District (between Thirty-fourth and Forty-second Streets in Midtown Manhattan). The sewing was sent elsewhere. As companies separated their sales and production sites, smaller business moved to the Garment District to be closer to showrooms. In addition, the area offered steel-framed, fireproof buildings and easier access to Pennsylvania Station, the main entry point for buyers visiting the city. By the early 1950s, anywhere from 65 to 80 percent of garment manufacturing took place in this area. Many of the firms that did not move north left for neighboring states where costs were lower.[30]

The garment manufacturers that remained produced standard, low-fashion items, such as women's and children's underwear, blouses, skirts, and sportswear. These firms benefited from SoHo's lower rents and from being relatively insulated from style trends. As garment firms left SoHo, businesses dealing with low-value paper and textile wastes replaced them. These businesses joined the wholesalers, some of which remained in the area for decades, and warehouse firms that moved to the area to find cheap space.[31]

By the first decades of the twentieth century, SoHo's built environment and industrial economy had reached the state in which it would remain for the much of the next sixty-plus years. During this period, SoHo businesses were mostly family owned, and an individual firm or family usually owned its loft building, either using the entire space or leasing out individual floors. There were no major property holders in the neighborhood, and investment in individual properties occurred in a piecemeal fashion.[32]

Research into one SoHo building, 80 Wooster Street, by SoHo resident and architect Shael Shapiro and journalist Roslyn Bernstein, reveals the types of businesses and progression of building ownership in SoHo during this period. The site that is now 80 Wooster Street contained a boardinghouse until the property was sold to Abraham Boehm and Lewis Coon, real estate developers active in Lower Manhattan, in 1894. The partners commissioned a cast-iron loft building to be built on the site the same year at a cost of $85,000. Over the next four decades multiple businesses and individuals owned the building, including a watch case manufacturer and a machine company. In 1944, the Feldman family, owners of a cardboard box recycling business called the Surfred Corporation, bought the building as an investment. The family then sold the building to the Miller Paper Company, a tenant in the building that specialized in decorative papers, in 1946. The company was sold to George Maciunas and his Fluxhouse group, an artist cooperative (see chapter 2), in 1967. The firm then bought a more modern loft across the street (at 73 Wooster Street), in which they continued to operate until 1993.[33]

The history of one well-documented SoHo firm, the earlier-discussed Weiss & Klau, provides further insights into the nature of SoHo business during the late nineteenth and early twentieth centuries. Weiss & Klau was founded in 1898 and operated in SoHo through the early 1960s. The company's family-based ownership, manufacturing focus, and long tenure meant that it had much in common with a large number of local enterprises. Most important, Weiss & Klau provides some of the most compelling evidence of the challenges that businesses faced when operating in loft spaces.

Weiss & Klau produced, marketed, and sold simple but useful housewares. Over the decades, the company's product lines included asbestos potholders, chair and table pads, wall coverings, "self-adhesive plastic products for shelving and other household uses," venetian blinds, window shades, and industrial fabric. Weiss & Klau had a strong record of success throughout the first half of the twentieth century. Only five years after its founding, Weiss & Klau outgrew its first headquarters and leased a second loft space at 203 Canal Street. The company originally occupied the top three floors of the building but only a year later rented the entire structure, using pulleys and ropes to move the raw materials and finished products of its oilcloth-manufacturing and distribution business in and out of the loft. In 1897 the company would add space in the adjacent buildings at 205–11 Canal Street.

The firm purchased its first SoHo building in 1911, a substantial six-story loft at 462 Broadway.[34]

In the first years of the 1920s Weiss & Klau developed a novel product, Oilcloth Ensemble (essentially a set of matching tablecloths, runners, doilies, and chair covers). Its popular Florenteen line allowed the company to flourish in the following years. In 1922 executives Nathan Klau and David W. Klau earned $56,000 and $50,000 per year, respectively, which amounts to roughly $782,000 and $699,000, respectively, in 2015 dollars. Throughout the Great Depression and World War II, the company was able to consistently add employees, and executive compensation barely slipped. Business was so good that in 1941 Weiss & Klau bought the loft building adjacent to its first factory space, 462–64 Broadway, for $111,000 (a sum equivalent to nearly $1.8 million in 2015 dollars).[35]

Weiss & Klau continued to expand throughout the early postwar era. Realizing that the market for oilcloth was soon fading away, they began to move into different product lines. They earned a major government contract for venetian blinds in 1951. This change in orientation led to an important expansion for Weiss & Klau. In 1953 the company purchased the manufacturing plant and business of the Coated Products Division of a firm called the Interchemical Corporation, located in semirural Buchanan, New York. It is significant to note that Weiss & Klau invested a substantial amount of capital in a company and plant outside of SoHo.[36]

The firm continued to grow in the late 1950s and '60s, but some of this growth came from businesses headquartered outside SoHo. Weiss & Klau earned contracts from the New York City and Brooklyn Boards of Education for window coverings in 1955 and 1962 and established a pension plan for employees in 1963. Additionally, in 1962 the company developed a relationship with a warehousing concern in suburban Mount Vernon, New York, to distribute wall coverings to institutional customers. Throughout the 1950s and 1960s, Weiss & Klau paid a dividend to its shareholders (mostly family members) and even donated a portion of the company's income to the David W. Klau Foundation. In 1960 the corporation had about five hundred employees, $13,907,000 in sales, an operating income of $752,000, and an investment income of $142,000.[37]

By the early 1960s, Weiss & Klau found itself in a distinctive situation. On the positive side, the company had undertaken numerous recent expansions, boasted a positive balance sheet, and had established a lengthy history of business success. The company owned two loft buildings plus a plant upstate and operated in diverse markets. Yet there were warning signs about the firm's long-term prospects in SoHo. The company's most substantial investments had been in businesses and plants outside the neighborhood—indeed, outside New York City altogether. While Weiss & Klau achieved success selling products such as window coverings, shelf liners, and industrial fabrics, these were not sectors on the cutting edge of the postwar economy. In fact, they were exactly the type of products that could be easily outsourced. The firm had invested substantially in local real estate and in machinery for its specific business and location but had been operating in the same type of building since the 1880s.

Weiss & Klau's circumstances were typical of SoHo firms in the early 1960s, when artists migrated to the area. One of the major sources for this information is Chester Rapkin's study of the neighborhood, which provides a thorough census of industrial and commercial activity. Overall, the neighborhood was dominated by textile, manufacturing, and waste recycling firms. There were 650 businesses located there employing 12,700 workers. The largest percentage, at 26 percent, were textile and apparel firms that provided jobs for 42 percent of all the area's employees. Manufacturing firms such as Weiss & Klau comprised 21 percent of SoHo firms and employed 22 percent of workers. These firms included manufacturers of toys and dolls and mechanical and electrical products, as well as small machine shops.

A quarter of the firms in SoHo, employing 10 percent of neighborhood workers, were engaged in the wholesale trades. Businesses in the waste industry dominated this category. They included those that would buy textile scraps, such as mill ends and other remnants, and then sort, clean, and bale them for use as wiping cloths. Others bought wastepaper and baled it for sale to paper mills, mostly for the manufacture of paperboard, or bought used cardboard boxes, sorted them, and resold them to industrial users and retail stores. As much of their activities consisted of storage, firms in this category were most often located in older, smaller loft buildings on West Broadway and Mercer Street that were less efficient for manufacturing.

A further 17 percent of firms and employees worked with printing, paper products, chemicals, and rubber and leather items. Printing firms included photoengravers, platemakers, and bookbinders. Several SoHo businesses manufactured envelopes, folding boxes, and other types of containers. These companies supplied wholesale paper dealers in SoHo when the quantity required was too small to be ordered directly from the mill. Much of the printed material produced in SoHo was promotional. Printers found SoHo appealing because of its location near advertising agencies, corporate headquarters, and marketing departments of large firms in the Lower Manhattan Financial District or Midtown. Finally, another 11 percent of SoHo enterprises and 9 percent of workers were concentrated in a variety of retail and service activities such as restaurants, trucking companies, and dry goods businesses.[38]

The structure of SoHo employment had a definite geographic distribution, which was rooted in the neighborhood's historical development. The area's larger and more stable businesses tended to occupy the larger loft buildings along Broadway, the street where the most substantial industrial structures had been built. Smaller and more marginal firms clustered on the side streets to the west, where lesser firms had built smaller structures during the nineteenth century. Generally, wholesaling establishments were located along West Broadway and Mercer Street, while retail stores occupied much of the frontage of the east-west side streets, as well as some of the shops along Broadway. Approximately 30 percent of SoHo firms were located in the larger and more efficient buildings on the blocks between Broadway and Mercer Street, particularly along Broadway. Half the jobs in SoHo were housed on three blocks along Broadway.[39]

Broadway also boasted one of three major concentrations of the ladies' and children's undergarment industry firms in New York. The area was considered the second most important concentration of undergarment manufacturing businesses in the city, producing $2.8 million worth of merchandise in 1967. The industry employed 3,500 people on Lower Broadway, nearly one-fifth of whom lived in Lower Manhattan. Businesses tended to value their low-cost Broadway lofts, remaining in the area in spite of poor elevator service and loading facilities, among other disadvantages. Most workers were women, at 95 percent of the labor force, according to one survey of a local union, and this type of manufacturing attracted a large number of unskilled workers, including newcomers to the city and country. In 1967, approximately 30 percent of the work force was Spanish speaking.[40]

SoHo employees tended to work producing goods, be part of small firms, and range from unskilled to semiskilled. Approximately 83 percent of the neighborhood's employees were involved in production, and the largest single employment group in the area was that of sewing machine operators. In terms of skill level, workers in the textile industries tended to be skilled, while manufacturers employed both skilled and unskilled workers. Wholesaling and warehousing employees were predominantly unskilled. Among nonproduction workers, clerical workers, executives, and professionals predominated. SoHo employees averaged $1.79 per hour at a time when the minimum wage was $1.15. Wholesaling employees earned the highest wages in SoHo, while textile employees earned the lowest. Low unemployment insurance rates in SoHo indicated that area employment was stable, and workers were long tenured. Twenty percent of employees were African American, 40 percent were Puerto Rican, and 40 percent were white. A large percentage of the latter group was Jewish, Italian, Irish, and Slavic. Finally, 47 percent of SoHo workers were women.[41]

Revenues were modest, but most SoHo firms were older and stable. The average neighborhood business tallied gross revenues of $312,000 (more than $2.4 million in 2015 dollars). As of 1962, more than 75 percent of SoHo companies had been in existence for more than ten years—and more than a third of those for more than twenty years. Only 10 percent had been in business fewer than five years. The firms in SoHo were significantly older as a group than similar businesses in the rest of Manhattan. The net worth of local businesses was modest, averaging $41,000 (more than $318,000 in 2015 dollars). Yet these companies did possess a higher net worth compared with all Manhattan enterprises in the same industries.[42]

Perhaps the strongest commonality among SoHo businesses was their difficulties adapting twentieth-century industries to nineteenth-century loft space. Before 1900, moving goods vertically via powered elevator was far more efficient than moving them horizontally. Elevators provided a relatively fast method of transporting goods from place to place compared with slow hand trucks or carrying materials by hand. Vertically oriented industrial buildings were also more practical during the nineteenth century because a large, central source, such as a steam engine, usually provided power for an entire building.[43]

Yet while some SoHo firms successfully navigated around the inefficiency created by central power sources, it was much more difficult to find solutions to the problems of multistory loft buildings. Many SoHo workers' only job was to move goods around in lofts, and businesses estimated that materials handling costs constituted 6 to 10 percent of wages. With limited space on each level, 48 percent of firms spread out operations to multiple floors, meaning that they relied on elevators to receive raw materials, ship out finished products, and move items vertically. This practice led to long waits for elevators and crowding in the lobbies of many buildings. Multiple-floor operations also created work space layout issues. For example, if a firm created a horizontal production line, with raw materials coming in one end and finished goods leaving the other, the final product would end up as far away from the elevator as possible, requiring it to be carted back to the other end of the floor. Some firms tried orienting their production in a horseshoe shape, but this proved difficult in lofts that were 25 feet wide on average.[44]

Inefficiencies in SoHo lofts did not disappear after goods left the building. Although the density of the area allowed for convenient connections to suppliers and customers, trucks bringing supplies or picking up deliveries found the neighborhood streets inadequate. SoHo was located near the major truck route that connected the Holland Tunnel (leading to New Jersey) and the bridges linking Manhattan to Long Island and Brooklyn. An average of 3,500 trucks entered or left the area each day to pick up or make deliveries. Yet almost half of SoHo's firms reported that they could attend to only one truck at a time. In addition, there were no off-street loading facilities for trucks, which meant that they had to park parallel to the sidewalk or back up across it to load or unload adjacent to a building. Trucks with substantial

FIGURE 4. Aerial view of trucks and vans on Greene Street in SoHo. (Photograph by John Dominis. "Living Big in a Loft," *Life*, March 27, 1970.)

trailers might find it impossible to back up to a building without "breaking the rig," or forcing the cab of the truck parallel to the trailer. For the most part, trucks had to park parallel to the curb, which took up even more space and led to further crowding and blocked traffic, creating additional delivery inefficiencies.[45]

Weiss & Klau represented an extreme version of the physical problems faced by all SoHo firms. In the 1960s, the company was doing fairly well, though not completely thriving, and one could imagine it remaining solvent for several years if the company's headquarters had not literally collapsed in 1966. Because of the limitations of its loft, Weiss & Klau quickly went from profitable to insolvent. The collapse of the Broadway loft motivated city officials to investigate the safety of industrial lofts in general. New York mayor John Lindsay, who arrived to inspect the scene, said the floors were "badly overloaded" and estimated that the building had been burdened by two and a half to three times the permissible weight. Buildings Commissioner Charles C. Moerdler complained that only one inspector was assigned to the neighborhood dubbed "Hell's Hundred Acres," leaving many who worked there in peril. William Oppenheim, vice president of Weiss & Klau, noted that the last inspection of the building, in February 1963, had found no violations. Yet one press account reported that "Touring the wrecked building Moerdler noted that floors wobbled as he walked. He asked a fire chief 'how much more of this stuff is there around here?' 'There's plenty of it,' was the reply.'" As a result, the buildings commissioner announced what he called "Operation Overload," which involved "twenty-one teams of one fireman and one buildings inspector" assigned to "check buildings in the area bounded by Chambers and Houston Streets, west Broadway and the Bowery" the next day.[46]

The collapse of the loft building was also fatal to Weiss & Klau. Because the accident seriously damaged equipment and inventory, the company soon found the "continuance of operations at that location virtually impossible." Because of the damage, as well as the unusable space in the company's two loft buildings, the company's manufacturing operations came to a standstill in the weeks following the accident, and the company was unable to fill customers' orders. At the end of the month, the buildings department ruled that the collapsed building could not be used until it was fully reconstructed. Consequently, "Weiss & Klau's officers decided that it would be too costly to try to continue operating all of its businesses on a makeshift basis pending the complete reconstruction of the building or the moving of operations to a new, comparable building." Within a few weeks, about 335 employees (out of a total of 400) were given notice of termination. By November 31, 1966, only 11 employees remained.[47]

Soon after, the company liquidated its assets. In January 1967 Weiss & Klau sold its window shade business to Breneman, Inc. for $800,000. In March it sold the self-adhesive business to the Clopay Corporation for $375,000. In November, Weiss & Klau sold its Industrial Fabrics Division to Empire State Coated Fabrics Corporation, at a discount, for $247,007. The loft buildings were sold to Chatham Associates for $400,000. At this point, Weiss & Klau ceased to operate in SoHo. Although it briefly kept its upstate facility open, by September 1968 the corporation was dissolved and sold to the American Cyanamid Company for over $20 million. Proceeds from the liquidation brought its shareholders, all relatives of the company's original founders, gross proceeds of more than $3 million.[48]

Weiss & Klau was a valuable company but one that was doomed by its investment and operations in SoHo lofts. According to most observers, SoHo lofts were old, insufficient, and literally dangerous to their tenants. They also stood in a neighborhood located next to a major university, an upper-income residential area, and the city's Financial District. Thus, it is easy to imagine how lofts became targets for replacement through urban renewal throughout the 1950s and '60s.

Washington Square Southeast: Industrial Renewal in Greenwich Village

The first attempt at renewal in loft districts took place in the section of Greenwich Village adjacent to SoHo, in the area between Houston Street (the northern boundary of the neighborhood) and Washington Square Park. In the early 1950s, Robert Moses, New York's "master builder" of highways and housing projects and chairman of the Mayor's Slum Clearance Committee (among other agencies), teamed with leaders of New York University (NYU) to plan and advocate for Washington Square Southeast, a Title I urban development project south of Washington Square Park.[49] The project resulted in the demolition of seventeen acres of buildings to make room for the Washington Square Village and University Village housing developments.

The area of Greenwich Village south of Washington Square Park shared some important similarities with SoHo. It contained many of the same types of loft buildings and housed many of the same industries. Yet unlike SoHo, industry was adjacent to some homes, and there were residents to fight renewal plans to raze the area. The area in question also sat immediately south of New York University, an institution in a prime position to back a renewal project. Like their peers at the University of Chicago, Case Western Reserve, and Columbia University, administrators at NYU sought to shore up the neighborhood surrounding their campus and expand the size of the institution at a time when the university was becoming an increasingly important part of the city's (and country's) postindustrial, Cold War economy.[50]

Robert Moses initiated the project in late 1952 by meeting with NYU Chancellor Henry T. Heald. The two men expressed mutual interest in a plan to construct a housing development in the area bounded by West Broadway and Mercer, and Houston and West Fourth Streets, using federal Title I urban renewal funds. The plan was to convert these nine square blocks of mixed-use properties into three superblocks, each containing three high-rise housing projects surrounded by plazas and parkland. The development would replace the neighborhood's current structures with one thousand low-density housing units and university buildings. Heald and Moses expected the city to obtain the land through its powers of eminent domain and then use federal urban renewal funds to clear it, building the housing projects through a development corporation founded expressly for that purpose. City leaders, Moses, and NYU would guide the corporation to build the structures as they saw fit. In this case, the project would provide housing for middle-class residents, many of them likely associated with NYU.[51]

Central to the project was the idea that the industrial and commercial "slum" area in southern Greenwich Village should be replaced with more modern and useful structures that would help the city prosper in a postindustrial age and generate higher tax revenues for the city. Representatives from NYU believed that the development would upgrade a "predominantly old commercial and industrial" district where "many of the buildings are deteriorated, the land coverage is high, and almost all of the structures have outlived their usefulness." The area was made up of buildings used "for loft purposes, light manufacturing, stores, etc.," which the project's backers did not view as viable businesses in the long term.[52] In February 1953, NYU agreed to pay $15,000 to $20,000 for a site plan for the slum clearance project (the amount later came to closer to $25,000). After the city condemned the land, the plan was for NYU to take title to the northernmost three blocks by July 1, 1953, complete the demolition of existing structures in three to four years, and begin construction of new buildings on the site soon after.[53]

However, a coalition of middle-class residents, area homeowners, and local businesses quickly organized to oppose the project, arguing that it would replace a vibrant mixed-use area, including lofts that made a valuable economic contribution to the city. They noted that Washington Square Southeast would require the demolition of nine city blocks and the forced relocation of close to two hundred residents, as well as eleven hundred businesses employing fifteen thousand workers. Village resident Samuel Duker objected

FIGURE 5. Map of urban renewal activity, Manhattan, New York City.

to the characterization of the neighborhood as a "dead loss," arguing instead that the "slum" area to be replaced was a "pulsating business center containing several thousand small enterprises which give employment to thousands of people, including hundreds from the vicinity who walk to work daily." Although it was not home to big corporations, and most companies utilized rented spaces, he argued that these enterprises were incubators where "the small manufacturer gets his start."[54]

In turn, NYU's support for the project was based on the premise that university buildings would replace the economic contributions of area light industries housed in obsolete lofts, thus supporting the city's postindustrial economy. Anticipating arguments for cultivating a knowledge economy in New York, NYU officials stated that "Greenwich Village is known throughout the world as creative cultural center" and that "a major contributing factor to this reputation is the location of New York University at Washington Square." They argued that the university provided creative stimulus and stabilizing influence to the neighborhood and that its continued presence in the area would act as a boon to its real estate. NYU staff agreed with the contention that the structures in the project area were obsolete and should be replaced by others supporting its mission.[55]

Despite the objections of Village residents, the City Planning Commission gave its approval to the Washington Square Southeast project on December 10, 1953. The project's opponents next worked to convince members of the Board of Estimate to vote against it.[56] As the board's January 14, 1954, hearing approached, community groups contended that the project would threaten local businesses and affordable housing. Protestors included members of the Commercial Building Owners' and Tenants' Association of Lower New York, whose spokesperson Charles Pagella maintained that the businesses in the project area served "the necessary requirements for adequate space at reasonable rents." He objected to Chancellor Heald's assertion that there were no reasonable objections to the housing development, arguing that the project area's "manufacturers of paper boxes, envelopes, zippers, elastic bands, sewing machine parts, men's and boy's belts, hats, umbrellas, brushes, house slippers, lamps and lamp shades, luggage and elevators" were a valuable resource to the city. They argued that if forced to move, "80 per cent of the firms will either go out of business or move to more favorable areas outside the city."[57]

Yet others contended that it would be best to replace this Lower Manhattan industrial slum. In an editorial on January 13, the *New York Times* played down the effect of businesses moving, arguing that "there seems little doubt that they can find comparable quarters elsewhere" and that "there is no future, except a downhill slide, in the area chosen for this development."

In addition, Louis H. Solomon, president of the Chamber of Commerce of Greenwich Village, argued in an editorial in the *New York Herald-Tribune* that the area southeast of Washington Square Park was a "real industrial slum" because there had been no money spent in it for decades and landlords did not have enough capital to rehabilitate their structures.[58]

In the end, the Board of Estimate approved the Washington Square Southeast project over the objections of Village residents, businesses, and organizations. The support of NYU and Robert Moses carried the day over the protestations of Villagers, many of whom made up the sixty speakers and one thousand spectators at a meeting on the project in January 1954.[59] By 1958, the Washington Square Village Corporation had constructed two seventeen-story buildings stretching the entire three-block length of the project site. NYU developed the southern portion of the site, which came to be known as University Village, where three thirty-two-story towers designed by well-known architect I. M. Pei opened in 1966.[60]

Although ultimately unsuccessful in stopping the Washington Square Southeast project, Village residents did encourage decision makers on the national level to question the rationale for, and operation of, federally funded urban renewal projects, specifically those that targeted industrial areas. In April 1955, the Sub-Committee on Small Business of the US House of Representatives held hearings on the Washington Square Southeast project. Representatives from the Washington Square Neighbors, as well as the Mayor's Committee on Slum Clearance and the Triborough Bridge and Tunnel Authority (an organization closely controlled by Robert Moses), spoke at the hearings. Committee members were concerned that the Washington Square Southeast project was built despite the fact that the Small Business Administration had recommended against it. In his report on the hearing, committee chair Wright Patman, a Democratic Congressman from Texas, called for policy changes that would prevent similar residential projects from being built in industrial slums. He noted that current urban development law "makes no mention whatsoever of aid to small-businesses men," which was an important omission because "moving a business entails a great deal more than does moving a family. Costs are often higher. In some cases suitable markets are left and new markets are yet to be obtained." He said that policy should be changed so that "small-business concerns should be remunerated for their moving expenses, costs of installations, and their allied expenses." Although the committee's report on the Washington Square Southeast Project concluded that the project was valid, it recommended that the federal government do something "to prevent the recurrence of such inequities to small-business concerns."[61] Although no action was taken as a result of the hearings, people were clearly beginning to question the rationale behind this form of industrial renewal.

It is also worth noting that Washington Square Village was not the only industrial slum clearance project planned for the area. When giving its final approval to Washington Square Southeast, the City Planning Commission voted to table the proposed Simkhovitch Houses as a concession to its opponents. Simkhovitch Houses were to be a middle-to-low-income housing project south of Washington Square. The development (really two projects, one paid for by the city and one funded by the state) was planned for the area enclosed by West Houston Street, West Broadway, Broome Street, and Sixth Avenue, and would have resulted in the destruction of some of the lofts on the western boundary of SoHo. The project called for housing 1,440 families at a cost of $9 to $12 per room per month and 432 families at $19 to $20 per room per month.[62] Clearly the project's backers believed that moderate-income housing was more important to the city than the industrial and commercial loft buildings located in this part of SoHo.

SoHo as Industrial and Commercial Slum

In 1962, SoHo experienced another, closer, brush with urban renewal: an attempt to raze the entire neighborhood and replace it with a middle-income housing project. Some civic groups, unions, and city leaders believed that the neighborhood's nineteenth-century loft buildings were physically outdated and destined for economic failure. Consequently, they saw the area as the perfect location for an urban renewal program that would keep the middle class in New York.

SoHo was an even more maligned industrial area than southern Greenwich Village. This view is best exemplified by *The Wastelands of New York City*, a 1962 planning study produced by City Club of New York, an organization founded during the Progressive Era and dedicated to efficient city government. The report sought "to determine the essential characteristics of large run-down commercial areas in lower Manhattan." Specifically, the study concentrated on "the so-called 'Valley'" industrial area, immediately north of Canal Street and east of West Broadway," which encompassed SoHo. The report used the term "Valley" in reference to the low building heights and low real estate values nestled between the high-rises of the Financial District and Midtown Manhattan. Additionally, the group studied the "Hudson Street to Greenwich Street section south of Canal Street" in what would be known as Tribeca a decade later. The study's findings were clear from its cover, which was filled with "For Rent" and "For Sale" signs hanging from lofts.[63]

The Wastelands of New York City

A Preliminary Inquiry into the Nature of Commercial Slum Areas, Their Potential for Housing and Business Redevelopment

THE CITY CLUB OF NEW YORK
6 West 48 Street, New York 36, N. Y.

FIGURE 6. Cover image of *The Wastelands of New York City: A Preliminary Inquiry into the Nature of Commercial Slum Areas, Their Potential for Housing and Business Redevelopment* (New York: City Club of New York, 1962).

To study SoHo, the organization's president, I. D. Robbins, interviewed every tenant in select blocks to get a sense of "the exact borders of the enormous commercial slum" that City Club estimated contained "600 run down commercial buildings [that] covered 45 acres." Visiting thirty buildings in the large block bounded by Spring, Broome, Mercer, and Greene Streets, the study found 264 factory and warehouse workers and 103 white-collar workers (a number that included salespeople), but also 79,550 square feet of vacant space, constituting 15.4 percent of real estate in the area.[64]

Overall, the report was unflinching in its condemnation of SoHo's prospects. It argued, "such areas are true wastelands of our city. Such space is so inefficient and unsanitary that industry avoids it even at extremely low rents." It concluded, "there are no buildings worth saving among the thirty studied" in SoHo, and though the surrounding neighborhoods had "been described as teeming with workers, they have relatively small working populations." Although some industries, such as waste recycling, might need large amounts of cheap loft space, "there is certainly no reason why such industries, paying the lowest rent and employing almost no one, should occupy some of the best locations in the city's inner core, blessed with every convenience of public service including transportation." The City Club said that building owners were unhappy in their locations and just hoped to be bought out by the city during urban renewal. In the end, they found, there was no reason "why the city should abstain from undertaking programs of housing and commercial redevelopment." In bold letters they declared, SoHo "should be regarded as a commercial slum and a better use should be found for the land it occupies."[65]

The City Club of New York was not the only entity that hoped to see redevelopment in SoHo. That same year, Manhattan borough president Edward R. Dudley proposed a plan for a middle-income housing project in SoHo, although it never came to fruition. Later in 1962, however, another civic group proposed a development that gained more traction. MICOVE, "an organization of 5,000 families in search of homes," commissioned an architect to produce a plan for a thirty-one-acre housing development in SoHo. The MICOVE project had its share of supporters, including the United Hatters, Cap and Millinery Workers' Union, an organization with close ties to New York's Liberal Party. The union hoped that the project would bring needed middle-income housing that employees working in nearby industrial lofts could afford.[66]

It was University of Pennsylvania professor of city and regional planning Chester Rapkin, author of the 1963 study on the South Houston Industrial Area, who saved the area from potential destruction. The study, commissioned by the New York City Planning Commission in response to the MICOVE housing project proposal, laid out a vision for the neighborhood that countered the City Club and others who saw SoHo as collection of outdated buildings. Instead, Rapkin argued that the area was a vital industrial incubator with viable industrial enterprises that provided employment for a significant number of New Yorkers, especially low-income minority workers who would have had a difficult time finding jobs elsewhere.[67]

Rapkin found that in spite of the deteriorating condition of many buildings, SoHo businesses made a significant contribution to the economic life of New York. The area contained machine shops, industrial wholesaling, dry goods, apparel, and printing firms, and companies making chemicals, rubber, leather, paper products, and plastic dolls. Overall wages, average weekly earnings of workers, and the hourly wages in South Houston compared favorably with workers in similar industries nationally. Area establishments did $203 million in business in 1960 and exhibited a pattern of growth in recent years.[68]

Even more significantly, perhaps, the report highlighted the importance of the South Houston Industrial Area to people of color in New York. It stated that a "large proportion of the employees in the South Houston Industrial Area come from the city's minority groups." Furthermore, owing to the ongoing shift from manufacturing to white-collar employment in New York, and the migration of industrial employment away from the city, minority workers in the South Houston Industrial Area would have had a difficult time finding other comparable employment if the community were to lose manufacturing due to urban development. When firms moved away from SoHo, Rapkin found, they tended to hire new employees, making it even more imperative that city leaders preserve these businesses to keep jobs in New York.[69]

The news from the Rapkin report was not all good, however. It cited the inefficiencies of industries in SoHo's multistory buildings, comparing them unfavorably to the horizontally oriented production setups of newer factories and warehouses. These inefficiencies, combined with the high price of bringing buildings up to fire code, would mean that the renovation costs of many SoHo lofts would total more than their current values. In addition, rehabilitation could lead to increased rents, making some more marginal businesses unviable. However, in spite of its problems, Rapkin remained committed to preserving SoHo as an industrial area, as he felt that its economic contributions, particularly in terms of minority employment, would be difficult to replicate elsewhere.[70]

Soon after the publication of the study, the New York City Planning Commission (CPC) published its own report concurring with Rapkin's findings. The CPC contended that the city should work to preserve SoHo because of the overall decline in manufacturing in New York during the preceding decade. During the four-year period from 1954 to 1958, sixty-two thousand production jobs were lost in Manhattan and twelve thousand more in the other boroughs. Yet, the report stated, "In this small but vital part of the New York Metropolitan Region are concentrated 29% of the Region's total manufacturing employment, and 53% of the City's total." Although "New York City must accept the fact that its old loft buildings which for years have been providing reasonably priced accommodations for small industries cannot continue forever" and "age and obsolescence are bound to take their toll," the CPC still argued that efforts to preserve manufacturing jobs in SoHo were warranted: "It is incumbent upon the City to concern itself with the full implications of this trend and take what steps are needed and appropriate to reverse or at least decelerate the outward flow of industries and jobs."[71]

However, the CPC also noted that a significant portion of this job loss came as a result of private development as well as urban renewal efforts, like those proposed for SoHo. The report put it bluntly: "During the past four years over 5 million square feet of Manhattan's industrial floor space have been demolished, and the overwhelming preponderance of industrial displacement has resulted from urban renewal projects and various kinds of public improvements." Moreover, the situation was not going to get better anytime soon. "Presently committed urban renewal projects in Manhattan call for the demolition of an additional 9 million square feet of loft and factory space." In the three and a half years from January 1959 through June 1962, 396 buildings with 5.8 million square feet of manufacturing space were demolished, and 87 percent of this total was in Manhattan.[72] In short, the CPC concluded, "industry is presently the scapegoat of urban renewal."

Like Rapkin, the City Planning Commission also highlighted the importance of SoHo jobs to New York's African American and Puerto Rican populations. The city already had what the CPC described as an unemployment problem among minority groups because, although "firms which move outside the City may retain some of their employees . . . racial barriers often prevent Negro and Puerto Rican employees from obtaining housing accommodations near the new plant locations." Moreover, the CPC continued, "production workers are especially vulnerable, and these comprise a large proportion of the workers in loft areas of Manhattan like the South Houston Industrial Area." As a result, the city "in its own economic self-interest and out of clear moral obligation must scrutinize very carefully any proposal involving further displacement of industry."[73] Not surprisingly, the City Planning Commission came down strongly against urban renewal in SoHo.

Interestingly, given its future history, part of the City Planning Commission's rationale for rejecting SoHo as an urban renewal site was its unsuitability as a residential neighborhood. They believed that building apartments south of Houston Street would "place housing in the worst kind of environment," as it would be separated from other residential developments (Washington Square Southeast) by busy West Houston Street and surrounded on all sides "by the same kinds of old loft structures as are contained within the

South Houston area itself." Moreover, "the delivery and shipment of materials and products through the rear entrances of the deep buildings fronting on Broadway" made the area noisy, and any housing would butt up against the "unsightly facades" of lofts "in an advanced state of dilapidation."[74] Ironically, these same facades would lead to SoHo's designation as a landmark district less than a decade later.

Due to Rapkin's findings and the City Planning Commission's analysis, no housing projects were built in SoHo. In June 1963, New York mayor Robert Wagner decided against an urban renewal project in the area south of Houston Street. City officials' desire to preserve jobs for low-skilled African American and Puerto Rican workers won out over the arguments of the middle-income cooperators, who said that the area was a collection of blighted structures.[75]

Industry, Artists, and Renewal in SoHo

In this manner, SoHo's industrial past and efforts to renew industrial slums in New York shaped its postindustrial future as an artist colony and gentrified neighborhood. Artists moved into SoHo right as groups were beginning to question and resist urban renewal efforts across the city, nation, and the Atlantic World. The defenders of industry in SoHo were able to save the area from the wrecking ball, helped along with an overall weariness with renewal projects in New York. Much of the City Planning Commission's rationale for rejecting the MICOVE housing project was that renewal projects had already inflicted too much damage on the city as a whole, and on industrial areas in particular. Civic leaders were also less eager to build another housing project in SoHo after the long, protracted debates and protests over Washington Square Southeast, as well as general opposition to urban renewal in the city.

Yet despite Chester Rapkin's warnings about the real struggles of loft industry, there were no plans in place to help these job-providing enterprises survive in an increasingly postindustrial landscape in New York. SoHo businesses were worth not replacing, but it was unclear how, or if, they might be saved. In this manner, the renewal era in SoHo was also one of the first instances when government inaction—a factor that would become increasingly important in the neighborhood's growth—strongly influenced its development. SoHo was saved by the failure to act on urban renewal plans, and little was done to shore up the area in the ensuing years. Although the City Planning Commission proposed programs to aid industrial businesses and increased code enforcement, neither took place. The lack of help for industrial firms likely increased vacancies and sent building owners to rent to any tenant they could find. Without code enforcement, city agencies mostly ignored the neighborhood. Consequently, in the coming years artists were able to find vacant lofts in SoHo and rent them without anyone detecting this illegal practice.

What remained in SoHo was a mix of family-owned businesses, firms with substantial investments in local real estate that wedded them to an increasingly obsolete locale. While some of the companies were successful, most of them operated on the margins of the postwar economy. They continued to turn out needed products, but their long-term futures were likely not to be in SoHo.

At the same time, the built environment that was left behind was conducive to adaptive reuse. The lack of large industry in New York may have prevented the sector from having many compelling defenders, but it also meant the city was covered with smaller, apartment-like lofts, not massive factories. This was the built environment in which a new form of artist-led redevelopment occurred in SoHo.

Finally, with all the focus on industrial renewal in SoHo, there is one group that is conspicuously absent from the story: artists. Although they later made their voices heard during protests over the Lower Manhattan Expressway (see chapter 3), no artist or artist group stood up against the proposed housing developments in SoHo or Greenwich Village. Nor did the City Club of New York, Chester Rapkin, or the City Planning Commission even mention the presence of artist tenants in industrial lofts. In fact, the latter went out of its way to disparage the very idea of housing in SoHo. There could be several reasons for this omission. Perhaps researchers simply did not encounter any artists in lofts. This is possible, as there were likely only a few hundred artists living in SoHo at the time. Because living in lofts was illegal, as will be discussed in the next chapter, any artists whom researchers encountered might have misrepresented their status or not answered the door. Yet it is more likely that policy makers found the artists they encountered to be either too few, or too unimportant, to mention.

2

Making the Artist Loft

Stephen Antonakos moved with his family from Greece to the United States in 1930. After a stint in the armed services during World War II, he studied art at Brooklyn Community College and eventually rented a studio on Twenty-ninth Street in New York City's Fur District, beginning a career in painting and sculpture that continued up to his death in 2013. In 1963, Antonakos sought out a larger space and ended up renting a loft on SoHo's Greene Street, signing a lease for $200 per month. The building was a fourth-floor walk-up with a freight elevator. He and his wife, Naomi, who worked at New York's Fischbach Gallery, would bring their grocery cart up and down the stairs. Guests, such as art dealer Ileana Sonnabend, would make the same trip up to the loft.

In 1967, the couple learned of a larger loft available as part of a cooperative forming in a building on the corner of West Broadway and Prince Street. Although they had five more years left on their lease, Naomi Antonakos went to look at the place. As she put it, "I rang the doorbell and a very intimidating man answered and said, 'What do you want?' I said, 'I need to see José on the fourth floor.' That was something I made up on the spur of the moment." There was graffiti all over the elevator, and when she arrived on the fourth floor to examine the unit, she noticed fluorescent fixtures hanging from the ceiling on chains, a row of bathrooms in the southeast corner, and workers making silk-screen print T-shirts. She took a quick look around, and when someone approached her, she asked, "Where's José?" After he responded, "He ain't here," she made her escape. Yet Naomi Antonakos had time to notice the loft's impressive size and the windows lining two walls. As she put it, "It felt okay, it felt good." The couple bought into the cooperative and moved into the loft. She remembers, "It was incredibly inexpensive from today's point of view. It wasn't cheap, but it was doable."[1]

Jared Bark moved to 398 West Broadway in 1968. Originally from Palo Alto, California, Bark completed graduate studies in sculpture at Hunter College in New York before going to work at Bellevue Hospital as part of his alternative service requirement as a conscientious objector during the Vietnam War. Like Stephen Antonakos, Bark first lived in a small loft space in the Fur District in Midtown Manhattan. At the same time, he worked in the Mercer Street loft of sculptor and Hunter faculty member George Sugarman. Some of Bark's fellow students from Hunter were living in an artist cooperative at 80 Wooster Street, which gave Bark an entry into the neighborhood. The growing artist community and the low cost of lofts inspired him to move to SoHo. He could get more space for less money, and the built environment of the area was inspiring. To Bark, "West Broadway in particular was a very light, light-filled, airy street. It had a certain less-claustrophobic feeling than West Twenty-ninth Street. It really was kind of dreary up there." He rented two adjoining lofts, together measuring more than three thousand square feet, above the garage and storage facility of a company called Hoffman Boiler Works. Rent was $200 per month and dropped to $190 the next year. He stayed in the space for the next four years before moving to another loft at 155 Wooster Street, in a building owned by SoHo gallery owner Paula Cooper, and started a framing business there.[2]

Jack Ceglic and Joel Dean, two of the founders of the famous Dean & DeLuca gourmet food store, relocated to SoHo in 1969. Needing more space for Ceglic's painting, the couple moved from a small apartment on Twelfth Street in Greenwich Village. Ceglic studied painting at the Parsons School of Design and was sharing studio space with several other artists on LaGuardia Place, just north of SoHo. He would often walk south of Houston Street and notice galleries opening and lofts for sale. After looking at a few spaces, Ceglic saw an advertisement in the *Village Voice* for a loft on Wooster Street. He went to visit and was impressed with the loft's light. Ceglic and Dean quickly jumped at the opportunity to purchase the loft.[3]

Artists came to SoHo because they needed inexpensive places to live and produce art. They made homes in SoHo because it was convenient: space was cheap and plentiful, and despite the lack of traditional retail businesses, the area was only a few blocks from Greenwich Village, near subway stations that could whisk them to jobs, museums, and other amenities uptown. Yet living in SoHo was also a challenge. Creating a residential loft out of an unused industrial space required a substantial amount of work and was extremely risky: not only could it be physically dangerous but residing in SoHo was also illegal, and any investment in a loft could be lost on the whim of a city inspector or landlord.

Taking these challenges into consideration, it is remarkable that a group of relatively poor artists created a new housing form in former industrial space. They did so by transforming the very features that made lofts increasingly obsolete for industry into the hallmarks of a new type of living space: the residential loft. Through hard work and ingenuity, artists (and smaller numbers of nonartists) converted what amounted to factory interiors—cavernous rooms filled with decades' worth of accumulated trash, old paint, and machinery—into attractive, light-filled apartments and work spaces. Through their renovations and interior design choices, SoHo artists also developed a new loft aesthetic that blended art and industrial space, urban life, and minimalist serenity. Artists were willing to put up with the difficulties of living in lofts because of the community that developed around them, a population that nurtured their creativity and supported their decision to live in a loft both practically and emotionally.

Though the neighborhood was a frequent target for urban renewal, the loft homes that SoHo residents created shared some similarities with the urban renewal projects built in Washington Square Southeast and beyond. In SoHo lofts, artists found the "sun, light, and open space" promised by the modernist architecture of superblock housing.[4] However, artists chose to live in a neighborhood that was the antithesis of what urban renewal attempted to create. SoHo residents found beauty and usefulness in places that were antimodern: a congested, economically obsolete neighborhood built on a nineteenth-century street grid and homes that were old, potentially hazardous, and located in a mixed-use area. In this manner, artists were able to find some of the benefits of modernist housing in a neighborhood frequently declared a slum.

Yet the decision to reside in the industrial slum of SoHo was practical. People who moved to SoHo in the late 1950s and early 1960s were not looking to make a profit through real estate investments: it would be hard to imagine a less secure investment than a SoHo loft. Like their fellow New Yorkers who moved to "Brownstone Brooklyn," artists saw beauty in the historical architecture of SoHo and were attracted to living in a neighborhood with a diversity of uses: industrial, commercial, and, thanks to their presence, residential. There was also an authentic grittiness to SoHo that many new residents appreciated.[5] Yet, in contrast to Brownstone Brooklyn, a search for authenticity was not the primary reason that most artists chose SoHo. Artists were attracted to the affordable present of SoHo, not its imagined history. It was the practical necessities of the art and real estate markets that made SoHo attractive.

Beyond the affordability of lofts, artists came to SoHo to be part of the burgeoning artistic community forming in the area. As urban planner Elizabeth Currid-Halkett argues, artists benefit from residing in close proximity to one another because of the opportunity it provides for informal social interaction and the formation of support networks. The ability of creative thinkers to meet, mingle, and exchange ideas and contacts is critical to creative production and the cultural economy. Artists gravitate to specific neighborhoods because their density and walkability encourage informal social interactions. Currid-Halkett writes that artists value "environments that allow for consistent and spontaneous human interaction." SoHo's distinct residential landscape made these forms of social interaction even easier. Since artists shared space with industrial businesses, they were the only people in the neighborhood on weekends and after working hours. Naomi Antonakos recalled that in SoHo in the 1960s, "you could know the whole art world," or at least feel like you did.[6]

SoHo's creative community also contributed to the creation of the residential loft. It was the critical mass of artists in the neighborhood that provided the expertise necessary to renovate factories and warehouses into homes. SoHo residents relied on community networks for the labor and know-how they needed to renovate their lofts safely and affordably. Artists worked on other lofts for free or could be hired at low cost. They provided expertise in plumbing, electrical work, and basic construction. In SoHo, the loft was a commodity that resulted from these social networks.

The neighborhood's close-knit artist community gave residents the emotional support required to live in the neighborhood illegally. Under the state Multiple Dwelling Law, any building with more than two residential units qualified as a multiple dwelling, which meant that it needed to have toilets, two means of egress, fire-retardant hallways, fire escapes, sprinklers, and other similar health and safety measures required for residences. Most early loft apartments did not possess these amenities. Even more problematic was that as soon as a building had two residential units, the Multiple Dwelling law applied to all units in the building. This meant that if an artist moved into a loft that still had some industrial tenants, its owner would technically have to bring all the lofts in the building up to residential standards. Even if they had the money to do so, it would make little sense for landlords to renovate industrial lofts to meet residential building codes. Moreover, these types of renovations might not have been physically possible in nineteenth-century buildings.[7]

New York City's prevailing zoning ordinance, enacted in 1960, outlined where commercial, industrial, and residential units could be located. In the postwar years, the city underwent a building boom, and the City Planning Commission had a difficult time regulating the built environment under its original 1916 zoning ordinance. The updated 1960 plan limited and sorted land use in Manhattan by making adjustments to use district boundaries, including ones that outlined where industry and housing could be located.[8] Making loft residences legal would have required changes to local zoning use districts, as well as alterations to the physical structure of the buildings.

Nevertheless, faced with a decreasing rental market for industrial lofts, owners of industrial buildings frequently leased to artists looking for large, inexpensive studio space. However, if an owner signed anything with an artist, it was likely a commercial lease that allowed the holder to work but not live there.[9] Although this arrangement allowed some artists to use lofts as separate studios, most did not have enough money for two rent payments. Thus, many artists ended up living in their SoHo work space illegally, leaving them vulnerable to eviction. The community of like-minded artists in SoHo also provided the support network to live in a fairly hostile environment, with city inspectors and landlords posing threats to their homes and investments.

The Artist Community Forms: Artists' Migrations to SoHo

By the early 1960s, there was a significant artist community in SoHo. Data on the size and composition of the artist enclave during these early years are hard to come by, but by 1968 the New York City Planning Commission found that artists occupied 211 lofts in a twelve-block area south of Houston Street. The commission estimated that 250 artists lived in this area but admitted that it was a conservative figure, as determining a population that deliberately hid itself from view was an inexact process. The SoHo Artists Association (SAA), an artist advocacy group, claimed to have a mailing list of more than 500 members in 1970, and most artist groups and local observers estimated that roughly 2,000 artists lived in SoHo at the time. Taking into account family members, the number of residents living in SoHo was likely 5,000 to 6,000 at that point.[10]

The SoHo artist community grew in unison with the flourishing art scene in New York that developed in the decades after World War II. In the late 1940s, an American avant-garde developed around abstract expressionism and broke from the formal traditions that had shaped previous artistic activity, shifting the cultural center of the West from Paris to New York. The ascendance of New York art was rooted in the growth of the United States as a superpower in the postwar era. To many observers, the growing prestige of the gestural paintings of Jackson Pollock and Willem de Kooning and the color-field canvases of Mark Rothko and Barnett Newman, among others, reflected the nation's standing as the most powerful country in the word. Moreover, New York artists' "emphasis on risk-taking, freedom, and personal discovery" helped "promote the message that American art best symbolized freedom and democracy's triumph in the post–World War II era."[11]

This art was deeply rooted in New York. In the period from 1948 to 1960, New York became, by near-universal agreement, the world center for artistic experimentation, a position that one could easily argue it has never relinquished. It did so thanks to the work of commercial and cooperative galleries, curators, art schools, and artists themselves. These artists included de Kooning, Rothko, Pollock, and Joseph Cornell, who put New York at the center of the art world in the 1940s and '50s. Newman, Donald Judd, Andy Warhol, and Fairfield Porter continued New York's successful run of artistic innovation through the 1960s. It was a time of extraordinary creativity. New York artists pioneered a flurry of revolutionary new techniques, including Rothko's floating rectangles, Pollock's manic splatter-paint abstractions, and Cornell's sculpted boxes. Starting in the 1950s, a thriving art scene developed around Tenth Street in Greenwich Village, with artists congregating at the Cedar Tavern and showing their work at cooperatively run galleries in the surrounding neighborhood. Museums displaying modern and abstract art also thrived. The Guggenheim Museum's iconic Frank Lloyd Wright–designed building opened on the Upper East Side in 1959, and the Museum of Modern Art continued to teach large numbers of New Yorkers about contemporary art. As critic Jed Perl had observed, by the 1960s, "culture was big business, museums were breaking their attendance records, and modern art was part of the mix." Art and art collection was part of this big business, and artists and art dealers could point to numerous examples of people who had attained success in the art world. Although the vast majority of artists still toiled in obscurity, during the postwar era, "success was no longer an abstraction, a daydream, a compact between you and your friends. Success was now something a lot of people rubbed up against and of which many at least got a taste."[12]

Residing in SoHo allowed artists to be close to the neighborhood most closely associated with this surge in New York art, Greenwich Village. Although the Greenwich Village gallery scene had been stagnant for several years by the 1960s, the area still had some of its cachet, and there were other local institutions, such as Judson Church and New York University, that provided teaching opportunities, display spaces, and gathering places for artists.[13] Residing in SoHo gave artists the opportunity to live in homes that were even more affordable and spacious than Village buildings, for which were there was still substantial residential and commercial demand, while having access to the social and artistic amenities of the neighborhood.

The large, open interior spaces available in loft buildings were particularly attractive to artists. SoHo industrial space was perfect for housing the outsize pieces that that New York artists were creating in the 1960s and '70s. Lower Manhattan artist and Artist Tenants Association (ATA) chair James Gahagan noted that artists settled in lofts because they were "singularly adaptable to their special needs." Lofts' ample windows provided natural light, and their open floor plans and high ceilings gave painters, sculptors, and dancers space to work. A *New York Times* reporter mused in 1962, "There seems to be some sort of mystic interaction between the size of a loft and the square footage of the work painters and sculptors turn out these days." In 1970, a *Life* reporter observed that SoHo lofts' "45-foot"-long rooms and "sixteen-foot ceilings" were perfect for artists "intent on painting canvases as large as billboards or sculpting pieces the size of automobiles."[14]

The architecture of SoHo also influenced the art produced in the area. As gallery owner Louis Meisel said, "The artists were down here working in

FIGURE 7. Rosemarie Castoro working in her SoHo loft, 1976. (Photograph by Robin Forbes. Reproduced by permission from Archives of American Art, Smithsonian Institution.)

these big cavernous spaces. And because they had the space they started to work larger." For Stephen Antonakos, the high ceilings of his loft gave him space to work, and its openness focused his attention on the "inner person," which was the subject of many of his paintings. James Wines produced sculptures in his five thousand-square-foot loft using large, chain rigs and welding equipment, moving the works out the window via pulley when they were done (as many local businesses did with their products).[15]

Lofts also appealed to artists because they could be rented cheaply. In 1960, when the average rent for a New York apartment was $78 per month, SoHo resident James Gahagan observed that SoHo artists generally paid $50 to $125 per month for much larger lofts.[16] Moreover, because they were big enough to use as both studios and residences, the real cost to artists was even lower, which was important because most New York artists did not earn high incomes. Analysis of data from a 1964 survey of members of the Artist Tenants Association found that artists in Lower Manhattan had a median income equal to only 63 percent of the overall median income for artists in the city, which was $5,200.[17]

Artists were able to find large, cheap lofts in SoHo because the area's deindustrialization left many of these spaces vacant. Indeed, the artists often found lofts in places where local industry struggled most. For example, owners of businesses that turned old rags into cloth or pulp into new paper often owned their buildings. When these businesses declined, the owners often rented unutilized lofts to artists. Such was the case with two partners in a waste recycling business at 113 Greene Street, who tried for eighteen months to find higher-paying industrial tenants before deciding to rent to artists. By 1968, artists occupied 25 percent of the square footage in lofts along Greene Street, which was a center for the waste industry. In contrast, artists occupied only 11 percent of loft space in the rest of the area.[18]

The New York City Planning Commission in 1964 found that industrial decline directly shaped the geography of the SoHo artist colony. They observed that artists lived in lofts "increasingly being abandoned by manufacturing tenants as dysfunctional of the demands of modern industry." This was particularly true when it came to smaller lofts less than twenty-five hundred square feet. For these landlords, "the choice was either to rent to artists or allow the building to go into bankruptcy requiring eventual demolition." As a result, "the relationship between artists and industry has been complementary. The artists have filled vacancies and saved buildings from bankruptcy and demolition." Artists first moved to the northwestern portion of the neighborhood, particularly near West Broadway as well as Greene Street, where lofts were smaller and industrial vacancies higher. Larger loft build-

FIGURE 8. Map of artist occupancy in manufacturing buildings in SoHo, Manhattan, 1968.

ings in eastern SoHo, especially along Broadway, had the fewest number of industrial vacancies and lower numbers of artists.[19]

Many SoHo artists moved into lofts that recently had housed industrial tenants. Visual artist and future SoHo shop owner Greg Turpan's first loft had been a cosmetics warehouse. While he lived on the fourth floor, a company on the third floor was still manufacturing novelties, such as replicas of the Statue of Liberty. Similarly, art dealer Barbara Toll's loft had been a wallpaper factory.[20]

The area's unique architecture also inspired artists to settle into neighborhood lofts. SoHo residents found beauty in the neighborhood's nineteenth-century industrial buildings as well as the distinct streetscape. Turpan remembered, "We weren't just drawn to these things because they were empty factory spaces in these bland buildings. When you look at these buildings and see these cast-iron facades, it was like being in Paris or something. So that in itself was a big part of that too; architecturally this was compelling." Painter Mary Heilmann, a longtime loft resident, said, "The architecture is so beautiful that I think that it has really influenced the way I think about work and where work goes when it leaves this place."[21]

The ability to live in a light-filled apartment was also a significant attraction. The relatively low height of buildings prevented the cavern effect that deprived many Manhattan structures of adequate natural light. Moreover, major SoHo streets such as West Broadway were particularly wide, allowing more light to reach inside lofts. Curator Barbara Haskell moved to SoHo because she wanted to replicate the "wide open spaces and a lot of light" of her native California. Ceglic and Dean "decided on this one particular building because of the light." Stephen Antonakos was aware of how light-starved New York could be, and he made sure to find a space with adequate illumination. His loft on the corner of West Broadway and Prince Streets gets sunlight from multiple directions and can feel like it is hovering over the street, with little to interrupt the rays streaming in from all sides.[22]

SoHo's Artist Residents

SoHo artists were generally well educated and from fairly stable financial backgrounds. Sharon Zukin found that artists, specifically those in SoHo, "were brought into the white collar workforce" due to increased levels of education, opportunities for wealth due to art sales, and government arts funding in the 1960s and beyond. Sociologist Charles R. Simpson found that SoHo artists were members of the middle class who "hoped for economic respectability as a component of their artistic ambition."[23]

The artists who moved to the neighborhood were mostly young and had some connection to New York. As SoHo resident and author Richard Kostelanetz noted, most people moving to SoHo were in their twenties or thirties. They knew enough about New York to understand how to transform a loft, a new and relatively rare form of housing in need of substantial renovation, into a feasible and attractive place to live. They also likely knew someone else who lived in the area, making the challenging transition to residing in an often-illegal loft home much easier.[24]

Most SoHo artists' introduction to the New York art world came from their experience in local colleges and art schools, having earned bachelor's and master's degrees in fine art from local institutions. For example, of the twenty artists who made up the cooperative A.I.R. Gallery in the mid-1970s, at least eight received bachelor's or master's degrees at schools that were part of the City University of New York system, while others had attended New York University, Cooper Union, the New School for Social Research, or Barnard College. Patricia Ann Norvell, who lived in a loft at 80 Wooster Street, was born in Berkeley, California, and received a bachelor's degree from Bennington College in Vermont before coming to New York to earn a master's from Hunter College. Susan Lewis Williams was born in Chicago and attended the University of Wisconsin at Madison for her undergraduate education before earning a master's from New York University. She studied sculpture at Hunter College before moving to a loft at 152 Wooster Street. Artists at the nearby Prince Street Gallery had similar educational histories. The gallery's 1974–75 lineup of nine artists included four with degrees from City Colleges, one with a degree from Pratt Institute in Brooklyn, and one with a BA from Columbia.[25]

The pattern of completing higher education and having some familiarity with New York also held for some of SoHo's best-known artists before they migrated to the neighborhood. Playwright Richard Foreman was born in suburban Westchester and went to school at Brown (BA) and Yale (MA) before moving to New York's Upper West Side in the 1960s and SoHo in 1970. Richard Kostelanetz moved to SoHo himself in 1974 from New York's East Village neighborhood. Kostelanetz was also born in Westchester County, New York, and went to school at Brown, fitting the pattern of highly educated, familiar-with-New York, middle-class artist settling in the neighborhood.[26]

Not everyone fit into this pattern, however; residents took diverse routes to SoHo. Some were in SoHo almost since birth. Gallery owner Louis Meisel's father owned a paper company in SoHo, and he worked in the area as a youth. He even placed his conception at a building on Spring Street in 1941. Others came from the other side of the world. Yukie Ohta's father migrated to the United States from Japan after visiting the 1964 World's Fair and found a loft on Crosby Street because another Japanese artist friend was living there.[27]

Despite the higher education and relative affluence of SoHo artists, most did not support themselves solely through art sales. As a result, many worked a variety of side jobs, particularly in the field of art education, to support their lifestyle while giving themselves opportunities to create and sell their art. Prince Street Gallery's Tomar Levine taught art at the Ninety-second Street YMCA, and Irene Buszco taught at public schools in New York. At A.I.R., the story was much the same. Rachel Bas-Cohen, Judith Bernstein, and Louise Kramer were art instructors in Brooklyn and on Long Island, Blythe Bohnen taught art classes at the Metropolitan Museum of Art, and Loretta Dunkelman was a Head Start program instructor.[28]

The museum and gallery sector also provided employment for neighborhood residents, especially as the gallery scene expanded after 1968. Loft owner Barbara Haskell worked as a curator for the Whitney Museum, Barbara Toll ran Hundred Acres, a print gallery owned by SoHo gallery pioneer Ivan Karp, and Jared Bark opened a successful frame shop. Finally, others worked on their art and did odd jobs while their spouses worked full-time. Such was the case with Hirotsugu Aoki, whose wife worked as an English professor at the City Colleges of New York while the couple lived in SoHo. He painted and did film work along with some odd jobs. Eventually, this led Aoki to a career doing production and special effects for motion pictures.[29]

Others turned to the neighborhood's industrial sector for employment. Greg Turpan drove a truck for an electrical contractor and did some teaching at schools in Brooklyn as well as a few odd jobs. He also worked in a SoHo restaurant, E. H. Cast, a luncheonette with a predominant clientele of industrial workers. Most famously, perhaps, the noted American classical composer Philip Glass worked in his cousin's plumbing business in SoHo before his career took off and he could support himself solely through his music.[30]

Paying for a Loft

Illegality made renting or buying a loft problematic. Many artists, especially in the early years of SoHo, simply leased their lofts, paying rent to a building owner who assumed they were running an industrial business or, more likely, did not care what they wanted to use the space for as long as their checks cleared. However, in the late 1960s, artists began to purchase entire buildings in SoHo through cooperatives. Members of co-ops still faced possible eviction, but they would at least own a part of the building even if they couldn't live there (though owning a piece of a likely already-vacant industrial building was far from a strong investment). The shaky legal status of SoHo buildings also made obtaining financing for loft space difficult, requiring some creativity on the part of both building owners and artists.

In SoHo's industrial era, loft buildings were owned by individuals or holding companies that represented individuals or families. Because it was far beyond the means of most artists to buy an entire building, if someone wanted to own a SoHo loft, he or she could only purchase a specific loft unit (usually an entire floor) through a cooperative. New York City has a long tradition of cooperative ownership of buildings dating back to the late nineteenth century, when wealthy New Yorkers would band together to erect buildings made up of spacious apartments. In the first decades of the twentieth century, several groups of artists joined forces to construct buildings composed of duplex apartments with living spaces and studios. From the 1920s through World War II, both residents and speculators built upper-income cooperatives in Gramercy Park and the Upper East Side of Manhattan. At the same time, ethnic groups, working-class people, and labor unions built several nonprofit, limited-income cooperatives (where residents could not sell their units at a profit) in places including Jackson Heights, Queens, and Manhattan's Washington Heights. In 1955, New York State passed the Limited Profit Housing Companies Act, creating so-called Mitchell-Lama cooperatives, backed and supervised by the City and State of New York, designed to create more affordable housing for low- and middle-income New Yorkers.[31]

Buying a loft through a cooperative had several advantages. Although owners could technically be evicted from their loft, their title to the space was not threatened by any city or state action. More important, buying a loft meant that a resident had ownership over any renovations that he or she undertook to his or her property. However, some of the usual benefits of home ownership, such as mortgage tax deductions and the promise of property appreciation, did not apply to loft owners.

By buying a loft through a cooperative, one was essentially buying shares in a corporation that owned a specific building. The shares would entitle the holder to inhabit one unit in the building and also give the holder a vote in deciding if and when the cooperative would take on new members (new residents). The members would then take collective responsibility for maintaining the building. This model of owning and operating a building fit with the ethos of the close-knit community of artists forming in SoHo.

Yet the illegality of SoHo buildings made this process more complicated. SoHo lofts were zoned for industry, and very few had a certificate of occupancy. As Barbara Toll's uncle told her when she was about to buy into a cooperative in the 1970s, "You can't buy this, this is completely illegal. You're buying stock in nothing."[32] Her uncle had a legitimate concern because it was common for SoHo residents to take years to work out the issues regarding the legality of their cooperative homes. The illegality of loft homes also meant that it was nearly impossible to obtain traditional mortgage financing.

Numerous SoHo residents nevertheless formed cooperatives starting in the late 1960s. Perhaps the most influential person behind the local co-op trend was George Maciunas. Maciunas was a Lithuanian immigrant who studied art and architecture at Cooper Union before earning a BA in architecture from Pittsburgh's Carnegie Institute of Technology in 1954. He then returned to New York and immersed himself in the local art world, taking classes at the Institute of Fine Arts and the New School while working for several architecture firms. While studying at the New School, Maciunas became involved in the artistic work that would define his career. There he met other artists, such as LaMonte Young, George Brecht, and Allan Kaprow, who were interested in interdisciplinary performance art. In 1961 Maciunas coined the term *Fluxus*, which referred to a new international avant-garde art movement that fused elements of performance art, Dada, and a variety of other genres. Fluxus performance art events crossed disciplinary (and other) boundaries. Their "happenings" ranged from a group of people dressed as dentists cleaning the sidewalk in front of the Plaza Hotel with toothbrushes, to recordings of music made by water dripping into a bowl, to Maciunas saving the packaging for all the food he consumed in a year and gluing it to a wall.[33]

As the last piece indicates, Maciunas was interested in transforming daily life into art, and the relationship between the day-to-day life of the artist and the work that he or she produced was a major focus of his career. As a result, Maciunas began to turn his attention to the problem of housing, particularly among those who produced avant-garde art. As this work could not easily be sold (and if it was sold, it was not likely to be for much money), Maciunas sought to find a way to provide artists a space where they could live and work affordably. In 1963, he developed what he called his Fluxhouse Plan to provide "large unbroken spaces with high ceilings and adequate illumination" to artists by renovating "commercial lofts" formerly used by marginal business in SoHo.[34]

Maciunas planned to address this problem by organizing nonprofit cooperatives of artists. These cooperatives would allow prospective residents to pool their resources to purchase loft buildings that they could then use for living and working spaces. He ran multiple advertisements in the local press, claiming that if an artist could pay roughly $2,200 to $5,000 (about $1 per square foot) as a deposit for the loft space, he or she could enter into the cooperative. Eventually, members were expected to come up with approximately $50,000 each in fees to cover the purchase of the loft and the renovations required to turn these industrial spaces into habitable dwellings.[35]

However, there were several legal obstacles standing in the way of creating housing cooperatives in SoHo. First, living in SoHo was illegal, and although Maciunas claimed that he would work to change city and state regulations to remedy this problem, legalization would not come for decades. Moreover, according to real estate syndication laws in New York, to offer shares in a cooperative, the organizer or sponsor had to prepare documents including a cooperative offering plan, a copy of the bylaws, and a proprietary release, along with other financial details, and send them to the New York State Attorney General, who would usually approve or deny them in six months to a year. However, Maciunas did not do any of this, and he did not want to wait as long as was required. He organized the buildings as agricultural cooperatives (which were easier to establish than cooperative residences) and filed them with the New York Department of State.[36]

Nor was there much chance that the state attorney general would have approved the cooperatives that Maciunas formed because it was only after receiving down payments from future tenants that Maciunas actually went out and purchased buildings and began the process of forming cooperatives. This meant that Maciunas was collecting money for cooperatives that did not yet exist for buildings he did not own. Maciunas was able to obtain some grant funding from the J. M. Kaplan Fund, a major New York foundation with a focus on the arts and artist housing in particular, to cover some of his purchase costs. Yet the grant did not cover the price of the buildings he organized as cooperatives.[37]

Over time, Maciunas's failure to follow procedure, as well as his overall management style, led to tensions with both residents and the authorities. Maciunas neglected to adhere to the law when it came to the handling of payments he received from cooperative members. Since he viewed his Fluxhouse cooperative as one larger enterprise, Maciunas used payments that residents gave him for one building to put down payments on the next. Over time these practices caught up with Maciunas. Residents at numerous cooperatives he organized also grew tired of his controlling personality and of his failure to live up to promises he made about loft renovations (he insisted on being both co-op sponsor and general contractor). Several of the cooperatives severed ties with Maciunas. In 1974, the attorney general investigated his failure to properly register these cooperatives, as well as his illegal handling of cooperative fees. However, he continued his involvement in co-op loft conversions through partners until his death in 1978.[38]

Despite his flawed practices, Maciunas pioneered the practice of creating cooperatives of artists in SoHo, and he helped organize cooperatives in sixteen buildings over the course of a decade, including those at 465–69, 451, and 331 West Broadway; 33 and 80 Wooster Street; 16–18 and 20–26 Greene Street; 64–70 Grand Street; 131 Prince Street; and 469–75 and 453–55 Broome Street. Without him, at the very least there would have been fewer homeowners in SoHo, something that might have changed the future course of political advocacy and real estate development in the area.[39]

Maciunas was not the only organizer of artist cooperatives in SoHo. One of the other major figures in the cooperative housing movement was Peter Gee, a British-born New York pop artist. Gee helped renovate and redevelop twenty SoHo buildings, including the lofts of Aoki and of Louis and Susan Meisel. Aoki paid $18,000 for a cooperative Gee organized at 132 Greene Street in 1974. The space he purchased was completely raw; renovations were not included in the purchase price.[40]

Like Maciunas's, Gee's organizational methods were also somewhat informal. Gee formed the cooperative at 141 Prince Street in which Louis Meisel purchased a loft in 1971. At the time, Gee was renting the top floor loft of the building from Yehuda Ben Yehuda, a prominent local artist who owned the building. Yehuda agreed to sell the building to Gee, who could not finance the entire purchase himself. Gee then approached the other tenants, who agreed to put up amounts ranging from $15,000 to $60,000 to buy a share in the building as a cooperative.[41]

Financing one's share in a cooperative also often required some creativity. Due to the illegality of SoHo lofts and the novelty of living in a former industrial space, obtaining a bank loan was impossible. As upfront costs were relatively low, SoHo residents were able to use other methods to obtain the necessary funds. For example, Susan and Louis Meisel financed the $50,000 they paid for their share in 141 Prince Street by selling some possessions as well as art that Louis owned as part of his uptown gallery, including a valuable painting by pop art progenitor Larry Rivers. They had $37 to their name the night they moved in.[42]

Other SoHo residents financed their lofts through loans from family members and friends as well as by using personal savings. Ceglic bought his loft for $14,000 with money from savings and help from his mother and brother. Naomi Antonakos received an advance on an inheritance from her father to purchase her first SoHo home. That, combined with the money that her husband, Stephen, made from selling the fixtures in his previous loft, was enough to cover the cost.[43] She didn't even consider bank financing. The creative financing that loft buyers used continued over the decades. Turpan bought his first loft, at 347 West Broadway, for $48,000 in 1981 by borrowing money from a customer at the restaurant where he worked.[44]

Other times, the decline of local industry and the development of artist cooperatives went hand in hand. Frits de Knegt befriended the Castellano brothers, owners of a paper recycling company across the street from his art delivery warehouse at 420 West Broadway (a business that will be discussed in chapter 5). He let them know that when they were ready to retire, he and his partner would be interested in buying the three buildings that served as their base of operations. When retirement finally came for the Castellano brothers, de Knegt and his partner found tenants who were willing to pay $40,000 each for a floor in their cooperative, used the down payments to renovate the elevators and make some basic repairs for the building, and bought them for $395,000. Each tenant was then responsible for renovating his or her own loft.[45]

Indeed, when cooperatives purchased loft buildings (including the case of de Knegt), or in cases where residents bought single-loft spaces directly from building owners, most did so using purchase money mortgages. In a purchase money mortgage, a buyer gives the seller a mortgage on a property that replaces all or some of the purchase price. For example, instead of a buyer paying a seller $100,000 for a building and getting a loan from a bank for much of this amount, the buyer would pay the seller the $100,000 directly, with interest, in installments over time. The seller technically lends the buyer money to purchase the building. Buyers use purchase money mortgages when they have little capital or are unable to obtain credit.[46]

Examples of the use of purchase money mortgages abound in SoHo. For instance, at the Fluxhouse cooperative at 80 Wooster Street, George Maciunas used $21,000 in resident fees and took an $84,000 purchase money mortgage from the previous owners to cover the rest of the cost. Jared Bark used a purchase money mortgage to buy the space that housed his first frame shop because traditional bank financing "would have been impossible" owing to the tenuous legal status of SoHo lofts.[47] It is hard to find a SoHo loft that was sold without this means of financing (if it was financed at all) through the early 1980s, even in the case of units purchased by relatively affluent investors. Consequently, many loft buyers were not able to take advantage of important benefits afforded to conventional homeowners, such as low-interest-rate Federal Housing Association–backed mortgages.

Loft Renovations and Homes: Adding Value to Industrial Space

After purchasing lofts, artists had to do a substantial amount of work to turn them into habitable structures. To convert industrial space into homes, pioneering artists did much of the work themselves, learning how to put up drywall, install sinks and showers, and sand floors. To complete these renovations, artists once again took on some risk, both to their person and to their investments. A plumbing mistake could be costly, and a wrong move while completing electrical work could be deadly. Artists took on this risk because they lacked the financial resources to carry out necessary renovations any other way. Moreover, as artists and members of a tight-knit community of other loft renovators, they were able to draw upon a wide range of resources in the form of both labor and expertise in order to turn old factories into livable apartments.

To convert industrial spaces into homes, artists invested time, labor, and capital, adding value to their apartments in the process. As Jim Stratton pointed out in *Pioneering in the Urban Wilderness*, a 1977 how-to guide to loft conversion, turning industrial lofts into appealing residences took a substantial amount of work, money, or both. Before even starting renovations, artists often had to unearth the physical space of their new homes. Lofts frequently contained a "half-century of garbage" sitting in "every corner" that either had to be sold or, more frequently, disposed of. Even removing this industrial waste could be a problem. Trash service often was not available in SoHo, so renovators had to rent a dumpster, which was a risky proposition. In addition to the high cost, a dumpster filled with trash outside a loft building could draw the attention of building inspectors, who could evict them or ask for a bribe to overlook the violation. Industrial business owners also filled renovators' dumpsters with their own trash, sparing themselves the expense of disposing of it, as they knew that the illegal artist tenants could not easily complain to the police.[48]

Additionally, many lofts were in advanced states of disrepair. Loft renovators frequently had to connect their living spaces to a variety of vital systems, including gas, electricity, plumbing, and heat, and install or arrange for the installation of working elevators, new roofs, and fire escapes. Frequently, boilers had fallen into disrepair, and if the building was used for industrial purposes, landlords did not provide heat on nights and weekends when no industrial tenants were present. Electricity might be outdated DC current that needed to be rewired, and setting up power to a loft residence sometimes required bringing up new electrical service from the basement. Loft plumbing was often inadequate, and existing systems provided water suitable for industrial uses but not for human consumption.[49]

In order to make their homes more livable and valuable, artists invested either their time and labor, by completing the renovations themselves, or their capital, by hiring individual workers to perform various aspects of the job and even employing contractors to supervise the work. The first of these options was the most attractive financially to artists, but it required substantial knowledge of the intimate details of multiple systems. The specter of adhering to New York City building codes also hung over all renovations. Along with the confusion over whether residential lofts crafted from industrial buildings should adhere to industrial or commercial building codes, artists faced a choice of whether to incur the costs of meeting either city code. Having work done according to the law might increase the chance of a loft eventually being approved as a legal dwelling, but dishonest contractors often inflated their prices for work done "up to code."[50]

Local artists learned a substantial amount about home renovations as they went along. Jared Bark undertook several renovations. To make his lofts habitable, first in the Fur District and then in SoHo, Bark did simple plumbing, such as installing a shower with polyvinyl chloride (PVC) pipe. Electricity required a bit more care, but if jobs got too complicated, one could always hire someone local. Most SoHo residents did their own drywall work to install some walls in their lofts. As Bark explained, "You learned quite easily, and it was very exciting to feel competent at interior carpentry." To make factory floors livable, he recalled, "You'd go down to Zelf's and rent a floor sander and you'd buy these big sheets of sandpaper and you'd go spend a weekend or whatever refinishing your floor. It was awful work, but, you know we didn't do—I didn't do—a very good job at it, but I did a lot of it. I did at least two floors and it was virtually free, and buy polyurethane or something and paint the floor." Despite the daunting nature of loft renovations, for some it was a rather natural process. As Bark put it, "You know, one learned; it's like your friends taught you, you picked it up."[51]

Many of the early loft renovations in SoHo were not fancy. Jack Ceglic worked on his loft for two years, covering the battleship-gray paint with multiple shades of white, obtaining a few pieces of furniture, and building a kitchen, just enough to "live there happily." Others echoed this renovation strategy. As Hirotsugu Aoki said, "At that time, most of the artists weren't really fixing their places very nicely. Basically they needed a big space, and in the back of the space they set up a little kitchen or whatever." Fortunately, this type of renovation did not require much investment. Greg Turpan remembered that he could only afford to finish the floors at first. "There were holes in the ceiling... but you just didn't worry about that," he said. "You just did as much cleaning as you could and with what budget you had, normally minimal... it was far from perfect, but it was livable when we finished." However, these renovations were cheap. Turpan recalled, "I think we made our space livable for less than $3,000. And the rent I was paying was $300, which I thought was astronomical at that time."[52]

Many artists relied on the growing community in SoHo for the expertise required to renovate their lofts. Painter Mary Heilmann hired an "artist-type plumber" to run a waste line and install a simple bathroom. She sanded her floors, together with a group of artists, and relied on an informal network of artists working informally as plumbers, electricians, carpenters, and drywall installers. Naomi Antonakos recalled that locals would usually hire other artists to do carpentry, painting, and electrical work. Although these artist-renovators were paid, a community spirit still pervaded. She said, "It was kind of close to that spirit of artists doing things . . . it was money, but it was still a cooperative spirit, a community spirit." Art school connections could also help. Turpan, who attended Pratt, which had strong programs in both fine arts and architecture, said that "having gone to school with architects . . . everybody did things on their own."[53]

The Loft Aesthetic: Creating Homes Out of Industrial Space

In SoHo, artists not only crafted a new form of housing but also a distinct interior design aesthetic. Loft residents took advantage of their artistic talents, and the industrial features of their homes, to convert underused industrial space into what would become an increasingly valuable real estate commodity.

The loft of Gerhardt Liebmann, a photorealist painter and president of the SoHo Artists Association, exemplified the emerging SoHo interior design aesthetic. Liebmann's loft at 451 West Broadway was part of the Fluxhouse cooperatives Maciunas formed in 1968. Two years later, the artist gave City Planning Commission members a tour of his home and building. Liebmann recalled that, upon walking into the various co-ops, the planners observed:

> The noise and decay were left on the streets the minute they stepped into the artists' lofts. Huge, serene spaces were painted a buoyant white. Indoor gardens grew to the high ceilings, urged on by the light flooding through skylights and vast windows. The artists' loft homes made the usual, even the highest priced New York apartment seem like LeFrak Village at its pinched worst. These spaces were the size of two, two-bedroom Levittown houses and were in the heart of Manhattan.[54]

Liebmann's loft impressed his visitors because it was like no residence they had previously seen in New York. His large home was a combination of industrial grit and artistic chic. Liebmann was able to transform the features of his loft that made it a poor industrial space into amenities that contributed to a striking and attractive home. Like other neighborhood artists, Liebmann took spaces too small to be factories but large enough to be comfortable apartments and converted them into light, spacious dwellings. He then decorated his lofts with design touches that expressed his creativity and artistic acumen, highlighting the novel and attractive nature of his new residences.

Looking at each of these elements of Liebmann's home, we can gain a fairly complete picture of the distinctiveness of SoHo lofts, as well as understand their development as industrial, cultural, and residential spaces. First, lofts' industrial pasts were important to their physical form and development. Liebmann's loft was "huge," with "high ceilings," "skylights," and "vast windows." The spacious interior and large windows were vestiges of the light industrial enterprises housed there. Though SoHo lofts were cramped for modern industrial uses, they made for massive apartments that were extremely attractive to space-starved New Yorkers. According to the early guidelines that the city developed for loft apartments, lofts could be as large as 3,600 square feet—which was an immense amount of space by New York standards—before they were considered too big for habitation.[55] Lofts sometimes were so large that it was possible to build "a complete three room house in a loft, complete with peaked roofs with eaves," as one SoHo artist did. Liebmann's loft was no exception. A *Life* magazine photographer captured artist Robert Weigand doing stunts on a trapeze hanging from his loft's ceiling in 1970.[56]

The open nature of loft interiors also made them uniquely adaptable, and many artists used their newfound carpentry skills to create or take away

FIGURE 9. Robert Weigand hanging from a trapeze in his loft, 1970. (Photograph by John Dominis. "Living Big in a Loft," *Life*, March 27, 1970.)

rooms through the addition or subtraction of walls. As Naomi Antonakos described it, "we could put up walls and take them down, it was so completely flexible." Spaces could change physically or functionally. The birth of a child could inspire the creation of a new bedroom carved out of the living room. When the child left for college, the wall could be removed again to create an open office. Yukie Ohta grew up in SoHo with her mother and artist father, and she remembered that when a Japanese woman came to live with them and provide childcare, her father simply said, "Oh, another person! Let's build a couple of walls!"[57]

Cast-iron interior columns created entire floors of nearly uninterrupted space. For reasons both practical and stylistic, residents often left their loft's interiors as open as possible. Artists used these open floor plans to create inventive apartment designs wherein living rooms, studio spaces, kitchens, bedrooms, and dining rooms all flowed into one another. Often, the bathroom was the only room with walls. This openness also encouraged a minimalism of design that fit with SoHo residents' artistic sensibilities as well as their budgets.

Open indoor spaces were also ideal for displaying striking, almost incongruous apartment features. In Liebmann's loft, the artist planted "indoor gardens" that "grew to the high ceilings," urged on by the light flooding through skylights and vast windows. In addition, in the same way that galleries would later find SoHo loft space ideal for their purposes, loft residences used ample wall and floor space to display outsize works of art or multiple paintings. For example, Liebmann built "custombuilt nooks" to display "his personal collection of Eastern statuary" and constructed a "modern free standing fireplace" in the middle of his open living space.[58]

In addition, artists used their creativity and artistic skills to turn other industrial features, including large windows and brick walls, into part of a new loft interior design aesthetic. Oversize windows were relics of a time when artificial lighting in industrial spaces was insufficient. Brick walls and hardwood floors were vestiges of nineteenth-century construction and were less than ideal at a time when fire-safe glass and steel factories were the norm. Artists incorporated these inheritances of SoHo's industrial past into their apartments, choosing decorations that highlighted them, as well as furnishings that evoked their homes' earlier histories.

Numerous SoHo artists combined the industrial features of their homes, the minimalism that open interiors encouraged, and their own artistic touches, to develop an interior design style that future loft inhabitants would later emulate. Nobu Fukui, a Japanese American painter who worked mainly in acrylics, converted a sixth-floor loft apartment at 53 Greene Street into a

FIGURE 10. People at a party in Nobu Fukui's loft, 1970. (Photograph by John Dominis. "Living Big in a Loft," *Life*, March 27, 1970.)

home "that allows for the expression of his creativity," decorated in "oriental simplicity and serenity, in striking contrast to the industrial activities in the remainder of his building." In painter and printmaker Vivian Browne's loft at 451 West Broadway, the space's "absence of interior walls" allowed for "flexibility in her living and working arrangements" and made it possible for Browne to live and work "in open space surrounded by her work displayed on exposed brick walls."[59]

Minimally decorated space became a hallmark of the emerging loft aesthetic. SoHo artist Ron Westerfield impressed a *New York Herald-Tribune* reporter with the size, openness, and minimalism of his loft. Westerfield's home was deemed "sparse but delightful." Space was often left open, with uses blending together, as was the case in the loft of multimedia artist and SoHo Artists Association member Sam Wiener, who lived at 451 West Broadway and worked "on large mirror sculptures in his light and airy loft."[60]

In SoHo, tasteful decorations and the space afforded by lofts helped overcome the disadvantages of living in an industrial space. On the second floor of 131 Prince Street, psychedelic oil painter Tom Blackwell and his wife, Linda, converted an "immense" former zipper factory into a "uniquely handsome home" that was featured in *House and Garden* and *Life* magazines. The couple decorated their space with Tom's "brightly colored semi-abstract work" as well as a "pleasantly shocking contrast of American, English, Spanish Renaissance furnishings." The Blackwell family decided to buy an entire floor of a SoHo loft co-op building and spend the time and money to remove nine tons of trash after "the thought of all that floor space—3,600 square feet—kept haunting them." Despite street noise from the surrounding industrial neighborhood, the couple enjoyed "an enormous living area" in addition to a "spacious studio, hidden behind the vinyl-covered living room wall." A photo of their loft that ran in *Life* showed a vast living room with hardwood floors, art on the walls, and enough room for the couple's daughter to ride her tricycle inside the apartment, no doubt mollifying some observers who were used to a suburban lifestyle into acknowledging that loft living was suitable for children.[61]

Because of their size and interior openness, the homes that artists created in SoHo stood in stark contrast to the typical postwar-era dwelling. While Manhattan apartments ranged from single-room-occupancy dwellings in the Bowery to eight-room palaces with servants' quarters on the Upper East Side, much of the housing built during this period took the form of basic

FIGURE 11. Linda and Tom Blackwell at home in their loft, 1970. The loft had enough space for their young daughter, at right beyond white wall, to ride her tricycle. (Photograph by John Dominis. "Living Big in a Loft," *Life*, March 27, 1970.)

apartments in the modernist style. Whereas some of these residences were in prime locations or possessed commanding views, this era of apartment construction featured structures akin to Washington Square Southeast, which featured two-, three-, and three-and-a-half-room apartments. Units had no more than a basic living and dining room, kitchen, bathroom, and bedroom, or even less in the case of studio apartments. In newly built structures, there was an emphasis on privacy over open space, and clean lines and solid colors were the norm. In a sense, the footprints of these apartments were not much different from the typical suburban home built during the 1950s, which offered a living room, kitchen, bathroom, and two bedrooms on seven hundred square feet of space.[62] Although a person of means could always move to a more distinctive home on Park Avenue, a brownstone, or a single-family house in the outer boroughs, the type of residence gaining an ever-larger share in the Manhattan real estate market was a small apartment in a modernist tower. In contrast to these homes, artists' lofts were all the more striking and unique.

Thus, it is fitting that Liebmann favorably compared his loft to "Lefrak Village," linking the positive qualities of loft space to contemporary critiques of modernist architecture. LeFrak City, a series of utilitarian housing towers located along the Long Island Expressway in Queens, was a prime example of the type of housing designed for middle-class New Yorkers during this era: small, unadorned apartments stacked on top of one another, far from the center of the city. Liebmann's loft offered something different: light, large spaces and a design sensibility that was both forward thinking and borrowed from a premodernist architectural past.

Some nonartists saw this former industrial space as competing favorably with housing available in the suburbs. In this manner, SoHo artists created a new type of home that achieved both of the goals of the housing projects that once threatened the area: lofts revalued the city's industrial built environment and helped keep middle-class families in New York. For example, artist Arden McCamy built an elevated structure within her SoHo loft for her three children to sleep on while pregnant with her fourth child. She, her husband, and the children slept on beds raised into the air, leaving space underneath for other activities. She described the home as functional, rather than fancy, yet still comparable to suburban living, as she noted that if she had wanted anything more, she would have "gone to the suburbs." Loft dwellers Bill and Yvonne Tarr decided to move from suburban Scarsdale into a SoHo loft, where they would join "Bill's assortment of steel and bronze sculptures" in their "90-foot-loft studio." The Tarrs chose the large, adaptable space over a comfortable suburban home, despite the lack of garbage collection and the absence of a community school in SoHo at the time. The Tarr family used its loft space to enact some interesting interior design features, including a ground-level family room and bathrooms, "with a living-dining-bedroom combination on an elevated platform halfway between the loft's ancient wooden floor and a skylight reaching to the 16-foot ceiling."[63]

The Artist Community: Friendships, Labor, and Risk

With artists converting lofts into homes throughout SoHo, a strong united spirit began to pervade the area. The SoHo artist community was both a contributing factor to, and a consequence of, the renovation of loft space. Artists helped one another find lofts as well as renovate them, and these finished homes became the sites where artists socialized. Over time, the community became the center of the artistic activity and political advocacy that would drive SoHo's further redevelopment. Most important, perhaps, many SoHo residents credit the spirit of the neighborhood's artist community for allowing them to take the risks and put in the effort necessary to carve new homes out of industrial space.

Once they moved to the neighborhood, the unique nature of SoHo's residential population made the community even more tightly knit. Stephen Antonakos recalled that in the late 1960s, when the neighborhood's industrial businesses would close each Friday at 5:00 p.m., SoHo would essentially become a neighborhood composed entirely of artists. Until the next Monday morning, the area would take on a small-town feel, with only artists walking the streets "from West Broadway to Broadway from Houston to Canal." At that point, the area's artist community numbered in the hundreds, and it seemed that he and his wife "knew most everybody in the neighborhood" and that SoHo "seemed to be mostly artists."[64]

This community, small in number and bounded geographically, was further brought together by their common membership in the local art world. Naomi Antonakos remembered that all she and those around her would do was "make art and look at art." Similarly, Heilmann recalled "that we all lived near each other and had conversations, and the art world was small, you could almost walk to everything at that time and you could almost know everybody." As Turpan noted, there was a "type of camaraderie among these pioneers that were down there, and one made lots of friends that way. There was a sense of community that I don't think, at least I don't see, . . . exists anymore."[65]

It was easy to find out about gallery openings and performances, and when residents attended, they likely knew the artists and most of the people in the audience. As Barbara Toll recalled, "there were performances everywhere, all the time, you'd just hear it. Everybody who was working downtown, you'd say, 'Oh, you know the Grand Union is going to give a performance in such-and-such a loft,' and you'd go there with some people and sit on the floor, and suddenly these people who had on one sock and a hat would start dancing past you with nothing else on, or candles in their hair."[66]

Art happenings and social events often bled into one another. Toll said that "once the Spring Street Bar opened on the corner of West Broadway and Spring Street, everybody would go there after work and you'd meet up and hear about whatever was going to go on during the weekend." These social gatherings could be gallery openings, parties, or both. For example, Louis Meisel had a party for three hundred people for each opening at his gallery. Although these large gatherings evolved into smaller artist dinners and brunches over the years, everyone from SoHo locals to Salvador Dalí and his ocelot would show up to "spend the whole day talking art and everything else."[67]

Beyond the social nature of the neighborhood, the SoHo artist community developed a philosophy that stemmed from the countercultural impulses of these 1960s and '70s artists as well as the spirit required to pioneer in this industrial neighborhood. As Jared Bark put it,

> One thing is that there were so many energetic people, people of ambition and enthusiasm and schemes and plans and ideas who might in other generations have gone down more conventional pathways, those being, let me turn these talents, ambitions, and enthusiasms of mine into a successful living. That was so far from our minds! We were adolescent for a very long time and in a very exciting way. So the ferment was great and . . . the art community included in those days a lot of people . . . who in another generation would have been investment bankers, or lawyers, or doctors, or something else. But there was something so magnetic about living your life in a new and unprogrammed way that it attracted many, many people. And, of course, there were drugs too![68]

There was energy in the air and a sense that great things were being accomplished. Yukie Ohta described it as people feeling "like they were living in an important moment, but they didn't know what it was. I think they knew it was special only because they were making up the rules as they went along." Greg Turpan described it as "one of the great times in the history of New York City. It was so remarkably energized and creative," because of the art being produced as well as the neighborhood's social events. He recalled, "Lines were being blurred between art, photography, fashion, food, all of that, so it was incredibly stimulating. And I want to say that many of us who were not well-to-do and living kind of meagerly had some of the most fantastic experiences, both when we entertained ourselves as artists in lofts and got together with large groups of us to have parties; it was fantastic, very stimulating, so much fun." Some of this enthusiasm was a product of the times: the late 1960s and early 1970s. As Hirotsugu Aoki put it, the SoHo artist community was imbued with a "hippie culture, anti-institution type of feeling" that had its own value system.[69]

Finally, there was a can-do spirit that permeated the neighborhood. As a group of people who turned factories into homes and opened galleries and new businesses where there had been no similar enterprises before, they needed such an attitude. As Toll said, "We certainly never thought there were things we couldn't do. And I think that was true of everybody, the people who lived here, who thought of businesses, who were artists and tried to get their work out."[70]

One of the results of this countercultural, can-do spirit was an attitude toward risk that allowed SoHo residents to make what, objectively speaking, were somewhat questionable decisions to invest money, time, and labor into loft space. Bark recalled a conversation he had with a friend who had a keen mind for business when Bark was about to buy into a co-op. Bark figured that he and his fellow co-op members could get five thousand square feet of space for roughly $275 per month in a building that was technically illegal. The friend asked what they thought the place would cost if loft living were legal. They estimated it at $750 per month. The friend argued that the $475 difference, then, was the true cost of the space. That is, taking on the risks that came with living in an illegal space and doing much of the work to renovate these spaces themselves was costing the co-op members $475 per month.[71]

As it turned out, the artists were right in the long run. While standard real estate investors were scared off by the risk of loft properties, artists dove right in, assuming that there was a critical mass of people living in lofts and that the city would never evict them en masse. As Bark said, "These people are living the American dream. They're investing, they're bootstrapping." If evicted from their lofts, "the press on this would be awful for the City of New York, not to mention the destruction of the art community, which is important to the city's revenues. So in fact we were lucky in that we perceived accurately that this was a pretty risk-free investment, and so we got incredible bargains."[72]

In this manner, artists' renovation of lofts into homes reflects their privileged and marginal status within the city and its housing market. Many SoHo artists came from middle-class backgrounds and had the financial acumen and resources to invest in lofts. Their training as artists, which often included at least an introduction to metalworking and other skilled trades, was also helpful in renovating these properties. Yet, at the same time, it is likely that few people other than artists would have taken on the risks that SoHo residents did in converting lofts into homes. Those with standard work schedules, or with the means to live in places other than old factories and warehouses, likely would not have taken the chance or put in the labor necessary to transform lofts into dwellings.

Aside from the risk it took to turn lofts into homes, it is important to recognize the work that went into creating these novel residences. In the 1960s, there were no government incentives to renovate lofts, nor did anyone invest in converting industrial space into residences in a coordinated way. The transformation of industrial lofts into loft homes was the result of the work of individual artists who spent their time and energy, and often risked much financially, to pioneer this new type of residence. Artists created homes and studios in lofts out of necessity; they used space that was available and cheap, and they only converted their units into a livable habitat after considerable sacrifice. Although their actions were uncoordinated and unplanned, the unique qualities of SoHo lofts and the creativity with which artists converted them into homes led, accidentally, to a new form of housing and a novel way to revalue underused industrial space.

However, in the mid-1960s, there were still several obstacles to SoHo's evolution into a residential neighborhood. The first of these was the continuing issue of illegality. While many artists were content to live outside the sanction of the law, the area would not have transitioned into a stable residential area if loft housing had remained illegal. The law would have to be changed for this illegal artist colony to become the residential neighborhood of SoHo. Additionally, there was one last urban renewal project planned for the area, the Lower Manhattan Expressway, which threatened to completely remake the area and its built environment. It was not until the ultimate death of this project that the residential transition of SoHo would begin in earnest.

3
Gray Areas and Industrial Slums: The Lower Manhattan Expressway

Whether they realized it or not, the first artists in SoHo moved into the path of a bulldozer. From 1941 through 1970, some of the most powerful civic leaders in New York, including Robert Moses and several mayors, sought to build the ten-lane Lower Manhattan Expressway along Broome Street through the heart of the neighborhood. The push to build the Lower Manhattan Expressway intensified in the early 1960s, just as the SoHo artist community was forming. The person behind this renewed effort was David Rockefeller, president of Chase Manhattan Bank, brother of New York Governor Nelson Rockefeller, chair of the board of directors of the Museum of Modern Art, and head of one of the city's most powerful planning organizations, the Downtown–Lower Manhattan Association (DLMA).

To David Rockefeller and the DLMA, SoHo represented an area of depressed property values between the Lower Manhattan Financial District and Midtown Manhattan, the island's second corporate center. The DLMA's 1964 planning study, "Lower Manhattan Expressway: An Essential Key to Business Growth and Job Opportunities in Lower Manhattan and New York City," described "the general route of the expressway" as "an economic valley between the higher priced areas to the north and south. It is an area of lower development, low value to the owners and of low return in taxes to the City." The DLMA asserted that "the construction of the Lower Manhattan Expressway will unquestionably open up this depressed economic valley to new modern development" both by improving traffic and by creating an "air of accomplishment" to spur new construction.[1]

Efforts to build the Lower Manhattan Expressway complemented attempts to renew SoHo through the construction of housing projects, such as the Middle Income Cooperators of Greenwich Village (MICOVE) development, which inspired Chester Rapkin's report. The roadway was connected to a broader planning philosophy that emphasized the importance of retaining the middle class in the city. It was aimed at helping New York City remain competitive with suburban areas by making it easier for car-owning Manhattan residents to access local highways and river crossings. As the quotation from the DLMA's report indicates, however, the Lower Manhattan Expressway's backers saw an added advantage to the project. To DLMA head Rockefeller, the roadway's main benefit was that it would replace outdated loft buildings while giving the Lower Manhattan Financial District, with its banking firms and corporate headquarters, room to expand.

Yet the Lower Manhattan Expressway was never completed. The project faced formidable obstacles from the outset; its path would have taken the roadway through the dense heart of Manhattan, and no highway across the borough was ever realized. Yet the roadway was a real possibility for significant parts of the 1960s and '70s. Its backers were well funded and politically connected, and construction even began on one part of the project in 1963. In the end, however, the Lower Manhattan Expressway remained unfinished and was eventually tabled.

Plans to build the Lower Manhattan Expressway fell victim to the "freeway revolts" that developed across the United States starting in the late 1950s. Beginning in San Francisco and spreading to cities including New York, Philadelphia, Washington, DC, Memphis, Nashville, Miami, and Baltimore, urban residents fought back against unresponsive civic leaders and engineers to resist highway projects that they considered damaging to their communities, their health, and their cities' built and natural environments. Protesters turned back, or at least altered, plans for highways in several cities, redirecting funding to transit projects in some cases.[2]

The fight against the Lower Manhattan Expressway was an important part of the freeway revolts, one that has been chronicled in urban histories of the period.[3] It is a classic urban renewal confrontation tale that pitted Robert Moses and numerous downtown interests against aggrieved local residents, including Jane Jacobs and the growing SoHo artist community. David Rockefeller and the DLMA sought to bolster New York's urban core against urban decay to provide a fertile environment for private development in the inner city. Their efforts inspired grassroots resistance from residents and business owners who would have been displaced, many of whom saw the negative consequences of urban renewal on other neighborhoods. Project opponents questioned the views of civic leaders and "expert" city planners, developed their own studies and rationales for preserving SoHo and the surrounding area, and presented them to the court of public opinion. The battle against the project had many of the hallmarks of a successful freeway protest: it started early and featured persistent, well-connected advocates who used litigation and lobbying to delay the project until changes in attitudes and political leadership ushered in its ultimate defeat.[4]

The history of the Lower Manhattan Expressway also presents an opportunity to examine both the effects of urban renewal on a specific urban site and the development of a neighborhood faced with the wrecking ball. Efforts to complete the Lower Manhattan Expressway, as well as its failure, had profound consequences for the evolution of SoHo. Without the expressway plan's defeat, there is little chance the neighborhood would have developed in the manner it did. A ten-lane expressway cutting through SoHo would have flattened many of the loft buildings that artists had converted into homes, gallery owners had turned into exhibition spaces, and entrepreneurs had transformed into restaurants and stores. A major roadway slicing through the neighborhood would have altered its character and created a barrier that would have prevented visitors and residents from traversing the neighborhood on foot. Years of construction necessary to build the expressway would have had a severe impact on the area and certainly would have prevented it from gentrifying. Moreover, as initial plans called for an elevated highway, the structure would have blocked some of the sunlight that made the neighborhood so attractive to artists.

Yet because its backers were able to keep plans for the project active for so long, the area in the path of the Lower Manhattan Expressway experienced many of the negative consequences of renewal. Faced with the possibility of their buildings being condemned by the city, SoHo's industrial loft owners were loath to improve or even maintain their properties for decades. The project caused industrial vacancy rates in SoHo to rise and rents to plummet, thereby allowing artists to obtain affordable studio and living space. After the threat of the expressway was lifted, SoHo experienced a commercial renaissance based on investment in its undervalued loft buildings. Consequently, efforts to build the roadway shaped SoHo as much as the project's failure did.

The success of New York's freeway revolt enabled artists to redevelop SoHo lofts, creating a community that suited their needs and, in time, became attractive to a wider population of affluent New Yorkers. Due to their efforts, the neighborhood evolved into something more than an economic valley; in the decade after the death of the Lower Manhattan Expressway, it became a neighborhood where all New Yorkers, even the workers in David Rockefeller's Financial District, could visit, shop for art, and even live. In this manner, efforts at urban renewal created the conditions under which artist-led gentrification developed in New York.

Renewing Gray Areas: The Philosophy of the Downtown–Lower Manhattan Association

The Lower Manhattan Expressway was part of an overall effort by David Rockefeller and the Downtown–Lower Manhattan Association to support the neighborhoods of Lower Manhattan as centers of banking, finance, and trade. The DLMA formed in 1958 after the Downtown Manhattan Association, Inc., merged with the Committee on Lower Manhattan, Inc. The organization's membership included Lower Manhattan firms in the fields of banking and finance, including the American Stock Exchange, the *Wall Street Journal*, Lehman Brothers, Morgan Stanley, American Express, Goldman Sachs, Merrill Lynch, and AT&T.[5]

The group's goals were "to foster, promote and support the improvement and sound redevelopment of economic values" in the area of Manhattan south of Canal Street. These goals were both altruistic and self-serving. David Rockefeller, the association's chair, had a genuine interest in inner city redevelopment and a strong personal financial interest in Lower Manhattan. As executive vice president of planning and development, and later chair of Chase Manhattan Bank (one of the largest banks in the nation, which was long associated with Standard Oil and the Rockefeller family), Rockefeller was largely responsible for moving the bank building's headquarters to One Chase Manhattan Plaza in Lower Manhattan in 1961. The bank's heavy outlay in Lower Manhattan was a somewhat risky move due to the lack of investment in the area at the time, especially compared to the borough's other major business center in Midtown, which had better access to suburban commuter train service. As a result, Rockefeller looked to ensure the long-term stability of Lower Manhattan through the DLMA.[6]

Practically, the DLMA worked closely with government agencies to research, develop, and implement traditional urban renewal efforts, such as housing projects, highways, and transit routes. The organization acted as an "unofficial, knowledgeable advisor" to elected officials and government agencies. Though the group had "no governmental powers" and reminded outsiders that it was forced to "work with one city department or another to bring life to its plans," the DLMA was not far from the levers of power. The DLMA traced its origins to the plans of one of the city's most powerful figures, Robert Moses. After Rockefeller finalized plans for Chase Manhattan Bank's downtown headquarters, Moses recommended that Rockefeller create an overall development plan for Lower Manhattan. This suggestion gave rise to the DLMA.[7]

The DLMA had a profound, if indirect, impact on Lower Manhattan.

Major projects that shaped New York City, such as the World Trade Center and Battery Park City, were rooted in the DLMA's research and planning efforts, which served as guides for these schemes and saw others through to completion. The organization was not able to achieve all it wanted, yet some contemporary observers of New York's development argued that the face of the city was influenced more by the "benign robber barons" associated with the group than it was by government officials or city planners.[8]

Though several people were responsible for the organization's activities, David Rockefeller was its guiding force and public face throughout much of the 1960s and '70s. More important, he also provided the organization with its philosophy of urban growth and decay. Although Rockefeller believed that Lower Manhattan was still the financial capital of the world, he worried that "the 'flight to the suburbs,' the economic distortion of the remaining population groups left in the central city" (i.e., "white flight") taxed central cities to the point that their very survival was in question. Without a healthy central city, entire metropolitan regions were threatened. As Rockefeller put it, "We must think in terms of the irreplaceability of the central city and its function. As the tree is doomed to death once its core is rotten, so the city which is healthy only at the fringes cannot long endure."[9]

At the center of Rockefeller's philosophy on urban decline were "gray areas," places of decline near the prosperous core of the city. This term had its origins in *Anatomy of a Metropolis: The Changing Distribution of People and Jobs within the New York Metropolitan Region*, a planning study completed by Harvard University in 1959. The report itself expressed a concern with the "development in the 'gray' areas that comprise most of the less central parts of the Core."[10] Whereas the idea of addressing blight on the fringes of prosperity was nothing new to theories of urban development in the middle of the twentieth century, Rockefeller used this idea to inspire the DLMA to target not the areas of deepest urban decay but those struggling neighborhoods located near the core of cities. In a sense, he sought to rehabilitate the "Zones of Transition" of Robert Park and Ernest Burgess's ecological model of city growth.

In urban areas, Rockefeller observed, "The main problem arises, not at the prosperous core or at the outer fringes where growth is taking place, but in the gray areas between the two." To Rockefeller, "these gray areas are left behind, not in the sense of being abandoned, but in the sense of enjoying the best or highest use." Gray areas placed a strain on city government because municipalities were required to retain services that were out of proportion to the revenue generated in them. Even worse, gray areas could spread, threatening the entire central city.[11]

To "fix" gray areas, Rockefeller argued, city governments and private capital needed to upgrade the declining industrial portions of inner cities before they threatened the city's stable economic base. Rockefeller viewed Lower Manhattan's financial center, a "core that is still around with fine buildings and prime office space," as the key to the city's long-term financial stability. To support the growth of the Financial District, the DLMA supported efforts to replace light industrial buildings that ringed this center of business and trade. The organization asserted "that eventual business occupancy of the greater part of lower Manhattan will represent the most logical and economically sound use of land in the area." In the view of the DLMA, "Banks and trust companies, stock exchanges and brokers, investment and banking houses and insurance firms—these have made the narrow tip of Manhattan the center of international finance. This is the very heart-pump of America's free economy, circulating creative capital to the furthest reaches of the union."[12]

Rockefeller viewed SoHo as the gray area that most directly threatened the Financial District. He argued that the vibrant Lower Manhattan financial center was surrounded by "blocks still occupied in large part by four-story dwellings which over the years were converted to marginal commercial uses. The majority of them are over one hundred years old. In many instances only the ground floor is now utilized." To Rockefeller, the area had potential only as an extension of the nearby Financial District. He said of the "almost continuous strip of inadequately utilized land encircling the highly developed financial district" that "nowhere else in Manhattan is there such a well-located area available for redevelopment so close to such a concentration of highly improved and increasingly valuable real estate. Nowhere else is there such accessibility to underground and surface transportation."[13] The plan for the Lower Manhattan Expressway was key to realizing this vision of an expanded Financial District.

The Lower Manhattan Expressway

The idea of a Lower Manhattan Expressway had been brewing since the 1920s and, during the next fifty years, city leaders proposed, fought over, and even began building a highway across Broome Street in the southern portion of SoHo. Plans called for a road to allow cars traveling between Long Island and New Jersey to move quickly along the first limited-access highway across Manhattan.

There was nothing in particular that made the Lower Manhattan Expressway different from the multiple highway projects that reshaped New York during the 1940s, '50s, and '60s. Under the guidance of New York "mas-

FIGURE 12. Lower Manhattan Expressway, 1965. (Downtown–Lower Manhattan Association Records. Courtesy of Rockefeller Archive Center, 1979.)

ter builder" Robert Moses, roadway projects including the Belt Parkway, Brooklyn-Queens Expressway, Cross Bronx Expressway, Cross Island Parkway, Gowanus Expressway, Grand Central Parkway, Long Island Expressway, Major Deegan Expressway, Brooklyn-Battery Tunnel, Bronx Whitestone Bridge, Throgs Neck Bridge, and Triborough Bridge brought New York fully into the automobile age, spurring growth but often destroying older communities in the process. The Lower Manhattan Expressway was part of this vision for the future of New York and meant to complement these projects. However, whether it was because of the difficulty of building through Manhattan, the city's mostly densely built borough, or because other projects were more important, Moses and others waited longer to attempt to build a highway across Lower Manhattan. By 1962, the time that the project lurched toward approval, New York governor Nelson Rockefeller had removed Moses from the chairmanship of several state agencies he once held, depriving the master builder of much of his power, though not his control over arterial projects in the region.[14]

The history of the Lower Manhattan Expressway itself began in 1929, when a civic group known as the Regional Plan Association called for a highway across Lower Manhattan as part of its master plan for city highways. The City Planning Commission proposed roughly the same project in 1941: a highway connecting the Holland Tunnel and the West Side Highway to the Williamsburg and Manhattan Bridges along Broome Street. In the next two years, the Lower Manhattan Expressway won the approval of the New York State Legislature, which included the expressway in the State's Arterial Highway System. In 1946, the Manhattan borough president, the City Planning Commission, and the city's construction coordinator, Robert Moses, reached an agreement on a plan for a $22 million Lower Manhattan Crosstown Expressway. The city intended to acquire the right of way for the roadway in 1948 and complete the job in 1949. It was to have been the first of a series of five east-west highways across Manhattan, two in Midtown at Thirty-fourth and Fifty-seventh Streets and another at 125th Street. Yet the road was not constructed at that time due to lack of funds. The land for the project totaled $10 million, an amount far larger than the city could meet on its own even before paying for any construction costs.[15]

Plans for the Lower Manhattan Expressway gained new life in 1956 with the passage of the Interstate Highway Act. With federal funds available, the expressway's supporters were able to take additional steps toward construction. Perhaps anticipating approval of the act, in 1955 the Port Authority of New York and the Triborough Bridge and Tunnel Authority, under the leadership of Moses, conducted a joint study of arterial facilities in New York, which found an expressway in Lower Manhattan to be necessary to accommodate traffic in this congested area. In 1956, Moses worked with the City and State Department of Public Works to request that the project become part of the Interstate Highway System, making it eligible for 90 percent funding from the federal government and 10 percent from the state. An agreement was then reached between city and state officials on a route for an elevated expressway that would be built across Canal and Broome Streets, allowing the program to be added to the official planning map for interstate highways in 1958.[16]

Starting in 1958, David Rockefeller and the DLMA lobbied political leaders, researched and published reports, and spoke publicly in favor of the Lower Manhattan Expressway, arguing that the roadway would benefit the banking and financial services sectors in Lower Manhattan. When David Rockefeller spoke at a City Planning Commission hearing in 1959, he said, "We believe it to be in the interest of the city, the state and of the Nation, for the financial, trading and shipping complex concentrated in the tip of Manhattan to develop in a way which will permit it to serve its function efficiently." The roadway should be built, Rockefeller argued, because it would improve "the fluid flow of vehicles and the accompanying elimination of irritating traffic congestion" and support the "modernization and expansion" of Lower Manhattan and its 34 million feet of commercial office space, including 9.5 million feet of space constructed since 1950; this in turn would "enhance and promote the further development of the downtown community which will, we are convinced, result in a multifold net increase in business activity and productive job opportunities for our City's citizens."[17]

The highway's supporters viewed the SoHo neighborhood as an outdated, declining commercial area. The *New York Times*, which ran several positive editorials about the highway, reported, "In the path of the proposed new road are substandard tenements" and "a few substantial loft buildings and some run-down commercial property" that could easily be replaced. Robert Moses's office expected little opposition to the project, saying, "Only a hard core of tenement house occupants are expected to fight the improvement."[18]

However, plans for the expressway immediately drew criticism from people living in the neighborhoods surrounding SoHo. While members of the DLMA spoke in favor of the roadway in front of the City Planning Commission, local residents expressed concern over the two thousand families that would be relocated and the 365 retail stores and 480 nonretail establishments that would be put out of business. These concerns led Moses to ask the city to increase the compensation given to residents relocated by urban renewal projects. Additionally, after the City Planning Commission added the expressway to the city's master planning map in February 1960, Manhattan borough president Louis A. Cioffi ordered a study of tenants in the roadway's path. Both the Board of Estimate and the Federal Bureau of Public Roads pledged not to move forward with the project until the relocation issue had been resolved.[19]

City leaders saw value in both the planning philosophy of the DLMA and community arguments against urban renewal. In September 1960, the Board of Estimate gave its approval to the expressway, but Mayor Robert Wagner made it clear that the city would not take any additional steps to build the roadway. He appeared reluctant to face political fallout from expressway construction and relocations. In January 1961, the city delayed releasing a report that found that tenants and businesses could be easily relocated. Apparently not eager to undertake these relocations, Wagner did not draw attention to the report's findings.[20]

In early 1961, Mayor Wagner did allow the Board of Estimate to refer the project back to the City Planning Commission, which approved the acquisition of property for the expressway in May 1962. The mayor did not forget about the relocation problem, however, saying, "The city must and will face up to its obligations to render all possible assistance for the decent and humane relocation of the people who will be affected."[21]

With the expressway project going forward, opponents grew more vocal. Father Gerard LaMountain of the Church of the Most Holy Crucifix, located on Broome between Mott and Mulberry Streets, helped organize local residents against the project and involved local political leaders such as state senator Louis De Salvio. He was also partially responsible for enlisting Jane Jacobs in the fight against the Lower Manhattan Expressway. Jacobs, a West Village resident and prominent urban renewal opponent, was the most prominent of a group of local residents who objected to the project because it gave urban space over to auto traffic, changed the scale and density of the area, and displaced residents and local industrial businesses. In 1962, Jacobs helped form the Joint Committee to Stop the Lower Manhattan Expressway after a meeting at the Church of the Most Holy Crucifix. The group's membership included twenty-eight local "religious, political and civic organizations" opposed to the expressway. By the time the Board of Estimate held a hearing on the acquisition of property for the road that June, "it was given over primarily to hearing the opposition from the local tenants and local groups and some groups not with an immediate interest such as the West Village Association headed by Mrs. Jane Jacobs." In addition, a letter was read from Eleanor Roosevelt, who objected to the expressway because insufficient attention was given to the relocation of residential tenants. Due to these objections, the Board of Estimate reserved its decision on the property acquisition until August. That month, one hundred members of the Joint Committee to Stop the Lower Manhattan Expressway marched through SoHo to Gracie Mansion to deliver a letter to Mayor Wagner urging him to reject it. Their protests had an effect, as city leaders delayed any decisions on the expressway until after the November 1962 gubernatorial elections.[22]

Although their involvement was not extensive, at this juncture SoHo's new artist residents also protested against the Lower Manhattan Expressway. At the August 1962 Board of Estimate meeting protest, the *New York Times* reported that "bearded artists" and "loftmenschen" who created signs "so artistically competent" that they constituted an "outdoor art exhibit" hoped to convince the board to shelve plans for the roadway so that they could "hang on to their low-rent lofts." At a Board of Estimate meeting that December, sculptor and painter Harry Jackson, "a member in-residence of the Broome Street area loft colony," said, "in the last twenty years New York has become the focal point for contemporary painting," and the expressway would "destroy a series . . . of the most fecund neighborhoods" for art in the city.[23] Jackson argued if the expressway were built, artists would lose the opportunity to convert lofts into homes and studios, and a new way to redevelop urban space would be lost.

Using Highways to Fight Industrial Slums

Despite its growing population of artists, throughout the 1960s SoHo continued to be characterized as an industrial slum. The debates over the expressway occurred at roughly the same time that MICOVE proposed to replace SoHo with a middle-income housing project, and Chester Rapkin produced his study highlighting the benefits of local industry. David Rockefeller, the DLMA, and expressway proponents such as Moses did not share Rapkin's optimistic appraisal of SoHo businesses. Instead, they sought to portray the area as inefficient, outdated, and in need of upgrading through urban renewal.

In 1960, the amount of vacant loft space in SoHo had provided expressway proponents with the rationale for pushing forward with the project. A report prepared by Relocation Management Associates argued that the displacement of residents and businesses in the path of the expressway would not be problematic, as there was a "ready availability" of loft space in the area. The struggles of the neighborhood provided an opportunity for urban renewal: businesses along Broome Street could simply move to many of the empty lofts nearby.[24]

After the 1962 elections, the back-and-forth over the roadway continued, with SoHo industry at the center of the discussion. Opponents gained the upper hand in December 1962, when the Board of Estimate put off a vote on acquiring land for the expressway.[25] Additionally, Moses left many of his state-level posts by the end of the year to accept a position as head of the 1964 World's Fair, removing one of the highway's strongest advocates from key positions of power.[26] Yet the project was still on city, state, and federal highway planning maps, and its advocates were not ready to give up. In April 1963, Mayor Wagner moved to table the highway for good by requesting that the city remove the project from its official planning map. At the mayor's request, the City Planning Commission held a five-hour meeting on "demapping" the expressway. At the hearing, attended by Moses and Jacobs, representatives from the DLMA argued that, although 14.5 million square feet of commercial office space had been built below Canal Street since 1949, the area north of Canal Street (SoHo) was "not living up to its industrial potential." Although they acknowledged that parts of these "industrial loft areas" provided employment "particularly in the printing trades, to tens of thousands of persons," they contended that much of the area had been given over to "acres of industrial slums which are under-utilized and subsidized by the City and other industrial plants." Through the expressway, they believed "this area can be rehabilitated, giving jobs and employment to many more thousands in improved quarters and at higher pay" in the banking and financial industries, which would have room to expand from Wall Street northward. These arguments had an impact because after the hearing, the expressway remained on the city's planning map.[27]

Ironically, it was at this moment of near death that the only actual existing segment of the Lower Manhattan Expressway was constructed. In 1963, the city Department of Highways completed work on abutments, piers, and counterbuoyancy slabs that were needed if the planned depressed roadway's foundation were to be strong enough to support the creation of a new subway tunnel under Chrystie Street that was under construction at the same time. This segment cost an estimated $2 million and remained in place under a pile of dirt as debate continued.[28]

With some construction having been completed and the roadway still on the city's planning map, Rockefeller and Moses quickly worked to push the expressway forward. At Moses's suggestion, the DLMA's executive committee met with Mayor Wagner and worked with staff of the Triborough Bridge and Tunnel Authority to present a report in favor of the project to the Board of Estimate.[29] In response, the Jacobs-led Joint Committee to Stop the Lower Manhattan Expressway visited city hall to argue that the expressway would destroy ten thousand jobs in SoHo. Echoing Rapkin's report, they argued that "about half of the jobs destroyed . . . are held by Negroes and Puerto Ricans, minority groups that the city is attempting to help."[30]

For his part, Moses sought to create the perception that SoHo was blighted by highlighting statistics about building code violations, fires, vacancies, and declining assessments. He noted that one of five buildings in the path of the roadway was fully or partially vacant and that no new developments had been built since 1929. Perhaps in response to these arguments, Mayor Wagner allowed the approval process for the Lower Manhattan Expressway to move forward at the end of 1964.[31]

However, the DLMA was not able to convince an important rising star in New York City politics, John Lindsay, of the value of the expressway. Whether he did so for philosophical reasons or simply for political expediency, when the Congressman ran for mayor in 1965, he made the Lower Manhattan Expressway an election issue and threw his support behind the project's opponents.[32] Lindsay was elected that November, and by March 1966, information had leaked that the expressway was "definitely out" under the new administration. By July, the new mayor removed Moses from his position as City Arterial Highway coordinator, leaving the Lower Manhattan Expressway dead, seemingly for good.[33]

The Final Death of the Lower Manhattan Expressway

Yet, despite the scales being tipped against the project, the Lower Manhattan Expressway went through a final iteration before being permanently tabled. Although he ran for office on an antiexpressway platform, Mayor Lindsay attempted to revive the roadway plan, in part due to pressure from the DLMA and others who viewed the project as a pathway to job creation. Lindsay's actions met with resistance from residents, advocates for SoHo industry, and the politicians who supported them. However, in the end, it was the environmental impact of the project that led to its final demise.

Shortly after his election, Mayor Lindsay attempted to forge a compromise by developing plans for a four-lane roadway that would travel partially though tunnels and "open cuts" that were below ground but uncovered. The mayor hoped that this plan would prevent many of the community disruptions that would come with an elevated highway. The plan did not sit well with residents. Politicians, including New York City Council member Edward Koch and Greenwich Village Democratic leader Carol Greitzer, quickly organized protests.[34] Despite local objection, in March 1968, the Board of Estimate approved Lindsay's plan in principle, as did necessary state and federal agencies. The DLMA supported the new roadway in public hearings in front of the City Planning Commission and the Board of Estimate, arguing that it would create jobs and alleviate traffic. Urban renewal opponents continued to stress that development projects turned diverse commercial neighborhoods into single-use districts and gave pedestrian space over to automobiles, harming the city in the long run. Jacobs was charged with disorderly conduct after trying to break up a New York State Transportation Department hearing on the expressway at Seward Park High School in April 1968. She allegedly ripped up the stenographer's transcript and encouraged others to climb onstage and disrupt the meeting.[35]

By now opponents also noted that the new highway plan would harm SoHo's growing art community. In December 1968, architecture critic and preservationist Ada Louise Huxtable wrote that the Lower Manhattan Expressway threatened the loft that housed the Richard Feigen Gallery at 141 Greene Street, between Houston and Prince Streets. The building, which would have been demolished as part of the MICOVE housing project planned for SoHo, was now just over two blocks from the planned route of the Lower Manhattan Expressway.[36]

Loft residents also formed a lobbying group, Artists Against the Expressway, to oppose the highway and put forward their vision of SoHo's redevelopment. Led by SoHo resident Julie Judd, who was married to the prominent painter Donald Judd (himself an owner of an entire loft building in SoHo at 101 Spring Street), the group argued that the Lower Manhattan Expressway would threaten the six thousand artists estimated to live around Broome Street. Equally important, Julie Judd said, the road would halt the investment that area artists had made in rehabilitating local commercial property. She contended that SoHo artists were "not just a fly-by-night camp of gypsies—many own buildings individually or co-ops." Of course, if built, the roadway would threaten the community altogether. Judd said, "The expressway would kill the last suitable place in the city for lofts. There'd be scarcer space and higher rents. And we don't want to be urban renewed."[37]

Artists Against the Expressway soon joined with other organizations protesting the project. The group was present at a hearing held by Manhattan borough president Percy Sutton in May 1969 and later that month held its own meeting at the Whitney Museum of American Art to further protest the roadway's construction. Artist Barnett Newman, art dealer Richard Feigen, Museum of Modern Art architecture curator Arthur Drexler, and Metropolitan Museum of Art curator Henry Geldzahler were among the 250 group members who attended the meeting. At the event, Newman told the assembled crowd that he had already been pushed out of two lofts due to urban renewal and that his third was in the path of the expressway. He complained that his home was at risk because "do-gooders who are saving the city by speeding up traffic" were advocating a project that would lead to the destruction of his loft and the homes of artists living around him. By holding its protest at the Whitney Museum, the group directly linked the artwork created in SoHo to the art museums that brought the city both cultural and financial capital through art and tourism.[38]

In its protests, Artists Against the Expressway pointed out an irony of the project: that one of the expressway's main proponents, David Rockefeller, was also the chair of the board of directors for the Museum of Modern Art. As such, Rockefeller, one of the major art patrons in the city, was advocating a roadway that would destroy the artist community of SoHo. At the Whitney protest, Newman proposed that Artists Against the Expressway elect a committee to call upon Rockefeller "as a lover of art" and to ask him "to declare to us personally where his loyalty lies. He should have the opportunity to declare . . . whether he has some feeling for the artists who make the art. He should use his good offices on our behalf rather than in our destruction." Artists Against the Expressway originally wanted to have its meeting at the Museum of Modern Art, but when staff learned that one of the museum's trustees would be criticized, they denied permission for use of the auditorium.[39]

However, in the end, it was scientists concerned with the environmental impact of the expressway who got the project tabled for good. While Mayor Lindsay's plan for a below-ground road mollified some, he did not consider where the exhaust for all the cars using the "open cut" portion of the expressway would go. Deploying data collected by the city's Department of Air Resources in 1968, a group called the New York Scientists' Committee for Public Information found that air quality near the proposed roadway would be hazardous to the health of people living around it. The group stated that carbon monoxide levels around the roadway would be three hundred parts per million, enough to cause the physical collapse of some people near the road. By June 1969, the federal Department of Health, Education, and Welfare agreed to sponsor a more exhaustive study of the roadway's environmental effects. By March, Mayor Lindsay asked the federal government for funds to study an alternate roadway rerouting traffic around the southern tip of Lower Manhattan rather than across Broome Street. This project had the backing of many of the expressway's political opponents.[40]

In July 1969, Mayor Lindsay declared the Lower Manhattan Expressway dead "for all time." Despite the federal funds the city stood to lose by ending the project and the money the state had spent in 1963 to build the one 156-foot segment of the expressway, at the mayor's urging, the City Planning Commission voted in August 1969 to remove the Lower Manhattan Expressway from its planning map. In December, state legislators from Lower Manhattan introduced a bill to take it off the New York State planning map. Governor Nelson Rockefeller finally ended the project for good in March 1971 when he signed a bill authorizing this plan, thus eliminating federal funding for the road and ending any possibility that it would be built.[41]

The Lower Manhattan Expressway and SoHo Investment

By preventing the Lower Manhattan Expressway's construction, anti–urban renewal forces saved SoHo for loft residents, gallery owners, and entrepreneurs to build a new residential neighborhood in the area. However, the Lower Manhattan Expressway had another important effect on the neighborhood's development. Looming over the area for decades, the threat of the expressway project provided a strong disincentive for landlords to invest in their property, thus depressing values and providing artists with a large supply of inexpensive and often vacant lofts to convert into homes and studios. Although no comprehensive data on SoHo property values is available, evidence suggests that the expressway substantially depressed rents. In addition, with the expressway plan vanquished, art-related businesses owners felt more secure in investing in the neighborhood, leading to the area's commercial renaissance after 1969.

From the first inkling of the expressway plan, property owners in its path worried that the project depressed values and provided disincentives for property maintenance. In 1960, Barnett August, executive director of the East Side Chamber of Commerce, commented, "Building owners are asking us whether they should make repairs; tenants are concerned over prospective termination of their leases; people are wondering when they will have to move." Four years later, Harold H. Harmatz, the same group's chair of the board of directors, argued that the area had been in limbo for twenty years because of the indecision over the expressway. As a result, investors and owners had not rehabilitated their property, causing "erosion not only of property values but also part of our urban heritage." Though it ultimately remained on the city's planning map at that time, he celebrated the anticipated demapping of the roadway, saying, "at last this sword of Damocles has been removed so that we can proceed with our desire to upgrade our entire area."[42]

Deterioration of property values became even more of an issue as indecision over the expressway continued into the 1960s. In 1964, the Porter Flushing Realty Company brought suit in the Supreme Court of the State of New York asking the Board of Estimate to make a decision about the Lower Manhattan Expressway. The company said that "it ought not to be kept in suspense any longer regarding the city's plans for the project." Porter Flushing charged that political wavering over the roadway was responsible for the company's failure to get a $10,000 loan to improve its property. Later that year, Sidney Z. Searles, chair of the subcommittee on condemnation of the Association of the Bar of the City of New York, said that "millions of dollars of real estate deteriorated under the shadow of government seizure" since the project had been put on the city's master plan in 1941. "This area will remain in limbo until this project is demapped, and is an unusual hardship for the neighborhood and those of us who are committed to building a better lower Manhattan."[43]

With decreased property values came increased vacancies in the area around Broome Street. According to Robert Moses's Triborough Bridge and Tunnel Authority, 25 out of the 116 buildings along one stretch of the street were partially or completely empty in 1964. That same year, the DLMA urged the Board of Estimate to take action on building the expressway because "the owners of the commercial buildings within the right of way who have been unable to rent their properties and have been losing tenants because of the uncertainty will welcome positive action by the Board of Estimate."[44]

While Moses and the DLMA saw these vacancies as an argument for building the expressway, property owners saw the expressway as the reason for these vacancies and blamed a lack of government action on the project for lowering their property values and damaging their investments. In 1965, Alfred S. Friedman, a building owner at 125 Canal Street, planned to seek damages through legal action for the city's procrastination over the project. He claimed that the delay left property owners, tenants, and landlords in a state of inaction in which "their investments had withered." In Friedman's case, the number of tenants in his building had dropped from thirty to ten over the last twenty years.[45]

Taking the argument one step further, several observers said that the project had put the area on the path to becoming a full-fledged slum. In 1969, architecture critic Ada Louise Huxtable observed, "The social and physical fabric of the city along the proposed route has been deteriorating for the past 28 years. This is the blight that comes from being fingered for an expressway route, with the uncertain future of the area as its only certainty. Properties are not kept up; improvements are not made. Residential and business tenants share the insecurity that sends everything downhill." That year, the Reverend Gerard LaMountain of the Most Holy Crucifix Church argued that the city was systematically turning the area around Broome Street into a slum by hanging the threat of a highway over it.[46]

In turn, the devaluing of property along the route of the Lower Manhattan Expressway created an environment where artists could find low rents. In 1968, Ulrich Niemeyer moved to a loft at 462–64 Broome Street in SoHo, obtaining a ten-year commercial lease for $325. He was able to obtain a lease in large part because the building's owner, Joseph Mandel, likely never expected to have to honor it. According to Niemeyer, Mandel only leased space to artists to increase his rent rolls in the hopes of maximizing his compensation from the city if it seized his property through eminent domain to build the Lower Manhattan Expressway.[47]

Conversely, as soon as local leaders tabled the Lower Manhattan Expressway for good, SoHo underwent a commercial renaissance. Instead of industrial enterprises, it was art galleries and related businesses that opened in the neighborhood. The first major art gallery opened in SoHo in 1968, and the first major group of galleries to move from New York's Midtown gallery center to SoHo began operations in 1970. In 1970 and 1971, thirteen new galleries

CHAPTER THREE

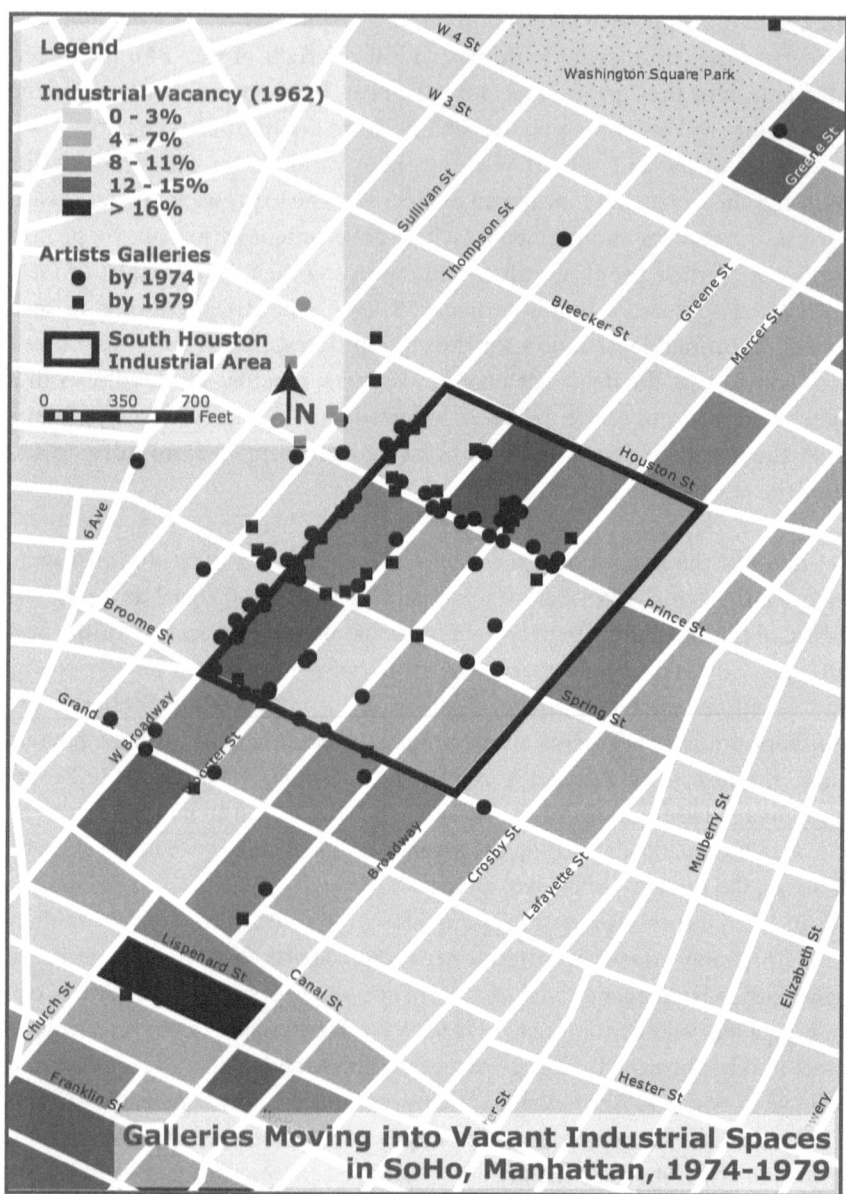

FIGURE 13. Galleries moving into vacant industrial spaces in SoHo, Manhattan, 1974–79.

and art-related businesses opened in SoHo, including several major Midtown galleries at 420 West Broadway. By 1973, when several years had passed with no mention of reviving the Lower Manhattan Expressway, there were twenty-four art-related businesses in SoHo. Eleven more debuted in 1974, followed

TABLE 1. Listing of SoHo Galleries by Opening Date

Name	Address	Date
Byrd Hoffman School of Birds/Byrd Hoffman Foundation	147 Spring St.	1964
Millennium Film Workshop	66 E. 4th St.	1966
Performing Garage	33 Wooster St.	1967
Elaine Summers Experimental Intermedia Foundation	537 Broadway	1968
Global Village	454 Broome St.	1968
Ontological-Hysteric Theater	491 Broadway	1968
Paula Cooper	115 Wooster St.	1968
55 Mercer	55 Mercer St.	1969
Bowery Gallery	135 Greene St.	1969
La Mama/La Mama Etc. (Experimental Theater Club)	74 E. 4th St.	1969
OK Harris Works of Art	383 West Broadway	1969
Sculpture Now	142 Greene St.	1969
Ward Nasse	131 Prince St.	1969
112 Workshop	112 Greene St.	1970
Buecker and Harpsichords	456 West Broadway	1970
Poster Originals Ltd./Mark LV Framing	386 West Broadway	1970
Prince Street Gallery	106 Prince St.	1970
A.I.R.	97 Wooster St.	1971
Andre Emmerich/Downtown	420 West Broadway	1971
Barnabu Rex	155 Duane St.	1971
Food	127 Prince St.	1971
John Weber	420 West Broadway	1971
Kitchen	484 Broome St.	1971
Leo Castelli	420 West Broadway	1971
Small Business	101 Wooster St.	1971
Women in the Arts	435 Broome St.	1971
Artists Space	105 Hudson St.	1972
Betty Cunningham	94 Prince St.	1972
Downtown Potters Hall	113 Mercer St.	1972
Film Forum	15 Vandam St.	1972
First Street Gallery	118 Prince St.	1972
Ken & Bob's Broome St. Bar	363 West Broadway	1972
Landmark Gallery	469 Broome St.	1972
Let There Be Neon	451 West Broadway	1972
Nancy Hoffman	429 West Broadway	1972
SoHo 20	99 Spring St.	1972
Spring Street Restaurant	162 Spring St.	1972
14 Sculptors	75 Thompson St.	1973
Chuck Levitan	42 Grand St.	1973
Colonnades Theater Lab	428 Lafayette St.	1973
Downtown Whitney	55 Water St.	1973
Green Mountain	135 Greene St.	1973
Holly Solomon	392 West Broadway	1973
John Gibson	392 West Broadway	1973
Louis K. Meisel Gallery	141 Prince St.	1973
Open Space	64 Wooster St.	1973
Rabinovich	74 Grand St.	1973

(*continued*)

TABLE 1. (*continued*)

Name	Address	Date
Razor Gallery	464 West Broadway	1973
SoHo Artists Theater	465 West Broadway	1973
Wbroadway/Alternate Space Gallery	431 West Broadway	1973
Ali's Alley	77 Greene St.	1974
Amos Eno	101 Wooster St.	1974
Anthology Film Archives	80 Wooster St.	1974
Azuma Gallery	143 Greene St.	1974
Center for Book Arts	15 Bleecker St.	1974
Hansen Gallery	70 Wooster St.	1974
Heiner Freidrich	393 West Broadway	1974
Noho Gallery	542 LaGuardia Pl.	1974
Pleiades I/Pleiades II	152 Wooster St.	1974
Susan Caldwell	383 West Broadway	1974
Viewing Room	72 Wooster St.	1974
African Sculpture Unlimited	145 Spring St.	1975
Braunstein/Quai	139 Spring St.	1975
Cayman Gallery	381 West Broadway	1975
Collective for Living Cinema	52 White St.	1975
DaSailvano	260 6th Ave.	1975
Drama Ensemble Repertory Company	108 Wooster St.	1975
Echo Gallery	133 Mercer St.	1975
Edward Won Graphics, Inc.	149 Mercer St.	1975
Environ	476 Broadway	1975
Frances Alenikoff/Eden's Expressway	537 Broadway	1975
Hudson Street Studio/The Silent Performer Workshop	1 Hudson St.	1975
Incorporated Gallery of Contemporary Craft	150 Spring St.	1975
Leslie-Lohman	55 Wooster St.	1975
Phyllis Kind Gallery	139 Spring St.	1975
Prince Street Bar/Restaurant	125 Prince St.	1975
SoHo Repertory Theater	19 Mercer St.	1975
Studio 505	39 Walker St.	1975
Vorpal SoHo Gallery	465 West Broadway	1975

by eighteen the next year,[48] further peppering the neighborhood with galleries and shops.

In this manner, the defeat of urban renewal once again saved SoHo for redevelopment at the hands of artists. Without the actions of Jane Jacobs, the Joint Emergency Committee to Stop the Lower Manhattan Expressway, and Artists Against the Expressway, among others, there might not have been buildings to renovate or a neighborhood to gentrify. If the project had been completed, Broome Street would be a highway. The street's industry, commerce, and pedestrian traffic would have been superseded by cars alone. This, of course, was the goal of slum clearance urban renewal: to remove the mess and complexity of urban life, the things that brought on decay and obsolescence, and provide order and efficiency. In all likelihood, the roadway would have prevented SoHo from evolving into what it became from the late 1960s onward: a mix of industry, artist homes, galleries, and shops, all existing in the same structures that had stood in the neighborhood since the late nineteenth century.

Yet without the threat of the Lower Manhattan Expressway, SoHo would never have developed in the way it did. Artists might not have found available lofts for rent, or found them in the numbers they did, without the depression in property values brought about by the threat of the Lower Manhattan Expressway. Resistance to urban renewal drew attention to its political, human, and cultural costs, which caused city leaders to look with greater interest at the urban development that artists sparked in SoHo through their conversions of loft buildings into homes. Their methods of adaptive reuse cost nothing to the city and, at least for a time, did not displace any residents or businesses. This became particularly important when artists later argued that their practice of converting industrial space into apartments should be legalized, something that would require the support of policy makers at various levels of government.

While the arguments of antirenewal activists and artists might have won the day, the David Rockefeller/DLMA vision for SoHo did not vanish. Few forgot that no matter how dingy its lofts were, SoHo was a short distance from Wall Street. When artists promoted their homes to the public as part of their advocacy efforts, they quickly developed a new concern: that wealthy New Yorkers might realize that living in a loft close to their jobs in the Financial District was a desirable option. As a result, both urban renewal and the city's expanding postindustrial economy would shape the development of SoHo and its artist community in the coming years.

4

Artist Organizations, Political Advocacy, and the Creation of a Residential SoHo

In February 1961, SoHo artists faced another threat that almost ended their nascent colony. This peril was not an economic downturn, the prospect of a highway, or even the early stages of gentrification. Instead, the culprits were some of the most mundane elements of urban governance: zoning ordinances and building codes. These types of regulations are meant to protect residents, and it was the issue of resident safety that caused an acute crisis in the SoHo artist community. In late 1960 and early 1961, a series of fires broke out in industrial lofts below Houston Street, leading to the deaths of four people, including three firefighters. Though none of the fires occurred in lofts where artists lived, these blazes led the New York City Fire Department and the New York City Department of Buildings to launch a series of inspections of SoHo structures.[1]

Although both agencies initially reacted to a series of code violations in industrial buildings, they soon made a surprising discovery: artists living illegally in these structures. The *New York Herald-Tribune* reported that city officials found at least 128 illegal apartments in the area containing "beatniks, complete with beards" living with "mattresses on the floor and works on Zen Buddhism," along with vermin and cockroaches. In turn, Deputy Assistant Fire Chief Thomas J. Hartnett wondered how anyone could stand living in this section of Manhattan, asking, "How do they get their milk delivered?"[2]

This "discovery" of SoHo residents reveals an important element of the neighborhood's early history: that the very idea of living in a loft was completely novel. Whereas lofts are now ubiquitous in urban areas worldwide, hardly any people considered living in former industrial space before the 1960s. Similarly, few observers saw artists as people with the power to transform neighborhoods or develop real estate, as demonstrated by the *Herald-*

Tribune's use of the word *beatniks*, the derogatory term for bohemians of that era, to describe SoHo residents; in that writer's view, they did not even rise to the level of artist. As mentioned in the previous chapter, local building and zoning laws made no allowance for people who wanted to live in industrial buildings. As a result, when they encountered loft residents for the first time, city officials did not celebrate the possible rebirth of a struggling industrial area at the hands of artists. Instead, they threatened them with eviction.

In response to the specter of eviction, artists organized themselves politically, forming lobbying organizations and using public demonstrations and boycotts to advocate for their housing needs. SoHo artists threw the entire weight of the New York art world behind their cause. Well-known artists such as Willem de Kooning and Isamu Noguchi, as well as curators and gallery owners, spoke out in favor of loft residents. Through their advocacy, SoHo residents worked to redefine the role of the artist in society in the minds of local leaders. They argued that affordable housing for up-and-coming artists was crucial to New York's future because artists were the backbone of its cultural economy, as well as the people who gave the city its reputation as the world's leading creative and artistic center.

In making these arguments, SoHo artists placed the arts at the center of the debate about how to redevelop cities at a time of urban crisis. By finding value and beauty in outdated industrial structures, they also reclaimed properties viewed as obsolete eyesores by urban renewal advocates. By pioneering new uses for lofts, SoHo residents created powerful arguments against slum clearance, particularly in industrial and commercial areas.

SoHo artists also shifted the terms of the ongoing debates over neighborhood preservation and rehabilitation. Although meeting the housing needs of lower-income populations in central cities had long been a preoccupation of policy makers, artists looked to demonstrate that they were a unique group—relatively poor people with distinct housing needs but who also had the power to drive the city's economy and give it its unique identity. They urged city leaders to help bolster one of the few things that New York still had going for it—its reputation for the arts—by allowing artists to live in the manner that best suited them: in converted industrial lofts with room to live and work affordably.

Though they fought to change zoning laws, rather than against slum clearance, artists developed powerful arguments that pushed the debate over the future of urban neighborhoods beyond the renewal/community defense paradigm that had dominated discourse up to that point. Unlike antirenewal protesters, who mainly focused on preserving their neighborhoods, SoHo artists posited a new future for their community. They argued that their efforts would revitalize an area shaped by deindustrialization and urban renewal. At the same time, SoHo artists placed the arts at the center of a debate over the future of their neighborhood. To SoHo artists, urban culture could do for SoHo what other urban development schemes could not: create a vibrant neighborhood that helped drive the city's economy and identity. Much like the backers of projects such as Manhattan's Lincoln Center, SoHo artists were staking out a place for culture in the city. The same New York artistic culture that could help the United States compete with the Soviet Union for cultural dominance globally could also help breathe life into moribund industrial neighborhoods.[3]

In the end, artist groups in SoHo achieved goals that were both modest and significant. Their advocacy led to changes in two regulations that allowed only a limited number of artists to live legally in a loft. Yet these laws were the first to make it legal for anyone to live in such a structure and the first to give government sanction to anyone, artist or otherwise, to live in any former industrial space. Moreover, these policies indicated that more New Yorkers were starting to support an argument made by SoHo activists: that artists had a unique power to reinvigorate neighborhoods long ago left for dead. Thanks to artist advocacy, policy makers began to connect artist housing and urban vitality, a link that would become the foundation of theories of creative place making and the creative class several decades later. Through their actions and words, SoHo artists made the case that art could be a force for urban change.

Fires, Illegality, and Evictions: The Early Years of SoHo Lofts

SoHo artists learned quickly that their tenancy in lofts was vulnerable. After the series of fatal loft fires in late 1960, Fire Commissioner Edward F. Cavanagh Jr. promised increased inspection and fire code enforcement in Lower Manhattan and SoHo. Previous inspections had shown that buildings in this area often did not contain sprinklers or other fire-prevention systems. Although the existence of an artist community in SoHo seemed to be far from his mind, the fire commissioner promised to conduct a more extensive survey of code violations in three thousand Lower Manhattan structures.[4]

Fire Commissioner Cavanagh had reason to worry about the safety of loft buildings. Although cast-iron columns gave SoHo lofts their unique open floor plans, they could also be a safety hazard. Because each column rested on the one below it, a single stack of columns running from the basement to the roof supported the whole building. Even under normal conditions, cast-iron columns were in danger of collapsing or cracking. Building owners had to worry about industrial equipment shifting or knocking out a column.

The risk of fire was even more troubling. Cast-iron columns were unable to withstand rapid temperature changes. A column that grew too hot too fast from a building fire, or too cold from the water used to put out that fire, could snap, collapsing the building. In addition, weak brick walls, older timber beams, and open elevator shafts meant that the overwhelming majority of SoHo buildings were not fire resistant.[5]

Public concern over fire safety in loft buildings grew after a man living on the second floor of a five-story commercial building at 275 Canal Street (near Broadway) died in a fire in February 1960, prompting another promise of inspections by Fire Commissioner Cavanagh. Although the tenant in this case was not an artist, and it appeared that he had been living in the building legally, the New York Fire Department paid increasing attention to residential units in Lower Manhattan. Cavanagh said, "nearly twenty persons, including two firemen" had been killed in fires in Lower Manhattan in the previous two years.[6]

SoHo residents faced a genuine threat of eviction as a result of these inspections. In 1961, well-known painter Romare Bearden claimed that he was the first artist evicted from his loft. At that time, a local artist group reported that one hundred or more artists had been evicted in the past year. Although it is unclear how many loft tenants were evicted from their homes, there was a risk of the entire residential population facing eviction.[7]

Even if they were not faced with eviction, living illegally created a variety of nuisances that made residing in SoHo difficult. Although some SoHo residents never thought twice about the legal status of their homes, others avoided placing houseplants near their windows that could attract the attention of city officials. Some even had movable beds and living room furniture that could be whisked out of sight at a moment's notice if an inspector came calling. Without a legal residential population, neighborhood residents did not have regular garbage service, and they had to walk to Greenwich Village to buy groceries. These peculiarities of SoHo living gave artists additional incentives to legalize their homes.

Organizing to Save Their Homes: The Beginnings of SoHo Artist Advocacy

A coalition of Lower Manhattan artists formed the Artist Tenant Association (ATA), an organization of "painters who have been told to vacate their studios in antiquated, low-rent commercial buildings that have not met fire department regulations." The group's goals included working with city and state officials to amend building and zoning codes to allow for loft residences.

The ATA kicked off its existence with a meeting at Greenwich Village's Judson Memorial Church on April 6, 1961.[8]

Although the bulk of the lofts that artists turned into homes were in SoHo, the artists who joined the ATA lived all over Lower Manhattan, and some resided as far away as Midtown. In addition, unlike the bulk of SoHo artists, some of the leading ATA figures had connections to Greenwich Village. Chair James Gahagan was active in the Provincetown Painters in Cape Cod in the 1950s, essentially a northern satellite of Greenwich Village, while member Robert Henry studied at the Hofmann School of Fine Arts, an institution that played a central role in shaping artistic production in the Village at midcentury.[9]

Although the ATA's concerns were practical—their first aim was to prevent evictions from lofts—they soon framed the issue of artist housing within the ongoing debates over deindustrialization and the city's need to strengthen its economy in a time of urban decline. Through the ATA, SoHo artists contended that some of the area's underutilized industrial space was best used as a center of housing for artists who contributed to New York's economy and status as a leading cultural center. They argued that New York City would become a "cultural wasteland" if city leaders continued to evict artists from these unique structures. ATA members warned that without artist housing in SoHo, artists would follow the many businesses and residents who had left New York City for the suburbs or cities farther west. The organization's leadership even went so far as to telegraph "the Mayors of Hoboken and San Francisco 'asking for asylum' if their 'cruel persecution' forced them to become 'refugees.'"[10]

In addition, SoHo artists worked to rehabilitate the image of the loft dweller from subversive outsider to important economic actor. Downtown artist Tom Hannan worried that the image of artists as beatniks prevented their grievances from being taken seriously. He said, "Artists are one of the few groups with a single identity. Because we're creative, people think we're all nuts. They call us 'beatniks' or 'kooks' and they think we don't take baths. There is a tremendous moral, middle-class anti-artist attitude in this town. Nobody wants to get involved with us." In response, the ATA worked to create an image of artists as hardworking, family-oriented contributors to New York's cultural and economic life. For example, Jim Gahagan stated in an interview with the *New York Times* that the five thousand to seven thousand artists living in Manhattan lofts were hardly degenerates. He countered, "We're Bohemians, but we're not Beatniks. We may be isolated from the social, economic, even the political values the rest of the country operates under, but we aren't isolated from people. We put up with substandard housing, we do part-time labor and a lot of other things. Most of us earn less than a thousand a year from our painting and sculpture, but we wouldn't change the situation." The article argued that artists who were "pioneering in what is unquestionably the most built up city on earth," were by and large "models of tranquility and respectability by comparison with those, say, of some television and advertising people. A fairly high percentage not only are married but have children." He even tried dispelling the myth of the decadent "loft party," which was described as possessing "all the orgiastic aspects of a rush-hour dash for a commuter train." Aside from providing evidence that artists were respectable economic contributors to society, by referring to artists as "pioneers" in the most built-up city on earth, the article implied that artists had the power to drive real estate development without the teardowns and other costs associated with urban renewal.[11]

In addition, the ATA argued that the city should encourage loft housing because artists made important contributions to New York's economy. In their public statements, the ATA highlighted the "big business" of art in New York, saying that a significant portion of the $500 million that Americans paid for art each year was spent in two hundred New York City galleries. SoHo artists also made explicit connections between Lower Manhattan artists and the well-known New York school of abstract expressionist painting. Even though only a few SoHo artists were part of this movement, they claimed that their inability to live in lofts threatened a school that brought cultural attention, and a good deal of profits from the sale and exhibition of art, to the city. Artist Basil King said, "Do you know what the New York School is? The New York School is the colony of artists they're talking about all over the world. Everywhere you go, you hear people saying The New York School . . . The New York School . . . But this is what The New York School is. It's just a bunch of painters painting in lofts."[12]

However, ATA members faced a challenge: when they spoke of the economic contributions of New York artists, the relationship of a group of relatively low-income artists in SoHo to the more lucrative formal art world was not immediately apparent. To better connect artist housing in SoHo to the New York art world, the ATA enlisted well-known artists, patrons of the arts, and representatives of the city's museum and gallery communities to their cause. In May 1961, New York art patron Eleanor Roosevelt supported the ATA's cause through a press release that read, "I find it hard to believe that the Administration and people of this great city, once they are informed of the situation, would stand idly by and allow artists to be dispersed." Metropolitan Museum of Art director James J. Rorimer asked the city to intervene to help local artists because "it is the work of the artist that contributes to the soul of the nation." In May 1961, the ATA organized a rally that drew three hundred "artists and art patrons," including *Art News* editor Alfred M. Frankfurter, sculptor Isamu Noguchi, abstract expressionist painter Willem de Kooning, and art critic Clement Greenberg, to a meeting at Washington Irving High School in Greenwich Village. De Kooning criticized the city for cracking down on artist lofts as well as Greenwich Village coffeehouses. Greenberg and de Kooning's presence lent an aura of authenticity to the Lower Manhattan artists' cause, and he likened the health of the arts to the economic and cultural well-being of the city. Fittingly, Greenberg also remarked to the press that he had put on a good suit to avoid being labeled a beatnik.[13]

"Artist in Residence"—The Beginning of Loft Policy

The ATA's advocacy efforts eventually captured the attention of Mayor Robert Wagner, who called for a policy allowing some of the artists to legally convert industrial lofts into homes and studios. The *New York Times* reported that the mayor took action after reading about their protests in the newspaper and grew concerned about their "charge that mass evictions were threatening New York's continued existence as a center of artistic life." At the urging of the mayor, Fire Commissioner Cavanagh met with representatives from the ATA in May 1961.[14]

However, SoHo artists still had a difficult time convincing city officials that their need for housing, and their contributions to the city's economy, were more important than the safety issues associated with living in industrial buildings. Cavanagh was still focused on the legal concerns associated with artists living in lofts. As the fire commissioner put it, "The loft-dwellers don't have a foot to stand on. The rules say what kind of building you can live in. I'd be indicted for maladministration if I don't carry out the rules. I'd like to leave them alone. I'm not afraid to live in a loft building and I know they're not." He remarked to the press that he liked art as much as the next person, but said, "I'd like to see it in a wholesome, safe atmosphere. It doesn't have to be wholesome even, as long as it's safe."[15] Despite meetings with Fire Commissioner Cavanagh and attention from Mayor Wagner, the ATA was not able to reach a satisfactory agreement with the city, leaving the threat of loft evictions in place.

In response to the continuing indifference to the artists' plight, in June 1961 the ATA organized an artists' strike. The organization enlisted its artists and art dealer supporters to remove their artworks from galleries and museums until the city and state legalized loft housing for Lower Manhattan artists. In addition to de Kooning, famous artists who pledged their support for the strike included Jasper Johns, Ad Reinhardt, Robert Motherwell, Alex Katz, and Fairfield Porter.[16]

The ATA also pledged to enlist as many of the city's four hundred galleries as possible to cement the connections between SoHo artists and the city's cultural economy in the minds of policy makers. The ATA requested that its members not participate as artists in any public activity in New York, including exhibiting, appearing on TV or radio, or lecturing. It also asked participants not to send their work to any gallery or museum in New York, nor show their work in studios, nor attend exhibitions at galleries or museums, and to withdraw works on loan or consignment if possible. Finally, the ATA asked that artists encourage colleagues living outside of New York not to send or show anything in the city. SoHo artists sought to remind the public that the art they made in their loft studios ended up for sale in galleries, and unless city leaders took action to legalize loft residences, the economic benefits of gallery sales might be lost.[17]

The threat of an artists' strike led to an agreement that created the first legal protections for artists living in loft buildings. On August 15, 1961, ATA chair James Gahagan and Robert Bobrick, the organization's counsel, met with city officials, including buildings commissioner Peter Reidy, acting fire commissioner George Mand, housing assistant to the mayor Hortense Gable, and acting city administrator Maxwell Lehman. The goal of the meeting was to reach an agreement in advance of the ATA's September 11 strike deadline.[18]

As a result of this meeting, a policy agreed on by Mayor Wagner on August 15 and announced to the press on August 22 spelled out the conditions under which artists could use loft buildings in Lower Manhattan. The agreement allowed artists to live in commercially zoned buildings as long as there were two means of egress and no businesses that created excessive fire hazards, such as those that manufactured paint and plastics. The artist also had to send a letter notifying the commissioner of buildings that he or she was occupying the premises. In addition, artist tenants were required to place an eight-by-ten-inch sign on their loft's exterior that read *A.I.R.* The letters stood for "Artist in Residence." Each sign also indicated to first responders where to find residents in case of an emergency and to buildings department inspectors where they should focus their inspections to ensure that artist studio residences were safe.[19]

The agreement between the ATA and the city was significant news. Local papers and national art journals such as *Art News* reported on it. *Art News* wrote, "For the first time, New York artists, most of them vanguard, have joined together as a political pressure group in order to influence legislation to their own advantage, with the formation this summer of the Artist Tenants

Association." The periodical reported on the notable artists who signed onto the ATA's pledge and quoted Mayor Wagner as saying, "The artist working in New York is assured of the city's continuing interest in his welfare and in his work."[20]

Wagner's policy was the first public action that recognized the right of artists to live in lofts. The mayor developed the policy for practical reasons. Never a public figure who relished conflict, Wagner probably saw the action as a way to avoid evicting artists and help a population in need with little effort or expenditure. Yet, aside from these practical issues, the action was also an indication that the mayor, as well as other public officials, recognized the unique housing needs of artists and their importance to the city's economy and image as a center for the arts.

However, this arrangement was temporary and incomplete. The policy was not rooted in statute; it was only an informal agreement between artist groups and Mayor Wagner regarding which city laws would be enforced. Consequently, its application was spotty at best. Only three months after the policy was announced, four artists were threatened with eviction for not bringing their lofts up to commercial building code. Jim Gahagan responded, saying, "For 50 years, these buildings were used for commercial purposes without sprinkler systems. Now that the artists live in them, the Fire Dept. demands that the landlord install sprinkler systems. If the Fire Dept. is going to throw industrial and factory code at the artists, then they can never comply." Moreover, he claimed that having to install sprinkler systems would lead to prohibitively high rent, violating the spirit of the agreement between the ATA and the city.[21] Efforts to legalize loft living, it seemed, would have to continue.

Zoning Change, Loft Value, and Postindustrial Artist SoHo

While these early policy changes demonstrated that artists were garnering more political support, government actions legalizing loft residences were incomplete and temporary, leaving artists vulnerable to eviction. The Artist in Residence program was never truly a success. According to the ATA, in the years between 1961 and 1963, fewer than one tenth of Lower Manhattan artists applied for and obtained A.I.R. status. This was due in part to the difficulties involved in becoming an official artist in residence and the continuing fears among some artists that registering with the city and displaying a sign alerting the world to their presence would have made their residences a target for theft, as well as for unscrupulous building inspectors looking to extract bribes. These concerns, and the fact that state regulations allowed only two loft residences per building, served to keep A.I.R. enrollment down. More important, the city's agreement with the ATA only applied to structures that were zoned for commercial use. When, in 1963, the city rezoned the area south of Houston Street as an M1–5 light industrial zone, the city stopped accepting A.I.R. applications in SoHo.[22]

Consequently, the ATA began its grassroots organizing afresh. It once again organized a coalition to support its efforts, but one that now included politicians and housing advocates in addition to artists, critics, and curators, indicating that a wider group of influential people was paying attention to the issue. In February 1964, the ATA organized a meeting at Greenwich Village's Judson Memorial Church at which two hundred of its members gave their support to a state bill that would amend the State Multiple Dwelling Law to allow for artist loft residences. McNeil Mitchell, a Greenwich Village Republican, and Assembly member Alfred A. Lama, a Brooklyn Democrat-Liberal, sponsored the legislation. The bill itself came as a result of ATA members working directly with representatives from the state legislature. The group reported that it was collaborating with State Senator Mitchell to change the Multiple Dwelling Law as early as December 1962.[23]

The involvement of Mitchell and Lama gives some indication of how policy makers viewed artist tenants. The duo was best known for the Mitchell-Lama Limited-Profit Housing Companies Law, which encouraged the construction of middle-income housing in the city through the provision of state-backed mortgages for such projects.[24] Thus, at this juncture, it is likely that city and state leaders viewed artists at least in part as a moderate-income group whose housing needs local leaders could meet through appropriate policy.

The next target of artist advocacy was the New York State Multiple Dwelling Law. In spite of the decision by the mayor's office to ignore the city's zoning ordinance to let artists live in commercial buildings, the New York City Department of Buildings still had to enforce the state laws governing residential structures. This meant holding artists and their landlords to the state laws governing buildings containing multiple dwellings, including the safety standards of apartment buildings.

To push for changes to this law, the ATA staged a multipart protest that combined public demonstrations by rank-and-file artists and a boycott by better-known members of the New York art community. On Friday, April 3, 1964, the ATA's previously threatened artist strike became a reality, and eighty New York galleries closed to protest "recent enforcement of commercial zoning regulations" that prevented artists from living in lofts. Artists argued that without legislation allowing them to live in SoHo, they would be forced to leave the city, taking the economic contributions of art gallery sales with them. As loft resident and sculptor Ron Westerfield put it, "This is the end of the line for New York artists. If we have to get out of the lofts, we'll be finished."[25]

Critic Irving Sandler made the connection between loft living and New York's status as the world's art center explicit: "Many of the artists who will participate helped turn New York into the art capital of the world. Now they will be reduced to pounding the streets, begging for the right to live and work here." Even though New York artists, including the abstract expressionists, "added to the cultural stature of New York since 1945," the city was preventing the growth of new art movements by failing to legalize loft housing. He continued, "Instead of pointing with pride to the achievements of these masters, our city regards them and the younger artists who hope to emulate them as undesirables." If their housing needs are not met, Sandler argued, "larger numbers of artists will be driven from New York. Such an exodus would prove disastrous to the reputation of the city as a cultural center. But what is even worse, it could harm American art today."[26]

On April 3, the ATA also launched its most public protest to date, organizing a march attended by one thousand artists at City Hall. The march was meant to highlight the $500 million in revenue the arts community brought to the city each year, economic activity that was threatened by the lack of legalized loft housing. While the march was going on, recently elected ATA chair Jean Pierre Merle met with representatives of the City Planning Commission and the Department of Buildings, as well as city councilman at large Paul O'Dwyer of Manhattan, about the zoning changes that would legalize artist residences in Lower Manhattan.[27]

Thanks to these protests, city leaders began to take artists, their housing needs, and their ability to contribute to the city's economy more seriously. Artists' protests and advocacy were increasingly effective, as ATA members began to work directly with policy makers on legislation legalizing loft residences, demonstrating the growing acceptance of their vision for Lower Manhattan. In April 1964, the ATA met with a committee comprising members of the New York City Planning Commission, Buildings Department, City Administrator's Office, and Office of Cultural Affairs for the purpose of "studying the present problem, arriving at an equitable solution, and planning future housing."[28]

In May 1964, local leaders put their support for artists, their housing needs, and economic contributions into policy by amending the New York State Multiple Dwelling Law to permit "certified artists" to live in New York lofts. The nonprofit group Volunteer Lawyers for the Arts remarked that the amendment represented "the first official public policy statement enunciating a commitment to prevent the exodus of artists from New York City." The law demonstrated that the ATA's arguments connecting artists' ability to live in SoHo lofts with New York's status as the world's cultural capital were beginning to take hold. SoHo artists helped pass the legislation by working with their connections in the state legislature, most notably State Senator Mitchell. The drafters of the law reasoned that the large amount of space artists require, combined with the fact that "financial remunerations to be obtained from pursuit of a career in the visual fine arts are generally small," made it difficult for artists to work in New York in light of the city's high housing costs. Therefore, the state had to act to keep artists living and working in New York by legalizing loft residences.[29]

However, the 1964 amendment to the Multiple Dwelling Law did not unambiguously support artists' housing. There were tensions in the law itself between the desire to preserve industry and the impulse to encourage loft conversions as a form of housing development. The amendment required buildings to be classified as entirely industrial or entirely residential. It did not allow for the typical conversion pattern in SoHo, in which industries occupied larger and more commercially viable lower floors while artists lived in relatively cramped upper stories. The law required that loft residences adhere to residential fire and safety codes that were, in the opinion of the Volunteer Lawyers for the Arts, "economically prohibitive." The policy also made it legal for "a person engaged in the visual fine arts, such as painting and sculpture on a professional fine arts basis," to live in a loft. Artists doing so had to be certified by "an art academy, association or society, recognized by the municipal office of cultural affairs or the state council on the arts." This definition appeared overly restrictive to some and untenable to others, as the New York City Department of Cultural Affairs did not have a mechanism for determining who was an artist and in fact did not put one in place until 1971, when a more comprehensive SoHo zoning resolution required it.[30]

Moreover, although the state changed the Multiple Dwelling Law to allow for certified artists to live in commercial and residential buildings, the law applied only to districts with specific city zoning designations (M1 and C8), which limited the number of loft buildings in which artists could live legally. The city also refused to accept any further registrations to the A.I.R. program in these areas. The ATA asked the city to survey the neighborhoods that allowed for loft studio residences and those that did not in order to determine the availability and demand, but negotiations soon broke down. The ATA staged a protest at the reopening of the Museum of Modern Art as a result of this decision, but no further action from the city was forthcoming.[31]

New York was so adamant in its decision not to expand areas where artist housing would be allowed, or to accept further A.I.R. applications, that, according to the ATA, only 286 artists were registered to legally live in loft buildings by 1967.[32]

Artists and Urban Development

As the piecemeal nature of the loft policy and problems with its enforcement indicate, city and state leaders had not adequately addressed the issue of loft housing in New York. Likely, they did not fully understand the demand for, and the particular legal and physical barriers to, loft living among artists. During this time of debates over urban renewal, when policy makers were increasingly aware of the challenges of keeping industrial businesses in the city, they were also reluctant to enact any policy that could threaten the industrial businesses still housed in lofts.

Policy makers worried that increasing the ability of artists to live legally in lofts could develop into a zero-sum game. If too many artists lived in lofts, they could conceivably take up the spaces where job-producing industrial businesses could locate. If loft policy were too restrictive, artists might leave the city, and industrial loft space might remain vacant anyway, harming both industrial business owners and the city's cultural economy.

Artist advocates understood this political balancing act, and from the beginning of their legalization efforts, they argued that the benefits that loft conversions brought to the city were good for industry as well as the economy as a whole. Members of the ATA stressed that artists were able to upgrade urban neighborhoods, achieving many of the goals of urban renewal without most of the costs. A 1962 ATA publication stated, "With artists' ingenuity they transformed vacant, rundown light manufacturing lofts at their own expense into safe, adequate studios. In this process they have improved property, eliminated fire hazards, and solved their own living problems without relying on Federal, State or City funds."[33] Moreover, artists were able to achieve this upgrading of SoHo's built environment and stabilization of its economy without affecting its industrial tenants, who were operating under the threat of urban renewal.

Others noted artists' dual role as potential urban renewal victims and people with the ability to generate many of the goals of slum clearance with few of the costs. A 1964 article in the *Nation* on loft advocacy in Lower Manhattan observed that many local artists been pushed out of affordable housing by government-sponsored redevelopment projects. Because of their need for "extravagant amounts of space by slide-rule criteria" and their low incomes, artists "naturally gravitate to the older sections of town, where more expansive accommodations of an earlier age are standing in slow dissolution," exactly the types of locations that were frequent targets of urban renewal projects. Once in these older sections of town, "they produce, in effect, lively oases in a neighborhood of slums" and since "no community was ever blighted by painters and sculptors, they have an instinct for renewal." This instinct was particularly important in a time of white flight and suburbanization, as when "everyone else is going to the suburbs . . . artists are urban creatures" who often bring great benefits to urban neighborhoods.[34]

Thus, much like the advocates of urban renewal projects in and around SoHo, artists sought to convince city leaders that by upgrading SoHo lofts, they were improving New York's economy by producing new housing, creating new jobs, and preserving old ones. Yet, unlike advocates for projects such as highways and housing developments, SoHo artists developed a way to upgrade the area's industrial built environment while avoiding the human and economic costs of urban renewal. Artists' ceaseless efforts to change laws to secure legal recognition of their right to turn deserted industrial lofts into their living as well as work spaces played a key, if initially unanticipated, role in pioneering new strategies for urban renewal.

Yet, carrying this argument forward, it is not hard to see where conflicts could emerge. If artists' actions resulted in eliminating slums and upgrading neighborhoods, they were also helping to increase the value of local property. If this pattern continued, it would not be long before this increase in the cost of area lofts became an issue, both for artists and the industries with which they shared space. In anticipation of this potential conflict, artists had to demonstrate that they were adding to the city's cultural economy without detracting from its industrial one. They did so by reasoning that by renting vacant portions of industrial buildings, they allowed building owners to stay financially afloat and businesses employing the city's minority populations to stay in business. Even those who purchased loft buildings could argue that they were putting money into the pockets of industrial building owners, who might have other neighborhood enterprises or prefer to use these funds to relocate to a more efficient building.

Both policy makers and artists realized that the balance between artist housing and industry remained precarious. Industry saved SoHo from the urban renewal wrecking ball, allowing artists to cultivate new methods of upgrading loft buildings and adding value to these structures. Yet, a very real possibility existed that residential and industrial uses would soon come into conflict, resulting in industry being pushed from SoHo in much the same way that urban renewal advocates intended.

In the coming years, this risk of this conflict would be exacerbated by another factor that would shape SoHo's development: the growth of an art gallery district downtown. Soon after the first policies that legalized loft housing, art dealers and some SoHo artists began to see the benefits of spacious and inexpensive loft space for the display and sale of art. With art galleries came visitors, and businesses catering to visitors soon followed. In time, a thriving retail scene developed, making SoHo a more attractive place to live but also providing another potentially profitable use for loft space, further threatening the remaining industry in the neighborhood.

5

Moving Art Downtown

Paula Cooper's path to opening a SoHo gallery began as it did for many art dealers in the neighborhood: with a job at an established gallery uptown. The child of a naval officer, Cooper (then Paula Johnson) spent her childhood in Greece, Italy, Germany, and France before returning to New York in the late 1950s to work at the World House Gallery at Fifty-seventh Street and Madison Avenue, close to what was then the center of the gallery world. After two years arranging the gallery's auctions, sales, and exhibitions, she set up her own short-lived enterprise, the Paula Johnson Gallery. She then served as the director of the Park Place Gallery, a cooperative on LaGuardia Place just to the north of SoHo, from 1964 until it closed in 1968. Later that year, she founded her own gallery for a second time, this time under her married name.[1]

With little money to spend, Cooper searched for a storefront where space was cheap and plentiful. She first focused on the area between Fourteenth and Canal Streets, looking at several industrial properties, including a former pocketbook factory and a sweatshop, which she hoped to turn into a showroom. Eventually, she narrowed her search to SoHo. Cooper was attracted to the neighborhood due to its affordability and because it would allow for a showroom that would provide a sharp contrast with the established galleries of Midtown Manhattan. Cooper did not want "a store-like gallery like all the uptown galleries had become." Instead, she imagined "a much more open fluid place" where collectors, artists, and casual visitors could mingle and view art. She saw the open loft spaces available in SoHo as ideal for this purpose. Finally, and perhaps most important, she wanted to be near where artists lived. In 1968, Cooper rented two contiguous lofts on the third floor of 96–100 Prince Street in SoHo, right next to Fanelli's, the neighborhood's most popular bar, for $300 per month. Next, Cooper focused on turning her loft into a gallery. She took out a $3,000 loan from a bank (she asked for $5,000, but the bank wouldn't give it to her without collateral), some of which covered the security deposit on her loft, artwork, and announcements for her first exhibition. The rest went toward renovating the totally raw loft space she rented. Cooper constructed walls and built a display shelf along the front windows. Without the money to hire help, getting the gallery ready for business was a community project. Cooper swept the floors, and a friend of one of her artists made and manufactured lights, which Cooper and her artist friends spent days assembling on the gallery floor. The gallery's floors were renovated because one of Cooper's artists, Bob Hewitt, did a piece that involved stripping and fixing the floors in one area of the gallery.[2]

When it was completed, the Paula Cooper Gallery was large and sparse, with five thousand square feet used to display painting and sculpture "unsuited by intent and size to intimate indoor space." It contained "two white rooms which look north over Prince Street" that were "spacious enough to accommodate large architectural pieces." The gallery thus was able to specialize in "large outdoor painting and sculpture." However, there was also an area of the gallery to exhibit drawings and models for these large sculpture projects as well as photographs and slides of existing outdoor works.[3]

As the gallery was coming into shape, Cooper faced another problem: who would actually come to SoHo? No other gallery owners had their only showroom below Houston Street, and the area was filled with trucks, workers, and a few scattered artists during the day. On weekends and at night, the time when visitors came to art galleries, the streets were totally deserted. All of Cooper's friends told her that she was crazy to open there. Yet she believed that if the art was good, people would come.

Of course, Cooper had an ace up her sleeve: the New York art community. The gallery's first show on October 22, 1968, was an art benefit for the Student Mobilization Committee to End the War in Vietnam. The artists showing that evening would not have been out of place in an established uptown gallery or the Museum of Modern Art. Noted curator Lucy Lippard organized the show, which included works by Carl Andre, Dan Flavin, Sol LeWitt, and Donald Judd, among others. Yet the atmosphere at Paula Cooper was entirely "downtown." The subject matter was edgy (it might have offended some viewers), and the mood was open and informal, a feeling that matched this unfinished space located in the empty industrial neighborhood of SoHo.[4]

Paula Cooper was at the vanguard of a major change in where and how art was displayed, bought, and sold in New York City, a place already established as the center of the art world. On the most basic level, the Paula Cooper Gallery was one of the first major galleries to open in SoHo during the late 1960s and 1970s. Her efforts, along with the work of other early gallery pioneers, set off an explosion of art display in the neighborhood. While the New York press followed five major SoHo galleries in 1970, by 1973 there were more than eighty galleries in SoHo and its surrounding neighborhoods. By 1979, there were one hundred galleries in the area, and two guidebooks had been written on the local art scene.[5]

Moreover, when art came downtown to SoHo, it became more accessible, community-oriented, interdisciplinary, and visitor friendly. Cooper exemplifies some of the major trends that shaped SoHo and New York art in the late 1960s and early 1970s. She conceived of her gallery not as a sales floor but as an open and accessible space where anyone including collectors, artists, and casual visitors would be welcome.

Further, when Cooper saw the potential in loft space for the display of art, she began a trend that changed how art was shown in New York and worldwide. The physical nature of loft space was ideal for displaying the type of outsize works that New Yorkers, including SoHo artists, were producing during this era. Cooper and other SoHo gallery pioneers invented the sparse, high-ceilinged, white-walled art gallery with interior columns that one now sees everywhere art is presented and sold. Soon, loftlike space became the canonical form of display for modern art.

SoHo likewise transformed the geographic relationship between artists, art galleries, and art patrons. Art dealers came to SoHo to be around artists, and both found ample loft space to rent due to the neighborhood's continuing deindustrialization. An important point is that galleries opened in SoHo to be closer to the area's arts scene, not to be near their customers. This meant that a large portion of the artist and art gallery community occupied the same neighborhood for the first time in the history of New York. The low cost of space and the dense population of artists and galleries led to the creation of a distinct arts community where an artist could show works in commercial galleries down the block from his or her loft, or rent inexpensive loft space to open a cooperative gallery and show his or her own work. At the same time, both for-profit and cooperative arts institutions presented performance art, dance, and music created by the diverse artists in SoHo.

Local artists and art dealers did not seek out their patrons; they brought them to SoHo. SoHo's commercial galleries found customers among an international community of art collectors, institutional buyers (such as museums and universities), and corporate purchasers who either visited local galleries or sent their representatives to buy art. The artists who formed SoHo's cooperative galleries, which were less dependent on sales, brought monetary support for the arts to the area, first by using their own sweat equity to establish and operate nonprofit arts institutions and then by garnering state and federal arts funding for these establishments.

SoHo's collection of commercial and cooperative galleries also brought substantial numbers of visitors to the neighborhood. While some sought out painting and sculpture, others traveled to the area to experience various forms of artistic performance, including dance, theater, music, and interdisciplinary performance art. SoHo's commercial galleries hosted performances, and artists established several cooperatives (and some for-profit venues) dedicated to performance. SoHo's galleries, jazz lofts, dance companies, and interdisciplinary alternative spaces all sought to bring people to their doors to experience their art, or even to participate in its creation. These venues formed a vibrant and increasingly popular arts scene in SoHo.

Yet because of the diverse funding sources for SoHo galleries and arts organizations, visitors were not essential for the financial success of these institutions. As a result, those who traveled to SoHo could experience a museum-quality pop art retrospective, or an avant-garde performance piece, without the pressure to buy anything. Sometimes outside parties funded the gallery's operation, and in other instances the art displayed defied commodification. Crowds quickly grew, creating a potential customer base for businesses catering to these artistic tourists, which gave the SoHo gallery scene an impact beyond the art world. It was local galleries that drove the area's commercial renaissance and contributed to its continuing redevelopment.

The Birth of the SoHo Gallery Scene

Art galleries quite literally transformed the area south of Houston Street into SoHo. It was the neighborhood's developing art gallery district that caused the name "SoHo" to come into popular usage. The first time a journalist used the moniker in the *New York Times* was in 1970, in an article covering the March opening of the Reese Palley Gallery at 93 Prince Street. At that time, there were five major art galleries in SoHo, and the *New York Times*' "Downtown Scene" column gave regular updates on SoHo gallery shows.[6]

The rise of the SoHo gallery scene corresponded with the rise of New York and Lower Manhattan art to even greater levels of international prominence. From the end of World War II through the 1960s, New York became the unquestioned international art center. This artistic acclaim led to monetary success, as several New York artists, dealers, and collectors became wealthy from the sale of contemporary art. Galleries opened in SoHo just as the art market took a dramatic turn upward. This upsurge is generally associated with the 1973 Scull auction, the sale of fifty works by noted collector Robert Scull that brought in more than $2.2 million (more than $11.6 million in 2015 dollars). At the auction, Jasper Johns's *Double White Map* alone sold for $240,000 (nearly $1.3 million in 2015 dollars). By this time, many of the artists from the auction had works for sale in SoHo.[7]

Because of the vitality of the New York art scene, along with its built environment and arts community in New York, SoHo quickly grew to rival the more established Midtown gallery district, near East Fifty-seventh and Seventy-ninth Streets and Madison Avenue, in size, scope, and importance. Galleries came to SoHo for many of the same reasons artists did: to be close to those producing art and to take advantage of the area's large, inexpensive, former industrial spaces. For example, at his gallery's opening in 1970, Reese Palley said that he was able to find "more exhibition space than the Whitney Museum," at a much lower cost than equivalent rentals on Fifty-seventh Street.[8]

Gallery owners also established their businesses in SoHo to be close to artists—one of the unique elements of the neighborhood's history. The city's previous gallery districts grew as a result of their proximity to cultural institutions, buyers, and transportation, not artists' studios. New York's Fifty-seventh Street commercial gallery center flourished in large part due to its proximity to the Museum of Modern Art and because it was close to the homes of wealthy patrons on the Upper East Side of Manhattan, the offices of business leaders of Midtown, and Grand Central Terminal, through which buyers from around the country could travel to the city and look at art.[9]

In the 1950s, several galleries did open on Tenth Street between Third and Fourth Avenues in Greenwich Village, then New York's major center for artistic activity. However, these galleries were not designed as profit-making institutions. Some were designed as nonprofit cooperatives, such as the Tananger, Brata, and Reuben Galleries, and nearly all of them struggled financially and artistically, in large part because successful Village artists such as Jackson Pollock showed their work at established galleries uptown. At Greenwich Village galleries, according to critic Irving Sandler, "sales were not expected and in fact were rare. But selling did not matter much: what counted was the approval of other artists."[10] Additionally, Greenwich Village was already a densely inhabited, largely residential neighborhood that lacked vacant storefront space, preventing a robust gallery scene from growing close to nearby artist studios.

In contrast, numerous galleries moved to empty storefronts alongside artist lofts in SoHo. Appropriately, some of the first area galleries were outposts of established Midtown galleries. Richard Feigen, an uptown art dealer with a gallery on Eighty-first Street and Madison Avenue, was the first to open in the neighborhood, establishing a branch on Greene Street in 1967. Feigen, like many Uptown art dealers, was "faced with the problem of squeezing outsize wares into brownstone galleries of shoebox width." *New York Times* art critic Grace Glueck noted, "To accommodate, say, the massive constructions of Chryssa and Lee Bontecou, the giant canvases of Frank Stella, Larry Poons and Robert Irwin, narrow-gauge galleries such as Pace and Castelli must dismantle stair rails, remove door frames and hoist whole shows through windows." Additionally, art dealers were already renting warehouse spaces in other parts of the city to store works not on display. Sometimes this meant that collectors would have to visit several locations to see works they were considering purchasing. Feigen's solution was to "meet the art more than half-way" by opening an annex "right where the work is made—the 'in' artists' loft district downtown." He opened a gallery in a former button factory on Greene Street near Houston Street, a building that included "three floors of unbroken 'live storage' space, a loading dock and an elevator made for giant crates."[11]

Feigen assumed that visitors would be sparse. He originally planned to show work to the public only on Sunday afternoons and did not intend to put on full-scale art shows in this new space. However, people were already starting to come to his loft gallery, most often while visiting local artists' studios or enjoying the amenities of nearby Chinatown. Feigen said, "The area's become a Sunday hangout for collectors. They like to go loft-hopping and stop for a Chinese lunch. The painting atmosphere's there, and it puts them in a buying mood." He hoped that other galleries would follow his lead, but even if not, the ability to sell art in SoHo was not yet of central importance. Feigen told the *New York Times*, "The original Feigen Gallery will still remain in its uptown spot" because there "he sells the small Picassos that keep things going."[12]

Then along came Paula Cooper in 1968. Because she was the first person to open a SoHo gallery that was not connected with an established uptown location, the *New York Times* declared, "Paula Cooper is probably more responsible than any one person for the surfacing of the South Houston scene." It was her gallery that helped foster and draw attention to the "liveliest concentrated art activity in America" and "New York's first conspicuous art scene since 10th Street."[13]

Next came Ivan Karp, who established OK Harris Gallery at 465 West Broadway. Karp, a "former star salesman at Leo Castelli," a gallery most noted for its role in promoting and selling work by pop artists (and a future SoHo tenant), moved to SoHo in 1969 "to be in fresh territory, where the artist themselves work." Karp also lived in the area and knew the type of

FIGURE 14. SoHo gallery exhibition installation, 1976. (Photograph by Robin Forbes. Reproduced by permission from Archives of American Art, Smithsonian Institution.)

rentals that could be obtained at low prices. When he decided to open his own gallery, within a week, Karp recalled, he "found an enormous space on West Broadway, an abandoned warehouse with seven thousand square feet. The exhibition space in Leo's gallery was about five hundred square feet, and I had always thought that substantial. I first considered that this enormous space could be divided and still be the largest gallery in the world—at less than $600 a month." Karp opened his gallery, named after a fictional character "who wears a zoot suit and a gold chain—the kind of sharpie who might come suddenly to town and deal in art"—on a "serene and neighborhood street" directly across from a box factory where artists might pass by and say hello.[14]

Next, two additional established art dealers moved to SoHo. Max Hutchinson, an Australian gallery owner with locations in Sydney and Melbourne, created a massive three-floor showroom at 127 Greene Street in 1969. Reese Palley Gallery, the fifth to locate in SoHo, opened at 93 Prince Street, a block with "grimy lofts and rag reclaiming plants and dingy candy stores," in 1970. Having looked for a gallery space on Madison Avenue, he found the atmosphere there to be "anti-art and anti-artist," so he decided to move to SoHo and sell art "among the artists." At Palley's opening, Karp greeted his new neighbor, saying, "Another flourishing gallery is the best possible thing that could happen to the downtown art scene . . . The bigger the extravaganza here, the better."[15]

Then, in 1971, the uptown art community established a larger beachhead in SoHo at 420 West Broadway. This building contained branches of two well-regarded eponymous Midtown galleries, André Emmerich, which had a space at 17 East Sixty-fourth Street, and Leo Castelli, also located at 4 East Seventy-seventh Street, as well as galleries run by Ileana Sonnabend, Castelli's ex-wife and an established European art dealer, and John Weber, formerly associated with Midtown's Dwan Gallery.[16]

The galleries at 420 West Broadway had connections to both the art world and the industrial functions of lofts. The art dealers at 420 West Broadway found their way to SoHo via The Hague Art Delivery, a company founded by Dutch American partners Frits de Knegt and Wouter Germans (see chapter 2) that did work for Castelli's gallery. The company's main job was moving art for Midtown dealers, but because of the outsize nature of contemporary art (the pair's first big job was to move James Rosenquist's eighty-six-foot-long painting *F-111*), the company needed substantial warehouse space. After quickly outgrowing several smaller warehouses, the company rented a one hundred-square-foot, four-story garage on 108th Street and Amsterdam Avenue. Because they did not need all four stories, the Hague's partners convinced Leo Castelli to lease one of the garage's floors and consolidate his warehoused artworks here. Castelli eventually had some gallery shows in the warehouse. Later, art dealers John Weber and Virginia Dwan also rented floors.[17]

Yet in 1970, the City of New York informed the company its 108th Street warehouse would soon be condemned to make way for a housing project (which was never completed). The company looked for new space. The company's broker soon called about a building on West Broadway. De Knegt recalls having to look on a map to even locate that street. Though neither partner wanted to go to this "no man's land," both were so impressed by the amount and quality of space available that de Knegt and Germans were soon trying to figure out how they could purchase 420 West Broadway for $275,000. They went to Leo Castelli and Virginia Dwan, who each agreed to buy a floor. Soon, Emmerich joined the group, as he needed room to house the large Morris Louis canvases he was struggling to display in his Fifty-seventh Street gallery. Dwan subsequently dropped out, and Weber took over. Castelli then brought Sonnabend into the building, and the galleries of 420 West Broadway were born.[18]

It is hard to overstate the importance of these galleries in the New York art world, and of the Castelli in particular. Before moving to SoHo, Castelli's gallery held the first solo shows by Robert Rauschenberg and Jasper Johns in 1958 and the first Frank Stella and Cy Twombly exhibitions in 1960. The gallery put up the first exhibit of Roy Lichtenstein's comic book paintings in 1962 and the first exhibition of minimalist sculpture by Donald Judd in 1966. In 1964, Andy Warhol and James Rosenquist joined the gallery. Dan Flavin joined Castelli in 1970, Ellsworth Kelly in 1973, and Claes Oldenburg in 1974. Castelli's first season at 420 West Broadway included art shows by Robert Rauschenberg, Bruce Nauman, Cy Twombly, a concert by Philip Glass, and a group exhibition of works by Twombly, John Chamberlain, Donald Judd, Roy Lichtenstein, Robert Morris, Frank Stella, and Andy Warhol.[19] With art of this quality being displayed locally, gallerygoers in SoHo could experience shows on a par with the Metropolitan Museum of Art or the Museum of Modern Art. With established artists came high sales. For example, in 1976 alone, receipts at Leo Castelli Gallery totaled more than $2.5 million (more than $10.3 million in 2015 dollars).[20]

As the SoHo gallery community grew, the trend of dealers looking to establish a casual "downtown" identity by opening branches near SoHo artists intensified. One prominent SoHo gallery owner was Nancy Hoffman. Hoffman had worked at an uptown gallery, French & Company, which had considered moving its operation downtown along the lines of Richard Feigen. However, the gallery decided to move in another direction, and she chose to open her own gallery in SoHo. Hoffman had knowledge of the area because she had spent time visiting artist studios, and on studio visits she was impressed by the artworks she saw and the rooms in which they were created. As she recalled, "they were these open loftlike warehouse spaces, they were pretty raw, and at the time quite affordable." Although the space she found for a gallery at 429 West Broadway was "a real lemon, it was really a mess," Hoffman could see its potential for beauty; moreover, it could hold large works of art. Hoffman remembered seeing a sculpture and thinking, "Oh wow, that will work great in the gallery because we can fit that" without "some sort of crazy hoist . . . it can go right in the front door." After only two weeks, Hoffman was able to collect the $50,000 she needed to get the business up and running, $30,000 of which went toward renovations. After *New York Times* critic John Canaday wrote a favorable review of her first show in December 1972, the gallery was off and running.[21]

The same year, Betty Cunningham made a similar journey to SoHo. Cunningham worked for Reese Palley, himself one of the neighborhood's gallery pioneers. One day in 1970, when Cunningham was coming back from lunch, Palley announced that he was closing his gallery. She went across the street to talk with bar owner Mike Fanelli and wondered, "What should I do?" Fanelli provided the answer: "You're moving upstairs." Although people told her she was crazy, two years later, Cunningham opened her gallery on the floor above Fanelli's bar. The growing artist and gallery communities gave Cunningham confidence that she would succeed.[22]

Louis Meisel had run a gallery on Seventy-ninth Street and Madison Avenue in 1968, but by the early 1970s he was eager to transfer his operation to SoHo. He was so enthusiastic that he did so in 1972, a year before his lease uptown ended. He placed a sign in his window on Madison Avenue and Seventy-ninth Street telling would-be visitors to come downtown to the loft he had bought at 141 Prince Street.[23]

Meisel sought to create a casual, open atmosphere at his gallery, even as he was dealing in art on a high level. As he described it, "I came down to SoHo, I put on a pair of jeans and a work shirt and my cowboy boots," and welcomed "anybody that walked in the door to talk to me, weather it was a collector or a noncollector." Meisel believed that people felt too intimidated to walk into galleries uptown, and he created a welcoming atmosphere that brought people such as Charles Saatchi and Donald and Mera Rubell, soon to be some of the world's best-known art buyers, into his gallery to begin their collections.[24]

Before any art could be sold, SoHo gallery owners had to physically convert their loft spaces into functional galleries, which was no easy task. There was little difference between these "start-up" art dealers and loft owners when it came to renovation. Hoffman, for example, had rented what had been a heavy-duty sheet metal manufacturing shop. Among the items that had to be removed to open up usable space were eleven bathrooms, a great deal of manufacturing detritus, and a number of partitions. Hoffman put in a new floor and walls, renovated the ceiling on the first floor to expose the attractive wood beams overhead, removed the name "Stanford Sheet Metal" from the facade of the building (only to find the name of a wine merchant from the 1880s underneath), kept a staircase and hoist to the basement to haul up paintings, and installed racks for storage. Hoffman was in the gallery every day, "cracking the whip" to make sure contractors completed renovations before the scheduled opening.[25]

Cunningham did not even have the luxury of hiring contractors. She painted her loft's floor rather than sand it because it was cheaper and, with the help of friends and gallery assistants, covered up a shaftway in the middle of the gallery floor (ironically, the same sort of renovation that eventually led to the collapse of Weiss & Klau). Again, these renovations were not risk-free for artists or gallery owners. One of Cunningham's artists, Ross Bleckner, was seriously injured when he got his foot caught between a gallery floor and a hydraulic lift. Even the art could cause problems. Much as the operations of industrial businesses sometimes risked building integrity, Cunningham remembers that a Richard Serra sculpture fell against a cast-iron column in a building Leo Castelli had rented to show some of his work, breaking the column and requiring the evacuation of the building.[26]

Supporting SoHo Art—Commercial Galleries

SoHo's for-profit commercial galleries formed the backbone of the local art scene. Yet these institutions were also integrated into a broader community of artists, patrons, and buyers. SoHo's commercial galleries showed art created both locally and nationally, and they sold pieces to collectors, businesses, and institutions across the country and around the world. A visitor to a for-profit gallery in SoHo could see world-class art in an open, casual atmosphere. Yet commercial galleries did not depend on weekend browsers for sales. The result was an environment in which a large number of galleries opened in the same neighborhood but did not depend on the patronage of visitors for their success.

Art shown in SoHo was top quality, in large part because local galleries displayed works from around the world in addition to art produced in the area. This high level of art pervaded the entire neighborhood. In addition to the museum-quality work on display at Leo Castelli, the art shown at less-established galleries such as the Paula Cooper Gallery was also highly regarded. Even in the first years after she opened, several of the artists Cooper represented were well respected and relatively established. They included sculptors Forrest (Frosty) Myers, Keith Hollingworth, and Chris Wilmarth, and painters Edwin Ruda and Harvey Quaytman. The artists taught at art schools across the country, showed their work in such museums as the Whitney Museum of American Art, the Museum of Modern Art, and the Art Institute of Chicago, and had fellowships from the Guggenheim Foundation and the National Endowment for the Arts (NEA). Paula Cooper also represented some SoHo artists, including Rosemarie Castoro, who lived at 151 Spring Street, David Diao at 496 Broome Street, and Forrest Myers, who lived just north of SoHo. Yet, many times, the gallery was equally dedicated to serving as a showcase for an international avant-garde.[27]

Other SoHo galleries exhibited a similar mix of local artists and imported talent. Nancy Hoffman's first show featured an artist from Northern California and one from Southern California. Betty Cunningham showed mostly New York artists at the beginning, though some resided outside SoHo in other parts of the city, such as the Meatpacking District, the Bowery, and the Lower East Side. The bulk of Louis Meisel's stable of photorealist painters hailed from around the country, including California and Chicago, and showed their work along with works by artists from New York.[28]

Wherever the artists came from, the sales from art in SoHo commercial galleries could be substantial. Although the gallery atmosphere at Paula Cooper was casual, its sales were not. In 1968, the first year of its operation, the gallery tallied gross receipts of $73,484 (almost $500,000 in 2015 dollars) and reported a profit of $21,811 (more than $148,000 in 2015 dollars). A sampling of the sale prices of works displayed at the Paula Cooper Gallery from 1968 to 1979 (see Table 2) shows that some artists sold large numbers of works at the gallery, more than one hundred in some cases. The average sale price for artists' works ranged from modest to substantial. For example, Mark di Suvero's sculptures sold for an average of more than $6,000 each (almost $41,000 in 2105 dollars).[29]

In spite of its visitor-friendly atmosphere, visitors to the Paula Cooper Gallery were not its main customers. Collectors, museums, academic institutions, and corporations from across the United States made up the bulk of her clients. Cooper was linked to a national network of collectors, including Frank Porter of Cleveland, Betty Blake of Dallas, and Patrick Lannan, a philanthropist based in Florida.[30]

Museums, government agencies, and foundations also bought art from Paula Cooper. The gallery sold pieces to the Smithsonian's Hirshhorn Museum and Sculpture Garden, the Walker Art Center in Minneapolis, the Whitney Museum of American Art in New York, and several university art museums. In addition, foundations and government agencies served as a market for the Paula Cooper Gallery. The gallery sold an Edwin Ruda painting to the Port Authority of New York and New Jersey, and it negotiated with

TABLE 2. Average Prices of Works at Paula Cooper Gallery, 1968–79

Name of Artist	Works for Sale	Average Sale Price
James Dearing	9	$1,789
Mark di Suvero	27	$6,284
Jeremy Gilbert-Rolfe	18	$2,980
George Kuehn	40	$1,738
Forrest Myers	27	$3,398
Ulrich Ruckriem	11	$3,053
Edwin Ruda	140	$2,354
Doug Sanderson	58	$594
Joseph White	3	$433
Chris Wilmarth	69	$1,848
Kes Zapkus	131	$3,055

the New York State Council on the Arts (NYSCA) for the sale of Forrest Myers sculptures for public installation. The Woodward Foundation and the Lannan Foundation bought from the gallery, and Paula Cooper often relied on foundation grants to support performance pieces staged in the gallery.[31]

This pattern of outside support extended to other SoHo galleries. Nancy Hoffman had "tripartite support for the gallery: private collectors, institutions, like museums, and corporations." The 1970s was "the beginning of the blossoming of consultants putting collections into corporations, collections into law firms, collections into banks, it was a nascent moment for corporate collecting," and galleries such as Hoffman's benefited from this trend. Karp wrote that "eight to 10 percent of my business comes from museum purchases, and 15 to 20 percent from corporations," with the remainder coming from sales to collectors across the country. Similarly, Cunningham sold art to Chase Manhattan Bank, IBM, and McCrory Corporation.[32] In 1972, the first full year he was open in SoHo, André Emmerich sold to buyers from California, Florida, Illinois, Kansas, Massachusetts, Michigan, Missouri, New Jersey, New York, Ohio, Oklahoma, Texas, and Wisconsin, as well as South Africa and Germany. This was not surprising, as the artists the gallery represented—such as Hans Hofmann, David Hockney, and Franz Kline— were figures with New York and international connections who often sold paintings broadly.[33]

SoHo's Nonprofit Arts Organizations

SoHo was home to a large number of nonprofit cooperative galleries that substantially expanded the local art scene. Much like the neighborhood's commercial galleries, SoHo's nonprofit arts organizations did not rely on gallery visitors for their income. Artists established cooperative galleries as places to show their work, but the gallery itself did not take in any money from the sale of art. Instead, dues from members covered monthly rent, and artists who showed in cooperatives hung their own artwork, cleaned the gallery, and handled their own publicity, among other tasks. In addition, many SoHo nonprofits received partial funding through grants from NYSCA and the NEA. As a result of these diverse funding sources, cooperative galleries were places to see up-and-coming artists and new works without pressure to purchase anything.

Artists contributed to SoHo's commercial sector through the capital and labor they provided to its nonprofit arts organizations. SoHo's cooperative galleries were modeled on Greenwich Village's Jane Street Gallery, founded in 1944, at which artists paid monthly fees in exchange for the opportunity to regularly show their work. Beginning with the opening of the 55 Mercer and Ward Nasse Galleries in 1969, cooperative galleries and nonprofit arts organizations quickly spread in SoHo, including the 112 Workshop and Prince Street Gallery in 1970; A.I.R. and the Kitchen in 1971; First Street, Bowery, Landmark, and SoHo 20 Galleries in 1972; the 14 Sculptors and Westbroadway/Alternative Space in 1973; and Pleiades and Cloud in 1974.[34]

Again, the sale of art to casual visitors was not critical to the financial health of cooperative galleries. These institutions did not deduct proceeds from art sales; all funds earned from sales went into the artists' pockets. Although visitors to cooperative galleries did buy some art, and prices were lower than at commercial galleries, sales were not high. For example, in 1975 the average sale price for an artwork at a Prince Street Gallery show was around $400, and the bulk of exhibitions had an average sale price of under $1,000 ($1,760 and $4,400, respectively, in 2015 dollars).[35]

While commercial galleries were founded to sell art and turn a profit (even if it was a modest one), the founders of SoHo's nonprofit and cooperative galleries had other, often anticapitalist and countercultural, aims. Looking back on its history, *Artforum* editor Joseph Masheck described 55 Mercer as "ever-struggling." Yet, it was access, transparency in what work was exhibited, and the ability to show innovative new work in an environment not completely dictated by the whims of the art market that inspired the artists of 55 Mercer. As member Stephen Rosenthal explained, "Galleries provide a limited forum and only one that relates to art as commodity. They are insufficient in their presentation of the range of living art: what should be seen, when and how. Profits dictate styles." The ability to display work in museums was not helpful in this regard. Museums were governed by ideology, and "more and more barricaded behind walls of institutional bureaucracy," Rosenthal asserted. As a result, he said, "the artist may spend his life as a cabinetmaker, working to furnish museums. He is the weakest link in the chain of the art world, the most expendable."[36]

SoHo's A.I.R. Gallery had a similarly political mission. It touted itself as the first cooperative gallery of female artists in the United States and worked toward providing "greater opportunities for women to exhibit their work." The gallery did "not exist to make a profit," and did "not plan to become profit making by taking fees from the sale of work." Its main goal was to teach and "redefine existing attitudes about the quality of women artists' work." The gallery's founders created A.I.R. to respond to a hostile environment for women artists in the United States. According a survey released at the gallery's founding, 95.4 percent of shows at leading New York galleries were of male artists' work; only 18 percent of commercial galleries across the nation displayed women's art; the Metropolitan Museum of Art and Guggenheim Museum had yet to do a major one-woman show; and the Museum of Modern Art only had four such shows from 1942 to 1969.[37]

Because they were not designed to make money, cooperative galleries stayed afloat through use of artists' labor and capital as well as government arts funding. The majority of a cooperative gallery's budget usually came from member dues, which consisted of onetime initiation fees for joining a cooperative and monthly payments that allowed members to regularly show their work and keep the majority of profits from their shows. In addition, members were required to donate the time and labor required to keep the gallery running. A.I.R.'s founding members helped build and paint walls, rewired the building, removed rusting pipes and radiators, and contributed up to $150 each to pay for more complicated renovations. When the gallery opened, each member contributed $21 toward its $350 monthly rent. In exchange, members earned participation in one of the twenty two-and-a-half week, two-person shows that A.I.R. held throughout the year.[38] In addition, A.I.R. members kept the gallery's books in order, completed basic maintenance, staffed the gallery once a month (or found a replacement), and raised additional money through foundation grants and direct appeals to supporters. In advance of a show, exhibiting artists were responsible for writing press releases; creating, mailing out, and paying for advertisements; designing, printing, and mailing invitations to their opening; and ordering wine. Before the show could open, artists needed to write and print their own résumés, put out guest books, create price lists, and hang their own artwork. When the show was on, they had to change their own lightbulbs, patch any scuffs on the walls, sweep up at the end of the day, and take the garbage out. When the exhibition was over, they needed to take their art off the walls and ready the gallery for the next show.[39]

The differences between SoHo's commercial and cooperative galleries were often blurred. Commercial gallery owners Hoffman and Cooper spent long hours in their spaces, supervising renovations or sitting on the floor with friends getting announcements into the mail in the early days of their galleries in a manner similar to cooperatives. Cooper would ask passing artists to help her hang works, and Cunningham's commercial gallery space was so big and her staff so small that she often had to run around her gallery finding people or checking information while buyers waited on the phone.[40]

The quality of the work shown in cooperative galleries, as well as their financial stability, fluctuated considerably. Cooperatives such as 55 Mercer, SoHo 20, and A.I.R. were secure financially, covered regularly in the press, and seen by many in the art world as on a par with some of SoHo's commercial galleries. However, some other cooperatives were not as respected, or as successful. As an article in the *SoHo Weekly News* pointed out, "Here we are presented with a turnabout system wherein a co-op, by virtue of an initiation fee paid by artists, may remain viable, even if none of its members sells a damn thing. The artists may end up eating broiled roaches but the gallery survives, and there is always a surplus of transparencies in the files with eager owners on the waiting list." Yet, without sales, cooperatives could be financially vulnerable. Even with the financial contributions of artists, some cooperative galleries struggled to stay afloat. In 1973, Tom Boutis, a member of the artist-run Landmark Gallery at 469 Broome Street, reported that the operation was "running on the edge of a precipice." Despite the investment of $13,000 worth of renovations by its six members, and a desire to eventually turn a profit, it would take an annual income of $73,000 from the sale of art for the gallery to break even.[41]

As a result, most cooperative galleries sought government arts funding to support their operations. Nearly all SoHo cooperatives were nonprofit organizations with tax-exempt status, allowing them to apply for government arts funding and pursue tax-deductible donations from individuals, grants from foundations, and gifts from corporations. SoHo's cooperative galleries benefited from a strong climate for arts funding at the federal level. The area's artist colony formed in the years immediately preceding the founding of the NEA in 1965. The NEA grew out of government efforts during the Cold War to highlight American artists' freedom compared to their counterparts in the Soviet Union. Conceived during the Kennedy administration and formally established by President Lyndon Johnson, the NEA grew considerably in the late 1960s and '70s. President Richard Nixon increased NEA funding from $7 million in 1968 to $64 million in 1974, just as the first art galleries were opening in SoHo. At first, the NEA did not fund avant-garde art, as the organization saw itself as a protector of the Western tradition and a guardian against communism. Under Presidents Gerald Ford and Jimmy Carter, the NEA began to fund feminist art, performance art, and video art—exactly the kind of work shown in SoHo galleries. Given the importance of the city in the national arts scene, New York artists and institutions in New York garnered a large percentage of federal arts funding. In the late 1960s, it was not uncommon for close to 95 percent of NEA grants to go to New York artists.[42]

Further exploration of the role of government arts funding in SoHo provides a way to expand on Sharon Zukin's analysis of the neighborhood's development. Zukin argues that federal and state arts funding was central to regularizing artists' employment and bringing them more solidly into the middle class, which in turn caused other members of the middle class to become more comfortable with the idea of living like an artist, making it easier for them to envision moving into a loft. An additional consequence of government arts funding was the support it provided to SoHo nonprofit arts institutions. This funding was instrumental in allowing the neighborhood's nonprofit cooperative galleries to contribute to SoHo's artistic community and attract additional visitors to the area.[43]

At the same time, New York City artists could also obtain funding through the New York State Council on the Arts. Governor Nelson Rockefeller, a major patron of the arts, founded NYSCA as a temporary state agency in 1960, and the organization became an official state agency in 1965. Like the NEA, NYSCA increased its size and scope while SoHo was transforming into an artist enclave. Governor Rockefeller increased NYSCA's budget from $2.2 million to $20.1 million in 1971.[44]

In turn, arts funding from the NEA and NYSCA, along with member dues, kept SoHo cooperative galleries in business. It was common for these cooperatives to have little or no outside income. For example, in 1975 all but $34 of SoHo 20's $9,368 of earned income came from member dues. The First Street Gallery's income came entirely from member dues and government sources from 1973 to 1975.[45]

Although not all SoHo cooperatives were as reliant on government support, state funding made up a significant portion of most budgets. A.I.R. was founded as a 501(c)(3) nonprofit in 1972, and the organization obtained its first NEA grant the same year. Throughout the 1970s and early 1980s, A.I.R. relied on NEA and NYSCA funding to cover supply costs, a traveling exhibition series, speakers' fees, and monthly salaries for staff members required to expand its operations. Grant funds represented a significant portion of its budget. For example, half of A.I.R.'s 1977 budget of $28,950 came from $15,000 in government grants.[46]

SoHo Performance: Dance, Music, Theater, and Performance Art

SoHo was also a site for innovative, interdisciplinary, performance-based art. Nonprofit "alternative spaces," established commercial galleries, and organizations dedicated to specific genres of performance, hosted performance art, dance, and music created by the growing and diverse SoHo arts community. Dance performances, concerts in "jazz lofts," plays, and a wide range of happenings in alternative spaces drew people into SoHo to experience artistic phenomena in large, sparse interiors. Unlike paintings or sculpture sold in galleries, these art forms were often noncommercial in nature and relied on outside funding. Yet, whether it was to experience the art or even participate in it, performance venues sought to bring people through their doors, helping to create a vibrant, and increasingly visitor-focused, arts scene in the neighborhood.

While SoHo was coming into its own as an artist colony in the 1960s, performance art was becoming an increasingly respected artistic medium. As critic RoseLee Goldberg wrote, "It was in the 1960s that an increasing number of artists turned to live performance as the most radical form of art-making, irrevocably disrupting the course of traditional art history and challenging the double-headed canon of the established media—painting and sculpture." During this time, much contemporary art incorporated performance elements. By the 1970s, "performance art became the predominant art form of the period." SoHo was one of the centers of performance art, and avant-garde pieces brought visitors into the neighborhood in greater numbers. SoHo loft spaces were fertile ground for the growth of this art form, as most of the "experimental new work in music, dance, or live events found its audiences" in "art spaces—first in smaller galleries or so-called alternative spaces," which abounded in SoHo.[47]

Much of SoHo's performance art took place in unadorned lofts, and events brought together multiple types of artistic endeavor. These spaces were often cooperatively owned and artist run. Alternative spaces hosted innovative, avant-garde events that pushed the boundaries of artistic media and often incorporated performance. SoHo became fertile ground for the creation of this a boundary-pushing art, as the dense and tight-knit artist community encouraged collaboration between artists working in various media. The physical openness and adaptability of lofts also made them well suited for performance art. Judson Memorial Church, located just to the north of SoHo, was one of the early centers of performance art, and some of its most noted practitioners, such as Meredith Monk, were based in the neighborhood.[48]

One of SoHo's best-known alternative spaces was 112 Workshop, which Jeffrey Lew and Alan Saret started in 1970 after New York University canceled artist Steve Paxton's dance performance at its Loeb Student Center because it involved "fifty nude redheads." Lew invited Paxton to instead stage the performance at his loft at 112 Greene Street. According to Lew, "at least three hundred people showed up, walked up the six floors. And we got rid of all my furniture and started giving performances there." After securing financial help from an art buyer, who agreed to pay the rent for two years, and the serendipity of the rag recycling business downstairs closing up shop, 112 Workshop was born. The space's first show featured Richard Serra, Richard Van Buren, and Gordon Matta-Clark.[49]

Much as was the case with galleries, loft architecture was central to how alternative performance venues conceptualized their role as display places for art. Lew envisioned 112 Workshop as an open, raw space where artists could make drastic alterations to the interior. Upon choosing the loft, Lew said that he was "not going to touch it, except to put in basic things like doors and lights." Lew believed that "space is always involved with the work that goes in it," and he did not want to restrict artists' use of it in any way, particularly those artists who found "the clean, well-lighted galleries uptown" inadequate for showing their work. Frequent collaborator Matta-Clark took advantage of the space the most, "activating the structure on every level." Living in the basement at the time, Matta-Clark said he "started treating the place as a whole, as an object." In his artwork, Matta-Clark dug into the floor, uncovering the gallery's subterranean recesses. He grew plants throughout the gallery in "impossible places," including a cherry tree in a hole he dug in the basement floor. He also filled an elevator shaft with a "matrix of glass bottles" he found on the street to bring sunlight downward into the building's basement.[50]

The flexible space encouraged the blurring of disciplinary boundaries: 112 Workshop was a place where "distinctions between art forms naturally began to break down" and artists explored all aspects of performance. Dancers and musicians came to 112 because they could use the space in any way they liked. Moreover, performers often used the paintings and sculpture already on display as "ready-made sets for concerts." The gallery also hosted avant-garde dance by Suzanne Harris, performance pieces by Tina Girouard, avant-garde theater by the group Mabou Mines, and shows by musicians of all types, from Louisiana jazz musicians to the Philip Glass Ensemble.[51]

The workshop's function as a place for artistic experimentation also provided another valuable role for the neighborhood, serving as a farm system for more profitable commercial galleries. "Many came to 112 on the advice of commercial dealers who were unwilling to take chances with new talent and saw the alternative spaces as a proving ground," wrote Robyn Brentano and Mark Savitt, authors of a history of the gallery. After showing at 112 Workshop, many artists were eventually signed by commercial galleries. In this sense, alternative spaces demonstrate the symbiotic relationship that existed between cooperative and commercial galleries. The former would create attention for new artists while the latter could then sell their work through their networks of buyers and patrons once they were established.[52]

Because the art shown at 112 Workshop included large numbers of abstract pieces that could not be sold, the organization relied heavily on government arts funding for its operational costs. NYSCA generously supported 112 Workshop because it was "offering a variety of avant-garde and experimental exhibitions and performances not often seen in commercial galleries." The organization found their work to be "of mixed quality but high interest, with a definite orientation with working with the Soho neighborhood." The National Endowment for the Arts provided 87 percent of 112 Workshop's total income in 1975–76, and 66 percent in 1976–77. Through the late 1970s, the gallery did not engage in any real fund-raising from corporate or foundation sources, instead relying on government funds and individual contributions (the organization received $4,500 in contributions in 1976–77). After it received its allotment from the NEA, 112 Workshop usually asked NYSCA for the remainder of its operating budget, with some success. NYSCA supported the organization because it played "an active and useful part in the general 'alternative exhibition' picture in New York," but was concerned that it "consistently relies only on government support for operating funds."[53]

Similarly, dance was a central element of SoHo's performance art scene. When the SoHo Performing Arts Association organized the SoHo Dance Festival in 1977, it found that SoHo had nearly as many dancers and choreographers as painters and sculptors. Dance thrived there despite the many challenges that its practitioners faced in profiting from this art form. As the *SoHo Weekly News* wrote, "you can't take a dance home with you the way you can a painting or sculpture—a real drawback in this cash-and-carry, art-as-status society. You can't speculate in dance: since it can't be owned, it can't appreciate in monetary value. The benefits of art-oriented commercialism of SoHo have passed the dancers by."[54]

Dance grew in SoHo in part because dancers found that loft spaces were uniquely suited to their performance needs. SoHo choreographers created works in their lofts and developed dances specifically designed to be performed in loft galleries and performance spaces as well as in the dancers' homes. Michelle Berne, one of the organizers of the SoHo Dance Festival, said, "Loft dancing is, after all, not just a prelude to dancing in a 'legitimate' theater. Dances are made to be seen in specific spaces; the space is integral to the choreography."[55]

SoHo's commercial galleries used dance to draw visitors as well as to provide a venue for artistic expression. Established galleries, such as those of Paula Cooper and Ileana Sonnabend, hosted dance performances. Cooper saw hosting performances as part of her gallery's artistic mission. She said, "I have this space and performers needed space." Cooper believed that artists were interdisciplinary in their thinking—"they read, they go to the cinema, they listen to music, they're very broad and broad-minded"—so it was natural to host events that would appeal to the artist community in SoHo and beyond. Performances were not designed to generate revenue. Some were free and others required a nominal entry fee (such as $2 for a dance at Paula Cooper in 1976). Perhaps due to this low cost, audiences could be substantial, up to 150 in some cases. Nonprofit alternative spaces, such as the Kitchen and Performing Garage, also hosted dance. SoHo dance took on diverse forms, including "solo improvisations to rock music, heavy on acrobatics" performed by nude dancers, improvisations to whatever happened to be on a record player, dances featuring wailing and pot shaking, or dancers reputedly tracing the shape of numbers on the floor of a loft.[56]

Because many artists lived and rehearsed in the same types of spaces that hosted performances, it was not uncommon for them to open their lofts to the public. As was the case with Off-Off-Broadway Theater in the 1960s and '70s, some of the most avant-garde work took place in people's homes.[57] For example, Douglas Dunn's two-week run of "Performance Exhibit 101" took place entirely in the artist's loft at 508 Broadway. It involved "turning [his] home into a museum and putting [himself] on exhibit every day for hours." During the piece, Dunn lay on a raised platform while visitors moved around him on a walkway that divided the room. Prolific and critically acclaimed SoHo choreographer Meredith Monk also regularly held dance performances at her home at 228 West Broadway. Her group was appropriately named "The House." Monk's work included pieces set to classical music and unaccompanied voice and dance in her large, light-filled, unadorned loft space. Trisha Brown, who lived at 541 Broadway, hosted a performance in which a dancer went about a daily routine, giving the audience time to take in the impressive space.[58]

Soon, SoHo gained considerable renown for the quality of its dance. For example, an issue of the *SoHo Weekly News* reviewed a dance at a loft on 168 Mercer Street in the same article that it covered a performance of the American Ballet Theater at the Metropolitan Opera House. By 1976, the SoHo dance scene had become so successful that plans for constructing formal theaters emerged. That year, Alwin Nikolais and Murray Louis, whom the *SoHo Weekly News* described as "giants of modern dance," announced their intention to move to SoHo. They planned to convert an old fire station at 155 Mercer Street into a three-hundred-seat theater with two large dance studios. It never fully came to fruition, but a smaller Joyce SoHo Theater now exists in the location, an offshoot of one of New York's best-known dance companies.[59]

World-renowned performance groups, including the Byrd Hoffman Foundation, established their headquarters in SoHo and hosted numerous well-attended performances in the neighborhood. Byrd Hoffman was established in 1974 as a venue to promote the experimental dance and performance pieces of Robert Wilson, "a unique American artist of international renown." In the early 1970s, Byrd Hoffman rented three floors of a loft building at 147 Spring Street to serve as its headquarters and main performance space. Over time, its director, Ann Wilson, worked to develop the facility as a community center for artists that would also conduct workshops for adults and children in body movement, dance, and theater. Its two hundred members included students, actors, dancers, sculptors and painters, writers, composers and performing musicians, and employed and retired people, ranging in age from eight to seventy-four years. Though the foundation earned income from ticket sales, a significant portion of its budget came from government and private sources. For instance, the group's 1972–73 revenue comprised $4,462 in individual contributions, $16,800 in foundation grants, $12,000 from the NEA, and $19,790 from NYSCA, helping make up for the more than $22,000 difference between the group's expenses and its income from ticket sales.[60]

Visitors to SoHo could also hear world-renowned musicians in intimate loft concert venues. In SoHo, one could see a jazz luminary in a living room or some top-flight classical music while sitting on a gallery floor. For example, the SoHo Ensemble, a classical music group, "played a concert to some 120 or rapt listeners, sitting on the floor and window sills of the bare OK Harris Gallery on West Broadway" in 1973. OK Harris regularly hosted these classical music performances, despite the fact that they "taxed the live acoustics of the gallery to the utmost." Along with dance performances and gallery shows, Paula Cooper hosted chamber music performances in her gallery, most notably two concerts by the Chamber Music Society of Lincoln Center in early 1978, an event for which she charged $4. The opportunity to see an internationally acclaimed group in such an intimate setting created an atmosphere that the *SoHo Weekly News* described as like "Times Square on New Years Eve." The concerts drew nearly three hundred people each, despite the fact that seating was only on a "flimsy foam-rubber cushion" on a "bare wood floor."[61]

Although some musical activity took place in SoHo galleries, jazz lofts were the primary venues for music performance. The term "jazz loft" encompassed a wide variety of performance venues, from clubs run by prominent artists such as saxophonist Ornette Coleman to sporadic concerts in living rooms. The New York press ran regular features on jazz lofts, and the venues drew substantial crowds. Coleman was perhaps the biggest name, attracting hundreds to loft performances. His Artists' House at 131 Prince Street, which opened in 1972 and later moved to 105 Hudson Street, was a cornerstone of the SoHo jazz scene. Also popular was Sam Rivers's Studio

Rivbea, at 24 Bond Street. Rivers's venue, which opened in 1972, hosted four hundred concerts per year. Beyond these clubs, SoHo's loft jazz scene was wide and varied. In addition to Coleman's and Rivers's clubs, the nine jazz lofts in SoHo in 1977 included Jerome Cooper, Environ, Charles "BoBo" Shaw, Ali's Alley, George Lewis & Muhal, Axis in SoHo, and Jazzmania. These clubs varied in popularity. While in some lofts, "the musicians onstage literally outnumbered the listeners," in others, "it might be hard to get a seat."[62]

The small size of the venues was also an attraction. At Sam Rivers's Studio Rivbea, for example, the performance space was located below the Rivers family's loft, creating a sense of intimacy. People sat on floor pillows, low mattresses, or park benches. In between sets, people could walk upstairs into the Rivers's living space. Thus, for two or three dollars, visitors could hear music as well as mingle with artists and their families. The family atmosphere, including the "presence of young children," made the space relaxed and comfortable, even for women who were "worrying about the traditional attitudes towards women going to jazz clubs alone."[63]

In this manner, the adaptability of loft space, along with the density and diversity of the area arts community, created a varied performance scene. In SoHo, one could view art in a gallery but also listen to world-class jazz in someone's living room or see avant-garde performances presented in front of an architectural sculpture. Commercial galleries, government arts funding, and the sweat equity of artists supported these activities, which all took place in open, accessible settings that welcomed all.

Gallery Visitors and SoHo Retail

Visitors flocked to SoHo's commercial galleries, artist cooperatives, and performance spaces. Gallery director Michael Findlay observed that his business saw "the kind of numerical turnout you get uptown" for a show in 1969, the second year that art galleries existed in SoHo. He noted, "In the beginning, the people who came were the people who were used to going to artists' studios. [Collector Joseph H.] Hirshhorn will still climb three flights of stairs to look at an artist's work." Gallery visitors quickly expanded beyond this early group of devoted collectors. Ivan Karp of OK Harris saw his gallery attract a "remarkable" crowd of affluent people, who included "lacquered matrons in Peck and Peck pants suits" who were not all dedicated patrons of the arts. Similarly, SoHo art dealer Joan Washburn remarked, "Soho galleries attract a different collector, a more general public, with greater attendance than uptown."[64]

By 1971, weekend art browsers numbered in the hundreds, and most were not traditional art patrons. A local periodical, the *SoHo Statement*, reported, "Saturday afternoons in SoHo have become almost a ritual—like Sundays in the park—for hundreds of uptowners who spill off the subways at Prince or Spring, bring out their handy little artmaps and begin the gallery-circuit tour." Wealthy suburbanites were even making their way to SoHo, as "tour buses filled with culture hounds . . . from Westchester and Scarsdale" were seen in the neighborhood. John Weber remembers that the galleries at 420 West Broadway attracted "twelve or thirteen thousand people" who "came through like a swarm of locusts, stopping traffic all up the street" the weekend they opened.[65]

However, casual gallery visitors were necessary to the success of a gallery, even if they did not account for a significant portion of sales. As the publication *Art Gallery* noted, galleries needed both buyers, who were "an absolute necessity" to a commercial establishment, as well as "floaters." Floaters were "considered a necessary nuisance by most dealers." By increasing gallery attendance and making the art on display appear in demand—"making the scene," as the article put it—floaters could increase demand for, and the prices of, art.[66]

Thus, SoHo art galleries worked to attract a large number of visitors to their doors but did not need their sales to stay in business. From the perspective of the floater, SoHo galleries were free cultural attractions, places where one could spend the day looking at the latest from the art world without paying an entrance fee or feeling pressured to buy art. As a local paper the *Villager*, wrote, "The gallery then becomes essentially a free museum, a showcase for contemporary work, sponsored by the dealer."[67]

The idea of galleries as free museums is an apt analogy, as even commercial galleries saw their enterprises as having an educational mission. Paula Cooper asserted, "It's very important that people see art, and that they be affected by art." To Cooper, even though visitors "may not be able to buy art . . . it really changes their lives enormously, and that's what's important. It's not that people can buy art, it's what art does." Nancy Hoffman said, "We've always considered one important aspect of the gallery to be educational. You almost convert some percent, even if it's a tiny percent, of people who visit into buyers and owners because they fall in love. They get bitten by the art bug."[68]

Attracting crowds was also important to SoHo cooperatives. In addition to artists seeking buyers, the galleries worked to attract guests because of their reliance on government arts funding. To compete for state arts dollars, organizations had to present their artwork as having a public benefit and show that they were "exposing the viewing public to the most interesting and dynamic art being produced." NYSCA was quick to turn down funding requests that it decided only benefited artist members. Thus, cooperative galleries had to attract cultural tourists, and the limited data that exist indicate that SoHo gallery audiences were often substantial. For example, the Spectrum Gallery estimated that its total audience was sixty thousand in 1971–72 and ninety thousand in 1972–73.[69]

Similarly, alternative spaces hosting performance needed to draw visitors. In turn, government arts agencies justified their funding of alternative spaces in part due to the audiences these organizations reached with their works. Audiences at venues such as the Kitchen, one of SoHo's major avant-garde alternative spaces, could be sizable. For instance, 12,000 people attended a series of video exhibitions in the Kitchen's 1977–78 season, and 4,000 attended shows as part of an arts development program that same season. The next season, the Kitchen drew 6,600 people for thirty-five musical performances, while forty-five dance shows brought about 4,275 people to the flexible theater space. With so much going on, programs in one area inspired increased attendance in another. "Visitors to an exhibition are intrigued with the sounds of a rehearsal and often return for the evening concert," NYSCA staff noted. In addition, the Kitchen drew people from outside the SoHo artist community. As NYSCA staff reported, the nucleus of the Kitchen's audience consisted of "artists, basically downtown people," but NYSCA's own analysis indicated, to the surprise of many in the organization, that "the audience is becoming much more diversified and that many come from other parts of Manhattan as well as New Jersey." The gallery's staff attributed this diversity to increased coverage in the *New York Times*, including reviews and listings in the weekend section.[70]

As witnessed by the Kitchen, dance could also draw visitors to SoHo, even for avant-garde performances. Reporting on the Byrd Hoffman Foundation, NYSCA wrote, "one would not expect large audiences for these pieces, but the crowds have come." For example, six hundred people attended six shows by Cindy Lubar and Gary Reigenborn in 1979, filling the loft space to 80 percent capacity.[71]

Local entrepreneurs soon took note of the large groups of visitors traveling to the neighborhood. These art-savvy, relatively affluent visitors had money in their pockets after a day of browsing in galleries or taking in a performance in an alternative space—money they could spend shopping or dining in the area. It wasn't long before businesses opened to cater to this previously untapped customer base. It was these businesses that demonstrated the link between the art market and the development of a "gentrified" retail sector in SoHo.

At the same time, as numerous neighborhood performances took place in homes, the crowds of art lovers who came to SoHo were able to see residential lofts up close. They doubtlessly noted the lofts' ample size, open spaces, and distinctly decorated interiors. Soon some of these visitors began to view a SoHo loft as a viable housing option, driving up demand for local real estate and changing the dynamic of urban development in the neighborhood.

6

Real Estate and SoHo Politics: Loft Promotion and Historic Preservation in Lower Manhattan

In May 1970, the recently founded SoHo Artists Association (SAA) worked with the city's Department of Parks, Recreation and Cultural Affairs to establish a new event: the SoHo Artists Festival. Festival visitors could view art shows and performances throughout SoHo—in lofts, in galleries, and on the street. More than seventy artists opened their homes to the public, showing paintings, sculpture, and mixed-media creations. Theater companies put on free shows along Houston Street as well as in galleries and lofts. Dance performances were held indoors and out. Artists screened films in lofts and galleries, and rock music shows featured multimedia art. The festival's program made clear the explicitly political message: "All of this creative work was done underground, because artists have never had the legal right to use these lofts, the only spaces suitable for artists' working, housing and storage problems." The SAA made the following request of festivalgoers: "To help us, sign one of the petitions you will find throughout the Festival area, and we will send it to Mayor Lindsay."[1]

To many visitors, the ability to see the inside of SoHo lofts was more intriguing than the festival's art or political goals. As a *Village Voice* reporter wrote, "Perhaps part of the enjoyment is the vicarious living you can do as you clamber through lofts and living rooms and bedrooms and studios and among the people who live and work there. And you feel and breathe the energy and excitement of the birth of a new community, rather than the more usual death of one area or another of New York."[2] Such statements about loft homes were fairly common throughout the 1970s. During this period, the attractiveness of SoHo lofts increasingly shaped local politics, infusing them with a language of real estate and urban development. Similarly, as the decade progressed, the debates over the legality of lofts shifted from a focus on housing for artists to the loft as a vehicle for neighborhood transformation at a time of urban crisis.

It was artists themselves who were behind this change in orientation. Local artist groups realized that the lofts they transformed from decrepit industrial relics into lovely homes were appealing to a broader public and used this attraction to bolster their political advocacy. In their continued efforts at loft legalization, artist groups infused a language of real estate into their political advocacy and highlighted the improvements that loft renovators had made in SoHo. The result of their efforts was both an increased legalization of loft residences and added attention to the loft as a trendy type of home.

Most directly, SoHo residents invited an increasingly large group of people into their lofts through art festivals, organized tours, and articles in the local and national press. Although loft visits were ostensibly about buying art or changing policy, guests enjoyed the unique and stylish homes that artists created. Artist groups quickly caught on to this attraction and exploited it to increase attendance.

At the same time, architectural preservationists increased public awareness about the historic significance of the buildings' cast-iron exteriors. Their efforts led the New York City Landmarks Commission to declare the SoHo Cast-Iron Historic District a landmark in 1973. This designation resulted in a rehabilitation of the image of these once-derided structures. The actions of artists and historical preservationists were mutually reinforcing. While artists' renovations of loft buildings reworked the interiors of obsolete factories into attractive homes, historic preservationists helped further increase the value of SoHo buildings by convincing the public that they were historically significant as well as attractive on the outside.

While artists began their advocacy efforts by contending that they were a low-income population with unique housing needs, they quickly realized that city leaders were more receptive to another argument: that their conversion of lofts into homes should be encouraged as a new form of urban development. Beginning in 1970, to achieve the goal of legalizing their loft studio residences, artists and artist organizations not only mobilized to win recognition as important contributors to New York City's global status as a center of artistic innovation (and consumption) but, increasingly, as people who attracted precisely the sort of high-income, highly talented, creative professionals and entrepreneurs upon whom the city's economic future would depend. This development was of great interest to urban leaders at a time when residential growth in New York was in short supply.

Real Estate and Artist Politics: The SoHo Artists Association

When SoHo artists founded a new political organization, both loft legalization and local real estate were central to its operating philosophy. This new group, the SAA, was a spin-off of the Artist Tenants Association (ATA) formed in 1970. The SAA's goals were tied to the multiple positions artists occupied in the SoHo real estate market. "An association of artists living in the Soho area," the SAA stated as its purpose to "represent, protect and serve the interests of artists who own or rent lofts in this area." Similar to that of the ATA, the SAA's main function was a political one, to "act as a spokesman for artists in any dealings with any private or government agencies involved in regulatory or legislative activities that would affect the status and character of this district, such as zoning, planning, and inspection." Yet, in a change from earlier organizing efforts, the SAA's goals also included protecting artists against real estate interests that would turn "a potential Montmartre," or thriving and affordable artist community, into "another high-rental, fashionably bohemian Greenwich Village." The group met at 451 West Broadway, an artist

FIGURE 15. Meeting of the SoHo Artists Association, 1970. (Photograph by John Dominis. "Living Big in a Loft," *Life*, March 27, 1970.)

cooperative that was home to several SAA members, including chairman Gerhardt Liebmann.[3]

SoHo artists restarted their lobbying efforts at a particularly fraught time in the history of New York City. After the ATA's artist strike and the state's passage of an amendment to the Multiple Dwelling Law in 1964, New York had moved into one of its most tumultuous periods. There was a sense that the city was becoming ungovernable, leaving municipal authorities incapable of providing even basic services. In the first year that Mayor John Lindsay took office, 1966, New York experienced its first transit strike, which left the city nearly paralyzed for two weeks, and became embroiled in a major controversy over the establishment of a Civilian Complaint Review Board for the New York Police Department. In 1968, the city faced a two-week-long sanitation strike that caused garbage to pile up in the streets for fifteen days. Also in the anxious year of 1968, growing racial tensions were exposed in a confrontation between residents of the African American neighborhoods of Ocean Hill–Brownsville and the largely Jewish United Federation of Teachers over control of neighborhood schools. This controversy occurred during a time of great racial change in the city. From 1940 to 1970, New York's African American population increased from 458,000 to 1,668,000, and its Puerto Rican population grew from 61,463 to 811,843. At the same time, suburbanization and white flight reduced New York's white population from 6,977,000 to 6,048,000. During this era, neighborhoods, including Brooklyn's Brownsville and East New York, Manhattan's Lower East Side, and much of the South Bronx, saw their populations rapidly change from majority white to almost entirely African American or Puerto Rican.[4]

Beyond individual controversies, there was a palpable sense that the city was spiraling out of control. Though there had always been stories of crime, poverty, and disorder in New York, from 1965 onward there was widespread concern that the city's moral order, infrastructure, government, schools, and place in the national hierarchy of cities were in precipitous decline. The crime rate was up, the economy was down, and the end of the crisis was nowhere in sight.[5]

This political landscape presented opportunities and risks for artist advocates. With city and state government often in turmoil, controversies over artist housing flew under the political radar. Distracted policy makers meant that the pace of change was slow, but the tumultuous 1960s and '70s also gave artists opportunities to exert influence over policies that were not seen as critical to the functioning of the city. Moreover, city leaders were more receptive to artists' arguments that their actions were breathing new life into neighborhoods at a time of overall decline in New York.

Into the fray stepped the SAA, whose initial membership was made up of artists who lived in a small group of SoHo cooperatives, many of which were organized as part of George Maciunas's Fluxhouse efforts (see chapter 2). Members included painter Ken Ewers, who lived at 465 West Broadway, and painter Mel Reicher, architect Shael Shapiro, and artist Ely Raman, who all lived at 80 Wooster Street. Others, such as Jeff Mitchell, a photographer; Jim Stratton, a writer who later authored the "Keeping Aloft" column in the *SoHo Weekly News;* Vivian Browne, a painter; Karen Husey, a designer; Pierre Jouchmans, an architect; and Jay Rosenfeld, along with Liebmann, all lived at 451 West Broadway. The group's original membership also included jazz legend Ornette Coleman, who lived at 131 Prince Street, and Julie Judd, wife of painter Donald Judd, who lived at 101 Spring Street.[6]

Since many SAA members owned their lofts as part of cooperatives, they invested time and money in their properties, and thus they had more to lose if they could not live there legally. Moreover, the SAA's membership fit the general profile of the educated, New York–savvy, middle-class artist. This was a group with connections to the broader art world and the political knowledge to effectively campaign for policy changes that would make loft living legal.

The SAA's planning philosophy was to maintain the SoHo artist community by preserving the neighborhood as a mixed-use district, which would protect it from large-scale development, whether by urban renewal or private developers. The SAA sought to save both SoHo's "marginal industry employing low skilled minority group workers" and artists' loft studios in "historically and architecturally significant buildings." The SAA reasoned that while loft buildings allowed for low rents and flexible living-working arrangements for the artists, "the industry prevents the area from being re-zoned as a residential one, which would lead to assemblage redevelopment and would eliminate the artists. The low skilled jobs are a powerful political argument for retaining the area." Yet the SAA was also worried about the possibility that concern with protecting the neighborhood's industry would cause it to "revert to an enforced commercial district" devoid of artists.[7]

The group's statements in support of mixed-use districts and local industry were in keeping with the arguments of figures such as Jane Jacobs and Chester Rapkin. Yet the group broke new ground by directly arguing that the real estate value SoHo artists added to industrial buildings through loft conversions was positive for the city. As SAA cofounder Robert Weigand (previously featured in *Life* hanging from a trapeze in his loft) argued, "after all the atmosphere we create is part of what attracts high-caliber people here to live and work."[8]

Artists' success in advancing their argument that the conversion of industrial lofts into homes would benefit the cultural life, economy, and real estate market in New York was reflected in the political support that they gained for legalizing these conversions. The SAA worked in conjunction with city officials and representatives from the art world, such as renowned artists, curators, and art dealers, in order to gain legalization for artists' loft studios. As the SAA outlined in its planning philosophy document, SoHo artists had "political connections and organizational acumen which has halted demolition and redevelopment of the area so far." The group's patrons included Mayor and Mrs. John V. Lindsay; Senator and Mrs. Jacob Javits; John Hightower, director of the Museum of Modern Art; Thomas M. Messer, director of the Solomon R. Guggenheim Museum; John I. H. Baur, director of the Whitney Museum of American Art; Theodore Rousseau Jr., curator of the Metropolitan Museum; and Larry Aldrich, director of the Aldrich Museum in Connecticut.[9]

The SAA's members used their political and social connections to achieve their reform goals. In particular, they worked with the Citizens for Artist Housing (CAH), a group of advocates based on the Upper East Side of Manhattan who actively supported the cause of SoHo artist housing. The group's leader, Doris Freedman, and a small group of advocates appear to have done much of the organization's lobbying for artists' housing. In fact, the "citizens" of the Citizens for Artist Housing appear mostly to be notable figures who lent their names to the group to give its actions more weight. Although some of these famous members may not have done much on-the-ground work to change zoning laws in SoHo, attaching their names to advocacy efforts represents another way in which the formal art world contributed to the development of a residential SoHo. At most, these figures wrote letters in support of legislation or attended legislative hearings. Perhaps some even spoke to decision makers with whom they were acquainted. However, one cannot discount the power that a list of their names on the organization's stationery likely had on city officials looking to preserve the financial and cultural position of New York.

The membership of CAH included notable figures from New York's artistic and political worlds. The group was cochaired by curator Klaus Kertess and pop artist Peter Blake. It included noted artist Donald Judd and his wife, Julie, as well as artists Roy Lichtenstein and Robert Rauschenberg, gallery owners Leo Castelli, André Emmerich, Richard Feigen, and Paula Cooper, and representatives from the Museum of Modern Art, Metropolitan Museum of Art, Brooklyn Academy of Music, New York State Council on the Arts, and New York City Department of Parks, Recreation and Cultural Affairs. CAH was also responsible for enlisting the legal assistance necessary to draft successful legislation regarding artist housing in SoHo. The organization had the help of the Volunteer Lawyers for the Arts, a pro bono legal assistance group. The Volunteer Lawyers then worked with the SAA and City Planning Commission (CPC) to draft the eventual legislation covering SoHo artists.[10]

After lining up support from both political decision makers and cultural luminaries, the SAA targeted the main impediment to loft legalization in 1970: the New York City zoning resolution. This law divided the city into ten types of residential districts, eight types of commercial districts, and three types of manufacturing districts. SoHo was zoned as an M1–5 "Light Manufacturing District," designed for the manufacture of apparel and textiles, electronic equipment, and wholesale service facilities. In short, M1–5 districts contained the types of businesses the Rapkin report attempted to protect. New residential development in these areas was prohibited.[11]

To lobby for changes to the zoning resolution, the SAA's leadership petitioned members to send letters to the CPC and encouraged them to attend public hearings on the issue of Lower Manhattan zoning. When the CPC approved a change to the zoning resolution, the SAA, along with CAH, organized a letter-writing campaign to the New York City Board of Estimate, the body that gave final approval to legislation such as zoning resolutions. Members of the SAA also frequently consulted with the CPC to formulate new zoning resolutions allowing for artist housing in SoHo lofts. "An atmosphere of mutual respect" pervaded at these collaborations, and members of the two groups came to know each other on a first-name basis. Much of the goodwill between them came through the actions of Michael Levine, a city planner whose 1968 study on artist housing and industry in SoHo for the CPC would later prove critical in furthering loft housing legislation.[12] Additionally, it could not have hurt to have Mayor Lindsay, known for his support of the arts, among the group's patrons.

As a result of these meetings, in October 1970 CPC chair Donald Elliot presented a new zoning plan in which the forty-three-block M1–5 Light Manufacturing Zone in which SoHo was located would be divided into two new M1-A and M1-B districts. The M1–5A area corresponded to the northwestern portion of the neighborhood, roughly centered on West Broadway, where lofts tended to be smaller, and the artist population and industrial vacancy rates were higher. Under the proposal, it would be legal for artists to live in any loft smaller than 3,600 square feet in an M1–5A district. Additionally, any artist living in a loft larger than 3,600 square feet who moved in before September 1970 would be allowed to legally remain. Although additional artists' residences in the M1–5B district would be prohibited, any artist resident who rented a loft smaller than 3,600 square feet on or before

September 1970 could remain as long as he or she obtained a special permit. Finally, all artist cooperatives in both zones would be legalized.[13]

The fact that the CPC proposed the zoning resolution demonstrates SoHo artists' success in convincing city leaders that their housing needs were worth addressing. Yet the zoning resolution also demonstrates policy makers' continuing concern that residential loft conversions could threaten industrial jobs. The prohibition on conversions of lofts in buildings larger than 3,600 square feet was an attempt to preserve the neighborhood's larger lofts, which the CPC believed were better suited for contemporary industries. According to the SAA, Elliot "pointed out that the Commission believes it has made an extreme concession with possibly dangerous future consequences for the welfare of the blue-collar employing industry of this area; that no other city had made such extensive or such unique concessions to a single group; that in a city where space is at an all-time premium, this concession will prove embarrassing to them in the future; but they are making it because they recognize the need and importance of artists." For its part, the SAA worked to convince the CPC that artists were not threatening industry but simply filling spaces it had vacated. As the SAA's Weigand pointed out to the CPC, "building owners are dependent upon the artist occupants to pay the building maintenance costs."[14]

The CPC's final decision reflected some remaining desire to preserve industry and an increasing wish to promote the arts and the city's cultural economy. The CPC, and eventually the Board of Estimate, approved a zoning ordinance allowing artists to legally occupy lofts in SoHo in January 1971. Mayor Lindsay drafted a statement to be read at a public hearing, stating that "the creation of a SoHo artists district will insure New York's position as the art capital of the nation and one of the great creative centers of the world." In June 1971, the state legislature passed another amendment to the State Multiple Dwelling Law that relaxed fire and safety regulations for converted buildings and required that lofts comply with safety standards set for converted buildings, rather than those mandated for residential structures, making it easier for residents to comply with the law. As artists were still the only people allowed to live in renovated lofts, the regulations also clarified how they were to be certified, giving most of the responsibility to the New York City Department of Cultural Affairs. SAA member Shael Shapiro and CAH representative William C. Shopsin drafted the legislation.[15]

Developing a process of artist certification was a necessary, albeit odd, step in the process of loft legalization. Suddenly New York City was in the business of determining who was or was not an artist. According to the Volunteer Lawyers for the Arts, the Department of Cultural Affairs "established criteria for certification based on two factors: "(1) the artist's need for space and (2) his or her commitments to art." The Department of Cultural Affairs Certification Committee was composed of twenty artists and nonartists who reviewed artists' application for certification and recertification. The committee included SoHo painters, composers, choreographers, and filmmakers, curators from major local institutions, and gallery owners such as Paula Cooper. Many artists went through the process of becoming "certified artists" in order to legalize their homes. For example, Barbara Toll submitted slides left over from her MFA graduate show to the Department of Cultural Affairs as part of her certification application. Susan Meisel, a painter and fabric designer, remembered, "I held my slides up in front of somebody's face, they said, 'Yes, you're an artist,' stamped my card, and handed it to me. I was now a card-carrying certified artist."[16]

Even as their homes were becoming fully legal, artists realized that they were soon likely to face another dilemma: rising loft prices. In April 1970, the *New York Post* reported, "With the recent influx of galleries in the south of Houston area (now dubbed 'SoHo'), general interest in lofts is up again. And non-artists, charmed by the relative low rents and generous spaces, are now competing for the little space that's left. This added to the area's new-found glamour has started to raise rents to uptown levels."[17]

One month later, the *New York Times* reported that in SoHo, "buildings that sold for $30,000 ten years ago are now going for $150,000." In July, another article's headline dramatically summed up the situation: "Costs for 'SoHo' Lofts Are Rising Drastically." The article stated that although they had to live illegally and travel to other neighborhoods to buy food or dump garbage, residents were paying several thousands of dollars in "fixture fees" just to move into lofts. The article also noted that some loft buildings were selling for as much as brownstones on the Upper West Side. There were also further indications that other types of professionals were moving into lofts, as an unnamed artist in the article said that "prices of lofts have been driven up by Madison Avenue advertising men who want to live among artists and can afford to pay higher rents."[18]

For its part, the SAA was aware of these trends. Liebmann wrote in 1970, "Artists are trail blazers whose Art becomes Fashion. They are followed by the Beautiful People who find it chic to live in a loft, especially when the artist has shown by his talents how superb a life style can be led in gobs of space. With the housing shortage in New York the problem is exacerbated."[19] Weigand worried that a special zoning designation for the most heavily populated section of SoHo would concentrate and accelerate residential development in the area. He argued:

> The formation of the M1-A zone is the first step to insure the redevelopment of SoHo. The concentration of artists north of Broome Street will insure redevelopment for residential use. The natural trend, which we must fight strongly against, is for artists to take over industrial space, and then non- or quasi-artists to price them out. . . . Special designation of this area, which is closest to the village, will greatly accelerate the residential pressures there. It will also enable someone to point out how many artists there are here versus how few there are elsewhere, and thus argue that artists don't need to be elsewhere. The area south of Broome will be redeveloped for industry and the area north of Broome will become the south Village.[20]

Weigand proved to be prescient. Although residential pressures prevented industry from retaining a foothold south of Broome Street, the concentration of artists and their residences in a corner of SoHo eventually contributed to its residential redevelopment and the rising costs of loft apartments in the neighborhood.

Visiting SoHo Lofts—Experiencing Loft Space

Though they worried about the rising popularity of lofts, SoHo artists were responsible for promoting them to a wider population. Starting in the late 1960s, SoHo artists exposed people from outside the community to renovated lofts through informal visits, organized tours, and festivals. At these events, artists showed off their homes and art to aid in their advocacy efforts and sell their work, but the result of these efforts was to expose visitors to the attractive and potentially valuable nature of loft homes.

SoHo loft visits were part of a longer tradition of collectors and patrons frequenting artists' studios. As an essay in a 1978 retrospective book on a SoHo festival stated, "The admission of the public to the studio is a logical extension of the photographic documentation of the creative act and the studio that has been built up in the twentieth century by, for instance, Dora Maar's coverage of Picasso's *Guernica*, Alexander Liberman's photographs of studios and famous artists."[21] However, visits to SoHo lofts were unique in that they were most often part of artists' political advocacy efforts. In addition, SoHo loft visits allowed a wider range of art patrons into studios that were also homes. Consequently, loft visits exposed a large number of relatively affluent art supporters to a new type of interior residential space for the first time.

Loft visits began on a large scale due to a series of art festivals that artist groups employed as part of their advocacy in the late 1960s and early 1970s. The first of these festivals, called Ten Downtown, began in 1968—perhaps not coincidentally the year that plans for the Lower Manhattan Expressway

FIGURE 16. Prince Street art fair, 1976. (Photograph by Robin Forbes. Reproduced by permission from Archives of American Art, Smithsonian Institution.)

were on the path to extinction. Ten Downtown was an informal tour of artists' lofts, which residents would open up for the day in order to sell work and display the vibrant-yet-still-illegal community that was growing in the area. By 1973, the event drew six thousand people for what the *New York Times* called the city's "walk-and-climb-athon par excellence."[22]

On a larger scale, the SAA organized the SoHo Artists Festival, a yearly event cosponsored by the city's Department of Parks, Recreation and Cultural Affairs. The aim of the festival was to make New Yorkers aware of the "unparalleled concentration" of thousands of artists in the South Houston Planning District" and aid in advocacy efforts for zoning laws that would allow them to live and work in SoHo lofts. The festival also exposed thousands of New Yorkers to SoHo's art galleries and interior spaces. As SAA president Liebmann noted, part of the advantage of SoHo was the ability of a collector, or any visitor, "to stroll from the gallery where the art is shown to the loft where it is produced." The "concentrated number of lofts close together" allowed patrons as well as casual visitors to see a large number of loft homes in a short period of time. The festival was a major success, drawing crowds of more than ten thousand, according to one estimate.[23]

The SoHo Artists Festival showcased the neighborhood's cultural importance as well as the advocacy efforts of the SAA. The *New York Times* reported that the "three-day festival . . . flowered in the dingy blocks of SoHo, the burgeoning artists' community in downtown Manhattan. Crowds came, music filled the air, and there was dancing in the streets." *New York Magazine* reported that the normal weekend quiet of SoHo was replaced as "streets were full of gaping uptowners and suburbanites, most of them puffing up and down steep old staircases." Moreover, "according to the positive view," attendees "came away with a feeling that here in these shoddy blocks was a cultural brotherhood that had to be preserved against the incursions of great corporate glass. These weekenders would now be allies in the fight to keep SoHo for the artists; a whole army of them had been gained in 48 hours, and a few paintings had been sold to boot."[24]

Although the aim of the festival was political, its unintentional effect was to allow thousands of nonartists to experience eye-catching renovated loft interiors. The SoHo Artists Festival gave visitors the opportunity to view seventy lofts throughout the neighborhood. A highlight of the event was, as *New York Times* art critic Grace Glueck put it, the ability to gain "some candid exposure to the inventively improvisational ways for loft living." Throughout the event, visitors could watch outdoor performances by artists, dance groups, and drama companies, which took place in the streets and on top of buildings. These events all kept visitors moving throughout the neighborhood, experiencing its numerous interior and exterior spaces.[25]

Artists realized that encountering loft space often left quite an impression on visitors. Liebmann brought members of the City Planning Commission into his loft in 1970—the same officials with whom he had worked over the preceding years on loft legislation. He realized that impressing them with the loft home he created would create a greater impact than any verbal argument about the vibrant arts community in SoHo or its importance to the city.[26]

SoHo artists did little to discourage the appeal of loft housing. They recognized the desirability of their homes and organized events specifically designed to display lofts. They intentionally advertised the opportunity to visit homes, and their promotional materials often blurred the line between political pamphlet and real estate listing, highlighting square footage, recent renovations, and interior design.

Similarly, the SAA helped organize loft tours that sought to enlist New Yorkers to their cause. For example, in 1970, the SAA planned a fund-raiser for English in Action, a nonprofit whose goal was to assist immigrants in learning English by engaging them in conversations. The event was "a unique opportunity to see the living places and working places as well as to talk to and meet the artists themselves." A brochure stated, "Beyond the grubby facades of the 19th century industrial buildings, these artists have created spacious, tastefully decorated homes."[27]

The SAA emphasized the lofts' distinctive design elements, including Liebmann's indoor rock garden, greenhouse, and collection of "eastern statuary displayed in custombuilt nooks" that was "warmed by a modern free standing fireplace." One could sense Sam Wiener's "creativity . . . in every corner" of his "light and airy loft." At Steve and Ann Fernandez's home at 451 West Broadway, which they converted from a former rag factory over the course of two years, "ceilings arched over sophisticated modern furniture create an interesting effect in this warm and charming loft." In the same building, the SAA drew attention to the unique "exposed brick walls" and "absence of interior walls," allowing "for flexibility in her living and working arrangements" in Vivian Browne's home. The living room at Manny Ghent's four-bedroom apartment at 131 Prince Street "dwarfed" a grand piano, and the loft had ample living and play space for his four children. "Curved brick walls divide his kitchen, dining, living and sleeping areas" in Charles Leslie's neighboring loft. In all the lofts on the tour, art that owners produced or collected enhanced minimalist space to create uniquely decorated interiors. This art included large mirrored sculptures, brightly colored semiabstract works, and collections of Mogul, African, and European and American art bought on filmmaking trips around the world.[28]

Tours of SoHo often drew upper-income professionals with an interest in art and the means to pay more rent than the typical artist. These tours included outings organized by university alumni groups. For example, in 1971 the Cornell Alumni Club organized a loft tour through the SAA. Alumni were able to view art, see the loft spaces where artists practiced their craft, and purchase their work. Visiting loft interiors was the big selling point. The organizers advertised the tour as "an opportunity to see where the artist creates his works, an area not normally open to the public. The art will represent what is being done in New York today. . . . Acquisitions of art are welcome." Though there was an explicit political element to the tour—programs mentioned that the SAA was "currently involved in lobbying for proposed legalization before the City Planning Commission which would officially legalize the presence of artists in the area as residents"—it also showed off the neighborhood's architectural, commercial, and artistic amenities to two hundred participants. Visitors were given a map of the area "locating the artists and galleries, and a description of their work" and were able to explore neighborhood galleries and lofts at their leisure. The day finished up with a wine-and-cheese reception at one of SoHo's first galleries, Reese Palley.[29]

The tour exposed Cornell alumni to loft interiors, cast-iron facades, local businesses, and art aplenty. Visitors walked around the neighborhood, climbing the stairs in buildings identified by a red Cornell SoHo decal and "signs outside the building that prominently display location of lofts." The alums started the day in a "typical family loft" in an artists' co-op at 161 Greene Street, and perhaps imagined the possibilities for their families inhabiting similar loft space. They then moved north along Greene Street, where they could observe industrial businesses coexisting with the neighborhood's artist population. Reaching the corner of Greene and Grand Streets, explorers continued north on Greene and visited thirty artists' lofts on Greene and Prince Streets and West Broadway. The loft visits included Nobu Fukui's rental home at 53 Greene Street and lunch in a "typical loft" at the co-op at 451 West Broadway. Finally, the program encouraged visitors to walk east on either Grand or Prince Streets to Broadway, where they could view SoHo's historic buildings and their cast-iron facades. Buildings on the tour included the Singer Building on Prince Street and Broadway and the Haughwout and Roosevelt Buildings near the corner of Broome Street and Broadway. After making their way north through a valley of historic buildings and artists' lofts, the alumni could visit galleries along Prince Street and West Broadway, including Reese Palley, Paula Cooper, and 55 Mercer.[30] In this manner, members of the SAA inadvertently taught visitors about various ways they could potentially enter the loft market. Additionally, the Cornell graduates served as tastemakers, spreading the word about loft living to their similarly affluent friends and acquaintances.

The connection between artist advocacy and wealthy SoHo visitors was even more explicit during another 1971 tour that served as a fund-raiser for the American Jewish Congress. The event, which cost $125 for a lecture about the New York art scene and a bus tour through SoHo, brought women who "wore hats and tiny veils and although a few had come in pants suits, most wore minks, tiger and seal fur coats." Many visitors bought $75 sculptures from Clement Meadmore, along with more expensive items, and helped raise more than $10,000 for the American Jewish Congress. CAH director Doris Freedman led the tour.[31]

Observers noted that loft visitors were impressed by SoHo artists' homes. During a visit to Weigand's loft, a tour participant identified by the *New York Times* as "Mrs. Herman Mars" admired "a Plexiglas table in front of a sofa, the wood and canvas campaign chairs, an antique desk and the floor-to-ceiling bookshelves beyond and structural cast iron column." Another visitor, "Mrs. Marvin Roth," commented, "What a marvelous room—so warm and personal—and this is the last place you would expect to find it."[32]

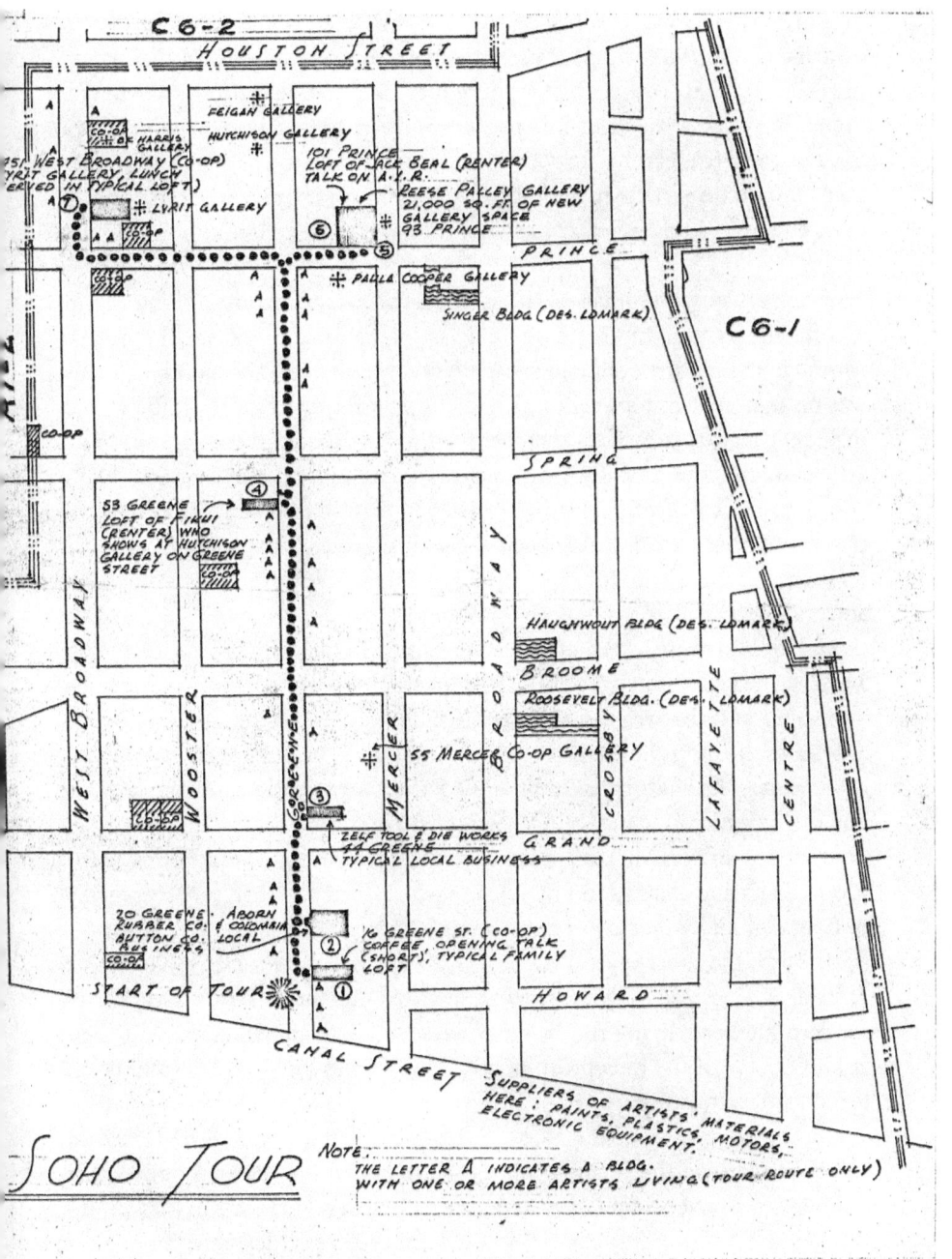

FIGURE 17. Map for an art-themed tour of SoHo, May 2, 1971. (Courtesy of Soho Artists Association records, Archives of American Art, Smithsonian Institution.)

Furthermore, the number of New Yorkers who visited loft homes was dwarfed by the "virtual loft tours" that tens, if not hundreds, of thousands of readers embarked on thanks to the local and national press. Starting in the early 1970s, a series of loft profiles in local and national publications showed their readers the attractive residences that artists had created in former industrial spaces. Much like artists festivals in SoHo, these loft profiles were encouraged by advocacy groups trying to legalize living in industrial lofts.

Artist advocacy influenced the 1970 *Life* magazine feature "Living Big in a Loft," the first major article on SoHo in the national press (see chapter 2). Although the piece mentioned artist advocacy in the neighborhood, its focus was on the "sixteen foot ceilings" and "45 foot rooms" that could be found inside the apartments of artists lobbying for legalization of their homes. The article's highlighting of Robert Weigand's home and Bill and Yvonne Tarr's choice to relocate from suburban Westchester to SoHo focused on the real estate potential of loft space. Even the article's title, "Living Big in a Loft," focused the reader's attention on the large, impressive homes that artists created in SoHo.[33]

SoHo lifestyle articles highlighted loft features that would be attractive to a broad, magazine-buying public. Besides emphasizing the space in lofts like Weigand's and the wealthy suburban origins of families like the Tarrs, the articles dwelled on the elements of loft homes that would appeal to middle-class readers. As Sharon Zukin has noted, these articles indicated that a "new cult of domesticity" was developing in lofts. This domesticity was reflected in descriptions of "oriental rug[s], track lighting, polished wood floors, comfortable sofa and chairs and a bicycle in the background" that were reassuring to potential middle-class loft inhabitants."[34]

In 1970, the same year of the *Life* magazine article and the SoHo Artists Festival, a *New York Magazine* profile reported that SoHo artists had "set up modern kitchens, living rooms, bedrooms and bathrooms along with their studios." One of the lofts prominently featured was Liebmann's open, comfortable, light-filled space.[35]

By the beginning of the 1970s, SoHo artist groups were well versed in displaying lofts to the general public. Not only had they created homes that appealed to a variety of middle- and upper-class New Yorkers, but they intentionally used this lure to plan events and engage in political advocacy. Most likely, members of the SAA did not want to encourage the wealthy visitors to move in next door. However, the group did explicitly work to promote both their homes and the lifestyle they lived in them to a variety of outsiders.

Fighting Development through Advocacy

Yet it was not long before local political groups faced the negative impacts of their efforts at loft promotion. Two events in 1972 brought some of the consequences of neighborhood promotion and real estate development in SoHo to the foreground. These incidents were the short-lived effort to rename West Broadway Jackson Pollock Place and the proposed construction of a twenty-one-story Sports Palace in SoHo.

Possibly inspired by the success of the SoHo Artist Festival, in February 1972, August Heckscher, commissioner of the Department of Parks, Recreation and Cultural Affairs, proposed to rename the main commercial street in SoHo, the stretch of West Broadway from Canal to Houston Streets, Jackson Pollock Place. The commissioner noted that this would be the first street in the city named after a modern American painter. The *New York Times* observed that this action came because "the city has been encouraging the development of SoHo as an art community."[36]

Backers of the proposal supported the renaming for reasons both cultural and practical. Commissioner Heckscher backed the name change using arguments that echoed those made by the ATA in its advocacy efforts in the mid-1960s. He spoke of the meaning that Jackson Pollock Place would have "not only for Soho, but for all of New York and the international community." Gallery owner André Emmerich noted that naming streets after cultural heroes was common practice in Europe and that there were multiple streets named Broadway, causing confusion. However, local artists believed that Emmerich was only in favor of the plan due to the attention it might bring to his gallery, located at 420 West Broadway.[37]

In contrast to Emmerich, a number of local artists and other community members fought the proposal. At a meeting of Planning Board 2 later that February, reactions ranged from "howling laughter to hot rage." Some expressed artistic objections to the plan. Larry Tierney of the SAA argued that because some SoHo residents were abstract expressionists themselves, they felt they were in competition with Pollock. Artist Marty Greenbaum noted that Pollock was part of a different aesthetic and asked, "Why put the kiss of death on Soho by associating it with another time?" Gallery owner Ivan Karp was concerned that the street name would associate SoHo with commercial art, making it "Greenwich Village South." As a result, "the artists would become victims of a voyeuristic society that would come to stare at the bohemians and weirdos" and be subjected to "mobs of tourists looking for artists wearing cute berets."[38] Although plans to rename the street were quickly shelved, this was an early instance of SoHo residents and business owners expressing concern with the overpromotion of the area.

Later that year, a more tangible threat to the neighborhood emerged: a plan to build a skyscraper-like sports club in SoHo. Developer Charles Low hoped to construct a twenty-one-story Sports Palace with tennis courts, skating rinks, a swimming pool, and other athletic facilities (as well as parking for more than two hundred cars) on space occupied by a parking lot on West Broadway between Canal and Grand Streets. The project did have some local backers, including New York University and members of the local Italian American community, who argued that development would be good for what they referred to as "the Village" (not SoHo), particularly after the shadow of the Lower Manhattan Expressway had hung over the area for so long. However, local artists were strongly against the project. In November 1972, after the Board of Standards and Appeals approved a zoning variance for it, artists contended that the Sports Palace was "as an eyesore that would spoil the character of the neighborhood, send rents up, and draw real-estate speculation and heavy traffic to the area." Much as was the case with Jackson Pollock Place, artists worried that the project would "lure tourists, spur commercialism, and ultimately destroy the SoHo colony that has developed within recent years." Liebmann went so far as to say, "If this goes through, it means the end of SoHo."[39]

Artists were concerned that the project signaled that SoHo was ready for the type of large-scale investment that it had not seen in decades, something that would upset the fragile balance in the area that allowed them to find suitable places to live and work. The high membership prices and plentiful parking spaces available indicated that Wall Street employees would be important clients at the Sports Palace, triggering fears that downtown money would soon start to encroach on SoHo. Furthermore, as the *Village Voice* reported, the SAA feared that "the city, realizing the area is becoming too expensive for light industry, will abandon the artist housing experiment there after all." Already, artists worried that the project was the first sign that they were going to be forced out of the area and become yet another "real estate casualty."[40]

In the end, the Sports Palace was never built. It is unclear whether this was because of the decision to make SoHo a landmark district or simply because a twenty-one-story sports complex was untenable. Although what the ultimate impact of a completed Sports Palace in SoHo would have been is unclear, the proposed project demonstrated that SoHo artists were beginning to have concerns about the attention their neighborhood was gaining from tourists and real estate investors. In short, they were worried about becoming victims of their own success.

From Eyesore to Outdoor Museum: Landmarks and SoHo Building Exteriors

While SoHo artists invested their time, labor, and money to convert formerly run-down industrial lofts into beautiful homes that attracted the attention of art lovers and other visitors, historic preservationists and advocates for the importance of cast-iron architecture worked to convince the general public that SoHo buildings were aesthetically pleasing and architecturally important. They did so through tours of cast-iron buildings and efforts to make SoHo a landmark district. Although their goals were to get policy makers and ordinary New Yorkers to see the importance of cast-iron buildings at a time when many of them were targets of urban renewal and development, the effect was also to further increase their value as real estate.

Before the middle of the twentieth century, preservation movements in the United States traditionally came from two distinct sources: private efforts to preserve historic structures, such as Mount Vernon and Independence Hall, and federal protection of the nation's natural features and landmarks through the National Park Service. These efforts began to merge in 1949 with the establishment of the National Trust for Historic Preservation, whose members linked the preservation efforts of the federal government and the private sector through advocacy and management of certain federally recognized historic properties. Preservation efforts gained additional impetus from reactions against urban renewal and private development in the postwar era. By the 1960s, works such as Jane Jacobs's *The Death and Life of Great American Cities* and the National Trust for Historic Preservation's *With Heritage So Rich*, which illustrated well-regarded architecture that had been destroyed by development, gave the historic preservation movement additional momentum. Members of Congress incorporated the recommendations of the latter book into the National Historic Preservation Act of 1966, which created the National Register of Historic Places and promoted the establishment of local historic districts. The Preservation Act both contributed to the creation of entire historic districts in municipalities across the country and urged states and localities to take a more active role in preservation.[41]

The law required that the establishment of historic districts and the enactment of legal protections on individual structures had to originate at the local level. In this case, New York was one step ahead of Congress, as the city passed the Landmarks Preservation Law in 1965, creating a Landmarks Preservation Commission as an official city agency (it had formerly existed as an advisory body). The commission designated landmark districts in Brooklyn Heights and Greenwich Village that same year.[42]

Historic preservationists saw cast-iron buildings as both historically and aesthetically important. Architectural historians viewed the buildings' cast-iron fronts as the first step toward the steel frame that was eventually used to support the modern skyscraper. In addition, the buildings' "repeated, rhythmic iron framing of oversized glass windows" provided a stylistic forerunner "to the modern glass and metal wall" of the late twentieth-century building. The slender cast-iron columns that supported the floors were also attractive and often contained fluted Corinthian capitals ornamented with gold paint.[43]

However, preservationists were most attracted to the facades of cast-iron buildings. Architects working in cast iron copied Renaissance designs and painted their buildings in light colors meant to emulate stone. Facade designers also took inspiration from Renaissance Italian and French architecture and achieved elegant cast-iron motifs. Many SoHo buildings were decorated with "ornate iron or marble fronts" that were "modeled after Italian palazzi." The nineteenth-century buildings featured "fantastic craftsmanship" that included handsome columns set between windows on building exteriors and ornate facade details. According to critics, these architectural features made SoHo a pilgrimage site for European architects and historians.[44]

New Yorkers working to preserve cast-iron structures were quick to take advantage of the city's new law. In 1966, the Landmarks Preservation Board petitioned the Housing and Redevelopment Board to save New York's first cast-iron building built by James Bogardus, dating from 1848, saying, "It is not generally known to the public what a magnificent heritage our cast-iron commercial buildings represent. These early buildings of iron exerted a major influence on the development of iron technology and paved the way for the advent of the skyscraper." Although much of New York's stock of cast-iron buildings remained standing, the Landmarks Commission worried that it would increasingly become a target for redevelopment, as its buildings often fell into disrepair, housed industries nearing obsolescence, and were located in areas city seen as declining. As if to confirm the commission's fears, developers tore down an entire section of well-preserved cast-iron buildings on Worth Street to build a parking lot in 1962.[45]

Policy makers first got involved with the preservation of SoHo buildings during the debate over the Lower Manhattan Expressway in the 1960s (see chapter 3). Preservationists challenged the roadway on the grounds that it would destroy the historically and architecturally significant cast-iron buildings along Broome Street and throughout the rest of SoHo. *New York Times* architecture critic Ada Louise Huxtable, an outspoken supporter of architectural preservation and cast-iron architecture, became a public figure in the fight against the roadway. Huxtable consistently highlighted the significance of SoHo's buildings and kept efforts to preserve the structures in the public eye. In 1965, Huxtable pointed out that the highway's proposed path across Lower Manhattan would destroy some of the area's most architecturally significant cast-iron buildings. The road threatened "the blocks between Canal and Houston Streets from Wooster to Mercer Street," which "are considered the richest stand of Victorian Architecture of the Civil War Era in the city, and one of the best survivals of 'The Iron Age' in the country."[46] When the stalled roadway plan was revived in 1968, Huxtable again cautioned that "the route is fixed where it will do the most possible harm and architecture damage," in part because it threatened Greene Street, "a uniquely intact enclave of iron architecture."[47]

Similarly, Mayor Lindsay used New York's Landmarks Preservation Law in his efforts to stop the Lower Manhattan Expressway. In February 1966, one month after he took office, the mayor led the Board of Estimate in ratifying the landmark designation of the E. V. Haughwout Building, a nineteenth-century commercial loft building in SoHo that stood in the path of the roadway. According to the city's landmark law, once a building became a landmark, it could not be altered without a succession of steps to make every effort to preserve it. Despite expressway proponent Robert Moses's objection that the structure was "directly in the right of way of the Lower Manhattan Expressway," the Board of Estimate approved the landmark status with only two dissenting votes. The *New York Times* later claimed that the possible destruction of the Haughwout Building "tipped the scales against approval" of the highway.[48]

After the death of the Lower Manhattan Expressway, the most vocal advocate for cast-iron architecture was Margot Gayle, who founded Friends of Cast Iron Architecture in 1970. Gayle worked in public relations for New York City and wrote an architecture column for the *New York Daily News* while championing architectural preservation causes. She first encouraged the city to preserve Greenwich Village's Jefferson Market Courthouse in 1959 (and to convert the building into a library in 1967) and then lobbied for the Landmarks Preservation Law in 1965 before turning her attention to cast-iron architecture in 1970.[49] Friends of Cast Iron Architecture grew to 1,000 members by 1974 and held regular tours of the "gracious cast iron, columned buildings" located throughout the neighborhood. These tours sometimes drew more than 150 people. In addition, Gayle's 1974 book of photographs, *Cast-Iron Architecture in New York*, brought increased attention to SoHo buildings. Thanks to the group's efforts, SoHo architecture gained renown, so much so that the *New York Times* dubbed the neighborhood the "city's largest outdoor museum, made of cast iron."[50]

SoHo buildings gained another level of recognition when the entire neighborhood became a landmark district in 1973. Margot Gayle conducted much of the research for the official report outlining the notable architectural character of the area.[51] The designation meant that none of the roughly five hundred buildings in the twenty-six-square-block area from Houston to Canal Streets and West Broadway to Crosby Street could be torn down or altered without the approval of the Landmarks Preservation Commission. The Commission credited "a group of artists who moved, in the 1960s, into what then seemed to be a doomed neighborhood. They have given it a new life, making feasible the preservation of an irreplaceable part of our cultural heritage." The report continued, "This recent conversion of abandoned lofts into artists' residences, studios and galleries has added new vitality to the area." Because artists transformed lofts into homes, opened galleries, and created art, "the social, cultural and economic history of the District has been, and is again becoming, as varied and colorful as any to be found in New York City." More important, this artist-driven rehabilitation made the district an example of "one way in which the core of an old city can be given new life without the destruction of its cultural heritage," without resorting to costly and painful urban renewal projects. The report argued that if the neighborhood "continues to succeed as it has during the past few years, SoHo may well provide a wider lesson. With a little imagination, effort and ingenuity, exciting alternatives to demolition can be found for the stagnant and decaying areas of our cities. These alternatives have the further advantage, which 'slum clearance' lacks."[52]

One cannot overestimate the impact of the landmarking of SoHo on the neighborhood's future development. The recognition of SoHo as an area containing lovely, historically significant buildings increased the area's appeal and value as a residential neighborhood. In addition, the reported architectural beauty of the buildings carried beyond the artists already living there to the broader New York population. More significant, landmarking effectively precluded high-rise buildings from being built in SoHo. As City Planning Commissioner William Goldstone pointed out, one of the significant architectural qualities of the area was its uniform building height: a taller building would destroy the historic character of the district.[53] Moreover, the designation prevented large developers from entering the local real estate market. If any developers were eyeing SoHo for a large-scale housing development to serve the needs of Greenwich Village residents, Wall Street bankers, or any other population, the landmarking of SoHo thwarted these plans. As a result, loft owners had to work with the buildings as they were. This allowed a new model for development based around adaptive reuse, not replacement, of industrial structures to arise in SoHo and encouraged those living and working in lofts to use the space creatively. Moreover, without the ability to significantly alter SoHo buildings, residential development would have to proceed in the same piecemeal, loft-by-loft manner as it had for years. This left artists and industrial business owners in the best position to potentially benefit from an upturn in loft demand. Moreover, since the landmark designation prevented new housing stock from being added in SoHo, increased demand would lead to even higher property values.[54]

The appeal of cast iron helped draw more people to SoHo. Neighborhood guidebooks published in the late 1970s listed the dates when notable buildings were erected, along with other pertinent information (such as hours and addresses), in their listings of galleries, shops, restaurants, and performance venues. The guidebooks also included numerous photographs of building exteriors and pointed out attractive facades as highlights of neighborhood walking tours. *Anderson and Archer's SoHo*, published in 1979, included a column icon to indicate architecturally interesting buildings that readers were encouraged to visit. An entire section of the guide was dedicated to photographs, addresses, and maps of buildings with notable exteriors.[55]

In turn, the lure of cast iron and the possibility of living in a landmark district encouraged some New Yorkers to move to SoHo lofts and undertake their own interior renovations. Hanford Yang, an architect and a professor at the Pratt Institute School of Architecture, moved into a "Landmark Loft in SoHo" in 1974. He was attracted to this space in large part because of the cast-iron building in which it was located, which he said he thought "forecast the American architectural style." In addition to its exterior charms, the loft's interior space and the possibility of innovative design strategies drew Yang to the loft. His apartment had an "enormous expanse of 35 by 80 feet of living space." There, Yang "worked out a three-level scheme with his bedroom on the top level, the kitchen-dining area on the middle level and the 35-by-50-foot living room on the lower level." The living room was "vast" and "light-filled" and occupied the majority of the living space. In addition, the three-level floor plan "provided plenty of wall space for his collection of contemporary American art."[56]

The efforts of preservationists in promoting SoHo building exteriors and the work of SoHo artists in rehabilitating loft interiors were mutually reinforcing. By converting the interiors of industrial lofts into attractive homes while leaving the exteriors intact, SoHo artists created a viable new use for buildings that preservationists saw as historically important and worth saving from demolition. By promoting the exteriors of loft buildings as attractive and historically important, preservationists gave nonartists another reason to pay attention to, and consider living in, a SoHo loft: the chance to make a home in an appealing and historically important building. People who decided to move into a loft apartment had to spend substantial amounts of time, money, and effort to create a new home. Being able to do so in a building that architects, historic preservationists, and especially the New York City Landmarks Preservation Commission deemed beautiful and architecturally significant likely made more people willing to participate in this undertaking.

Lofts and Gentrification

In the period after the defeat of urban renewal projects in SoHo, artists and local business owners provided a more permanent solution to the problem of what to do with SoHo's loft buildings. The value that artists added to loft buildings through their renovations demonstrated that a viable new use for SoHo lofts existed, as evidenced when New Yorkers beyond the artists' circle found loft living desirable, and prices of residential lofts soared, indicating that SoHo real estate was fast becoming an industry in its own right. Thus, not only did artists help save the neighborhood's built environment from renewal and redevelopment, but they also rehabilitated this space so that it could be reclaimed and recycled as profitable housing stock.

This redevelopment was far from natural. What occurred in SoHo was not a simple movement of capital from an area of high value to one of low value, nor was it an inevitable result of a reaction among urban liberals to the values of the suburbs. The neighborhood's development depended on the advocacy work of artists and preservationists, as well as the area's specific architectural inheritance. Without artists and preservationists publicizing as well as rehabilitating the image of these structures, city residents would not have known about the benefits of loft living. Similarly, without the impressive loft spaces available in SoHo, few would have paid attention to the neighborhood. Its unique industrial spaces also contributed to the new interior design aesthetic that artists brought to the masses through tours, festivals, and the press.

Artists themselves played a significant role in promoting their own neighborhood. On one hand, one can hardly blame groups such as the SoHo Artists Association for doing what they could to legalize their homes and protect their investments. However, by turning art festivals into de facto open houses and by encouraging the press to come into homes to write lifestyle pieces, local artists did much to encourage the public at large to learn about the benefits of loft living. The neighborhood's gentrification was in many ways an unintended consequence of its politics. In addition, through publicizing the positive effect artists had on struggling urban neighborhoods, the SAA helped created a link between artists and urban change just as gentrification was coming into the scholarly vernacular.[57]

Some SoHo residents were already growing wary of the effect that the promotion of the neighborhood had on its development. Jared Bark and some of his fellow artist friends felt that the push for legalization was mostly due to efforts of the "more bourgeois wing of the artists community," those who had bought lofts and "were trying to make it safe for investment." During the SoHo Artists Festival, when politicians and artists were lauding the rebirth of SoHo, he thought, "Oh God, this is the beginning of the end! And, it was, in fact."[58]

By the mid-1970s, SoHo artists had transformed lofts into distinctive homes, partially legalized the practice of living in former industrial space, and promoted this new type of housing to a more general public. New art galleries had opened in the area, and SoHo was becoming a destination for art buyers and art lovers. As SoHo became a more established residential and commercial area, the "bourgeois wing of the artists community" would have greater influence, changing the nature of lofts, influencing what types of stores located in the neighborhood, and alerting an even wider audience to the benefits of loft living and the amenities of SoHo.

7

The Embourgeoisement of SoHo

Art galleries hold numerous attractions for visitors. Yet it is rare that the highlight of any gallery visit is a trip to the bathroom. However, such was the case at art dealer Alexander F. Milliken's 1977 show in his SoHo loft. According to *New York Magazine*, the event in his combined home and art gallery involved "a party full of patrons down from the East Side to look at sculpture" but who kept slipping away to the gallery owner's bathroom "to ogle and then show it to anyone who hasn't yet made the discovery." The bathroom in question, "a sybaritic sight to behold," was "as big as an uptown bedroom" and "entirely paneled in cedar and wonderful smelling, like a sauna. A four-by-five foot Jacuzzi fills one corner, with a platform for body bronzing under a built-in sun lamp in another. Over the door there's a chinning bar—custom made—and a spray hose for hair washing over the sink." It was inevitable that the art exhibition would become a de facto open house, as visitors had to walk through the living space to reach the gallery area and offices.[1]

This combination bathroom showcase and gallery show was emblematic of several changes taking place in SoHo in the middle of the 1970s. In the first years of the decade, the SoHo gallery community exploded, expanding from a handful of showrooms to the city's most vibrant art scene. At the same time, thanks to the work of artist advocates, housing in SoHo was legal for a wider population, and neighborhood promotion had focused the attention of larger numbers of New Yorkers on the SoHo artist community and the innovative loft homes that they created.

As the number of residential lofts and galleries increased, the nature of lofts, as well as the reasons people visited SoHo, began to change. As SoHo artists became more successful, and more affluent artists and nonartists moved to the area, lofts became increasingly upscale. This development led to articles in the local and national press about the neighborhood's striking homes, exhibiting the loft lifestyle to a wider audience. Attendees marveling at Milliken's bathroom fixtures could go home and shop for interior design products inspired by the industrial aesthetic of lofts, browse grocery stores set up like gallery spaces, or visit boutiques selling artistic commercial products.

At the same time, SoHo's industrial sector continued to decline. Despite the positive view presented by Chester Rapkin in his 1963 report on local industry, the area's shaky industrial base had weakened steadily in the following decade. Numerous businesses closed up shop or left the neighborhood, and more lofts were vacant. This increase in vacancy opened up rental space for homes, galleries, and shops, allowing SoHo's residential and commercial sector to expand even further.

As a result, during the middle years of the 1970s, a shift began that would transform the local economy and redefine the neighborhood's dominant industries. First, a number of businesses opened that catered to SoHo gallery visitors. This well-educated, affluent group wanted to eat between gallery visits and was in the market for art-inspired products, such as prints or boutique wares that were cheaper than items sold in galleries. By the mid-1970s, restaurants and boutiques were opening in large numbers.

Simultaneously, lofts became the sites of, and inspiration for, several new commercial enterprises. Groundbreaking retailers such as Dean & DeLuca used loft space to display their gourmet food and professional-grade cookware to the public. As SoHo-style housing became more popular, loft renovations became an industry in their own right. Finally, businesses in SoHo and beyond began to sell products inspired by the industrial aesthetic of lofts.

By the end of the decade, SoHo lofts were increasingly upscale and visible due to coverage in the press. Businesses catered to gallery visitors and people interested in decorating lofts or outfitting homes with loft-style products. The loft lifestyle had become a commodity, and an increasingly upscale one at that. All these elements represented an overall embourgeoisement of SoHo retail and of the neighborhood as a whole. Yet this change did not come about because of upper-class outsiders moving to SoHo or due to a concerted effort on the part of corporate interests. Artists themselves, through their loft renovations, businesses, and the increasing visibility and success of both their art and retail enterprises, remade SoHo into a more upscale neighborhood that attracted a wider population.

Industry and Industrial Decline in SoHo

The changes occurring in SoHo were rooted in a reconfiguration of SoHo industry that took place throughout the 1970s. Whereas in the early 1960s city leaders saw signs of health in SoHo's industry, by the end of the decade the economic picture was far bleaker. The neighborhood experienced increasing numbers of business closures, job losses, and vacant lofts due to the continuing deindustrialization of New York and the American urban north as a whole, as well as the particular challenges created by SoHo's built environment and the specific struggles of businesses situated in the neighborhood.

Deindustrialization created a unique geography that allowed artist-led residential and commercial growth to occur in tandem. The neighborhood's vacant loft space made it possible for galleries to open near artist homes and then for shops catering to both artists and gallery visitors to be established. The ready supply of vacant lofts also encouraged greater numbers of artists (and nonartists) to move into lofts once occupied by industry. In each case, the neighborhood's density and the unique nature of rental space shaped its growth, fashioning a distinct place in which distinct homes, galleries, and stores developed into a densely organized, vibrant, mixed-use urban neighborhood.

Along with the rest of New York City, SoHo's industrial sector was in an overall state of decline by the late 1960s and early 1970s. While one-third of New Yorkers were employed in industrial occupations in 1950, this proportion fell to one-fifth by 1970, with the number of New York manufacturing firms declining by almost half from 1958 to 1977.[2] Both contemporary observers and recent scholars noted the general pattern of downward industrial employment "that extended from New England across New York, Pennsylvania, and West Virginia, through the Midwest to the banks of the Mississippi." This decrease came as a result of industries that "automated production" or "relocated plants in suburban and rural areas, and increasingly in the low-wage labor markets like the American South and the Caribbean."[3]

Although the trend of deindustrialization was noticeable throughout New York, it was particularly acute in Lower Manhattan. The area was at a disadvantage in retaining industrial employment due to its high land costs as well as its nineteenth-century built environment. By 1969, city planners were already writing that "inevitably, white collar activities and housing are going to supplant manufacturing" in Lower Manhattan.[4]

The particular struggles of SoHo industry can be seen in a 1968 City Planning Commission (CPC) study designed to follow the 1963 Rapkin report. Whereas Rapkin presented a generally positive view of the area's industrial present and future, the 1968 study painted a picture of less-stable industry undergoing significant decline. The report found that in the five years since the Rapkin study, 11 of the 127 firms analyzed went bankrupt and 4 sold their stakes to other companies and closed. Even worse, the rate at which industrial businesses were moving from SoHo was increasing. Just 4 percent of businesses had relocated out of SoHo during the period of the Rapkin study, while 19 percent had moved out of the area five years later. Of the firms that moved from SoHo, a majority cited a "lack of contiguous space as one of the reasons for the move, and most probably the principal reason."[5]

Furthermore, industrial decline was rooted in the struggles of the specific types of businesses in SoHo. These industries, which included rag and paper recycling and the garment trades, fought to remain viable in the best of times. Now the marketplace in which they operated was becoming increasingly globalized, centralized, and technologically advanced, making area businesses even less competitive. The 1968 report put it rather bluntly: "Most of the firms in SoHo are small and old firms engaging in activities that are no longer necessarily promising lines of business." It used B. Kruger, a paper-cutting firm located at 163 Mercer Street, to illustrate the point. Kruger bought paper waste from larger paper mills and processed it into new paper. However, the business had fallen on hard times due to centralization in the paper industry. "In recent years big mills have been processing their own waste and selling the product on the market at the same prices as they sell unprocessed waste to firms such as B. Kruger." Company namesake Kruger reported that most firms in his line of work were going out of business and that he and his partners would close their firm upon their retirement. Further, the domestic paper waste business also suffered from competition from synthetic substitutes, such as plastic. Paper mills also increasingly imported bales of wastepaper, as well as the finished product, fiberboard, from abroad.[6]

Other SoHo businesses were also engaged in textile waste recycling, another industry bordering on obsolescence. Most local firms recycled cotton products. During the late 1960s and early 1970s, a substantial part of the textile industry transitioned to synthetics, decreasing the demand for recycled cotton and increasing chemical processing of cotton that prevented wastes from being recycled into paper. Additionally, high labor costs for recycled products in SoHo made them more expensive than textiles manufactured abroad, where companies could "enjoy a considerable wage differential in a labor intensive industry." Inefficient transit made it even harder for companies to remain solvent. One business owner said that only firms with easy access to freight transport, such as those with their own railroad sidings, would remain competitive. The CPC study found that at least one SoHo business moved to New Jersey specifically to gain access to freight train service. The lack of loading and unloading facilities was cited second most often as the reason businesses gave for moving out of the neighborhood.[7]

More lofts were vacated when industrial firms left New York in search of cheaper labor. For example, garment maker Sonjay Mills employed two hundred people in SoHo in 1962. During the next five years, the firm moved the bulk of its operations to Puerto Rico. By 1967, the company employed only eighteen people in New York. The wage differential played a large part in the company's decision to move. In its report, the CPC observed that such moves did not bode well for the long-term success of industry in SoHo. They argued that "not only has the industrial space been determined to be less adequate than in 1962, but furthermore the available labor pool has diminished." In addition, the report stated that the trend toward unskilled labor would make it harder for businesses to succeed in New York. To survive, "they will need to have ideal conditions such as minimal traffic congestion and single level plant operation," which was impossible in SoHo. That is not to say that the CPC believed that SoHo industries did not serve an important function. Its report found that the neighborhood was "even more intensive in its employment of blacks and Puerto Ricans" than in 1962. In 1962, 59.2 percent of the employees were African American or Puerto Rican, and by 1968 this figure had increased to 69.9 percent. The report noted that SoHo businesses were "still a prime source of employment for those of our city who would encounter difficulty of finding employment elsewhere."[8] Yet jobs for these populations were increasingly migrating away from the city.

The connections between artist housing, deindustrialization, and commerce in SoHo can be seen in the changing geography of the neighborhood. As Figure 18 demonstrates, there were larger numbers of empty lofts to the north and west of the neighborhood, particularly along West Broadway, which contained smaller lofts less attractive to industry. Conversely, the area along Broadway, with its larger lofts, had fewer vacancies. Similarly, the blocks with the highest concentrations of industrial vacancies contained buildings with larger numbers of artist residences. The pattern of artist residence corresponded with the growth of commercial businesses in SoHo. A large percentage of retail was located along West Broadway from Houston to Spring Streets, and along Spring Street and Prince Street from West Broadway to Greene Street. These blocks also contained some of the highest concentrations of artist residences and industrial vacancies.

When retail establishments joined artist galleries in the neighborhood, they followed the same geographic pattern. New businesses opened in areas where there was more vacant industrial space, indicating that they were

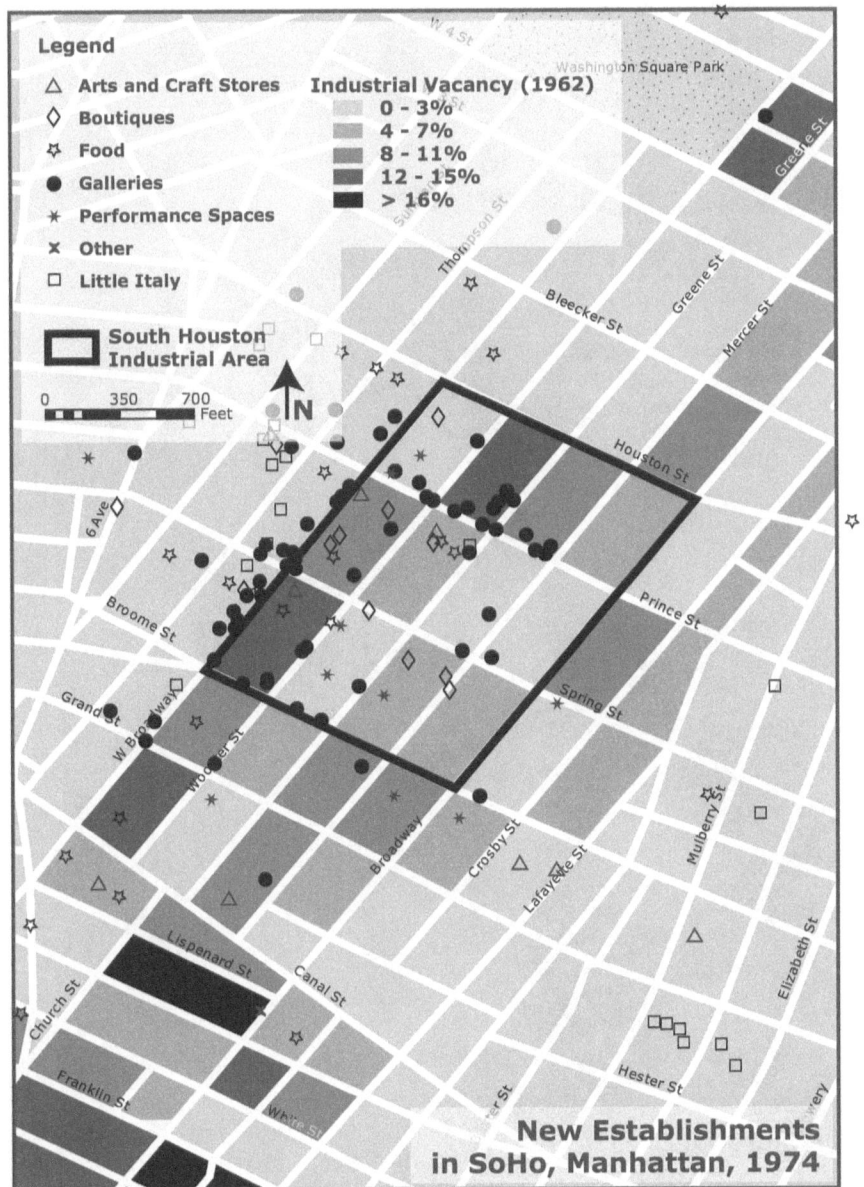

FIGURE 18. New establishments in SoHo, Manhattan, 1974.

migrating toward already-vacant lofts. As Figures 18 and 19 indicate, SoHo businesses tended to locate to the west and north of the neighborhood, as well as on its east-west blocks, where lofts were smaller and industrial vacancies higher. Shops and eateries also congregated around galleries, making it likely that they wanted to be near their customer base: SoHo's artistic tourists.

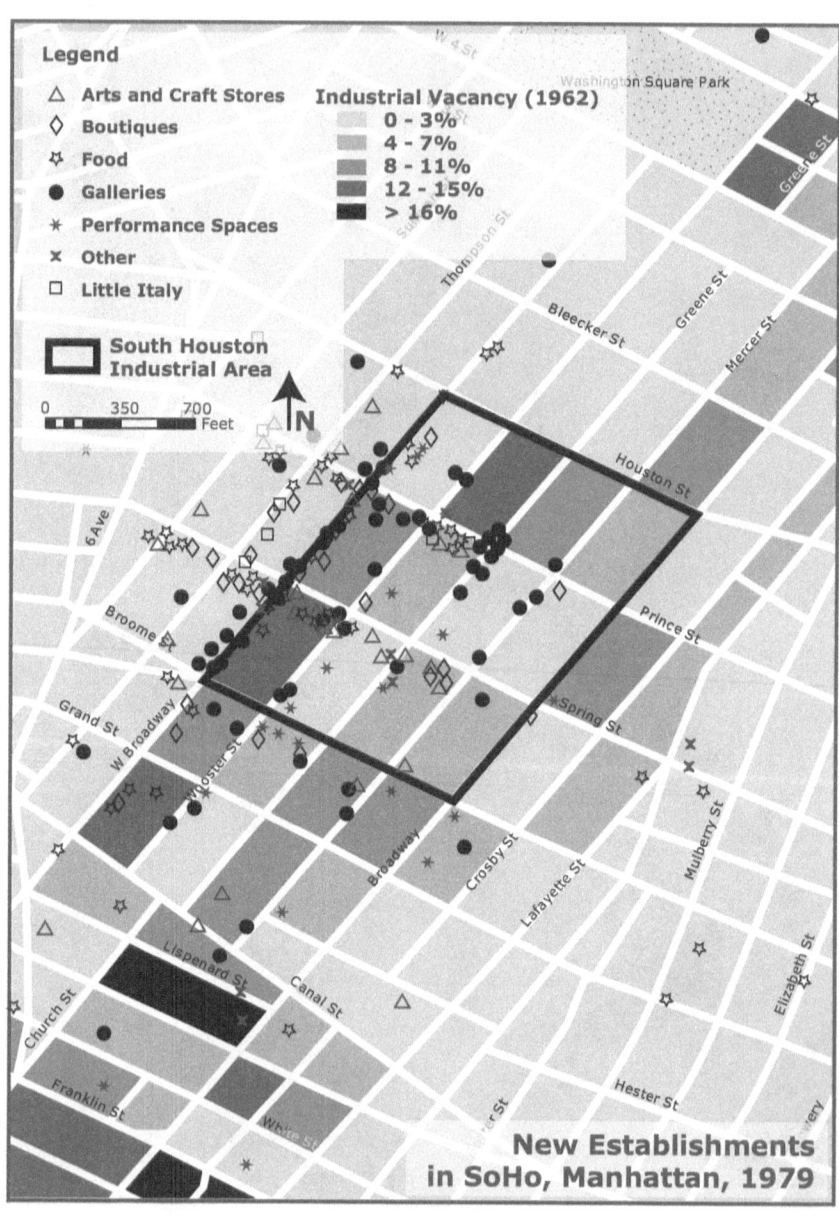

FIGURE 19. New establishments in SoHo, Manhattan, 1979.

Finally, the number and concentration of local retail establishments increased from 1974 to 1979, as SoHo's commercial and residential sector grew.

Art as Commerce: SoHo's Retail Landscape

As art galleries sprang up across SoHo, a new retail industry catering to their visitors grew. By the early 1970s, audiences for SoHo art were substantial. These art lovers were ideal customers, particularly because they did not often spend money on the art they traveled to see and thus had funds left for shopping and dining. As a result, commercial enterprises serving gallery visitors flourished.[9]

The local press soon noticed how the visitors to SoHo galleries became customers for other local enterprises. In 1973, the *SoHo Weekly News* described how area galleries and businesses were "crowded, colorful and progressively geared towards viewer-consumer needs." When gallery crowds descended on SoHo on Saturday afternoons, they could find "books and clothes" for sale "close to the galleries," and restaurants were "filled for lunch until late afternoon." Even the SoHo Children's Playgroup "had the foresight to set up a stall for drinks and homemade goodies which was patronized out of existence" soon after.[10]

By the early 1970s, SoHo had a flourishing retail district that included a florist, bookstore, health food store, and toy store. A few restaurants began opening as well, including the Cheese Store at 120 Prince Street, operated by Giorgio G. DeLuca, later a cofounder of SoHo's most famous food shop. However, the neighborhood's more artsy retail options defined the retail district. In June 1972, the *New York Times* reported on the neighborhood's "Downtown Frontier of Boutiques and Studios." By this time, clothing and design shops had opened near galleries and artists' studios in the "funky-chic environs once known as Hell's Hundred Acres." Galleries became a central part of this retail scene. While most SoHo visitors did not purchase expensive works of art, many SoHo galleries sold prints that were more accessible for the casual shopper. Art dealers liked prints because they did not cost much to produce, and buyers liked them because they were convenient and affordable. As the *Villager* observed, prints were "hangable above the couch and they can be had for two or three figures instead of four or five."[11]

Visitors could also purchase low-cost pieces of art from independent shops. At the 3 Mercer Store, shoppers could buy handmade levers with rocks for fulcrums, devices to evaporate water without heat, mechanical flying birds, and apparatuses made of balsa wood for amplifying sound. In crafting these items, proprietor Stefan Eins based his creations on Claes Oldenburg's sculptures and Marcel Duchamp's ready-mades. Products at the store were meant to straddle the line between junk and art. Eins said of his wares, "You can't point to the art, but the art is there." The journal *Art Rite* observed, "The 3 Mercer Street Store is just around the corner (literally and figuratively) from Canal Street, the bargain-basement/junk haven. Come in and browse around." Although they were artistic, items at the store were inexpensive, from 75 cents and up.[12]

SoHo's retail sector also contained a substantial number of boutiques selling one-of-a-kind and designer clothing. Their proprietors utilized some of the same techniques as SoHo artists, including printmaking, and took their inspiration from both local and international artistic trends. By 1974, there were eight boutiques in SoHo, including East Bank South, displaying its dresses in a gallery-like setting; Kathie Keller, which sold western ware constructed from silk scarves; Knobkerry, taking inspiration from fashions from Africa, Afghanistan, and India; Nana of SoHo, selling photo-printed T-shirts and low-cost French fashions; Paracelso, which sold Middle Eastern, Indian, and "Oriental" fashions; and Tales of Hoffman/Le Grand Hotel, offering shoes and custom-made skirts. The proprietors of Tamala took inspiration from SoHo artists (and garment industries) by designing their women's clothing in the loft above their store. Finally, at King Knitter, customers could purchase one-of-a-kind wearable works of art from owner Dione King, who sold knit sweaters for $200, vests for $75 to $100, and hats for $15 each ($960, $360 to $480, and $72, respectively, in 2015 dollars).[13]

Over time, even more boutiques set up shop in SoHo. In 1976, the neighborhood welcomed Harriet Love, a vintage clothing store that moved to West Broadway after twelve years in Greenwich Village. By 1978, several more clothing stores opened in the neighborhood, including WPA on Spring Street, Equator and Palma on Wooster Street, Church Street Surplus, and Merchant of Venice, and an expanded Tamala Design w/Bagel on Prince Street.[14]

SoHo had such a vibrant boutique scene that it encouraged some local industrial businesses to repurpose their products as fashion. Harold and Toby Gottlieb, owners of AA Fabrics at 34 Greene Street, transitioned their business from a rag distributor to a fabric retail house. Tellingly, AA Fabrics was the only commercial tenant remaining at its 34 Greene Street location by 1974, but Toby Gottlieb told the *SoHo Weekly News* he thought that the commercial "renaissance is great," and was "fascinated by the difference between their fabric-filled, business-like loft and an upstairs tenant's carefully cared for home." The *SoHo Weekly News* also reported on the "fetching products" that could be found at Allsteel Scale Corporation at 80 Spring Street. Allsteel started in the scale business in 1917 but, after finding it limited, began to sell other products, including industrial bags. The article's author suggested that the fashion conscious order Allsteel's heavy shoulder bags, designed for mail carriers and coal miners, to use as fashion accessories. The coal miner bags were particularly popular, retailing at $15. Mailbags, "just like those the mailmen carry," sold for $30 to $50.[15]

Additionally, artists opened restaurants that employed and catered to SoHo residents and later served the area's cultural tourists. The restaurant with the deepest connections to the SoHo artist community was Food. Gordon Matta-Clark and Caroline Gooden, artists who often showed their work at 112 Workshop, opened Food at 127 Prince Street in 1971. Food was connected to the SoHo artist community on every level of its operation. Local artists ran the kitchen, waited tables, and balanced (or failed to balance) the books. Food's goal was to be a "community based business whose goal was to support and maintain the art community of downtown Manhattan." Matta-Clark and Gooden viewed Food as both a community-building institution and a business that could provide needed income for artists. The restaurant's community impact was substantial. According to one estimate, three hundred artists worked at Food over the course of its history.[16]

Further, Matta-Clark viewed cooking as a means of artistic expression and thus blurred the line between cooking and art making during his time in the kitchen at Food. His creations included wiggling brine shrimp placed inside eggs for macabre effect (the meal caused several customers to abruptly leave the restaurant) and a "bone meal" featuring aspic and oxtail soup. At the conclusion of the meal, Matta-Clark had a jeweler create necklaces out of bones that diners could take home.[17]

Although Matta-Clark might have viewed Food as a work of art, the restaurant was also a commercial amenity that served SoHo's gallery visitors. In 1972, the *New York Times* observed that the "mink sheathed matrons" and suburbanites who came to see SoHo galleries also ate at the restaurant. To the newspaper, Food was part of the growing commercial landscape of SoHo. The newspaper reported, "Within the last year the art community, which had been composed of illegal squatters clandestinely pursuing their images in fear of eviction by building inspectors, has become legal through an act of the City Planning Commission. And in the wake of this legitimization have come more galleries, more people, restaurants, and rent increases."[18]

Food was not the only restaurant in SoHo that catered to wealthy visitors. The neighborhood's restaurant scene became increasingly upscale by the mid-1970s. At that point, many SoHo restaurants catered to a clientele that was far richer than the "starving artists" living nearby. In 1975 the *New York Times* reported that Food was serving "salads and crepes instead of okra soup and mashed eggplant," and was increasingly attractive to suburban tourists. Several other trendy restaurants with art world connections opened nearby, including Oh So Ho on West Broadway. The restaurant was "chic Chinese" or "Asian gourmet," serving food prepared by a Cantonese chef. Its owners, Maryann and Kwong Lam, imported Chinese films and made their own movies on the side. Kwong Lam even did a bit of painting.[19]

SoHo's dining establishments grew in tandem with its gallery scene. In 1975, two gourmet food emporiums opened in the neighborhood. De Roma's, a food specialty store, stocked imported beer, cheese, and three types of homemade pâté. Coffee Connection was an upscale coffee bean shop. Later that year, the *SoHo Weekly News* reported that SoHo "finally" had a café, Café Borgia II, on Prince Street between West Broadway and Thompson Street. In 1977, the food section of the *New York Times* nicknamed SoHo "brunchville," writing that the neighborhood offered "the city's highest concentration of delicious and original breakfasts against a zesty backdrop of open shops and art galleries."[20]

Some of these upscale restaurants also had connections to the art world. Noticing the crowds visiting SoHo galleries (including his own), Louis Meisel backed a restaurant called Chanterelle at 89 Grand Street in 1978. In time, the restaurant evolved into one of the city's most noted fine-dining establishments, and the first downtown eatery to earn a four-star rating from the *New York Times*.[21]

By 1977, it was hard to eat affordably in SoHo, as evidenced by a *SoHo Weekly News* article about finding cheap food in the area. The article's suggestions included lunch at a hot dog truck at Spring and Thompson Streets, frequenting sandwich shops such as Corner Restaurant on West Broadway, stopping by Dave's Luncheonette, or grabbing a bagel at the boutique Tamela Design w/Bagel. There were also some inexpensive Italian and Chinese restaurants, but affordable options were getting pushed out by restaurants catering to gallery visitors and, increasingly, wealthier SoHo residents.[22]

In this manner, the retail community that emerged in SoHo had its roots in, and also helped bolster, its residential and gallery scenes. Like galleries, SoHo shops were immersed in the arts, small-scale, innovative, and often artist-run. Food was similar to an artist cooperative that also functioned as a restaurant. Yet even this enterprise evolved into an amenity for gallery shoppers. Moreover, galleries inspired shop owners to settle in SoHo, which brought more visitors, indicating that the neighborhood was a safe place in which to invest. The growth of retail amenities also made SoHo an even more attractive place to live, drawing additional residents who then became potential customers for area businesses.

Lifestyle Articles: Publicizing the Upscale Loft

On May 27, 1974, the front page of *New York Magazine* declared SoHo "The Most Exciting Place to Live in the City." The issue chronicled SoHo's rise as an artist colony and served as a guide to joining the "uptown, out-of-town crowds" that "descend to do the galleries and the boutiques." However, the magazine had another audience in mind: those who might be interested in the attractive homes and upscale bohemian lifestyle of SoHo residents. Much of the issue highlighted distinctive SoHo lofts. Moreover, the magazine focused on the increasing affluence and material wealth of loft dwellers. The lofts featured were not mere functional dwellings for struggling artists. These SoHo lofts embodied a "robust middle class materialism" that prized interior decorations geared toward the wealthy. These included large, expensive fixtures, such as $1,200 king-size bathtubs, "acres of exotic plants," Steinway pianos, antique pool tables, imported eighteenth-century wood beams, twenty-four-foot-long leather sofas, and indoor fountains.[23]

Newspaper and magazine features on SoHo lofts became increasingly common throughout the 1970s. These articles both reflected and drove SoHo's development during this era. The media coverage reflected the fact that more and more successful artists and nonartists were moving to SoHo and creating attractive homes in the neighborhood. At the same time, the articles highlighted aspects of loft living that appealed to the middle and upper classes and provided evidence that increasingly affluent people were living in lofts.

While stories about SoHo lofts originally profiled the homes of lesser-known members of the Artist Tenants Association (ATA) and SoHo Artists Association (SAA), in part in an attempt to aid in the advocacy efforts of these groups, the pieces focused on the lofts of wealthier people, including nonartists. Even when these features profiled artists, they more often were practitioners who had achieved success that was apparent in their homes' lavish decorations. In its issue on SoHo, *New York Magazine* covered the loft of French artist Arman on West Broadway. Arman's loft reflected his artistic success; its kitchen supported walnut cabinets, modern appliances, and a collection of paintings of food, including Andy Warhol Campbell's Soup prints and Roy Lichtenstein's wedge of Swiss cheese.[24]

Over time, print-media features on lofts made it clear that this type of housing was evolving into a status symbol, as opposed to a way of meeting artists' basic needs for suitable studio space at low prices. Sculptor Ana Thornhill, the subject of a 1976 *New York Times* loft lifestyle piece, told the paper that she sold her art not to make ends meet but to finance renovations to her loft. The sculptor moved to her SoHo home for the large interior space

FIGURE 20. Child playing with blocks in a loft, 1976. (Photograph by Robin Forbes. Reproduced by permission from Archives of American Art, Smithsonian Institution.)

it provided for her sculpture and its uninterrupted interior rooms. Yet what was once a spatial necessity became a decorating luxury, as workshop space made room for interior design elements. Her loft impressed visitors with its open and verdant feel, which made it seem far removed from the dirty streets of SoHo's industrial past. Entering the loft was like "entering a conservatory." The apartment was filled with plants and Plexiglas divisions that allowed light to flow from the exterior windows into an interior gallery, creating a "living capsule."[25]

Other articles highlighted those who had achieved success through SoHo's

Pop in the kitchen: *Arman had professionals install his appliances, but he made the plastic stools stuffed with pages from "Screw."*

A Loftful Assemblage

Judging by his loft on West Broadway, there's not much of a gap between Arman's life-style and his art style. They are both summed up by the "motto" over his doorway—a photo-enlargement of the word *accumulate* with its dictionary definition: "to heap up; gather, as into a mass; collect. . . ." The French-born artist, whose assemblages of litter and garbage sell for between $5,000 and $20,000, has filled his five-room co-op with an accumulation of high and low art, camp, and junk. Sometimes it's in heaps, sometimes in orderly array, as in his kitchen (above). Lavishly equipped with Formica walnut cabinets and mechanized conveniences, the kitchen is also well stocked with Pop Art food: a wallful of Warhol's Campbell soups, Lichtenstein's wedge of Swiss cheese, and the glued-down *Dinner of Marcel Duchamp*, by Spoerri.

Arman bought his loft in 1970, along with the late Adolph Gottlieb (who had two floors) and the real-estate entrepreneur Jack Klein (who recently sold his floor to Ivan Karp of the O. K. Harris Gallery). Each partner paid about $100,000 a floor, which covered the purchase price of the building as well as extensive improvements: a new boiler, a new elevator (the large, uneconomy size), new floors, walls, and ceilings, closed-circuit TV surveillance of the front doors; and the cast-iron columns were encased in Sheetrock to satisfy the New York building codes.

Arman's monthly maintenance is under $500, a comparatively low sum for such space, thanks to the rent from a gallery on the first floor. But still, Arman says, the SoHo loft is "pretty expensive to use as a studio," and besides, his work with plastic "stinks and is unhealthy to breathe." So, since accumulation is his thing, he keeps a separate studio in the Bowery, not to mention an apartment in Paris and a house and studio in the south of France.

To remove special SoHo map, turn the next page and pull map down through staples.

FIGURE 21. Kitchen and eating area of Arman's loft, 1974. (Photograph by Steve Myers. "Lofty Living," *New York Magazine*, May 20, 1974.)

FIGURE 22. Long table in Louis and Susan Meisel's loft, undated. (Photograph courtesy of Louis Meisel.)

FIGURE 23. Kitchen in Louis and Susan Meisel's loft, undated. (Photograph courtesy of Louis Meisel.)

THE EMBOURGEOISEMENT OF SOHO   173

gallery scene and had used part of the proceeds to renovate striking loft homes. In 1977, the magazine *Town and Country* profiled Louis and Susan Meisel, who "squeezed" themselves "into 5,000 feet of much photographed space" above his aforementioned gallery at 141 Prince Street. Their loft's massive size and open floor plan allowed for "a studio for her; work space for him; a king-size water bed, and another bed with a normal mattress built into the floor; a huge dining-room table, and a typical free-standing SoHo kitchen, which includes a glass-fronted restaurant refrigerator to supplement the regular one; an antique pool table in the corner; ubiquitous plants; and where there is wall space—and there is plenty—art."[26]

As the 1970s came to a close, SoHo artists were increasingly living in luxury lofts that the local press brought to the public through lifestyle pieces. In 1978, the *SoHo Weekly News* profiled the home of Robert Mihalik, a sculptor, cabinetmaker, and "environmental designer," who was clearly a person of some means. Mihalik took off work for an entire year to do nothing but renovate his 2,400-square-foot loft. It was described as "$20,000 worth of sand-colored ascetic elegance," with a temple in the "entrance chamber" and "two 12-ft high sheetrock panels to divide rooms," letting in natural light. The loft's kitchen exuded "warmth and a sense of the past" with its "dark-stained wood beams along the low ceiling and two solid old doors—one of wormy chestnut and the other 17th century folding panels that once fronted a ground-floor shop in Rome."[27]

Other times, the incomes of artists' partners allowed for more elaborate loft renovations. In 1977, the *New York Times* published an article on the loft of architect Neils Diffrient and his wife, textile artist Helena Hernmark. The couple (who had barely beaten out pop musician David Bowie for the chance to purchase the loft) moved into the massive 3,300-square-foot home in SoHo, a space that they claimed was large enough for one to jog in. They implemented an open floor plan that allowed for artistic pursuits and interior design innovations. The only enclosed areas were the bathroom and a storage area. The loft also housed multiple large looms, 1,600 pounds of colorful wool, and a four-by-six-foot drawing board. The couple said that they were "turned down by roomy 5th Ave apartments when they found out they wanted to tear down walls and put in looms." The apartment also included a freestanding fireplace, modern furniture and antiques, a skylight to allow even more natural light into the kitchen, and custom cabinet doors. From the luxury here, it was clear that SoHo lofts appealed to those who needed them for more than just creating art.[28]

In this manner, lifestyle features on SoHo lofts demonstrated the evolving nature of loft space as a commodity. The articles both reflected and encouraged the spread of the loft lifestyle to nonartists. The very fact that people other than artists appeared in these features in the mid-1970s, just as the neighborhood's retail sector was exploding, is significant in its own right. The potential illegality of these homes was rarely, if ever, mentioned in these pieces. It is worth noting that artists and gallery owners were the ones creating these upscale lofts. Although some nonartists were making their way to SoHo, people in the art community were the most prominent residents using their wealth to design and furnish magazine-worthy spaces, not bankers or stockbrokers.

The Evolution of the Loft as a Commodity

As the 1970s progressed, the market for lofts and loft-related products and services expanded and evolved. As more moneyed artists and nonartists moved to SoHo, loft renovations became an industry, with companies advertising loft conversion services. At the same time, local businesses, most notably the innovative food store Dean & DeLuca, perfected the use of the loft space in retail design. Loft-style housewares began to make their way into stores across the city, helping to drive a trend toward the use of industrial products in interior design.

Whereas artists undertook most of the first loft renovations in SoHo themselves, many of the artists featured in lifestyle pieces on SoHo invested money, rather than labor, into their lofts. The growth of the loft renovation industry was a sign that living in SoHo was now possible for less do-it-yourself-inclined residents. Although only the most talented or dedicated artist renovator could turn a raw industrial space into a home, articles about SoHo lofts demonstrated to the general public that for enough money, anyone could live in a unique residence in the heart of the growing artist community of SoHo.

As lofts became more upscale, a mini-industry sprung up around loft renovations, replacing some of the economic value that industrial businesses in now-vacant lofts had once generated. In its 1974 issue on SoHo, *New York Magazine* featured SoHo residents who had undertaken costly renovations to their homes using contractors. One loft owner, Debora Remington, spent $30,000 (nearly $143,000 in 2015 dollars) renovating her loft. Alterations included stripping years of paint from the interior, exposing the loft's original cast-iron columns, and installing "a modern kitchen with walnut cabinets and a pass-through." The finished product showcased a "gracious array" of antiques. Remington's home does not fit with the image of a struggling artist in a 1960s SoHo loft. These loft renovations demonstrated the potential of lofts to provide luxury housing for anyone with means.[29]

Painter and printmaker Lowell Nesbitt, another artist profiled by *New York Magazine*, also invested substantial capital into renovating his loft. Nesbitt made his home in what the magazine called SoHo's most "status-y building," on West Broadway. He spent $25,000 (more than $119,000 in 2015 dollars) to renovate his loft into a space that visitors found "dazzling." The artists' massive apartment, which he "ingeniously subdivided into nine irregular-shaped living, working and display areas," included an octagonal white living room" featuring "a varied botanical world" including "turn-of-the-century French ceramic irises, and Nesbitt's own etchings of tulips."[30] Again, Nesbitt's loft demonstrated that a New Yorker with $25,000 could create a home to rival any suburban house or Upper East Side apartment, and in a building with status to boot. The fact that a loft building could have "status" showed the increasing appeal and value of loft homes.

By the mid-1970s, the media were outlining how wealthy loft renovators employed experts to complete their projects. It became increasingly normal to read of lofts with "three lawyers checking out the lease or prospectus" and "four architects trooping through with their sheaths of designs" for renovations.[31] When the *SoHo Weekly News* instituted a "Loft of the Week" feature in 1974, the paper chose fashion designer Valerie Porr's apartment. Porr hired an interior designer to create what the paper called one of the "most fascinating spaces in SoHo." With her designer's help, Porr crafted a loft with "white curved walls with a cantilevered drum that becomes a book-lined, brass-bedded bedroom kept discreetly hidden by white shutters suggestive of New Orleans." The large space contained twelve-foot bamboo, forty other plants, multicolored pillows gathered from her trips through Mexico and Central America, as well as "a pristine kitchen edged with an enormous butcher block table, cobalt blue glassware, a curved tile floor, "boldly painted dishes newly arrived from a Mexican factory," and a showroom for her artwork.[32]

By 1978, at least one company, Omnisolo Associates of West 57th Street in Manhattan, advertised itself as New York's "only professional consultant/co-ordinators for loft renovation." The company would arrange all aspects of renovation, "from contracting architects to the selection of materials & contractors, to the final clean-up." For those thinking about buying a loft through a co-op, companies such as the Walter Matzner Company offered property management to potential loft owners.[33]

In addition, local businesses capitalized on the loft aesthetic to display products, the most notable among them being Dean & DeLuca. Painter Jack

Ceglic used Dean & DeLuca as a canvas to experiment with innovative interior design, applying the same techniques as he did in his own loft. Ceglic's home was the subject of a feature in the *New York Times* in March 1974. He transformed a former toy factory into what the paper called "4,000 square feet of living room." The loft, painted with "eight coats of white marine paint," contained an open living area in the center, a kitchen with three large work islands with butcher-block tops, a dining area with a table built from an old work table that came with the loft, and a studio. To Ceglic, his loft "was all about the movement of space and how one views space." He never viewed the home as an apartment but rather as a factory that had been cleaned and polished, with no physical barriers between rooms (only the bathroom was enclosed). The open space allowed light to shine through from one area to another, and the loft's seventeen windows helped divide open areas into "rooms."[34]

In 1977, Ceglic, along with publisher Joel Dean[35] and Giorgio DeLuca, owner of SoHo's Cheese Store, opened Dean & DeLuca at 121 Prince Street, what fellow SoHo entrepreneur Greg Turpan called the area's "forward-thinking, aesthetically-driven food emporium" and "first church of food." Dean & DeLuca gained renown for its merchandise and interior design. The store's selection of gourmet merchandise is now common in upscale neighborhoods but was novel in the late 1970s. Dean & DeLuca sold cheeses from the United States and Europe, sourced the best produce directly from farmers, and introduced many new foodstuffs to New Yorkers. As Turpan put it, "nobody ever heard of a sun-dried tomato before Giorgio DeLuca and Joel Dean."[36]

The three owners also set out to create a store that expressed their vision for displaying and selling food. Much like early loft and gallery owners, Dean & DeLuca's founders had to renovate their loft space with minimal help and on a budget. Dean, DeLuca, and Ceglic did a lot of the renovations themselves, which led to one of the first innovations the shop made in displaying merchandise: metal shelving, then and now commonly used in walk-in coolers, to display merchandise. The shelving, suggested by Felipe Rojas Lombardi, the first chef responsible for Dean & DeLuca's prepared foods, had the advantage of not requiring a carpenter to install, and it allowed the trio to display merchandise with minimal visual distraction.[37]

The shelving added to the overall minimalistic industrial aesthetic Ceglic envisioned. Ceglic said that he designed the store "in a manner very similar to the way I was living, with the white space." Inspired by the open spaces of his loft, Ceglic took away as many of the store's interior walls and divisions as possible. He also painted the entire space, creating "a drama of the eventual goal of the store, which was the presentation of food." According to Ceglic, the shop had its own interior harmony and balance, causing the space to melt away in the mind of viewers, leaving them "absorbed in the world of food and cooking."[38]

To Ceglic, Dean & DeLuca was like a canvas to display the ideas of its founders. Ceglic used various shades of white to emphasize light and play with the colors and textures, much as one would with a painting. Gradations of white would make categories of food look and feel distinct while at the same time unify the space. Moreover, the whiteness brought the food to the forefront. As a painting does, the store had a message: to display the specialness of the food selected by Dean, DeLuca, and the store's chef. The design gave the store clarity, delineating food by shape and color (as seen at a farmer's market) and allowing the shopper to make sense of, for example, the more than three hundred cheeses that might be on display at a given time.[39]

The store impressed visitors. The *New York Times* wrote that the shop was "a handsome loftlike space with a certain Mediterranean aura." It was "white from floor to ceiling, glistening with freestanding chrome shelves, lighted by a rear skylight and high-up fixtures that make a Pyrex double boiler seem practically sculptural, becalmed by gently stirring overhead fans operating like silent dragonflies."[40]

While Dean & DeLuca was like both a piece of art and a loft home, it was also analogous to a gallery. Among the most memorable events at the store was its annual Christmas display. Lombardi would spend several days before Christmas hanging pheasants, birds, reindeer, and suckling pigs in the center of the store. As Ceglic described it, "It was a very beautiful thing that he did, it was just magic. He would wash the animals, they were stuffed with dry ice, the birds, their plumage was dressed and beautifully combed, the animals would hang for three days in celebration of the bounty of Christmas." Additionally, Ceglic would invent themes and story lines every Christmas, many of which were inspired by, or evoked, visions of old New York. For example, one year's theme centered on early twentieth-century millionaire gourmand Diamond Jim Brady and actress Lillian Russell. Ceglic would tell a story to the store's staff about how the two figures came into the store a few days before Christmas during a snowstorm. The store would provide food for Brady based on recipes from his favorite restaurant, Delmonico's, and lots of copper pots for Russell to buy for her friends. Ceglic would also paint a canvas to help establish the theme. As Ceglic recounted, this was akin to performance art, no different than the type that was going on in neighborhood galleries at the same time. But, as artistic as it was, this art was being done in the service of selling gourmet food and building a brand in the neighborhood and beyond.[41]

The founders of Dean & DeLuca developed the store with the artist customer in mind. Joel Dean reportedly felt that artists had a "great sense of living." They might not have the money to buy everything, but they wanted the best things, if just in the small quantities they could afford. However, SoHo visitors, particularly gallerygoers, were also an important market. The store sold not only to artists and people who liked art but also to "the wannabes" who might be more interested in shopping than art appreciation.[42]

The success of Dean & DeLuca and the draw of local galleries had a mutually reinforcing effect on area retail. As Ceglic remembered, visitors "were coming to the galleries and then particular stores opened with beautiful things very much along the lines of Dean & DeLuca." Local entrepreneurs realized that even though "people were coming to the galleries . . . they're not buying all of the art." So, they thought, "maybe they'll buy some of our *schmattas* [rags]."[43]

By the end of the 1970s, interior design companies were selling products specifically for lofts, or for people who wanted to bring elements of the loft aesthetic into their apartments. In May 1978, the *Village Voice* hosted what it called the "First Ever *Village Voice* Loft Expo" in two locations in Lower Manhattan. Displays included items designed to take advantage of lofts' unique interior spaces, such as "Stained Glass for Loft Living," or plants and hammocks to transform a section of a loft into something resembling a backyard. There were also purveyors of large bathtubs and whirlpools for oversize bathrooms, custom furniture, cabinetmakers, and contractors to turn raw space into a home. The expo included luxury kitchen appliance dealers, companies specializing in floor installations, and contractors claiming, "Lofts Our Specialty."[44]

In 1978, *New York Magazine* ran a feature spotlighting "re-used" products that fit well in lofts, which were, by nature, reused spaces. It advertised that these "industrial or commercial prototypes" were perfect for "furnishing an industrial-space-turned-home." The article included design products that evoked industrial themes, such as flower vases resembling industrial pillars and incandescent lamps that looked like car headlights. Other highlighted products were used adaptively, such as a plant stand turned into a sculpture–cum–clothes rack and storage units made of stackable boxes and baskets. Others were actual industrial products, including fishing stools used as chairs and film-production mast lights used to illuminate a large loft interior.[45]

The store that did the most with the loft aesthetic was Turpan Sanders, an innovative design shop opened in 1980 by Greg Turpan and David Sanders, that pioneered the use of several industrial products in interior design. At the forefront of an international trend, perhaps best exemplified by Joan Kron and Suzanne Slesin's 1980 work *High-Tech: The Industrial Style and Source Book for the Home*, the store was the first to stock products from both the commercial maintenance and restaurant supply industries for sale to the public. Similar to Dean & DeLuca, which used walk-in refrigerator shelving to display products, Turpan Sanders sold metal refrigerator shelving made by Metropolitan Wire (now called InterMetro) for use in the home. Long before Viking sold professional stoves to homeowners, Turpan Sanders sold Garland Ranges for home use.[46]

Turpan Sanders opened up whole new avenues for the distribution of industrial products and found innovative ways to display them in their stores. For instance, the shop used products from a company called Auto Poles, which made telescopic freestanding poles for commercial products, to craft transparent shelves that made items appear to be suspended in midair.[47]

Like Dean & DeLuca, Turpan Sanders had its roots in its proprietor's artistic modes of thinking. Much as Ceglic designed his home and store using his painterly sensibilities, artist Turpan would seek out industrial supply shops in SoHo and the Bowery to find utilitarian objects to use in his mixed-media works. Turpan said, "I was using these in my work, but at the same time I was so enamored with the functionality of a lot of these products in the industrial sector, and that's what led to my first retail venture."[48]

Turpan Sanders made an impact beyond the neighborhood. To Turpan, loft living in SoHo changed the way people thought about their homes and how to best design living spaces. Thanks to the influence of loft design, many homes were now more open and uncluttered—the perfect locations for the sleek, minimalist design products that Turpan Sanders sold. People in "all walks of creative life" came to shop in the store, and its design sensibility was soon recognized as far away as Milan and Paris.[49]

Similarly, more mainstream home furnishing stores sought to capitalize on the loft aesthetic, selling "loft" products to those residing in all types of homes. As the *SoHo Weekly News* put it, "Living in a loft gives you a whole new dimension in space and space relationships to work with. And because of this, the tendency is to go 'industrial' usually to great advantage functionally and visually." Home decorators could create such a look by purchasing design elements at industrial stores such as Cook's Supply Corps, or at stores specifically catering to loft dwellers, such as the Carpet Loft in Lower Manhattan. In addition, popular department stores, such as Macy's, also entered the loft decorating market. In 1979, Macy's advertised its own line of loft furniture, including "Thayer Coggin's tech-inspired stadium seating for loft spaces," costing $100 to $300 per stackable unit.[50]

Artists and the SoHo Renaissance

By the late 1970s, a New Yorker could be inspired by the loft lifestyle in a magazine feature, pay someone to renovate a loft for him or her, buy products designed for or inspired by loft homes, and shop in loft-inspired stores. SoHo was a popular destination for shopping, and more and more New Yorkers were finding SoHo an attractive place to live. All these developments had their roots in the neighborhood's artistic identity. Local shoppers were most likely gallery visitors, and loft homes had evolved from the functional dwellings that artists first created. Moreover, many of the lifestyle innovators in SoHo, the ones driving its development as a retail center, were artists who used their artistic skills and sensibilities to shape their new businesses.

Not surprisingly, not everyone was happy with the growth of the loft aesthetic as a commodity. In 1974, immediately after *New York Magazine* declared SoHo "The Most Exciting Place to Live in the City," Jim Stratton of the *SoHo Weekly News* feared that the article would accelerate an existing trend of upper-income professionals migrating there. He argued that the article's featured "decorator lofts" encouraged wealthy New Yorkers to "buy a loft in SoHo and send an artist to Brooklyn." He wrote that when wealthy visitors came to SoHo, such as "C.P.A.s and investment brokers," to visit artists' lofts, "it is not their art they look at . . . only their real estate."[51]

Others lamented the blurring of the line between commerce and fine art. When Victoria Falls, an "antique" clothing store, replaced the theater space of the Byrd Hoffman Theater dance company in 1978, the boutique opened with a fashion show by artist Richard Foreman. The *SoHo Weekly News* dance critic Wendy Perron expressed concern: "Next thing you know, Dean & Deluca will ask Robert Morris to build cheese displays. [Supermarket] Grand Union will retaliate by trying to get Joseph Kosuth to design their sale signs. And Miso, the dress shop, will up the ante by planning a fashion show for next season, to be choreographed by Merce Cunningham. The possibilities opened by marrying art and commerce are endless—and rather offensive." Yet, even while fretting about this commercialization, Perron reasoned, "Maybe it's not so strange, though, that in a neighborhood where culture is commerce—even the paper I write for, after all, is deeply enmeshed in the network that packages art for sale—a clothing store would use art to merchandise goods."[52]

By 1980, some SoHo residents were actively resisting the commodification of the loft aesthetic, which they saw as contributing to rising rents. A group of loft tenants staged a protest at Bloomingdale's new designer showroom, "Soho Loft: A Studio Environment Steeped in Sincerity." The exhibit contained a massive pine breakfront, a canopy bed, white overstuffed couches, and $3,000 lamps. As reported in the *SoHo Weekly News*, artists surrounded the installation during the protest, with one remarking, "This display is offensive to loft dwellers. . . . It makes loft living look glamorous and chic, and it's not!" Another said, "I moved into a loft when it had nothing, I put $10,000 into improvements and now my landlord is selling it for $100,000 and throwing me out." The protest was the first of a series of events organized by the Lower Manhattan Tenants' Association. The group hoped to stage a protest at a furniture exhibition at the Museum of Modern Art, another institution it felt was driving up prices by commodifying and glamorizing the loft aesthetic.[53]

It is hard to determine the agents and victims of change in SoHo. Certainly, some early pioneers suffered as a result of the growing popularity of its new retail base. Increasing neighborhood amenities brought with them higher rents, which likely forced some residents from SoHo. Additionally, the growing retail sector changed the character of the neighborhood, making it less of an artist colony and more of a commercial district that also housed artists. Too many visitors could even be a problem for gallery owners. As SoHo pioneer Betty Cunningham said, by the late 1970s the crowds were so great that it became hard for people to stay in her gallery long enough to fall in love with, and subsequently purchase, any of the art. By the 1980s, the situation had reached a point of crisis.[54]

Yet artists themselves caused many of the changes that SoHo was undergoing during this era. It was not stockbrokers and lawyers whose lofts were profiled in the press but increasingly successful artists and art dealers. Members of the local artist community started Food, Dean & DeLuca, Turpan Sanders, and other establishments that, for better or for worse, altered the nature of area retail and made the neighborhood more attractive to outsiders. These actions, combined with the advocacy efforts that pushed the neighborhood into the public eye, increasingly put artists at the forefront of gentrification in SoHo.

8

The Spread of Loft Living: Real Estate Development and Tenant Conflict in SoHo and Beyond

By 1977, the residents of 55 Walker Street were fed up. Over the past few years, they had noticed with growing concern that many of their neighbors had been leaving the building—forced out, most would say. Rents were going up and there was increasing concern that the building's owner, Eli Lipkis, was putting pressure on those who remained, mostly artists with favorable leases, to leave. The building's tenants had several more reasons to be concerned. Most had put substantial capital into renovating their lofts or paid previous tenants fixture fees to cover these costs before moving in. More important, everyone lived in the building illegally. The loft in question was in Tribeca, the neighborhood located in the "*Tri*angle *Be*low *Ca*nal Street" southwest of SoHo, and most tenants had moved into the area when all loft living was illegal and the building's owner had made no attempt to obtain a certificate of occupancy. Despite their tenuous status, the residents decided to take a stand. After Lipkis had asked for yet another rent increase, they decided to start a rent strike and take their landlord to court. The actions of the residents at 55 Walker Street were surprisingly common. As tenant Mario Pikus put it, "Go to Civil Court any day. You're going to find between 20 and 30 people who live in lofts."[1]

Throughout the 1960s and early 1970s, when artists moved into loft units vacated by industry, conflicts between landlords and tenants infrequently, if ever, occurred. Artist tenants were more worried about being forced from their homes by building inspectors than by rent increases. Similarly, loft building owners had incentive to keep their rent-paying residential tenants. Although they would have loved to replace an artist with a higher-paying industrial tenant, such renters were harder and harder to come by.

The situation changed in the mid-1970s. Whereas renting to an artist was only an emergency stopgap for loft owners in the 1960s and early 1970s, by the mid-1970s landlords realized that they could charge residential tenants higher rents. They began to see their low-paying industrial and artist tenants as impediments to profits rather than ways to keep their properties above water until higher-paying industrial tenants could be found. Residential loft demand increased both the rents that landlords could charge residents and the areas in which residential conversions took place. Loft demand pushed past the boundaries of SoHo and into the neighboring areas of Tribeca and NoHo (the area north of Houston Street to the northeast of SoHo) and beyond. Policy makers and local real estate interests took note and pushed for changes that would allow significant numbers of lofts to be converted into residences across Lower Manhattan.

The rise in loft demand also created a new and diverse group of loft speculators and developers. Longtime loft building owners with ties to SoHo industry, members of the neighborhood art community, and those who made their living developing real estate all invested in neighborhood lofts. Despite their varied backgrounds, property owners used many of the same tactics to exploit the rising market for loft residences. Some increased rents while others used the still-illegal status of some residents to push them out in favor of higher-paying tenants. Although their legal status was secure, low-paying industrial tenants faced some of the same problems. Building owners did not renew leases of many of these enterprises, or they demanded outrageous rent increases in order to clear out their buildings for more lucrative residential conversions. The illegal status of many loft rentals left them outside New York's rent control laws.

However, tenants fought back when SoHo building owners and policy makers attempted to expand residential conversions. Artists once again organized politically, but in contrast to earlier actions, they sought to limit any policy changes that would allow more people to legally move into lofts and inflate the already booming residential market. In particular, artist groups pushed back against any new policies that would make it legal for nonartists to live legally in lofts. In response to landlords' efforts to increase rents and force tenants from their homes, loft residents throughout Lower Manhattan turned their homes into battlegrounds, holding rent strikes, taking their owners to court, and bringing their cause to the local press. As a result, as the 1970s drew to a close, SoHo began to experience some of the conflicts associated with contemporary gentrification. It was clear that without meaningful policy change, the neighborhood was at risk of both losing its character and falling into real estate chaos.

Loft Demand in the 1970s

Changes in the demand for industrial and residential lofts fueled SoHo's development in the mid-1970s. Loft prices, both for rentals and entire buildings, shot up during this period, with nonartists fueling some of this demand. At the same time, people converted lofts into homes across a wider swath of Lower Manhattan, pushing the phenomenon beyond SoHo's borders. This action was problematic because SoHo was still the only place where anyone could legally convert a loft into a home. Finally, at mid decade it became apparent that residential lofts were no longer supporting industrial businesses by providing an income stream that kept some landlords afloat. Instead, the rise in demand for residential lofts threatened to push remaining industrial businesses out of the area.

The increase in demand for SoHo loft space coincided with some of the most intense years of New York's urban crisis. The city lost eighty-two thousand residents during the 1970s, and abandoned buildings were common across the city, most prominently in the Lower East Side and the South Bronx.[2] The South Bronx lost forty-three thousand housing units during the 1970s, many due to owners setting fire to valueless properties for insurance money: New Yorkers set thirty thousand fires in the South Bronx alone from 1973 to 1977. In 1975, the city nearly defaulted on its credit obligations, leading to a severe fiscal crisis, cuts to the city workforce, and a major drop in municipal services. The fiscal crisis left the city unable to adequately combat a rise in crime and control the explosion of graffiti in its subways. New York faced an image crisis as well. The films *Death Wish* (1974) and *Taxi Driver* (1975) created an entire subgenre of "asphalt jungle" and "New York exploitation" movies; the city was quickly becoming a stand-in for the nation's postwar urban ills. Launching what were perhaps the worst months in the city's history, the summer of 1977 brought the highest temperatures on record, the threat of the "Son of Sam" serial killer, and a twenty-five-hour blackout that exposed New York's crumbling infrastructure and social rifts. More than two thousand businesses were looted, and neighborhoods already affected by disinvestment and population loss experienced widespread damage. That October, a fire burned out of control during game two of the World Series at Yankee Stadium, creating the apocryphal tale that announcer Howard Cosell declared on national television, "The Bronx is burning."[3] Loft demand spiked at a time when bottom-up real estate development was scarce, good news was infrequent, and city leaders lacked the time and resources to address any negative policy consequences that might result from this upturn.

Loft prices rose steadily at the beginning of the 1970s and accelerated further at mid decade. According to figures reported in the press, mostly anonymously due to the still tenuous legal status of loft apartments, loft rents increased sharply starting in the mid-1970s. While SoHo lofts rented from anywhere between $100 and $200 per month in the 1960s, by 1970 (when the average rent for a much smaller average New York City apartment was $99 per month), SoHo rents were closer to $200 to $300 per month for a standard loft. By 1974, SoHo loft space cost closer to $350 to $450 per month.[4]

Scholars confirm the rising demand and rents for residential lofts throughout the 1970s. Sharon Zukin found that beginning in the late 1960s and early 1970s, rents in SoHo climbed toward, and eventually surpassed, the "acceptable market rent for a one-to-three room apartment for a Middle Class Manhattanite" of $350 to $450 a month. Zukin observed that rents increased abruptly in SoHo after 1968, and by 1970 average advertised rents of $300 to $400 a month outnumbered lower rents. Lofts began to rent for $500 to $800 per month in 1971, and by 1975 some renters paid $1,000 per month. By 1978, Zukin found that "the $800-$1,000-a-month rents dominated the market, closely followed, however, by $300-$400 lofts."[5] While lower rent lofts still existed, SoHo became an increasingly high-rent area during the 1970s, leading those in search of cheap apartments to look to other neighborhoods.

Analysis of property records from this period also demonstrates a rise in sale prices for loft buildings. As Table 3 indicates, it was not uncommon for properties in SoHo to double, triple, or even quadruple in price when sold from the late 1960s to the early 1980s. Although SoHo buildings could be had for less than $25,000 in the late 1960s and early 1970s, prices ran closer to the mid–six figures by the 1980s.[6]

By 1975, a *SoHo Weekly News* headline declared that the "SoHo Romance Is Over" due to rising costs. The paper argued that artists' work in converting lofts into attractive homes, and increasing their value in the process, brought on the neighborhood's decline as an artist colony. The paper contended, "In fact it was the artist himself who fouled his own nest. His bourgeois desires, his industriousness at fixing up his nest, his civilizing influence on a warehouse neighborhood made the invasion possible." As a result, artists were being priced out of their own community. The paper noted, "Very soon artists were not going to be able to afford to live in the area unless they were highly successful, privately wealthy, or employed full time." Besides the work artists put into converting lofts into residences, artistic tourism in SoHo played a role. "It's like part of Disneyland," one artist complained. "You know, they have Adventure Land. This is Art Land."[7]

In turn, nonartists who were attracted to the unique nature of loft space helped drive the demand for lofts. Observers noted that there was a

TABLE 3. Sale Prices for Select Buildings in the South Houston Industrial Area, 1968–1985

Address	Sale Date	Price ($)	% Change
489 Broadway	1970	50,000	
	1979	64,300	29%
	1984	325,000	405%
491 Broadway	1971	65,649	
	1975	147,369	124%
501 Broadway	1969	57,500	
	1982	100,000	74%
503 Broadway	1968	50,000	
	1982	140,0000	180%
535 Broadway	1967	55,000	
	1982	250,000	355%
	1984	230,000	−8%
547 Broadway	1979	170,000	
	1983	445,000	162%
565 Broadway	1968	13,517	
	1975	70,000	418%
	1977	119,247	70%
581 Broadway	1981	140,000	
	1981	825,000	489%
599 Broadway	1978	800,000	
	1981	2,370,000	196%
484 Broome St.	1970	250,000	
	1979	300,000	20%
492 Broome St.	1970	50,000	
	1976	120,000	140%
64 Greene St.	1968	13,500	
	1984	400,000	196%
68 Greene St.	1970	53,000	
	1980	120,000	126%
102 Greene St.	1967	20,000	
	1968	37,000	85%
	1975	37,016	0.04%
110 Greene St.	1966	50,000	
	1969	90,000	80%
139 Greene St.	1968	13,000	
	1973	56,000	331%
143 Greene St.	1969	4,000	
	1972	49,862	1,147%
79 Mercer St.	1966	27,500	
	1985	300,000	991%
103 Mercer St.	1967	20,000	
	1970	100,000	400%
127 Mercer St.	1971	125,000	
	1980	561,000	349%
169 Mercer St.	1969	43,000	
	1980	284,000	560%
137 Prince St.	1970	75,000	
	1971	108,947	45%

TABLE 3. (continued)

Address	Sale Date	Price ($)	% Change
143 Prince St.	1970	66,075	
	1973	137,000	107%
96 Spring St.	1973	135,184	
	1981	825,000	510%
118 Spring St.	1973	53,000	
	1983	600,000	1,032%
119 Spring St.	1967	40,000	
	1971	33,231	−17%
120 Spring St.	1969	12,500	
	1973	24,875	99%
145 Spring St.	1968	36,600	
	1973	80,000	119%
150 Spring St.	1966	20,000	
	1974	42,250	111%
	1979	162,042	284%
457 West Broadway	1970	97,000	
	1974	211,000	118%
465 West Broadway	1967	130,000	
	1968	124,500	−5%
477 West Broadway	1967	10,000	
	1984	200,000	1,900%
61 Wooster St.	1976	195,000	
	1983	1,445,000	641%
	1985	2,700,000	87%
64 Wooster St.	1971	374,338	
	1976	325,000	−13%
101 Wooster St.	1968	95,000	
	1977	110,000	16%
134 Wooster St.	1969	44,000	
	1972	106,000	141%
	1985	600,000	466%
135 Wooster St.	1968	37,000	
	1971	45,000	22%

"considerable appeal" for loft residences among "a significant number of young affluent non-artist households who also were not put off" by "SoHo's industrial ambience."[8] Although artists continued to move into lofts in and around SoHo, this new group of potentially more affluent loft dwellers did much to increase demand.

People in "creative" professions, such as advertising and publishing, who were not artists in the traditional sense of the word, found loft living increasingly attractive. Although hard data are difficult to obtain because nonartists could not live in the spaces legally, contemporary observers noticed an increase of nonartists living in lofts during the middle of the 1970s. In 1976,

Ingrid Weigand, a founding member of the SoHo Artists Association (SAA), wrote in the *SoHo Weekly News* that SoHo was "in the middle of a larger City and real-estate campaign to take over lofts and make them into fancy apartments for non-artists" because the "swinging single" and members of the "Madison Avenue crowd" were buying SoHo lofts at inflated prices. Whereas "$500 a month for 2,500 square feet is astronomical for an artist," it was "a bargain-basement price for a hip entrepreneur or art director who is already paying that for his one-and-a-half room, cubby size 'studio.'"[9]

Academics, particularly from local universities, also found homes in large, inexpensive, eye-catching lofts. SoHo resident and author Richard Kostelanetz reported that "Margaret Smith Burke, an NYU professor of educational psychology, bought into our co-op in 1975 with her husband, the visual artist Michael Burke, and stayed after he left. Annette Michelson, a professor of film, rented here in 1976; her colleague in film history, Robert Sklar, bought elsewhere in SoHo a year later." Similar to the creative professionals who increasingly made their homes in lofts, it was the more artistic academics who were drawn to loft living. According to Kostelanetz, professors at New York University's Tisch School of the Arts were more likely to live in SoHo lofts than were professors in the College of Arts and Sciences. Nevertheless, these relatively high-income academics helped increase loft demand.[10]

Compounding the problem, artists continued to move into SoHo and the surrounding area in greater numbers. A Department of City Planning report found that, of a sample of two hundred artists living in SoHo and NoHo in 1983, 20 percent had moved to their current residences from 1969 to 1973, 26 percent between 1974 and 1978, and 50 percent from 1979 to 1983.[11]

Investors began to take notice of the appeal of lofts to both middle-class artists and nonartists. A 1975 article in *Real Estate Weekly* alerted that "Artist-In-Residence Loft Conversion Can Offer Investment Opportunity." It highlighted the growing appeal of lofts to "the City's middle-income dweller" as well as the profits that could be made investing in this building type. Overall, the article stated, prices for lofts in Lower Manhattan had risen from $1 to $2 per square foot in the 1940s to $10 per square foot in the mid-1970s. The piece profiled Stephen Freidus of Andover Realty, who had helped twenty clients buy artist-in-residence properties attractive to "artistic professionals or professional artists," as well as another who paid $375,000 for a building at 20–6 Wooster Street that he then sold to individual owners as part of a co-op. It also chronicled the history of a building at 71–73 Grand Street back to 1941, when it was first sold by a savings bank, which had foreclosed on the property to an investor for $52,000. In 1946, it was sold again for $69,500. However, in 1974 an investor bought the building for $266,250 and filed plans for an alteration into artists' lofts. Six months later, the property sold again for $435,700. As Max H. Lustington of Murrimac Realty Co. observed in the article, "Just think! If the original purchaser had the prescience, he could have worked up his original cash investment of $10,000 into a profit of over $400,000."[12]

The demand for SoHo loft space also led to an overall increase in the area's population. In the two census tracts that encompassed SoHo, and some in the surrounding areas of Little Italy and Chinatown where there were more traditional apartment buildings, population decreased from 6,753 to 5,746 from 1950 to 1960, likely due to the threat of urban renewal. By 1970, the population had rebounded to 5,900, a modest increase of 154 residents that likely does not represent the numerous illegal tenants in SoHo at the time. However, by 1980, the number of residents captured by census data increased to 7,408, a 25 percent rise in ten years that would likely have been much higher if it took into account the large number of illegal tenants.[13]

At the same time, demand for loft residences pushed beyond the boundaries of SoHo. A 1975 Real Estate Board of New York study revealed that loft conversions were taking place extensively in SoHo and NoHo as well as in Midtown South from Fourteenth Street to Thirty-fourth Street.[14] A year later, the Department of City Planning found that close to half the loft buildings in the industrial areas of Madison Square, NoHo, and the northeast portion of Greenwich Village had undergone some conversion activity, along with one-third of industrial buildings in SoHo and Tribeca, and one-quarter in the Midtown South and Midtown commercial business districts.[15] Most of this conversion activity was illegal, as SoHo remained the only neighborhood where living in a loft had the sanction of the law.

In an ironic twist, it was exactly at this moment that industrial employment began to stabilize. Though manufacturing jobs in New York dropped by twenty-five thousand to twenty-six thousand per year between 1969 and 1975, they fell by only two thousand per year from 1975 to 1980. This meant that demand for lofts among industrial tenants remained steady as residential demand spiked. As a result, space in loft buildings quickly came at a premium.[16]

The Expansion of Loft Living?

As the demand for loft housing began to exceed the supply of legal units, investors and policy makers formulated a number of potential solutions. The city's real estate interests focused on the economic potential of loft residences and advocated for a general legalization of conversions. In contrast, members of the City Planning Commission (CPC) and the mayor's office prioritized industrial uses for lofts while recognizing the growing demand for them among a wider segment of the population. These policy makers sought a balance between artist housing, industry, and the new demands of the residential housing market.

The Real Estate Board of New York presented a plan for an updated loft policy in a 1975 study, *Residential Use of Manhattan Loft Buildings: Analysis and Recommendations*. The board urged the city to take advantage of "SoHo's spectacular transition from a declining industrial area to a mixed-use district containing artist/residents, and businesses related to the arts and its emergence as a world-renowned art center" that "triggered a demand for loft living among non-artists in other loft districts." It continued, "Loft living appears to be a truly viable alternative use for thousands of square feet of vacant loft space now on the market" and recommended that the city and state legalize loft living as widely as possible.[17]

The city's acute fiscal crisis and continuing deindustrialization made the public support of expanded loft conversions even more urgent. The New York Real Estate Board contended that the city should take advantage of a model through which "self-regeneration and renewal of entire districts" took place "without public expenditures," something that was sorely needed at a time when the city's fiscal crisis had ground to a halt the public sector's efforts to create housing. At the same time, the board did not look on New York's industrial future with great optimism. It found that foreclosures in Manhattan loft buildings increased sharply after 1973, from nine that fiscal year to thirty-six a year later. Furthermore, industrial buildings below Thirty-fourth Street in Manhattan housed 4.1 million feet of vacant space, a number that represented 31 percent of the total rentable space in those buildings. Like industry throughout the city and the region, SoHo businesses were moving to areas of the country that offered newer space at lower rents, areas where they could also take advantage of reduced taxes and labor costs.[18]

The Real Estate Board put forth several specific proposals, all of which would have expanded legalized loft residences in New York. Its suggestions included amending the New York City Zoning Resolution to allow loft conversions on the upper floors of all residential buildings smaller than 7,500 square feet and located below Fortieth Street in Manhattan, and changing the state Multiple Dwelling Law to make living in a loft legal for nonartists. The board did recommend that loft living in SoHo and NoHo be restricted to artists "to preserve the vital cluster of people and businesses connected with the arts which has emerged in the last few years." But it believed that loft conversions should be allowed in the rest of the city. The board also suggested changes in the procedures for gaining a certificate of occupancy for a loft, as along with provisions to protect the leases of industrial loft tenants from severe rent increases.[19]

While real estate interests focused mostly on the role of lofts in the residential real estate market, government agencies recommended balancing the needs of industry, landlords, and tenants. In 1976, the New York City Department of City Planning (DCP) and the Mayor's Midtown Action Office published *Residential Re-Use of Non-Residential Buildings in Manhattan*, which outlined these agencies' stances on loft conversions. Their priorities, in order of importance, were to "1. Insure the economic viability of industrial and commercial building types; 2. protect manufacturing jobs from the impact of unregulated conversion activity; 3. provide new housing."[20]

Instead of arguing for more conversions, the agencies' report expressed concern over the impact of residential lofts on industrial jobs. Despite the struggles of local industry, loft neighborhoods were still centers of industrial employment. The DCP and Midtown Action Office found that 74.6 percent of the 306,298 industrial jobs in Manhattan were in Midtown South, SoHo, NoHo, and Tribeca. Yet they reported that as of September 1977, 1,023 industrial buildings in Manhattan south of 59th Street, or 23.5 percent of all Lower Manhattan lofts, had undergone total or partial conversion to residential use.[21]

Moreover, the agencies were concerned that the bulk of loft conversions were still taking place illegally. Fewer than 10 percent of the buildings in their study (87 out of 1,000) had a valid certificate of occupancy. This "unregulated new form of housing development" left resident safety to chance and forced owners of cooperative units and loft buildings to operate in a climate of uncertainty.[22]

This lack of regulation was even more of a problem due to the entry of larger investors into the residential loft market. The DCP and Midtown Action Office observed that speculators were beginning to invest in lofts to take advantage of the relatively low cost of renovations and the potential for large profits. They found that developers had been entering the residential loft market on numerous levels. Artists and other small-time investors had been converting loft buildings in SoHo and Lower Manhattan for a decade. The report gave the example of a group that invested a relatively small amount of capital, $60,000, to buy a building at Twenty-seventh Street and Broadway, in which they planned to rent space to artists who could complete renovations of their own apartments. Because developers ignored building department regulations, the property did not have a certificate of occupancy and therefore did not benefit from any city tax-relief programs, such as those provided under the J-51 program.[23]

In contrast, some loft buyers acted more like formal real estate speculators. For example, a group of investors purchased two loft buildings at 73 Warren Street in Tribeca and 55 East Eleventh Street in Midtown South after obtaining $60,000 in private capital used as a down payment. The investors then secured a construction loan, renovated the buildings, and sold raw lofts as artists' co-ops. Each unit took up one floor, was two thousand square feet, and rented for $300 to $400 per month. These buildings had a certificate of occupancy and benefited from the J-51 program.[24]

Finally, larger developers also entered into the industrial conversion market. The DCP and Midtown Action Office reported that a group of "prominent real estate developers" purchased buildings at 88 Lexington Avenue in Midtown South and 160 Bleecker Street in NoHo. The group obtained $2 million in loans, put $1 million down, and got $3 million in other financing to convert the buildings into 170, 650-square-foot studio and one-bedroom apartments that rented for $350 to $600 per month. Since the investors were very concerned about their return on investment and had significant capital at stake, they obtained a zoning variance from the Board of Standards and Appeals so that the building was legal, and they were able to benefit from the J-51 program.[25]

In their policy proposals, the DCP and Midtown Action Office's overarching goals were to create a safe and stable mixed-use area, one where residents and industry could coexist under a set of functioning laws and regulations that would properly address the reuse of industrial buildings. Their aims included sorting out the overlapping city agencies governing loft conversions through the formation of an intergovernmental committee on loft conversions staffed by the Department of City Planning and the Mayor's Midtown Action Office, with cooperation from real estate, industry, labor groups, and local community boards. They hoped to accomplish these goals by making it easier for loft residents to obtain certificates of occupancy, enforcing existing building department codes and regulations, and increasing awareness of loft policy among developers, residents, and the public.[26]

Both reports found loft policy lacking but provided different rationales for its failure and proposed distinct solutions. The Real Estate Board of New York believed that the central issue was that demand for legal residential lofts exceeded supply. Its solution was to legalize enough lofts to meet market demand. Resident safety and preserving industry were not central concerns. On the other hand, the DCP and Midtown Action Office were dedicated to preserving a mixed-use industrial and residential area in Lower Manhattan through the enforcement of the current statute and the creation of new policies. Interestingly, neither study concentrated extensively on the needs of artist residents or the problems that rising loft rents could pose to current industrial and residential tenants.

The debates over loft policy quickly moved beyond the theoretical. Due to the large influx of loft tenants into the neighborhoods of NoHo and Tribeca (both immediately adjacent to SoHo), public officials had to consider whether expanding the right to live in a residential loft was good for the city and its economy. In these neighborhoods policy makers discussed the possibility of legalizing loft housing for nonartists. During the debates, a remarkable turnabout occurred: for the first time, artists contended that it was better for them to live illegally than for city leaders to further legalize loft living, which would have led to increased demand and further rent increases.

Government officials first addressed the demand for loft living beyond SoHo's borders in Tribeca, an industrial area once dominated by the butter and egg trades. By 1974, Tribeca already showed signs of following in SoHo's footsteps; it was dotted with loft homes, galleries, restaurants, and shops, as well as its share of vacant lofts. Like SoHo, Tribeca was also home to some attractive examples of cast-iron architecture, such as the building at 868–88 Franklin, with its "massive cast-iron pillars climbing six stories by the delicate contrast of the slender Corinthian leaf-topped columns on either side of the wide windows."[27]

Furthermore, by 1974, the neighborhood had already seen illegal conversion activity. That year, the recently created New York City Office of Lower Manhattan Development undertook a study that found that "a number of old loft, warehouse, manufacturing and office buildings," many of which had gained landmark status, had "been bought up by land speculators and real estate entrepreneurs for present and future residential conversions." As a result, real estate prices were as expensive as equivalent buildings in the high-rent areas of Midtown and the Upper East and West Sides. The report found that artists were often the first ones to reside in the neighborhood's lofts and often did so illegally. However, it reported that the "'illegal residence' situation will not persist" because "there are always those looking for unique and, at times, inexpensive dwelling units within Manhattan." The report recommended that the city quickly adopt a policy that would make loft residences legal for these nonartists.[28]

Residents found loft space in Tribeca as a result of the area's deindustrialization. In 1974, Jim Stratton of the *SoHo Weekly News* reported that a closer look at Tribeca "reveals a multitude of half-empty office buildings and warehouses where no artist has ever tread" due to the flight of light industry. He also wrote that the city itself had encouraged the flight of industry through its urban renewal policies. New York City officials had moved Washington Market, a fruit, vegetable, and dairy wholesaling market once prominent in the area, to the Bronx in 1956.[29] In fact, many people once called the entire area Washington Market. The new name "Tribeca" was a sign that the neighborhood was following in SoHo's postindustrial footsteps.

Thus, Stratton, among others, believed that Tribeca was ready to become the next SoHo. As he wrote in 1974, SoHo "gave the outside world the first clearcut indication in many years that there is still life and creativity in the 'dying' central city." Because SoHo also "proved the feasibility of converting unused mercantile space into entirely suitable housing," he contended that it was not possible for other neighborhoods, such as Tribeca, to redevelop in the same manner.[30]

The CPC agreed with Stratton, and in October 1975 it proposed new zoning ordinances for Tribeca and NoHo that would allow buildings in these areas to be "converted to productive use in a manner similar to the transformation of SoHo." However, in contrast to SoHo, the commission proposed that residency privileges in these areas would not be limited to artists.[31] Thus, for the first time, city officials considered legalizing loft residences for nonartists in a New York City neighborhood.

Of course, when contemplating opening up additional loft space for residences, city leaders did not totally ignore the plight of industry in Lower Manhattan. The CPC's new zoning proposal included provisions that would prohibit future residential conversions in the "Broadway Corridor," which contained larger lofts where industry was thought to be more viable. The plan also restricted conversions of the bottom two floors of loft buildings, thought to be more useful for industrial and commercial uses.[32]

Not everyone was so sanguine about Tribeca industry. In response to these efforts to preserve industrial jobs, writers at the *SoHo Weekly News* argued that attempts to protect industry in the neighborhood were misguided and would instead benefit real estate investors looking to profit from the rise in loft demand at the expense of artists. A 1975 editorial stated, "To believe that the city is merely misdirected in its notion of preserving the rag, garment and light manufacturing industries merely by setting up rigid conditions reserving space for them is to put a very polite face on the proposals. More important are the real estate, banking and construction interests." The paper argued that restricting the number of lofts that could be legally converted into homes along Broadway would only drive up prices for SoHo rentals, adversely affecting artists and benefiting property owners. Further, in a separate 1976 article, a staffer wrote that a proposal to reserve the bottom two floors of loft buildings for industrial tenants would drive artists out of SoHo: "Since manufacturing tenants are almost impossible to find, even at giveaway prices, the upper floors would have to carry the building, whether rental or coop units, putting an end to artists' housing in SoHo" by requiring residential tenants to pay even higher prices due to rising loft demand and limited supply.³³

The proposed zoning changes in Tribeca and NoHo also drew a negative response from local artists. In marked contrast to early policy proposals, where loft residents welcomed any changes that would legalize additional residences and prevent possible evictions, news of loft legalizations in Tribeca caused distress among artists. In December 1974, the Washington Market Community Association, a Tribeca-area group, organized a tour of the neighborhood for Manhattan borough president Percy Sutton, city council members Henry Stern, Miriam Friedlander, and Robert F. Wagner Jr., and Ira Goldman of the Office of Lower Manhattan Development. The group designed the tour so that the officials "could view firsthand the peaceful coexistence of loft dwellers and businesses in the community" and "resist intensive pressure from city and state agencies for rezoning and land use that would kill the growing loft community." In a November 1975 hearing on the proposed policies, local artists spoke out against the suggested changes, arguing "that the onset of legality and new housing standards in NoHo would, in addition to being a boon for real estate interests, open the area to a professional class that enjoys loft living," driving up rents in the process. One said that the situation in SoHo resembled one common throughout history, where "An artist finds a pigsty.... He rises above it because of his art and he's punished for it. And he's being punished again."³⁴

In early 1976, local residents reorganized the SAA and formed new committees. Loft tenants gained further impetus for organizing as a result of the CPC's decision to show the new zoning proposals to the Real Estate Board of New York for review but not to current loft residents. This action stoked fears that the new zoning proposals were designed to allow real estate interests to profit from the rising demand for loft residences at the expense of residents.³⁵

Tellingly, artists contended that they would rather continue to live in their lofts illegally because illegality dampened demand and prices for loft space. David Milne, a representative of the NoHo Artists' Association (formed in 1976), argued that NoHo artists "prefer to continue to live illegally if NoHo is going to be turned into high-income housing, which is what will happen if doctors, lawyers and other professional people are permitted to move into what they look upon as a fashionable, trendy place to live." The consequences of the increased loft demand resulting from legalization were foremost in artists' minds. The *New York Times* reported that although artists at the meetings appreciated "the chance to rent or buy space ideally suited to their needs, they are concerned that SoHo is becoming a tourist attraction and is sprouting discotheques and juice bars, which they regard as undesirable in a working and living neighborhood."[36]

This was a remarkable turn of events. For almost a decade, artists had formed political organizations, gone on strike, and marched on City Hall, all for the cause of loft legalization. Now many of the same people contended that they faced a greater risk of eviction at the hands of an unregulated real estate market than from a city official. They maintained that to keep their lofts, they would rather live illegally to keep some wealthier residents out of the loft market. This sentiment speaks to both the robustness of the real estate market for residential lofts and the inefficacy of regulations related to loft living. Artists felt strongly that they would be far more likely to be evicted by a speculator than a city inspector.

Much as they did in the early 1960s and 1970s, artists recruited notable representatives from the art world to argue that artist housing should be protected because of the important contributions the artists made to the city's economy. At a January 1976 hearing, representatives of SoHo's art community reiterated that Lower Manhattan artists provided important cultural and financial benefits to the city. Kent Barwick of the Municipal Art Society claimed that artists generated $3 billion in sales and $12 million in taxes a year. Louis Meisel argued that SoHo art brought greater tourist dollars into New York City because "art visitors spend more than any other tourists." He testified that visitors to SoHo and the surrounding areas spent more than those looking for art in other areas of the city, including New York's older gallery center, Madison Avenue. Other speakers said that "artists had created a thriving downtown art industry," and that the "art galleries, restaurants, theaters and stores supplying the raw materials used by artists had multiplied around the loft buildings," breathing new economic life into the city. Among the speakers was Ivan Karp, who said that developers looking "to prey on businesses and artists" by turning the city's loft districts into blocks of luxury apartment buildings threatened artists. He urged city leaders to protect and encourage New York's artist communities by passing zoning laws that were sensitive to their housing needs.[37]

In the end, the final zoning ordinance that was passed for NoHo and Tribeca in June 1976 embodied the tension city officials felt among providing affordable artist housing, protecting industry, and using loft conversions as an urban development technique. The ordinance allowed only artists to live in converted loft buildings in NoHo, and it expanded the number of properties in SoHo that artists could convert to residential use.[38] However, a separate zoning ordinance passed for Tribeca made it legal for the first time for nonartists to occupy residential lofts. These actions showed a growing awareness of the demand for lofts among a broader population and of the power of loft conversions to revitalize industrial neighborhoods. One measure designed to protect industry in Lower Manhattan also remained in the final zoning ordinance: a restriction that prohibited residences on the first and second floors of loft buildings, areas that were thought to be more attractive to manufacturing for commercial use.[39] This restriction demonstrated a continued ambivalence on the part of city officials toward loft living and a desire to prevent an increasing area of Lower Manhattan from fully transitioning from industrial to residential use. By limiting legal loft conversions in NoHo to artists, city leaders indicated a desire to both increase industrial job retention and provide housing for artists, while enabling the city to continue to reap the benefits of artistic production in SoHo and NoHo. However, in the end, the policies represented a significant expansion in legal loft conversions, indicating that city leaders were responding to the rise in loft demand among all New Yorkers.

Policy makers did not forsake the cause of real estate development altogether. In 1976 the New York State Legislature, with the support of the mayor's office, modified a long-standing tax abatement program in the New York City Administrative Code in order to cover, and thus encourage, conversions of industrial lofts into homes. Starting that year, the city's J-51 tax program gave substantial property tax reductions to landlords who converted their nonresidential buildings to residences. First started in 1955 to encourage building owners to install central heating and improve plumbing and sanitary conditions in their buildings, the program allowed owners to deduct the amount their property values increased due to renovations from the property tax bill for the next twelve years, and it abated taxes for at least fifteen years.[40]

The program demonstrated once again that city officials used public policy to encourage the conversion of industrial lofts into housing to spark residential development. Zukin argued that the J-51 program was among the important state interventions in the loft market that benefited large developers. She wrote that, in general, this program's effect was the turnover of loft apartments to higher-income tenants and that J-51 played a critical role in the deindustrialization of Lower Manhattan.[41] Moreover, when the administration of Mayor Ed Koch enacted a more extensive loft policy (see chapter 9), restrictions on the J-51 program were an important concession to both artist residents and industrial tenants.

However, other evidence indicates that the J-51 program's impact on New York real estate was somewhat muted. Although city leaders wanted to encourage loft housing, banks were not yet willing to invest substantial capital in this new housing form. The *New York Times* reported in August 1976, "Despite the bankers' professed interest in conversion, many real-estate owners say it is difficult to obtain mortgage money for conversions from the city's banks" even with the expanded J-51 program. For example, Lincoln Savings Bank, which had invested close to $100 million in J-51 properties in the mid-1970s, stopped investing in them two years later due to lack of profitability. As a result of the banks' reluctance to invest, the CPC found that only 3 percent of all industrial conversions (legal and illegal) received J-51 tax benefits in 1976.[42] In either case, for the second time in less than a year, city leaders took action to encourage loft conversions as a form of urban development.

Property Owners, Developers, and Residents: Loft Conflict in SoHo and Beyond

The rising demand for loft residences also led to a series of conflicts between landlords and tenants over specific loft buildings. Landlords sought to exploit the expanding market for residential lofts in Lower Manhattan by raising rents, or even by engaging in less savory practices, such as denying services or using the still-illegal nature of loft living as a strategy for replacing low-paying tenants with wealthier ones. In response, both residential and industrial tenants staged rent strikes, filed suits, and involved their elected representatives in their cause.

The unique nature of loft property ownership shaped the conflict between landlord and tenant in Lower Manhattan. Building owners included those who bought their property long before artists moved into the area. In addition, individual and small groups of investors bought loft buildings with the hope of converting them into profitable residential properties. These investors included gallery owners, art patrons, and artists who sometimes developed properties for other artists and other times for a combination of artists and nonartists. Companies with more substantial property holdings, firms that could be called real estate developers, invested in lofts by the end of the 1970s. However, large-scale investors did not dominate the market or drive the process of investment in SoHo.

Tenants and their allegiances also varied. Loft renters included artists, industrial businesses, and nonartists. Of course, all tenants wanted to maintain the use of their lofts at a fair price, which meant keeping rents low. All groups at times faced the potential of being replaced by a higher-paying tenant. Yet alliances and conflicts between tenants could also vary. Sometimes artists stood with industrial tenants against developers and new, nonartist tenants. Other times, artists and nonartist residents stood together against their landlords. Finally, upper-income artists could sometimes pay higher rents than industrial businesses and thus posed a threat to these enterprises.

Additionally, members of each group could act as either landlord or tenant. While some industrial businesses struggled to make ends meet at a time of increasing loft rents, some industrial business owners also owned lofts. These landlords often became involved in conflicts with their artist and industrial tenants over the price of loft space. While some artists feared being forced from their homes, other artists and people associated with the arts became landlords and battled with their industrial and artist tenants over the cost and legality of loft space. Some nonartist residents helped drive the rise in loft prices, while others found themselves in the same position as artists—vulnerable to fluctuations in rent and the speculative actions of landlords.

Loft owners who had purchased buildings before artists moved to SoHo were some of the first to profit from the increasing demand for lofts. Because artists rented otherwise vacant space, early residential tenants helped longtime SoHo landlords at least make more money, if not necessarily a profit, from their buildings. Yet, as demand for loft residences rose, building owners who possessed property zoned for industry soon became residential landlords. While many amicably coexisted with their tenants, and quite a few even helped artists become loft owners themselves, others began to act more like speculators. This often meant using underhanded means to remove both industrial and artist tenants to make room for wealthier renters.

An industrial building owner could act as a speculator by investing no money and following the law, at least some of the time. It was typical for building owners to rent "raw space" to artists illegally, leaving it up to the renter to install flooring, bathrooms, kitchen, and everything else necessary to make a loft livable. The customary practice was to allow the tenants who conducted such renovations to charge a new tenant a "fixture fee" to cover the cost of the renovations when the loft changed hands. However, the tenants had no legal ownership over their fixtures, and most did not even have a legal right to rent the space in which they lived. Thus, "a favorite ploy by certain loft landlords has been to offer an empty space and a long-term lease, sit back until the renovation has been completed, and then step in with a building inspector at his side to evict the hapless tenant for illegal living," later renting the property at a higher rate.[43] Thus, with no investment on their part, landlords could flip lofts for higher-paying tenants using current loft policy to facilitate the process.

As example of an industrial building owner turned speculator was Morris Moskowitz, whose tenants Ehrlich and Scarlet West accused him of threatening to evict them from their loft at 510 Broome Street in order to increase the building's rental income. Moskowitz's family owned the building before artists started moving into SoHo, and he almost certainly had no plans to rent to residential tenants when he got into the real estate business.[44] Speculating in residential real estate was something that Moskowitz likely did without prior planning. His transition into a residential landlord came about due to the unique circumstances in which he found himself as a SoHo building owner.

Yet Moskowitz soon became one of the longtime building owners who took advantage of the legal position of his loft tenants. The tenants in question said Moskowitz was reneging on promises to provide building amenities such as elevator service and heat seven days a week and was cutting back on necessary maintenance for important building structures, including fire escapes. This tactic was not unusual for the area. Even when they had knowingly rented lofts to people who planned to live in the space, landlords would fail to provide these services under the pretense of giving building amenities to only the "commercial" and "industrial" tenants who used the building on weekdays. The tenants accused Moskowitz of withholding building amenities in order to force out his residential occupants. The residents of 510 Broome Street noticed that Moskowitz advertised the property for sale in the *Village Voice* in 1975 and claimed that the building earned $60,000 in rental income per year, a figure that their rents inflated. In the end, Moskowitz decided not to sell the building, perhaps recognizing the potential for rents from residential tenants in the long term. His family owns the building to this day.[45]

The strike at 55 Walker Street also involved a longtime building owner. As in Moskowitz's case, it was unlikely that Eli Lipkis purchased his loft building to speculate in residential real estate. He bought 55 Walker Street in 1968 for $27,500, when loft living was illegal in Tribeca and residential demand in the area was low. Yet, as *The Village Voice* reported, when "the loft market took a sharp swing upward" in 1976, relations between Lipkis and his tenants began to deteriorate. At this point, tenants started to notice unusually high turnover in the building. When, in the winter of 1977, Lipkis demanded a general rent increase, asked tenants to pay an extra annual fee in addition to their rent, and granted only short-term leases, the tenants withheld their rent.[46]

The residents of 55 Walker Street fought back against their landlord's practices because they argued that it was their effort and capital that added value to the building's vacant industrial space and allowed Lipkis to profit from the increased demand for lofts. As resident Rebecca Pikus explained, when she arrived, "the floors had 100 years of dirt, grime, tar and industrial waste on them, many large holes and missing planks . . . dye-casting machines had left huge areas of lead burned and imbedded into the floor . . . walls were dark green military-surplus paint, all peeling from water leaks, with huge blocks of plaster falling or missing altogether from the sides. . . . The chains were missing from the windows, and they therefore did not open or close. The fire-escape window was also broken and did not open altogether. The old elevator shaft was caving in." Moreover, after Pikus spent $15,000 to renovate the loft, Lipkis reneged on his promise to grant her a long-term lease.[47]

The rent strike at 55 Walker Street led to more than a year of legal battles that resulted in a decision mostly favorable to loft tenants. First, a lower court ruled that Lipkis had to legalize his building by obtaining a certificate of occupancy before he could collect any additional rent. More important, a higher court decided that, despite the ostensibly illegal status of their lofts, the Multiple Dwelling Law covered the residents of Lipkis's building, giving tenants some basic legal protections and a basic right to inhabit their homes. However, the court's decision stopped short of giving them protection under local rent control laws or interpreting loft policy in a way that protected them in the long term, which left them vulnerable to possible later evictions and rent increases.[48]

Over time, not much changed with the building's transition to a revenue-generating residential property. Lipkis continued to own 55 Walker Street through the 1980s, and he even took out a loan in 1986 to make improvements. By 1988, the building was a condominium, likely catering to wealthier nonartist residents.[49] By then, Lipkis had become more involved in loft development. In addition to his attempts to turn 55 Walker Street into a profitable residence, in the late 1980s he purchased a building at 471 Broadway that was later converted to condos, and he sold a property at 48 Walker Street to loft condo developers.[50]

There were even cases where landlords who owned industrial businesses engaged in speculative practices against their industrial and residential tenants. A conflict at 1–5 Bond Street in NoHo pitted businesses owners against each other as well as older artist tenants and newer nonartist ones. The building, a landmark built in the Second French Empire style in 1871, housed a manufacturing concern, a cabinetmaker, and several artists and nonartists living illegally because the building was too large for legal residential conversion. The building sold in 1971 for $250,000. However, by 1980, the owner, Nathan Udell, who still ran a textile business in the building, claimed he wanted to sell his property so that it could be converted into artist living and work quarters. Thus, he wanted all manufacturing and nonartist tenants out of the loft. However, his tenants saw this move as a speculative one. In June 1979, Michael Geyer, an architect, rented a two thousand-square-foot loft for $425 per month and moved in with his wife and two children. Geyer claimed that the building's owner planned to sell the building to Thomas Rochon, an architect, and a number of investors, who in turn intended to sell cooperative lofts to nonartists for $80,000 to $150,000, resulting in a profit of $1.6 million. The owner applied for a zoning variance that would allow him to undertake this conversion legally. In turn, the building's tenants, including a hat manufacturer who had been in the building for twenty years, organized and fought the variance. Residents, such as twenty-five-year-old painter Michael David, argued that the owners could make a profit off the building if they rented all the space at current rates, while the hat manufacturer, Sam Benkel, claimed it would cost him $100,000 to move if evicted.[51]

Despite resident protests, the sale of the building did go through in 1980 for a relatively modest $259,000. However, by the mid-1980s, the ownership group, now going by the name Baco Development Corporation, had taken out loans of nearly $6 million, presumably to redevelop the property into luxury residences. By the end of the 1980s, the building was a condominium.[52]

Artists, or those associated with the arts, also acted as real estate developers and investors in SoHo and Lower Manhattan. Artists, dealers, gallery owners, and patrons used their inside knowledge of loft conversions to purchase buildings and convert lofts into homes. In a sense, nearly every artist who purchased a SoHo loft was a successful speculator. As loft prices were always on the rise, it would have been difficult to sell a loft without making a significant profit.

Because artists first saw the potential of industrial lofts as residences, they were in an advantageous position to make money in the real estate market. In 1970, many SoHo artists could rent space at the going industrial rate, which was $1 to $1.50 per square foot. With renovations that cost $3.10 per square foot, these artists could own an average-size finished loft in SoHo for $5,000. Artists who purchased lofts in cooperative buildings ended up owning property that quickly appreciated. In 1977, the asking price for a 3,700-square-foot loft was $70,000—five times what it cost in 1970.[53]

Artists could speculate in lofts with minimum capital. As the *Village Voice* noted, if artists could raise a certain sum of money—say, $4,000—they could buy a loft in a cooperative, paying one-third down on a mortgage that was arranged directly from the previous building owner. They could then spend two years or so making renovations to the loft and then sell it for double what they paid for it, recovering their initial down payment, paying off their debt, and pocketing a substantial profit. A real estate–savvy artist could then use profits on the sale of a loft (or two) to buy an entire loft building and sell shares to other artists as part of a co-op, generating even more profit. With minimal laws regulating this process, an artist could then rent the loft spaces in the building to other artist tenants.[54]

Although most art-related investors who rented lofts coexisted peacefully with their tenants, other came into conflict with both industrial businesses and artists. On one level, it makes sense that artists would want to profit from the real estate development they helped create. By inventing the loft home and helping to generate the tourism and commerce that fueled SoHo's growth into a thriving residential and commercial area, artists, more than anyone, deserved to profit from the rise in demand that occurred in the 1970s. Yet, at the same time, there is considerable irony in the fact that some artists actively encouraged SoHo's gentrification by speculating in residential real estate.

Some of the first people to enter into the neighborhood's real estate market were SoHo gallery owners. The group's connections to the art world, knowledge of the area, business sense, and experience either owning or managing lofts made them natural investors. J. Frederic Lohman, cofounder of the Leslie-Lohman Gallery, was also president of the SoHo Development Corporation, which invested heavily in local real estate. The company purchased a loft building at 427 West Broadway in 1970 for $200,000. In 1971, the year of one of the major legalizations of loft residences in SoHo, the company paid $200,000 for a property at 113 Spring Street, $114,000 for a loft building at 122 Spring Street, and $160,000 for one at 127 Prince Street. Finally, the group purchased a building at 22 Wooster Street in 1974 for $226,250. In all but one of these buildings, the properties became cooperative residences in the late 1980s or early 1990s.[55]

Art patrons were also involved in redeveloping SoHo lofts. Again, this is somewhat intuitive, as this group was both moneyed and knowledgeable about the Lower Manhattan loft scene. Museum of Modern Art trustee J. Frederick Byers, a real estate agent with extensive holdings in three cities, owned five buildings in SoHo by 1974. He called these investments "a labor of love, a marriage between art and real estate." His SoHo properties included the Kitchen performance and multimedia exhibition space at 484 Broome Street. He was well connected, having been born into the family of shipping magnate William R. Grace and married into the family of longtime CBS executive and philanthropist William S. Paley, himself a trustee of the Museum of Modern Art.[56]

Some property investors were simply artists without previous real estate connections. Although most entered into the loft market with little fanfare, some clashed with tenants over the prices, conditions, and legality of their lofts. Ironically, many of these tenants were artists themselves. Peter Gee, the loft cooperative organizer mentioned in chapter 2, was also a painter and silkscreen artist. The *Village Voice* reported that city records showed Gee as the owner of a string of buildings along Prince Street and West Broadway. However, Gee claimed that he only worked as a general contractor who oversaw the conversion of buildings and organized co-ops for a fee. Gee was not immune to conflict with residents. At 123 Prince Street in 1974, tenants argued that Gee reneged on a promise to renovate the lofts they rented, leading them to organize a rent strike. The residents lost, and Gee evicted them. He sold the building to artist Paul Serra for $110,000 in 1975 and helped him complete renovations. According to the *Village Voice*, after renovations, the finished lofts rented for $750 a month in 1977, a markup of 150 percent from the original price offered to artist tenants. By the mid-1980s, this building was also a cooperative residence.[57]

Those with art world connections were not immune to ignoring local laws and coming into conflict with industrial tenants and lawmakers. In 1977, SoHo gallery owner James Yu bought a massive property at 487 Broadway, on the corner of Broome Street. The thirteen-story building was "shaped like a huge rectangle with a narrow façade on Broadway and running the full block on Mercer Street." The upper floors were "an exquisite, eccentric eruption of Victorian terra cotta decoration," giving it the appearance of "a monumental slice of wedding cake." It had once held a silk exchange with a restaurant on the top floor. Yu sought to turn this building into an artist cooperative in 1977. Sale prices ranged from $28,000 to $42,000 per floor for raw space, with $400 to $900 per month in maintenance fees.[58]

Yu ran into complications because the building's industrial tenants stood in the way of his plans for an artists' co-op. Yu first angered the manufacturing tenants by not renewing their leases. Richard Meehan, who ran a machinery firm in the building, said that he felt he was being kicked out of the building so that Yu could form a co-op. Converting the building into residences also would have been illegal according to zoning regulations, which limited residential conversions to buildings with less than 3,600 square feet of lot coverage, which this giant building far surpassed. Yu might have been able to legalize his project by applying for a variance from the Board of Standards and Appeals. However, far into the project's development, he had not applied for one. As the *SoHo Weekly News* reported, another option was that "the shareowners can follow another SoHo tradition and not apply for a variance or a certificate of occupancy" and just convert the building to a residential co-op illegally and hope that city officials did not enforce the zoning regulations and evict tenants. Yu had reason to follow this strategy, as it had worked for thousands of SoHo residents up to this point. Not surprisingly, by 1984 the building was a cooperative residence.[59]

SoHo real estate was not only the domain of small-scale artist and industrial speculators. Larger-scale investors also entered into the residential loft market. However, more substantial real estate investors were never major players in the neighborhood during this period. Due to the complex legal framework governing residential, industrial, and artist residences in the area, it was difficult for an investor to buy a single loft building, let alone amass a portfolio of several local structures. It was the "schmatta guys," owners of textile or recycling businesses going back several generations, who dominated the SoHo landlord class.[60] Moreover, the SoHo Landmark District prevented many types of large-scale building projects, providing another disincentive for developers to enter the market.

Perhaps it is fitting, then, that even SoHo's most noted property owners did not fit the profile of the standard New York real estate mogul. This group included Jack Klein, known as the "loft king" of SoHo, who owned the leases to and managed several buildings through his Allhart corporation. As the *SoHo Weekly News* reported in 1976, "More than anyone else in the early 60s, he saw the potential for someone willing to act as intermediary between artists needing to find space and owners of the buildings who were not accustomed to dealing with artists. By his own count, he now owns or manages 15 buildings in the greater SoHo area." Klein became the "loft king" due to his "largescale conversion of lofts into living and working space" in the 1960s. By 1976, he was making his living buying, managing, and renovating loft buildings. Klein reportedly also served as a loft matchmaker for some of the best-known artists who settled in SoHo, including Jasper Johns, Robert Rauschenberg, Arman (see chapter 7), and Roy Lichtenstein.[61]

Klein started converting loft spaces for artists in 1962 after he became disillusioned as a stockbroker. He sought out industrial buildings that were occupied on the lower floors but had vacancies above. As long as building owners made some money off the empty space, he claimed, the owners did not care how it was used. He often had to convince owners to rent to artists, as "many of them distrusted artists and were afraid of attracting the attention of the Buildings Department inspectors." After a few years of acting as a rental agent for lofts, Klein bought the building next to his own on Jefferson Street, several blocks to the northeast of SoHo. Klein's projects pushed the boundaries of the SoHo artist enclave, and many of his loft properties were illegal. He rented out two loft buildings in the Fur and Flower Districts in Midtown Manhattan, which were not zoned for legal artist residences.[62]

Having rented to artists for more than a decade, Klein reportedly did not think highly of them. He viewed artists as dishonest, and he particularly abhorred the practice of renters charging new tenants fixture fees. Klein either forbade his tenants to set fixture fees or asked for a cut of the proceeds, as he accused many of them of charging more in fixture fees than they paid in renovations. He did not allow for a system by which tenants could profit off his property.[63]

Unsurprisingly, some developers who entered the loft market used the incomplete laws governing lofts to their advantage. In 1976 the Grand Sponsor Corporation began a project to convert four buildings that formerly housed the Baker Brush Company on Grand Street, an area where only artists were allowed to legally live, into 1,800- to 4,900-square-foot residences. The project concerned the *SoHo Weekly News*, which sent an undercover reporter to inquire about one of the lofts. The reporter claimed that when she asked the developer whether one needed to be an artist to live in the building, the property agent said, "We'll give you a paintbrush. . . . Anyway, we're all artists in our work." The paper was particularly worried that the developers seemed to be knowingly subverting zoning regulations to develop a co-op for non-artists. It reported that one of the developers, Irving Magot, said that the company would go after a variance to comply with SoHo zoning only after the cooperative was formed.[64]

The developers had a history of legally suspect residential conversions that worried some observers. One of the partners in the corporation, David Yagoda, had developed the co-op adjoining the Baker Brush buildings on the corner of Wooster and Grand Streets. During the conversion process, Yagoda applied for a variance from the Board of Standards and Appeals. Because "Soho zoning was discussed extensively during the variance procedure," the paper worried that the developers knowingly ignored laws.[65]

The Beginning of Gentrified SoHo?

By the waning years of the 1970s, SoHo, NoHo, and Tribeca experienced several interrelated developments. A rise in demand brought an increase in loft prices, a geographic expansion of loft living, and the entry of developers of various sizes into the local real estate market. Yet while the market for lofts was maturing, the legal framework governing these structures was not keeping pace. Although the policy changes in NoHo and Tribeca had made some attempt to both reflect the increased demand for loft residences and protect artist and industrial tenants, the overall legal framework abetted the worst abuses of the loft market. Clearly, reform was needed.

Additionally, although no one yet described the neighborhood as gentrified, SoHo was beginning to experience some of the negative outcomes associated with the gentrification process. Landlords and upper-income residents with a desire to live in the area were beginning to force out the area's original tenants, industrial businesses, and its first wave of "gentrifiers," SoHo's artists. For the first time, real estate speculators attempted to profit from the local residential property market. Although the neighborhood did not house lower-income residents of color, loft investment in SoHo threatened to dislocate a relatively low-income group, artists, as well as industrial businesses, which employed African American and Latino workers.

Furthermore, loft districts saw the beginnings of a movement from relative diversity to homogeneity. Aside from artists and industrial tenants, the other victim of the rise in loft demand was SoHo's status as a mixed-use neighborhood. As residential demand increased, loft districts became, at least incrementally, more upper-income and residential. This development was troubling for numerous groups. For artists, industrial residents kept down prices, kept out poseurs, and provided inspiration (and sometimes raw materials) for their artwork. For industrial businesses, artists provided additional rental income without threatening their existence. For planners, SoHo represented a welcome counter to contemporary urban renewal projects, most of which looked to replace mixed-use neighborhoods with single-use ones, such as housing projects or highways. Now it appeared that it might not be possible for residences and industry to coexist in the same neighborhood.

However, in other ways, the course of residential development in SoHo provides a counterpoint to the usual narrative of gentrification. The neighborhood's first displaced "residents" were industrial businesses, and investment in the area was disorganized and piecemeal. The story of residential development in the community is a complicated one in which residents, industrial business owners, and landlords all affected the outcome of a meandering process that led to the development of one of the country's first gentrified neighborhoods, and ultimately to a new form of loft-driven urban development.

Particularly notable was the absence of any large-scale developers. While large companies were involved in SoHo real estate, they were not pervasive. Individual investors, including artists and people who bought their buildings as individual properties, had just as much influence as the forces of big capital. Similarly, it was close to a decade after artists moved to SoHo before real estate developers became involved in the neighborhood in a sustained way. Even then, many of the major players in the SoHo real estate market came into their roles accidentally. Given the contemporary state of gentrification, in which upscale condo developers seem to follow artists and art galleries into disinvested neighborhoods in quick succession, the late and uncoordinated entry of developers into the SoHo real estate market is particularly striking.

Additionally, what is still distinct about residential development in SoHo is that living in a loft remained illegal for most SoHo residents from the late 1960s through the early 1980s. Thus, virtually all investment in SoHo property came at great risk, as eviction was still a legal possibility. Policy makers, relatively speaking, had little influence on this process, and even with the entry of larger developers into the loft market, state intervention was slow in coming. However, as residential lofts in SoHo and beyond became more lucrative and widespread, government officials sought to gain some control over residential conversions in Lower Manhattan.

9

Making New York a Loft Living City

Though plans for its construction were long dead, and the one existing piece of roadway was literally buried under mounds of dirt, in the late 1970s the Lower Manhattan Expressway once again became relevant to SoHo's artist community. This resurrection came as a result of one artist tenant, Ulrich Niemeyer. In 1968, Niemeyer was able to get a favorable ten-year lease from his landlord, Joseph Mandel, for a loft at 462–64 Broome Street. Niemeyer believed that the only reason he was able to sign the lease was that Mandel wanted to increase his potential compensation from the city when the property was condemned for the construction of the Lower Manhattan Expressway.

Niemeyer was not alone. Numerous artists who moved to SoHo in the late 1960s signed ten-year agreements with their landlords, the customary length for commercial and industrial leases in the area. These leases expired in the mid- to late 1970s, just as loft demand increased sharply. As a result, by 1979 an estimated 85 percent of loft tenants below Canal Street had leases that were set to expire over the next three years. With rents on the rise, many feared being priced out of their homes.[1]

When Niemeyer's lease was up in 1978, his landlord demanded a 300 percent increase in rent from him (he had been paying $325 per month). There was little room for negotiation: if residents at 462–64 Broome Street weren't willing to pay, Mandel threatened them with eviction. After all, Niemeyer and his fellow residents were living in a building without a certificate of occupancy. Like many loft tenants, Niemeyer and his neighbors fought back, and they ended up engaging in a twenty-four-month legal battle against their landlord.

In the end, the courts sided with Niemeyer. A state supreme court decision in January 1980 that found that evicting a tenant because he had a commercial lease would "ignore the reality of the situation as it has existed since the inceptions of their tenancies." Because all involved were aware that Niemeyer and his fellow tenants were living, and not just working, in their lofts, the court decided that they should be treated as if they were legally living in a residence. This meant that, like buildings that had a certificate of occupancy, residents were covered by rent stabilization laws, under which landlords could raise rents only 8.5 percent for a one-year lease, 12 percent for a two-year lease, or 15 percent for a three-year lease.[2] Making lofts subject to rent control was a wide-reaching decision, one that had the potential to affect every loft and loft resident in SoHo and beyond.

By the end of the 1970s, these escalating conflicts had shown a tangible effect on policy making, leading to the development of something closer to a formal loft policy. This policy emerged from lawsuits over loft conversions, which sometimes led to court decisions with far-reaching implications for who was allowed to live in a loft and under what conditions. Loft protests also drew the attention of local and state lawmakers, who increasingly moved to clarify and codify loft policy.

Yet, in creating a loft policy, government actors faced a dilemma. Thousands of people were living in lofts in SoHo and its surrounding neighborhoods by the late 1970s. Some of them had been making converted industrial spaces their homes for more than a decade. Yet, according to a survey completed by the CPC in December 1977, 91.5 percent of recent loft conversions in Manhattan below Fifty-ninth Street were illegal.[3] With so many people openly flouting the law, creating a policy framework that would not simply reward the worst abuses of the system, or result in mass evictions, was challenging.

Creating a rational policy regarding loft conversions was a challenge because the regulatory framework was extremely muddled. The New York City Planning Commission, New York City Department of Buildings, Board of Standards and Appeals, Landmarks Preservation Commission, local community planning boards, state and local courts, and the Board of Estimate, which included the mayor, the five borough presidents, and other elected officials, all had a role in creating and enforcing loft policy. Because city and state laws, as well as local statutes and codes, governed loft conversions, state and local elected officials also had a role in creating policy.

In formulating loft policy, judges, lawmakers, and administrators were confronted with several options. One was to enforce laws as they stood. However, taking current law at face value would mean evicting numerous residents. Aside from being cruel and politically unpopular, evicting loft tenants would mean losing the economic activity generated in SoHo and the loft real estate market. Another option would be to maintain the status quo by leaving laws as they were and continuing to enforce them selectively, or not at all. This solution pleased some residents and industrial businesses, but enforcement of existing policy neither prevented the worst abuses of landlords nor allowed the real estate market to function freely and efficiently. It also left residents vulnerable to the threat of eviction by city agencies as well as landlords. Furthermore, not acting would continue the potentially dangerous and embarrassing situation in which thousands of New Yorkers were living in residential lofts illegally in structures not covered by residential building codes.

Another alternative was to legalize loft living for everyone. This option would allow city leaders to exploit the growing power of loft conversions to revitalize neighborhoods at a time of real and perceived decline in New York. Representatives of the real estate community liked this idea, as did the numerous nonartists who had moved into lofts throughout the 1970s. However, many city and state leaders wanted to protect the remaining jobs in industrial lofts as well as the artist tenants who initially helped redevelop SoHo.

In the end, policy makers reached a compromise. By the early 1980s, the administration of New York mayor Edward Koch, the New York City Council, and state lawmakers created a set of policies that sought to strike a balance between the needs of local industry, artists, and the real estate market. The laws reduced tax breaks to developers converting lofts into homes, demarcated numerous industrial areas where loft conversations were prohibited, and left in place policies under which loft living was legal only for artists in several neighborhoods, including SoHo. The loft law also legalized loft conversions across much of Lower Manhattan, demonstrating that city leaders saw loft conversions as a development strategy that had the power to revitalize former industrial space. In time, they expected that these policies would allow others to convert lofts into homes, sparking SoHo-like residential and commercial development in other neighborhoods.

Loft Development and Public Policy: Conflicts with Policy Implications

By the end of the 1970s, continually rising demand led larger and savvier investors to enter the residential loft market. These speculators increasingly had the resources and incentive to use the ambiguous nature of loft policy to their financial advantage. In response, residents continued to fight back, and soon city and state leaders began to realize that the current situation was untenable. As a result, government agencies and elected officials joined with residents and industrial business owners in calling for a policy that would sort out this regulatory mess.

Creating a complete loft policy meant untangling multiple regulations and balancing the conflicting imperatives of several government bodies. Each area of New York City had a community planning board that recommended policies, including zoning regulations, to the CPC, which could approve or deny them. Before a zoning ordinance could go into effect, the Board of Estimate had final say. Courts also might overturn each of these agencies' decisions. The state legislature and governor had held sway over the city's Multiple Dwelling Law, and they and the New York City Council could pass any number of laws governing loft conversions.

The New York City Department of Buildings was in charge of inspecting lofts to determine whether structures were up to a building code set by the state legislature and to ensure that residents had a residential lease and buildings had a certificate of occupancy. Despite the attention paid to zoning changes in SoHo, the buildings department did not conduct large-scale inspections of lofts to ensure compliance with zoning or building codes between the early 1960s and late 1970s. The agency never had the political capital, will, or resources to regulate loft conversions and evict thousands of illegal loft tenants.

Wider-scale attempts to convert lofts into residences exposed other gaps in the legal framework. For instance, a landlord could apply for a variance to convert a loft to residences, even if local zoning ordinances prevented it. To do so, an owner would apply to the community planning board, which would then advise the CPC. Yet, both groups' decisions were only advisory, as the real decision came from the Board of Standards and Appeals, which tended to be more favorably inclined toward developers than the other agencies were. The Board of Standards and Appeals granted two variances for loft buildings in 1972, two in 1973, seven in 1974, and nine in 1975.[4] The Board of Estimate could then overrule the Board of Standards and Appeals, which it sometimes did. However, in some cases, the state supreme court overturned the Board of Estimate's decisions as a result of suits filed by building owners. Even policy explicitly addressing loft housing was inconsistent. For instance, throughout much of the 1970s, artist certification documents did not have addresses on them, meaning that tenants could apply for certificates of occupancy by claiming that fictitious artists lived in their lofts.[5]

Confrontations between investors and tenants involving multiple regulatory bodies and the courts escalated with the entry of more experienced property developers into the loft market. An important example of such a clash occurred at 260 West Broadway in Tribeca, an eleven-story Beaux-Arts commercial building at West Broadway and Beach Street purchased by Harry Macklowe for $690,187 in 1977. Macklowe was extensively involved in Manhattan real estate. Between 1968 and 1984, he bought twenty properties across the borough, including five in SoHo and Tribeca in 1974 and 1975. Macklowe added these properties to the collection of buildings he owned in more established real estate markets across the city, including Midtown, the Upper East Side, and Greenwich Village.[6] The fact that an investor would consider buildings in the fashionable Upper East Side along with lofts in SoHo indicates the ways in which the real estate industry was thinking about the neighborhood and its potential. Additionally, Macklowe's decision to invest heavily in the area in 1974 and 1975 once again points to these years as critical to the development of the SoHo real estate market.

After making his investment at 260 West Broadway, Macklowe sought to convert the top nine floors into residences. In this case, the conversions were still illegal, as the building's lot coverage was 11,500 square feet, well over the 3,600-square-foot limit. Further complicating matters, the building already had several illegal tenants before Macklowe made his purchase.[7]

Macklowe first tried to legalize residences in his building. In 1978, he applied for and received a variance from the Board of Standards and Appeals to convert the lofts into residences. In response, his tenants joined with local groups, including the Chambers-Canal Civic Association and Artists Housing Coalition, to oppose the variance. Although it would have permitted the current residents to live there legally, they believed that if Macklowe received a variance, they could not afford the rents he would be able to charge. Moreover, the CPC, Community Planning Board Numbers 1 and 2, and the SoHo Artists Association (SAA) joined the residents in their opposition. They then asked the Board of Estimate to overturn the Board of Standards and Appeals' decision, which it did.[8]

In typical SoHo fashion, Macklowe next attempted to use the ambiguous legal status of his building to his advantage. First he moved to evict the artists currently living there illegally, most of whom had commercial leases. Local artist groups also accused Macklowe of forcing the eighteen small businesses located in the building to sign thirty- to sixty-day cancellation clauses. The Artists Housing Coalition also accused him of attempting to resell the building for $1.8 million, a figure far higher than its value based on current rent rolls. Their thinking was that the building was worth more to a future investor empty of tenants and that evictions were crucial to this sale.[9]

In this case, because the Board of Standards and Appeals and the Board of Estimate could not agree on how loft policy should be implemented, the courts offered their interpretation. In June 1979, state supreme court justice

Herbert Shapiro ruled in favor of a suit brought by Macklowe, finding that the Board of Estimate had overstepped its bounds by overturning the variance approved by the Board of Standards and Appeals. As a result, Macklowe said he would move ahead with plans to evict the artists living in the building with illegal commercial leases by the end of the month. Not surprisingly, both manufacturing and artist groups reacted negatively to this decision. The vice president of the Chambers-Canal Civic Association (who was the owner of a cheese importing and processing firm) argued that the case demonstrated the failure of loft zoning (including the recent reforms in Tribeca), as the purpose of zoning was to keep large buildings for businesses. He believed that the decision would now allow developers to fully take over the area. Lori Antonacci of the Artists Housing Coalition urged the city to appeal. However, if there was an appeal, it was not successful; Macklowe maintained control over the property, and the building was converted into condominiums by 1981.[10]

Confrontations between tenants and loft owners continued, and calls for reform grew stronger. The next in a growing line of loft confrontations took place at a building owned by Martin R. Fine at 644 Broadway in NoHo. The *SoHo Weekly News* described Fine as "a controversial lawyer-turned-speculator-developer who in the last couple of years has been accumulating a mini-empire of lower Broadway manufacturing and commercial buildings with the intention of converting them to residential use." Fine owned four other properties on Broadway, including numbers 565, 640, 649–59 (a single building), and 684. He purchased 644 Broadway in 1978 for $86,000 and took out loans on the property totaling $530,000 over the next two years.[11] Outside SoHo, Fine's property holdings were substantial. Through multiple real estate holding companies, Fine built a portfolio of ten properties on the Upper East and West Sides of Manhattan, four in Midtown, three in the East Village, one in the West Village, and two in Tribeca, all purchased between 1975 and 1978.[12]

Fine's reputation for unsavory practices grew along with his real estate holdings. He first came to the attention of the SAA in 1977, when he tried to force manufacturing tenants out of his buildings by turning off the heat, discontinuing services, and shutting off the elevator. By 1979, it had become clear that Fine was purchasing buildings in SoHo for the purpose of converting them to residences without any regard for the law. Regardless of his extensive property holdings, the *SoHo Weekly News* reported that none of his buildings had received zoning variances despite the fact that several people, including Fine himself, were living in at least two of the lofts. Additionally, the newspaper accused him of forcing firms employing close to 160 people from his property at 565 Broadway.[13]

Fine argued that converting 644 Broadway into residences was better than allowing the property to remain vacant of industrial tenants. He applied for a zoning variance to transform the building into residential lofts in 1979. He argued that the Board of Standards and Appeals should grant a variance in this case because the building was obsolete for industrial use, even though it was located in the "Broadway Corridor" of larger lofts that were more attractive to industry. Fine contended that he bought the building at a mortgage foreclosure proceeding in 1977, when it was on its way to oblivion, and that despite its seven thousand-square-foot lot coverage, it was too small for manufacturing. As he said, "You can't even bring a hand truck into that building." He added, "there's a tremendous demand for living and there's no demand for manufacturing space."[14]

However, his opponents stated that Fine never made an attempt to find industrial tenants for the building and that he harassed current tenants in an attempt to make them leave. Although he denied that he planned to convert 644 Broadway into residences, the *SoHo Weekly News* reported that a real estate office had been set up in the building to show lofts to potential buyers. Fine advertised the property as the "Bleecker Renaissance" in the *Village Voice* and *SoHo Weekly News*, noting that co-ops would sell for $53,000 to $63,000. In addition, according to Sandy Hornick of the Department of City Planning's Manhattan office, Fine attempted to force the four industrial tenants from the building. These included S. K. Friedman and Sons, a retail clothing firm, which patiently waited for a new lease that never materialized, forcing them to rent in another building. Paul Metzler of Hi-Lo Manufacturing, another building tenant, complained that Fine provided no heat, poor elevator service, and no cleaning of the building. These practices forced at least one business, Devon Trading Company, to leave for New Jersey. Fine also allegedly harassed the Viola Farber Dance Company, an artist group renting in the building, by failing to provide heat, locking the doors, and shutting off the elevator. Farber filed harassment charges against Fine but later dropped them in exchange for moving expenses.[15]

Despite the accusations against him, and the opposition of the Department of City Planning and Community Planning Board Number 2, Fine was able to get a zoning variance from the Board of Standards and Appeals to legally convert 644 Broadway into lofts. In July 1979, the Board of Standards and Appeals agreed with Fine's contention that the conversion "has substantially improved the neighborhood and has induced many tax-paying middle class people back into the fabric of the lower Manhattan neighborhood, and has created a large number of jobs." In addition, the board called 644 Broadway "functionally obsolete" and claimed that its floors were not strong enough for industry, that its elevators and loading facilities were inadequate, and that to "upgrade the structure for manufacturing uses would be prohibitive." The board made this contention despite the findings in a New York City Department of Buildings report, which stated that the floors were sound for industrial uses and that the building had held manufacturing tenants since 1917 without mishap. Both Sandy Hornick of the Department of City Planning's Manhattan office and Doris Diether of Community Planning Board Number 2 spoke against the Board of Standards and Appeals decision. Hornick called it a "bellwether," and Diether criticized the board for being too "developer-oriented."[16]

As conflicts grew more frequent, elected officials became increasingly involved in conflicts between loft tenants and property owners. The three-year-long clash between residents and tenants at the Singer Building at 561 Broadway was particularly important in generating policy change. The controversy over the building involved protests by residents, genuine attempts by landlords to legalize residences, blatant disregard for loft law, petitions to the Board of Standards and Appeals, debates over the viability of local industry, and court intervention into fights over the future of loft properties.

The purchase of the Singer Building by a group of real estate investors quickly aroused the concern of its tenants, including manufacturing firms and artists living in lofts. Bernard Marson, Alexander Edelman, and Ira Weissman bought the building for $700,000 in 1977 from its previous owners, Samuel and Clara Paul, who had owned it since 1960. Weissman had been involved in other residential conversions in SoHo, and he believed that transforming run-down manufacturing buildings into housing for low-income artists was a form of public service. However, the sale immediately raised concern among the building's industrial tenants. Most notably, Joe Horn suspected that the building's new owners hoped to turn it over to residential use. Horn was the owner of the Hi-Style Hat Company, a garment manufacturer that had been in business for twenty-seven years and in the Singer Building for fifteen. He argued that the building was worth only $450,000 to a buyer who wanted to keep its industrial tenants, indicating that the investors hoped to transform the property into more profitable residences in spite of its location in a section of SoHo where loft conversions were illegal due to the units' large size and suitability for industry.[17]

The Singer Building's tenants turned their concerns into active resistance by working with artist political groups to bring the new owners' actions to the attention of government officials and the public. In August 1978, the SAA gave CPC chair Robert F. Wagner Jr. a tour of SoHo to convince him of the severity of the problem of illegal conversions. On the tour, which included the Singer Building, Wagner called its conversion "totally illegal" and promised future action. The CPC teamed with the New York City Department of Buildings to get a stop-work order against the building's developers in 1979. Yet work on the building continued. The building's owners had incentive to continue their renovations. Weissman of Lafayette Development Corporation, one of the new owners, noted that many of its thirty-six co-op residences had already sold for prices ranging from $27,000 to $60,000.[18]

By 1979, another party entered the loft fray: New York mayor Edward Koch and his administration, which had recently created the Mayor's Task Force on Loft Conversions. In July 1978, the task force issued an action plan on the loft issue that included recommendations for an enforcement plan to prevent illegal conversions, an accelerated inspection program for existing illegal loft residences, a review of and revisions to code requirements to provide for safe housing in renovated lofts, state legislation that would create an antiharassment measure to protect manufacturing tenants, relocation assistance to industrial tenants who were displaced by conversions receiving J-51 tax abatement, and incentives to upgrade industrial buildings for industrial uses.[19] In creating these initiatives, the Koch administration's goals were to bring loft conversions in line with current law, while protecting industry. Although these policies were not antiartist, it is striking that there was little mention of artist housing. These initiatives were also aimed at limiting the ability of developers, whether large or small, to create further illegal loft conversions.

The administration looked to make the Singer Building a test case for these new policy aims, both because of the threat that residential conversion posed to the building's industrial businesses and because of the blatant illegality of the conversion. The building's developers did not apply for a zoning variance from the Board of Standards and Appeals and started selling raw spaces as co-ops even after the stop-work order. In addition, there was evidence that this potential conversion had already forced industrial businesses out of the city and threatened several more. According to Hornick, there were 340 jobs in the building when its new owners bought it in 1978, but in 1979 the number had shrunk to 120. Jobs lost included those at Mr. Jerre Fashions, a garment manufacturer, which moved from the building to West Orange, New Jersey, taking 150 employees with it.[20]

With a stop-work order seemingly ineffective, the Koch administration took the building's owners to court and, in July 1979, won a temporary restraining order halting renovations. The suit accused the building's owners of never attempting to apply for a zoning variance and showing a "blatant disregard for the law" in their conversion of lofts to residences. Deirdre Carson, coordinator of the Mayor's Task Force on Loft Conversions, remarked, "If people see the city is serious about land-use policies and protecting its small business . . . then they will think a little more carefully about taking buildings which are not zoned for residential and attempting to convert them. . . . There's not much point in having any kind of a land-use policy unless you are prepared to enforce it."[21]

However, in November 1979, the Supreme Court of the State of New York ruled that the city's suit was premature and that the building's owners should have the opportunity to apply for a zoning variance with the Board of Standards and Appeals. However, the court did issue a temporary restraining order against the sale of more cooperatives. The move was significant for the building's owners, as the *SoHo Weekly News* reported that they stood to earn $1 million in profits from the sale of cooperatives in a building they bought for $700,000.[22]

Later that month, city officials joined a new group in opposing the Singer Building's conversion. For the first time, union leaders entered the loft debate. Robert F. Wagner Jr.—now deputy mayor—joined with members of the United Artists Housing Coalition and the United Hatters and Cap and Millinary Workers (the union that had supported the MICOVE middle-income housing project in SoHo) to speak out against the plan. At the hearing, John Ross of the Hatters Union represented forty union members employed by one of the three businesses in the building. He said, "New York City will undoubtedly lose industry and the garment workers [if] these real estate speculators are permitted to continue to break the law." For their part, the property owners claimed that they were being unfairly singled out among the many illegal loft converters in Lower Manhattan. They pointed out that 165 illegal conversions took place in SoHo from 1977 to 1979 and that eleven other buildings had received zoning variances from the Board of Standards and Appeals during this time.[23]

Yet, despite the disapproval of the CPC, Community Planning Board Number 2, several artist groups, and the Koch administration, the Board of Standards and Appeals approved the Singer Building's owners' request of a zoning variance in December 1979. City leaders were irate over the decision. The CPC's counsel, Norman Marcus, called the court's decision "horrendous" and predicted that the buildings department would sue to have the ruling overturned. City Council member Miriam Friedlander feared that "unless the city goes to court to stop it, the laws will be stepped on by these developers." Buildings Commissioner Irwin Frutchman agreed, saying, "This decision throws zoning laws open. . . . It's just a way for the owners to get around the law and profit from doing something illegally."[24]

SoHo's industrial businesses were another casualty of the decision. Joe

Horn said that the decision was the "straw that broke the camel's back," adding that the Hi-Style Hat Company would likely go out of business. Although the mayor's office did bring a suit to fight the Board of Standards and Appeals' decision, it was still in litigation six months later. By that time, Horn's lease had expired. As a result, the owners increased Horn's rent from $2,000 to $15,000 a month, presumably in an effort to get him out of the building. He found a loft that he could rent for $3,000 per month at nearby 440 Lafayette Street but estimated that the move would cost $50,000.[25]

The Singer Building once again highlighted the inadequacy of loft law but also brought about actual policy change. Because of this case and the Koch administration's growing awareness of the fractured and ineffective legal and regulatory framework governing loft conversions, the city budgeted $400,000 for loft zoning enforcement in the next year. This would be the first of several attempts by the city to exert some control over the conversion process.[26]

Additionally, residents' actions against their landlords—as in the Ulrich Niemeyer case—inspired the courts to act to set loft policy. As a result of Niemeyer's suit, the state supreme court decided that all residential lofts should be treated like legitimate residences and that nearly every inhabited loft was potentially legal and subject to New York's rent control law. However, no one was sure what the repercussions of the decision would be. Marvin Markus of the Rent Guidelines Board called it "a troublesome and weird ruling," and the Department of Housing Preservation and Development, which had authority over administering rent control, said it would take no action until the courts heard appeals of the case.[27]

While city and state leaders were slogging through this policy morass, tenants and cooperative boards developed an informal method for dealing with some of these legal ambiguities. One technique was the "loft letter." Most people credit lawyer Vincent "Oz" Hanley for first drafting it. Hanley moved to SoHo in the early 1970s when he was twenty-six years old and recently out of law school. He came to the neighborhood to see music and art, found it interesting, and rented a cheap loft with some artist friends. At the time, Hanley was working for Legal Aid and began to grasp some of the issues that SoHo tenants were facing. He would sometimes barter his legal services for renovation work on his loft. In the late 1970s, Hanley was involved in the growing conflict between landlords and tenants in and around SoHo. He represented tenants against landlords who brought eviction actions against them, as well as residents attempting to obtain certificates of occupancy. Hanley twice tried to buy a loft in SoHo, but co-op boards turned him down, likely because he was not an artist. Eventually, he bought a building in Tribeca, converted it to residences, and established a real estate law practice downtown.[28]

The "loft letter," developed by Hanley and other lawyers working in SoHo at the close of the 1970s, was generic purchasers' indemnification designed to protect cooperatives in SoHo and other loft areas from any liability for including an illegal tenant in their corporation. The letter, really text included in a purchase agreement, states that the purchaser agrees that he or she is buying a loft knowing that one occupant of the premises must be a certified artist. The tenant agrees that if the city takes action against the cooperative, he or she indemnifies the cooperative against the suit. So that cooperatives would not simply use the agreement to get rid of tenants they did not like, the agreement would come into effect only if the city took steps against the cooperative. Even if it did, the tenant could "cure" the violation, either by getting certified as an artist, selling his or her unit, or somehow getting a certified artist to live in it.[29]

Toward a Complete Loft Policy

As SoHo quickly changed into a real estate wild west, government leaders sought to develop a citywide loft policy to rein in speculators, provide a solution to the increasing number of illegal loft residences, protect affordable rents for artists and local industry, and at the same time encourage residential development. First, the city tried to get a more accurate sense of the extent of illegal loft conversions. In 1978, the New York City Department of Buildings began a comprehensive inspection of residential lofts below Fifty-ninth Street, an action that it had not taken since the 1960s. The inspections were in response to the previously mentioned CPC survey that found that fewer than 10 percent of recently converted residential lofts were legal. Inspectors from the buildings department visited a number of lofts from a list of nine hundred illegal conversions developed from the survey. Upon finding illegal loft residents, the buildings department sent a letter to tenants saying that premises had to be vacated within thirty days.[30]

Although the inspections did not result in any evictions, loft tenants were surprised and upset by them. In response, loft tenants formed the Lower Manhattan Loft Tenants (LMLT), a new advocacy organization.[31] At the group's first open meeting in January 1979, two hundred loft tenants had a heated exchange with John LoCicero, special adviser to Mayor Koch, among others, about the motivation behind the recent inspections. They also expressed their concern about the rise in loft prices led by the "Bloomingdales types" seeking loft homes. Lawmakers countered that inspections were aimed at giving residents more rights by forcing landlords to get a certificate of occupancy and making their lofts legal. However, tenants claimed that the inspections gave landlords an "excuse to jack up the rents and kick out tenants who object" or charge their renters for bringing their lofts up to code. They cited the case of a building owned by the Sylvan Lawrence Company, which threatened to evict twenty-five tenants unless they paid for renovations to their building. Amalie Rothschild, a Tribeca resident and member of Community Planning Board Number 1, spoke about the city's favorable tax policies and their impact on lofts. She said, "By encouraging J-51 conversions, you are accelerating the process whereby small businesses are also being forced out."[32]

Loft residents worried that government attempts at comprehensive reform threatened what was valuable about the Lower Manhattan artist community: the ability to live affordably in homes and studios close to other artists, galleries, and arts organizations. In response, the Lower Manhattan Loft Tenants organized a protest march that drew one hundred residents of SoHo, NoHo, and Tribeca, along with city council members Ruth Messinger and Miriam Friedlander. This time, however, protesters were not worried about urban renewal or city indifference but instead sought "protection for residents endangered by real estate development." At the march, the LMLT highlighted the increasing number of buildings below Canal Street that they claimed were being sold to speculators who failed to bring their buildings up to code, sent eviction notices, and demanded rent increases as high as 200 percent. They reported, "The result is a growing fear that developers—abetted by the city—are using the demand that they bring their buildings up to code as an excuse to evict artists and other moderate-income tenants in favor of residents who can pay much more."[33]

After the march, both artist organizations and city officials across numerous city agencies offered their own solutions to the zoning problem. The Lower Manhattan Loft Tenants prepared a proposal for legal changes that would allow more loft dwellers to be covered by the state's Multiple Dwelling Law. In its proposal, the LMLT contended, "loft rental tenants have done more than any other tenant group in revitalizing areas of the city at no cost to the city or the landlord. In spite of their efforts, they have received a minimum of community services and building services . . . residential tenants take for granted." Artists, unlike speculators, did not displace industry but instead moved into spaces "which could no longer be rented to commercial or manufacturing tenants . . . it is a misstatement to say that loft tenants . . . displaced small businesses and jobs from the city." City council member Stanley Michels, a progressive from Washington Heights–Inwood in northern Manhattan, introduced a bill to the city council that would require owners who rented residential lofts to file plans and apply for a certificate of occupancy within ten days or lose the right to evict tenants on the basis of land use. At the same time, the Mayor's Task Force on Loft Conversions was deciding whether to extend a recently issued ninety-day moratorium on legal action on loft buildings whose owners moved toward getting certificates of occupancy.[34]

While artists organized formal protests of city agencies, politicians joined with industrial tenants to highlight the effect of loft speculation on local businesses. In February 1979, New York City Council member Carol Greitzer held a press conference in front of 746 and 752 Broadway in NoHo to protest the efforts of developers to convert the buildings into loft residences. Developers under the name of Manoco, a partnership formed by members of the Manocherian family, purchased the buildings in 1975 for $600,000 and planned to spend $5 million to $7 million to convert the seven- and twelve-story buildings into 175 studio, one-bedroom, and two-bedroom apartments, each renting for a rate of $450 to $700. Greitzer argued that the conversion threatened two hundred jobs in the buildings alone. Overall, she believed that close to fifteen thousand jobs in eighty Midtown and downtown loft buildings were in jeopardy due to "imminent" loft conversions. Greitzer blamed the Koch administration for changes in the J-51 program that made lofts more attractive to developers, who she said were totally controlling the loft conversion process. Hornick of the City Planning Department's Manhattan office concurred, saying that between one-fourth and one-third of firms that were forced to relocate either closed or left the city. Since many of these companies employed minorities, he argued, the job loss was especially significant.[35]

The *SoHo Weekly News* tried to give a face to the industrial jobs threatened. The buildings at 746 and 752 Broadway were commercially zoned, allowing the conversion to proceed without the developer having to apply for any zoning variances. Even though the buildings were commercial, the paper wrote, its conversion still threatened jobs. One worker, Jesus Galdez, traveled each day from Marble Hill in the Bronx to his job paying $95 a week at Falcon Sportswear. Falcon Sportswear's owners, Charles Cohen and Miriam Shapiro, had been running a business in the building since 1961 and employed about fifty people. They worried that the extra expense of having to move would force them to close. Jerry Dvorkin, the owner of a garment business in the buildings, argued that the buildings' tenants should be allowed to stay because "the buildings they are evicting us from are in excellent condition for commercial use." Despite these concerns, however, the buildings were eventually fully converted to residences. The Manoco partnership owned the buildings until 2010, when it sold them for $18.4 million.[36]

With piecemeal, neighborhood-based regulations (and no overall loft policy) on the city level, members of the New York State Legislature sought to create some clarity. Senate minority leader Manfred Ohrenstein and Assembly member Edward Lehner led a daylong hearing on the loft issue in February 1980. They planned to sponsor a series of bills that would give loft tenants some protection from evictions and rent hikes by placing them under rent stabilization laws and making it illegal for a landlord to evict a tenant simply because the building did not have a certificate of occupancy. Senator Ohrenstein, a Manhattan Democrat, was particularly concerned about the loft issue, remarking, "Lofts have become somewhat glamorous in the press—a form of gentrification. Legislators have no true understanding of the problems faced by 10,000 people with little or no housing protection." The two legislators planned on sponsoring a loft bill in spite of expected resistance from the real estate lobby in Albany, along with possible disinterest among upstate legislators unfamiliar or unconcerned with loft zoning issues.[37]

Because of the continuing tension between industrial and residential uses of loft buildings, labor unions became more heavily involved in the debate over loft law. In 1980, a coalition of twelve garment, printing, and building trades unions joined with housing groups to speak out against the trend toward luxury conversions of loft buildings. John Ross of the United Hatters, Cap and Millinery Workers characterized the fight against residential conversions as a class struggle between artists and manufacturer-producers against the rich, who just wanted to live, but not work, in lofts. He argued that the city could lose two hundred thousand garment industry jobs over the next eighteen months, based on loft businesses that had expiring leases and whose landlords had not offered them renewal options. Ross lent his union's support to parts of the proposed loft legislation that would guarantee relocation expenses for businesses forced to vacate lofts, and provisions that would allow courts to grant a stay of evictions of up to eighteen months to give businesses time to move.[38]

The New York State Legislature did not act immediately on the proposed legislation. The bill was first delayed as a result of a dispute between Ohrenstein and Republican senator John Marchi of Staten Island on a separate issue. The Koch administration was also feuding with Ohrenstein and thus initially refused to throw its weight behind the bill. In addition, landlords, through the Association of Commercial Property Owners, lobbied against it. After it was clear that the legislature would not pass a comprehensive rent stabilization bill, a compromise was reached on a law that would limit rent increases to 8.5 percent in a one-year period, ease some standards for loft conversions, and provide some relocation benefits for businesses displaced by conversions in buildings where developers received a J-51 tax abatement. However, after the New York State Assembly passed the bill and Governor Hugh Carey promised to sign it, senate majority leader Warren Anderson said he wanted time to study it. He did not call the bill, and it never came to a vote. With the full loft bill still not having passed, in November 1980 the New York State Legislature passed a stopgap measure that gave loft tenants in certain buildings with leases that expired after June 11, 1980, the right to a one-year lease extension with a maximum 11 percent rent increase, banned landlords from evicting tenants based on zoning grounds, gave the city council the right to require developers to pay relocation benefits to businesses forced to move out due to residential conversion, and amended fire and building standards to make residential conversions of loft buildings easier.[39]

With the state legislature failing to pass a full loft law, the Koch administration—working with the Department of Housing Preservation and Development and the CPC, with input from the LMLT, Brooklyn Loft Tenants, and Chelsea Loft Dwellers—sought to enact policy changes at the city level. The plan included $400,000 for a Loft Enforcement Project, which would seek to halt illegal residential conversions, and a rent stabilization plan for lofts. The administration also proposed a rezoning plan that would make it possible for New Yorkers to legally convert lofts into homes more broadly throughout the city. The plan would require building owners to pay relocation grants to businesses displaced by residential conversion and would amend the J-51 program to prevent developers from getting tax benefits for residential conversions in industrially zoned areas. It would also amend the building code for loft conversions, making it easier for owners to obtain residential certificates of occupancy and legalizing their residences. According to Housing Preservation and Development Commissioner Anthony Gliedman, the plan would "put the force of law behind [tenants] in their desire to stay where they are, and have reasonable rents," and stop the legal "dogfight, apartment by apartment."[40]

This plan exhibited a tension between the desire to utilize loft conversions as a form of residential development and the attempt to bring some order to the loft conversion process while protecting artist pioneers and industrial tenants. As loft tenant groups noted, the proposal would open up as much as ten million square feet of loft space to legal residential conversion in SoHo, NoHo, Tribeca, and the Midtown Garment District by nonartists, as long as an equivalent area was set aside for manufacturing or commercial uses. The plan did reaffirm the manufacturing-only status of several strong industrial centers in Lower Manhattan and northeast Chelsea. It also maintained the policy under which only certified artists could live legally in SoHo and NoHo lofts. Yet members of loft tenant groups worried that legalizing more areas for loft living would make conversions seem more attractive to wealthy New Yorkers. Chuck DeLaney of the LMLT was concerned that the legislation would lead to a loft grab in Chelsea and Brooklyn and that it "would make a middle class person from Westchester think it's legal and OK to live in a loft." Others were concerned that the specter of a rent stabilization law would lead landlords to clear out as many of their tenants as possible to get new ones who could be charged more rent.[41]

Manufacturing interests were even more concerned about the Koch plan and expressed their fear that the city was giving over too much loft space for residential development, threatening industry in the process. Walter Mankoff, associate research director of the International Ladies Garment Workers' Union, said that his union would "do everything we can to convince the Board of Estimate to turn the plan down." He argued that the city's proposal to allow both manufacturing and residential uses in some parts of Midtown Manhattan would not work, since garment companies depended on nearby businesses for specialized services. He worried, "What must inevitably happen is that the residential uses will gradually push out the manufacturing.... We are all agreed that this plan, if implemented, would lead to the elimination of the garment industry from the city." Norman Hill of the A. Philip Randolph Institute, an organization of African American trade unionists, said the proposal would "result in an increase in housing—but only for upper middle class professionals." He reasoned that a city that lost six hundred thousand manufacturing jobs in the last decade should not pass a zoning plan that would allow more firms to leave. He argued, "With the flight of industry will come more unemployment for the city's unskilled, semi-skilled and skilled workers. Our city's welfare and unemployment rolls will continue to grow."[42]

The actions of the Koch administration to intervene in this situation are consistent with the mayor's overall philosophy. Koch was a Greenwich Village liberal, concerned at times with the plight of workers, minorities, and those involved in the arts. Yet he was also focused on bringing the city's budget back from near oblivion. To accomplish this goal, he focused on development, particularly in the field of housing. These conflicting objectives likely led his administration to intervene to protect loft residents and businesses while keeping in mind the need to preserve economic growth and housing expansion.[43]

The final city loft plan reflected the objections of the garment industry and industrial unions. The city agreed to reduce the space open to legal conversion from ten to seven million square feet and to rezone a portion of the Garment District as manufacturing-only to protect specialized firms, such as stitchers, that unions argued were critical to garment businesses.[44] The

Koch administration also promised to establish an Industrial Loft Advisory Council to be composed of business and (possibly) artist representatives who would hear loft conversion cases before the Board of Standards and Appeals. Koch placed two garment industry leaders in the Business Relocation Assistance Corporation and promised to appoint three new people to the Board of Standards and Appeals to prevent it from being prodeveloper. In April 1981, the Board of Estimate approved zoning changes that created new mixed-use zoning districts in manufacturing areas of Manhattan, including southeast Chelsea, the Garment District east, SoHo, NoHo, and Tribeca, and also reaffirmed the status of mixed-use areas in other parts of Manhattan.[45]

However, the state was still reluctant to pass a full loft bill. Despite the efforts of artist tenant groups and city leaders, along with a petition signed by luminaries such as Andy Warhol, Meryl Streep, James Rosenquist, Romare Bearden (the first artist who claimed to have been evicted from a SoHo loft), Murray Louis, Christo, Robert Rauschenberg, Joseph Papp, Leo Castelli, and Claes Oldenburg, the New York State Legislature did not pass a bill legalizing loft living until June 1982.[46]

That bill, known colloquially as the "loft law," brought legal clarity to multiple elements of loft policy and reflected a reluctant acquiescence by city leaders and loft tenants to Republican lawmakers and building owners on some points. It applied to loft buildings in which at least three units were residential as of April 1, 1981. The bill created a Loft Board tasked with regulating residential conversions and compensating industrial tenants pushed out as a result. The law also obligated loft owners to make their properties conform to the residential building code and created a framework through which they could pass the costs associated with renovations onto tenants over the course of ten to fifteen years. For a period of time, the newly created Loft Board would regulate loft rents, after which buildings would be subject to the city's rent stabilization laws. The city would also have the authority to apply the law to other nonresidential areas. Finally, the law stated that if a manufacturing tenant was forced out of a loft because of a building's conversion to residential use, then building owners had to pay $4.50 per square foot of space occupied by the tenant into a fund that the tenant could then draw from to defray relocation costs. However, if space was converted to commercial use, property owners were not required to pay those expenses.[47]

The goal of the Loft Board, according to its first chair, Carl Weisbrod, was to limit illegal conversions and provide some sort of balance between the rights of loft landlords and tenants. Weisbrod, who came to the board after leading the city's Office of Midtown Enforcement, sought to use civil enforcement techniques to stop illegal conversions before they started and to limit some of the worst abuses of the system. The goal was to bring tenants and landlords into compliance with the law before they built up financial or social equity in their units. On the tenant side, the board sought to regulate rents, give buildings a path to legalization, and create a formula through which artists could recover the sweat equity they put into their units. On the landlord side, the goal was to provide a sufficient expectation of a long-term return so that they would invest in their buildings, bring them up to code, and allow them to get certificates of occupancy. In the first years of its operation, the board temporarily froze rents, regulated what services loft building owners were required to provide to their tenants, and developed a formula by which tenants would be compensated for the value of their fixtures (though not, as they might have liked, for the full value they added to the loft by conversion).[48]

Perhaps more important, the work of the Loft Board served to regularize loft living across the city. As Weisbrod recalled, "the overarching issue and consideration was to what extent should this form of housing be considered as normal apartment living and to what extent it should be considered as a separate kind of housing." In the end, through the formal policies it created, the Loft Board helped make lofts a regular type of residence to be enjoyed by anyone with the inclination and the means to live in a former industrial space.[49]

The Loft Law and Gentrification

With the passage of New York's loft law, residential conversions of industrial loft space became a formal method of urban development. New York City's Loft Board regulated the seven million square feet that could be legally converted to residences in Manhattan. In addition, a state law was in place that, in time, would make residential lofts legal residences subject to all the protections of conventional apartments. In many ways lofts were not treated like other homes. The restrictions on conversions for significant portions of Lower Manhattan, the requirement that relocation fees be paid into a fund to help displaced industrial tenants, and the very existence of a Loft Board all point to the fact that lofts were a distinct housing form that still did not fit neatly into preexisting legal frameworks.

The city and state loft policies reflected the conflicting desires of policy makers when it came to these structures. On one hand, both parties clearly wanted to control the process of loft development and bring conversion activity within the law. There was also a strong desire to encourage urban development and respond to the growing residential real estate market in lofts.

Despite the protections in place for artists and industrial tenants, the enacted policy still consisted of a major expansion of legal loft living throughout the city. More important, perhaps, as a result of the policy, nonartists could live legally in lofts throughout much of Manhattan. The implementation of a citywide loft policy demonstrates that policy makers now thought of loft conversions as an urban development strategy with the power to revitalize neighborhoods throughout New York. The policy also decoupled the idea of loft living from the figure of the artist. Loft living was no longer strictly affordable housing for struggling artists but was now market-rate housing for everyone.

It is not easy to say whether the loft law encouraged or discouraged gentrification in New York's loft districts. Although political leaders eventually legalized many forms of loft conversion, their reaction to this new form of urban development was both slow and incomplete. Far from efforts to clear the neighborhood of undesirable residents so that it could be redeveloped, city leaders attempted to protect both artists and residential tenants in SoHo from the adverse effects of gentrification. City leaders and state leaders also approved a large expansion in legal loft living, indicating that they were not fully antidevelopment.

Property developers and speculators, frequently central characters in histories of gentrification, also played an important role in SoHo's growth. Yet, as a whole, they were late on the scene. Certainly, unscrupulous speculators affected SoHo. Martin Fine's decision to raise the rent on Joe Horn's hat company from $2,000 to $15,000 per month is perhaps the most egregious example of the type of ruthless landlord behavior that is often associated with gentrification. However, people had been living in lofts for decades before developers of this type emerged. Developers ultimately shaped urban change in SoHo, but they never drove this process.

Those adversely affected by loft development correspond with the groups usually associated with "victims" of gentrification in the United States. Both artist pioneers and minority workers were among those forced from their homes and jobs due to luxury development. Additionally, over time, small businesses were forced out of loft districts, and the minority presence in the area shrank due to a reduced industrial base. However, artists and industrial workers cannot be seen simply as hapless victims. Both groups brought substantial resources to bear in the battle over loft space. Artists influenced the final loft policy through their grassroots activism, political connections, and well-known members of the art world who lobbied on their behalf. Similarly, unions representing these mom-and-pop enterprises influenced loft policy a great deal.

The development of a loft policy also complicates our understanding of the role of artists in gentrification. Artists invented the loft in the 1960s but struggled to retain control over the development of loft districts throughout the 1970s and '80s. They continued to have a say in loft policy, and their actions as tenants were perhaps the most important factor in inspiring policy makers to act to regulate loft conversions. Yet, in the end, many artist tenants were likely unhappy with the policies created, and the fact that many new loft dwellers were nonartists indicates how much they had lost control of the process of loft conversion.

The geography of loft conversions in SoHo gives some support to the rent gap theory of gentrification posited by Neil Smith, with some caveats. This theory posits that gentrification takes place where the actual capitalized ground rent of a property differs from its potential ground rent. In some ways, the conflicts over individual lofts are a clear illustration of the rent gap.[50] The stories of these conflicts directly involve landlords replacing their lower-paying tenants with higher-paying ones as soon as the profit to be made exceeded the cost of removing the tenants. However, getting from actual rent to potential rent was not an easy process. Building location, lot size, local law, and the tenacity of tenants, as well as their political connections and the willingness of government officials to intervene in each case, shaped how much a developer could align his or her rents with the demands of the market.

Despite the similarities between much of SoHo's development and the notion of gentrification, it is interesting that it was not until the early 1980s that observers began to use this term to describe loft development.[51] Almost twenty years after Ruth Glass coined the term, SoHo finally attained the status of "gentrified." Having the concept of gentrification at their disposal shaped the actions of all parties in the conflict over loft space and policy. Rather than responding to strange demands by artists to legalize lofts, government officials saw themselves as intervening to both encourage the economic benefit of and manage the worst abuses of gentrification. Tenants saw themselves as "gentrification victims" and used this language in their protests. Developers believed that they were simply responding to the demands of the market and were, in fact, providing a service by encouraging the gentrification of a city left for dead only several years before. With loft conversions spreading across Manhattan and beyond, it was becoming apparent that they were in many ways driving the gentrification of New York.

Conclusion

Contemporary SoHo and the Neighborhood's Significance

A contemporary visitor to SoHo might have a hard time imagining that it was once an industrial area or an artist colony. Whereas the landmark designation passed in 1973 ensured that SoHo's cast-iron architecture has remained in place, the rest of the neighborhood has been fundamentally transformed. Today, SoHo is known as one of the city's most expensive areas, one of its most upscale shopping destinations, and one of the best places to spot European tourists.

Much has changed in SoHo since the early 1980s, but there are also many legacies of its arts colony days. One consistency is that many SoHo residents who bought cooperatives in the 1960s and '70s stayed in their homes, watching their early investments appreciate. Residents whose cooperatives owned the ground-floor retail spaces of their buildings made out particularly well. As the area's retail scene took off, the rents for these shops covered monthly maintenance fees and necessary building renovations. A 2008 change in federal tax law allowing cooperatives to earn more than 20 percent of their income from commercial tenants (as opposed to contributions from tenant shareholders) helped greatly in this regard.[1]

Although some early residents remain, nearly everything else has changed. Perhaps the biggest transformation in SoHo has been its evolution from a neighborhood of artists of relatively modest means to one of the city's hottest real estate markets. This process began gradually. A 1978 study by the Rutgers University Center for Urban Policy Research found that 81 percent of loft residents had a college degree (as compared to 10.6 percent in New York City as a whole), while the median income of loft residents was $22,253 (as compared to $8,935 in the city as a whole). By that time, only 35 percent of

CONCLUSION

loft residents were artists, meaning that new, presumably wealthier residents were living in lofts in greater numbers.[2]

By the 1980s, it was clear that SoHo and its neighbor Tribeca were attracting an even wealthier clientele. Because of its large lofts and the neighborhood's location adjacent to the Financial District, from the 1980s onward many Tribeca residents feared that powerful forces were "working to re-create the area as a northern outpost of Wall Street." A major question that permeated debates over whether to give Tribeca its own historic district designation in the late 1980s was "where does the financial district end and where does TriBeCa begin?"[3]

Since the 1980s, SoHo and Tribeca have evolved into two of New York's priciest areas. These neighborhoods had the highest median sale prices for New York apartments in 2012, at $2.3 million and $1.9 million, respectively. Part of this pricing is due to the large size of loft homes. (Only Midtown and, ironically, urban renewal opponent Jane Jacobs's West Village had higher prices per square foot.) Some of this change has come about because, as former Loft Board president Carl Weisbrod noted, in the corporate world, "senior management increasingly in New York now lives in Tribeca and even in Park Slope and Brooklyn Heights" in addition to Westchester and Connecticut. Additionally, "investment bankers are as likely to live in Tribeca or SoHo as they are in Greenwich or Rye or East End Avenue."[4]

Another change has been the disappearance of industrial SoHo. Simply put, industry could not compete with residential real estate. For example, in 2008, the DeLorenzo family, owners of a metal shop that had been in business since 1907, sold their loft building on Grand Street near West Broadway to condo developers. The family had bought the building in 1968 for $65,000, but with some family members wanting to retire and the realization "that the shop is worth more closed than open," they sold it for a price "more than the business ever made in a century."[5]

Interestingly, even with the runaway success of SoHo real estate, the issue of illegality still hovers over the area. Despite the almost-complete residential transformation of the neighborhood, much of the area remains zoned for industry or remains part of the special SoHo artists zoning district. At times, this policy has affected large projects. Donald Trump and his partners sought to build a condo building on the site of a parking garage at 246 Spring Street, but the area is still zoned for manufacturing. However, since zoning allowed for "transient hotels," the developers sold units that can be inhabited only for 29 days in a 36-day period, or for no more than 120 days per year. The rest of the time, the condos are rented out as hotel rooms.[6]

Other times, the still-illegal nature of some SoHo lofts has affected the entire neighborhood. In 2010, home buyers, banks, and city leaders began once again to pay attention to the fact that numerous nonartists lived in lofts zoned for artists' joint living and working quarters. With the ever-increasing prices of SoHo lofts, buyers and their attorneys balked at the prospect of purchasing an illegal dwelling. Said one local real estate agent, "At these prices, buyers' attorneys are very loath to advise people to put that kind of investment into something that's limited. . . . It's like a lien on the property." With the financial downturn and foreclosure crisis of 2008, "banks worry that if mortgaged apartments go into foreclosure, the artist rule may make them harder to resell." At the same time, the Department of Cultural Affairs began to turn down artist certification requests. The department had certified roughly 3,400 artists since 1971; from 2003 to 2008, it certified 164 artists and rejected 11. But in 2009 the department accepted 14 artists and rejected 14. In the first eleven months of 2010, there had been 14 acceptances and 6 rejections.[7]

As a result, some presumably wealthy loft owners acted like 1960s artists and pushed for further loft legalization. In 2012, a group of property owners formed the SoHo/NoHo Action Committee and raised $30,000 to conduct a survey to determine how many artists certified by the city still live in SoHo and how many retail spaces are being occupied illegally. Much like earlier artist groups, the organization contended that "it wants to legitimize what has already happened: SoHo's loft spaces are no longer just for artists, and their current residents and owners shouldn't have the uncertainty of being at odds with city zoning law hanging over their heads."[8]

The transformation of SoHo's retail sector has been even more profound. No longer just a place serving gallery visitors, the area has become an international destination for high-end shopping. Again, this process began early. By the late 1970s, SoHo's commercial area was expanding into adjacent districts. In 1979, the *SoHo Weekly News* observed that Thompson Street, to the west of SoHo, contained "more than a dozen new boutiques and galleries" and could be considered "part of an expanding SoHo shopping district."[9] In the 1980s, some of the area's retail pioneers were priced out. Steven Burger, who had run a men's boutique at 172 Spring Street since 1972, saw his rent increase from $1,100 to $5,000 a month in 1980. Burger said, "Before, it was driving out the little mom-and-pop grocery stores, but now they're going after the boutiques and the upper-middle-class things. . . . If that happens to a store like myself, what can replace it? There's no room for the little guy anymore."[10]

Galleries, particularly cooperatives, also faced financial pressures. For example, A.I.R. paid $350 per month when it first rented loft space in 1972 and had seen only modest rent increases. However, with SoHo real estate booming in 1980, the gallery's landlord offered a lease renewal at $2,200 per month for the first two years, eventually going up to $3,200 per month for the sixth year. Gallery members decided to move operations to 63 Crosby Street in 1981, with increases in member fees covering the purchase price of the new space.[11] Cooperative gallery 14 Sculptors had its landlord increase rent from $350 to $1,000 a month in 1981, forcing the co-op to close and become "a gallery without walls." Rising rents also forced the Prince Street Gallery, Green Mountain, and Bowery Galleries to merge into a four thousand-square-foot space at 121 Wooster Street. Even on the less-desirable second floor, the space rented for $1,100 a month with a 10 percent increase per year.[12]

Many of SoHo's commercial galleries left SoHo in the 1990s, although more due to the changing character of the neighborhood and the need for even larger spaces to house the works of a new generation of artists than because of rising rents.[13] Paula Cooper sold her SoHo space and moved her gallery to Chelsea in 1996, and Nancy Hoffman did the same in 2008. There are no more galleries at 420 West Broadway: all the original gallery tenants sold out and the upper floors have been converted into condominiums. Although there are some galleries left in SoHo, of the neighborhood's early gallery tenants, only Louis K. Meisel Gallery remains.[14]

As galleries closed, upscale retail establishments took their place. Today, visitors and locals often describe SoHo as an "upscale mall." This evolution started with Dean & DeLuca. As cofounder Jack Ceglic remembers, the store "brought merchants that thought of themselves as high end" to the neighborhood for the first time. Meisel observed that after SoHo became a major tourist attraction, businesses moved in hoping to take advantage of the foot traffic, made up "theoretically of people with money." Dean & DeLuca's 1986 expansion to a space on Broadway once again led the way for changes in the neighborhood, as the store anchored an emerging retail district in the larger lofts on the block, which today dominate the area's scene.[15]

Today, SoHo's retail district often puts strains on its residents. The *New York Times* reported in 2010, "The artists who colonized the neighborhood decades ago may have secured castles in the sky, but they have also found themselves surrounded by streets that are clogged by tourists and lined with giant retailers and luxury stores." As a result, the SoHo Alliance, an outgrowth of earlier local artist groups, has led a charge against the formation of a Business Improvement District in SoHo, a public-private partnership that collects assessments to help pay for local improvements, better sanitation, marketing, and beautification. Some residents fear that this action would simply hand more power over to retail businesses and real estate interests.[16]

As a result of these changes, some SoHo residents sought out other inexpensive places to live and work. Starting in the late 1970s and early 1980s, people looked for industrial spaces to convert into homes and studios in other parts of the city. In 1980, the *SoHo Weekly News* reported, "Priced out of Manhattan by the loft conversion boom that has sent rents skyrocketing, artists are finding less expensive space" in Williamsburg, Brooklyn, "a rundown neighborhood with plenty of vacant lofts, brownstones and row houses." According to the paper, "In the early 1970s, a handful of black and Hispanic artists moved into the neighborhood, but few landlords believed that large numbers of artists—and certainly not white artists—would be willing to settle in Williamsburg," a prediction that proved to be emphatically wrong. Prices in Williamsburg were low. Dave Clark and Wendy Oberlin paid $325 a month for a 2,300-square-foot loft apartment. Like their wealthier peers in SoHo, most artists in Williamsburg were living illegally.[17]

Artists also migrated to the industrial area of Long Island City, Queens. By 1980, there were approximately 250 painters, sculptors, musicians, writers, and craftspeople living in a community of 800 manufacturing, distributing, and warehousing firms integrated into a predominantly working-class Italian community. Long Island City lofts were impressive spaces. Jeanany Morley, a twenty-four-year-old photographer, found a three thousand-square-foot Long Island City loft with thirteen-foot-high ceilings and views of the Manhattan skyline. Newer artists followed established sculptors Isamu Noguchi and Roy Gussow, who moved to the neighborhood in the 1960s to be able to make noise late at night in large spaces while remaining close to subway stops and highways that would take them into Manhattan. The neighborhood also had amenities, such as Italian restaurants and workers' bars, as well as the up-and-coming arts center Project Studios 1 (P.S. 1). Yet, the *New York Times* reported, "Anyone anticipating a stampede for conversion for a SoHo type community will probably get a lot of opposition from artists, among others, who want to see rents kept accessible and believe artists have been priced out of other areas once boutiques and restaurants move in."[18]

By the early 1980s, there was evidence that the SoHo model of urban development was inspiring housing changes in cities worldwide. In the early part of the decade, residents in the Vieux-Montreal neighborhood of Montreal converted lofts into homes. As sociologist Julie Anne Podmore found, the Montreal press disseminated images and profiles of SoHo and Tribeca lofts and their residents (the same type of lifestyle article that the New York media created a decade before) that "constructed a model of possible locations, aesthetics and identities for particular social groups in the inner city." In turn, these articles and the image of the SoHo loft helped bring about the notion of the "loft as a domestic space" and "the re-coding of inner-city

CONCLUSION   235

industrial buildings . . . as potential live/work or domestic spaces." Developers transformed the London Docklands from a commercial and industrial district to an upscale residential loft district at roughly the same time. London's Clerkenwell industrial district underwent a similar conversion (after a brief time as a location for secondary office space) a decade later. Musicians and other residents of Sydney, Australia, converted warehouses into lofts in the late 1970s. In the first decade of the twenty-first century, a developer-led loft-conversion boom featured projects named "New York, New York" and "TriBeCa" that directly drew on Lower Manhattan loft's lineage.[19]

By the 1990s, loft living had spread throughout much of the United States. A 2006 article in *Realtor*, the magazine of the National Association of Realtors, found that loft housing had spread to cities as diverse as Chicago, Las Vegas, and Atlanta.[20] Some of these new lofts were in converted buildings, while others were newly constructed. Indeed, it is difficult to find a contemporary American city without residential lofts.

Beyond the spread of the loft, perhaps SoHo's most obvious impact on the landscape of cities has been the naming of neighborhoods elsewhere. SuHu (Superior-Huron) in Chicago, SoDo (South of Downtown) in Denver, SoCo (South of Congress) in Austin, SoFi (South of Fifth) in Miami, SoMa (South of Market) and NoPa (North of the Panhandle) in San Francisco, SoFo (South of Folkungagatan) in Stockholm, and Palermo SoHo in Buenos Aires—it is hard to find a city without a neighborhood whose name can be traced back to SoHo.[21]

As the two international examples indicate, city leaders, real estate interests, and the press will go a long way to fit the SoHo template, even borrowing English words or fully incorporating the name "SoHo" into their neologisms. In choosing these names, the area's boosters were hoping that their neighborhood would also have boutiques and wealthier residents. The areas named after SoHo might have been industrial, and loft buildings may have had a prominent presence. However, most of the neighborhoods have some sort of gritty coolness that inventors, brokers, or boosters are hoping to exploit.

This points to a broader question: Why have so many people invented neighborhood names that are reminiscent of SoHo? Few cities possess the an art community akin to New York's in the 1960s and '70s, cast-iron lofts are rare, and it would be hard to replicate the confluence of political and economic factors that allowed for SoHo's development. Yet many cities do have artists and art galleries, and ironically, the form of development created in SoHo does not need a large concentration of noted artists or galleries to occur. Since it was visitors to art galleries, not the galleries themselves, who generated the economic activity that drove SoHo's transition from an artist enclave to an upper-income area, all a neighborhood needs to emulate it is a way to keep galleries open—perhaps through art sales, government subsidies, or below-market rent—to draw visitors who have the potential to inspire development in the SoHo manner. Moreover, these neighborhoods do not even need galleries to undergo redevelopment. Often, a mere countercultural or "hipster" presence is enough to inspire visions of the type of real estate development that occurred in SoHo in the 1960s and '70s.

The desire to emulate SoHo's path to upscale residential enclave stems from an important element of its growth: the landscape left after the urban crisis of postwar American cities, deindustrialization, suburbanization, and the failures of urban renewal shaped the area's rebirth. The specific nature of deindustrialization in Lower Manhattan played a critical role in the neighborhood's growth. SoHo's industrial decline was rooted in its specific industries, such as rag and wastepaper recycling, warehousing, and light manufacturing, which were in a state of decline, as well as the general unsuitability of lofts for modern industry. Furthermore, deindustrialization in SoHo created a dense collection of vacant loft buildings close to the amenities of Greenwich Village, Little Italy, and Chinatown. These nearby residential neighborhoods made living in SoHo more attractive than taking up residence in an isolated, stand-alone industrial district.[22]

Artists themselves realized how the type of development they encouraged in SoHo provided a way for the city to prosper at a time of mass suburban exodus, and they sought to use this argument to their advantage. Throughout the debates over SoHo's future, artists highlighted the value of their own cultural capital to both replace the economic contributions of New York's vanishing industry and retain the middle class within the five boroughs. Artists noted that they helped make New York the world's leading artistic center, bringing the city money and prestige, and that they had the potential to redevelop real estate and attract affluent professionals to the city. Furthermore, it is likely that the decision to legalize loft living for artists and others was based on the desire to allow the redevelopment of SoHo to continue at a time of neighborhood decline across the city.

The form of development that artists pioneered in SoHo provided a way for cities to confront the urban crisis without the financial and social costs of slum clearance urban renewal. SoHo was very much a product of the reaction against urban renewal in the years after 1960. The neighborhood was almost a victim of urban renewal plans, and the growing backlash against slum clearance urban renewal caused these proposals to fail. Likewise, the mode of development that grew in SoHo was the antithesis of urban renewal. It was unplanned, and it stymied the attempts of experts or politicians to control

CONCLUSION 237

it, even to the present day. It relied on the reuse of local vernacular architecture that was far different from the international style often used in renewal projects. SoHo provided a distinctly urban alternative to the structures built through urban renewal. These projects mainly attempted to provide urban residents with amenities found in the suburbs, such as easy auto access, security, and a verdant, nonurban feel. SoHo was gritty, urban, dense, and all the more popular for it.

Of course, there are many cities across the country and around the world that have suffered from industrial exodus, population loss, downtown decline, and general urban crisis. For these cities, SoHo has served as either an explicit or implicit model for how these circumstances can foster urban redevelopment. Having a standard for the transformation of a neighborhood from industrial wasteland to artist enclave to hot real estate market, all at little or no cost to the city, has encouraged political leaders and real estate brokers to jump at the chance to encourage similar development.

Not all similarly named neighborhoods have shared SoHo's success because SoHo's growth was due in large part to the resiliency of New York and its economy during the 1970s and '80s. Despite the fiscal crisis of the 1970s, by the end of the decade the city's economy and real estate market was rebounding, reaching near boom levels in the 1980s. The deregulation of the financial industry and the record profits on Wall Street during the 1980s caused many New Yorkers to look to SoHo and Tribeca as places where they could both invest and acquire grand living spaces a short walk from work.

The attraction of Wall Street workers to lofts points to a broader link between artists and the middle class that developed in SoHo, one that anticipates the contemporary literature on the "creative class." In SoHo, one sees an example of artists creating an environment that wealthy professionals coveted. By inventing the loft, an attractive new mode of urban living, and helping to build an amenity-rich neighborhood in SoHo, artists created an atmosphere that attracted wealthy "creative" New Yorkers, such as "ad men," architects, and stockbrokers. Therefore, the history of SoHo demonstrates that it is perhaps the neighborhoods that artists create, rather than the artists themselves, that help draw and retain the creative class in cities. These middle-class New Yorkers sought a form of urban culture only artists could provide, and they flocked to SoHo as a result.

In the end, the most important lesson of SoHo might be that culture matters. Culture meant many things in SoHo. Artists created their own community culture that allowed them to renovate lofts and open galleries. The high culture of fine art brought capital, visitors, and attention to SoHo. It developed a mix of galleries, art-related shops, and dining options that gave it a distinct neighborhood culture that proved attractive to a broader population. It was also the fear of New York losing the one thing that it could cling to at this time of urban crisis, its place as the cultural capital of the world, that pushed policy makers to enact changes that allowed SoHo to develop, cementing the link between culture, the arts, and urban development in the minds of those interested in the fate of cities.

Acknowledgments

A research project that lasts the better part of a decade requires the support of many people who deserve great thanks. My family members have long been my biggest supporters in this endeavor. My wife, Christine Minerva, has gone above and beyond the call of duty by moving numerous times to support my academic career and by editing nearly everything I have written from age eighteen to the present, including several drafts of this manuscript. My sons, Niklas and Erik, whether they know it or not, had their early lives shaped by this book. I owe my love of urban history and culture to my parents, Anne and Greg Shkuda, who, before I could walk, took me on treks through Manhattan, on visits to art museums, and into quite a few art galleries. It is fitting that their first apartment and favorite 1970s restaurant play a role in this book. I am also grateful to my sister, Vanessa Shkuda, and in-laws, Jordy, Kathy, and Laura Minerva, for knowing when (and when not) to ask me about my "book."

Kathleen Neils Conzen was my intellectual guide throughout the writing process. I strive to one day be able to ask the type of insightful, productive questions she asks. James Sparrow and Neil Harris also shaped the project from its infancy to the present, pushing me to think bigger about the work and to make connections to ideas and historical actors beyond the twelve blocks of SoHo. Larry Rothfield encouraged me to reflect more broadly about culture and the arts. The project began as a paper in a seminar taught by George Chauncey, who, along with Mae Ngai, Amy Dru Stanley, Adam Green, and James Grossman, shaped my graduate education. The path to this book in many ways began in the tenth-grade AP European History class taught by Dr. David O'Connor, who first kindled my passion for analyzing primary sources and scholarly works.

Friends and colleagues along the way also provided immeasurable moral and intellectual support. Without the inspiration and encouragement of John Nielsen, Gavin Brockett, Lisa Andersen, and Matthew Perry, I would not have known what a historian was, let alone pursued history as a vocation. Phyllis Russell and the late John Fish stimulated my early thinking about policy and urban space. My graduate school classmates included Monica Mercado, Anthony Todd, Ross Yelsey, Melissa Borja, Peter Simons, Celeste Moore, Sam Lebovic, Jessica Neptune, Susannah Engstrom, Darryl Heller, Alison Lefkovitz, Sarah Potter, Mike Wakeford, David Spatz, and Jon Levy, who offered compelling conversations, insightful comments, and indefatigable moral support. My colleagues at the Office of Undergraduate Student Housing at the University of Chicago acted as sounding boards, collaborators, and friends. These colleagues included John and Karen Deak, Dan and Anna Steinhelper, Patrick and Heather LaRiviere, Lara Perez-Felkner and John Felkner, Katie Callow-Wright, and too many others to list here. Kate Lynch, Paul Eiss, Nico Slate, Joel Tarr, and Joe Trotter welcomed me into the History Department at Carnegie Mellon University (CMU). Special thanks goes to Caroline Acker for providing mentorship, orientation to Pittsburgh, and advice on this manuscript. Millington Bergson-Lockwood, Kevin McDonald, Kate Anderson, and Ross O'Connell provided camaraderie and intellectual support while at CMU. At Stanford, Ellen Woods, Parna Sengupta, and Michael Kahan kept me grounded in the humanities, while Scott Bukatman, Jonathan Berger, Jeff Chang, and Janice Ross pushed my thinking in new artistic directions. I am especially grateful to have had Michael Shane Boyle and Hillary Miller as colleagues, and I thank them for their feedback on this research. Alison Isenberg, Stan Allen, and Bruno Carvalho at Princeton gave me the opportunity to push my work, and career, in further interdisciplinary directions, and William Gleason, Fabrizio Gallanti, Lilian Knorr, Johana Londoño, Mariana Mogilevich, and Mario Torres helped me shape the manuscript into its final form. Beyond the institutions where I have worked, Suleiman Osman, Julia Foulkes, Sarah Schrank, Brian Goldstein, and Leon Botstein provided invaluable feedback, dialogue, and advice. Elizabeth Wampler consulted on several of the maps in this book and has been my on-call urban planner throughout the writing process.

I am also fortunate in having received tremendous support from institutions and foundations throughout my career. Special thanks to the Andrew W. Mellon Foundation; the Princeton-Mellon Initiative in Architecture, Urbanism, and the Humanities; and, along with the American Council on Learned Societies, my New Faculty Fellowship at Carnegie Mellon. I am also thankful for the generous support of the Social Sciences Collegiate Division

ACKNOWLEDGMENTS

and Office of the Provost at the University of Chicago for funding my graduate studies, and the New York State Archives Larry J. Hackman Research Residency and the Rockefeller Archive Center Grant-In-Aid program for funding my archival research. Finally, a grant from the Barr Ferree Foundation Publication Fund from the Department of Art and Archaeology at Princeton University supported the images used in this book.

My inquiries would not have gotten off the ground without the assistance of Frank Conaway at the University of Chicago Libraries, Robert Battaly and the staff at the Rockefeller Archive Center, and the gracious and helpful people at the New York City Municipal Archives, the New York University Libraries, the Archives of American Art, and the New York State Archives Research Center. I am also indebted to the SoHo residents who took the time to share their stories with me: Mary Heilmann, Yukie Ohta, Barbara Toll, Nancy Hoffman, Stephen and Naomi Antonakos, Jared Bark, Greg Turpan, Susan and Louis Meisel, Jack Ceglic, Betty Cunningham, Joel Name, Michelle Stone, Hirotsugu Aoki, Carl Weisbrod, Susan Penzner, Frits de Knegt, and Oz Hanley. Special thanks goes to Barbara Haskell, whose introductions opened the loft doors for me.

Finally, Robert Devens, Timothy Mennel, and Timothy Gilfoyle at the University of Chicago Press have been incredibly supportive editors who pushed the project to completion. I am thankful for their support and grateful to all those who helped make this project possible.

Notes

Introduction

1. "Follow the Drips of Paint," *New York Times* (hereafter cited as *NYT*), March 18, 2012, RE1; Robert Sullivan, "Psst . . . Have You Heard about Bushwick?" *NYT*, March 5, 2006. See also James E. Goodman, *Blackout* (New York: North Point Press, 2003).

2. Quoted in "Why Long Island City Hasn't Happened; Once, the Neighborhood Was Hailed as the Next SoHo; But Can You Build a Bohemia From Scratch," *NYT*, November 7, 1999. See also "Quiching Hoboken," *NYT*, March 23, 1982, B2; "Metamorphosis for Old Williamsburg," *NYT*, July 19, 1987, R9; "West Chelsea: Art Appears in the Latest 'Next SoHo,'" *NYT*, March 26, 1995, 48; "Once-Gritty Neighborhood Comes Alive: Some Feel Far West Village Area Could Be the Next SoHo," *NYT*, February 16, 1997, R5; "Moving Out: Seeking the Next SoHo," *NYT*, September 12, 2004, RE1; "Gowanus Is Counting on a Cleanup," *NYT*, October 3, 2014.

3. In addition to Ruth Glass's original definition of the term in *London: Aspects of Change* (London: MacGibbon and Kee, 1964), often-cited definitions of *gentrification* are by geographer Chris Hamnett (1984) and Herbert Marcuse (1999). See, for example, discussions in Maureen Kennedy and Paul Leonard, "Dealing with Neighborhood Change: A Primer on Gentrification and Policy Changes" (discussion paper prepared for the Brookings Institution Center on Urban and Metropolitan Policy, Washington, DC, April 2001); Winifred Curran, "'From the Frying Pan to the Oven': Gentrification and the Experience of Industrial Displacement in Williamsburg, Brooklyn," *Urban Studies* 44, no. 8 (July 2007): 1427–40; Michael Barton, "An Exploration of the Importance of the Strategy Used to Identify Gentrification," *Urban Studies*, published electronically December 3, 2014, http://usj.sagepub.com/content/early/2014/12/03/0042098014561723.full.pdf+html. For a discussion of race in gentrification, see Lance Freeman, *There Goes the Hood: Views of Gentrification from the Ground Up* (Philadelphia: Temple University Press, 2006).

4. Loretta Lees, "A Reappraisal of Gentrification: Towards a 'Geography of Gentrification,'" *Progress in Human Geography*, no. 24 (2000): 389–408; David Ley, *The New Middle Class and the Remaking of the Central City* (New York: Oxford University Press, 1996); Jon Caulfield, *City Form and Everyday Life: Toronto's Gentrification and Critical Social Practice* (Toronto: University of Toronto Press, 1994); Neil Smith, *The New Urban Frontier: Gentrification and the Revanchist City* (New York: Routledge, 1996); Jason Hackworth and Neil Smith, "The Changing State of

Gentrification," *Tijdschrift voor Economische en Sociale Geografie* 92, no. 4 (2002): 464–77; Neil Brenner and Nik Theodore, *Spaces of Neoliberalism: Urban Restructuring in North America and America and Western Europe* (Malden, MA: Blackwell, 2002).

5. Richard Lloyd, *Neo-Bohemia: Art and Commerce in the Postindustrial City* (Chicago: University of Chicago Press, 2005); Rosalyn Deutsche and Cara Gendel Ryan, "The Fine Art of Gentrification," *October* 31 (Winter 1984): 91–111; David Ley, "Artists, Aestheticisation, and the Field of Gentrification," *Urban Studies*, no. 12 (November 2003): 2527–44; Ley, *New Middle Class*, 24.

6. Sharon Zukin, *Loft Living: Culture and Capital in Urban Change* (Baltimore: Johns Hopkins University Press, 1982), 2. For other analyses of SoHo, see James R. Hudson, *The Unanticipated City: Loft Conversions in Lower Manhattan* (Amherst: University of Massachusetts Press, 1987); Charles P. Simpson, *SoHo: The Artist in the City* (Chicago: University of Chicago Press, 1981); Roberta Brandes Gratz, *The Battle for Gotham: New York in the Shadow of Robert Moses and Jane Jacobs* (New York: Nation Books, 2010), 95–119. Richard Kostelanetz also provides a compelling first-person history of the SoHo artist community in *SoHo: The Rise and Fall of an Artists' Colony* (New York: Routledge, 2003). The excellent one-building study, Roslyn Bernstein and Shael Shapiro, *Illegal Living: 80 Wooster Street and the Evolution of SoHo* (Vilnius, Lithuania: Jonas Mekas Foundation, 2010), will also contribute to my analysis.

7. Elizabeth Currid, "Bohemia as Subculture, 'Bohemia' as Industry: Art, Culture, and Economic Development," *Journal of Planning Literature* 23, no. 4 (May 2009): 368–82.

8. Ruth Glass et al., eds., *London: Aspects of Change* (London: MacGibbon and Kee, 1964), xviii.

9. Historical studies of gentrification include Suleiman Osman, *The Invention of Brownstone Brooklyn: Gentrification and the Search for Authenticity in Postwar New York* (New York: Oxford University Press, 2011), and Brian Goldstein, "A City within a City: Community Development and the Struggle Over Harlem, 1961–2001" (PhD diss., Harvard University, 2013).

10. This literature includes Arnold R. Hirsch, *Making the Second Ghetto: Race and Housing in Chicago, 1950–1960.* (1983; repr., Chicago: University of Chicago Press, 1998); Thomas J. Sugrue, *The Origins of the Urban Crisis: Race and Inequality in Postwar Detroit* (Princeton, NJ: Princeton University Press, 1996); Kenneth Jackson: *Crabgrass Frontier: The Suburbanization of the United States* (New York: Oxford University Press, 1985); Becky Nicolaides, *My Blue Heaven: Life and Politics in the Working-Class Suburbs of Los Angeles, 1920–1935* (Chicago: University of Chicago Press, 2002); Robert O. Self, *American Babylon: Race and the Struggle for Postwar Oakland* (Princeton, NJ: Princeton University Press, 2003); Matthew D. Lassiter, *The Silent Majority: Suburban Politics in the Sunbelt South* (Princeton, NJ: Princeton University Press, 2006); Samuel Zipp, *Manhattan Projects: The Rise and Fall of Urban Renewal in Cold War New York* (New York: Oxford University Press, 2010); Samuel Zipp, "The Roots and Routes of Urban Renewal," *Journal of Urban History* 39, no. 3 (May 2013): 366–39.

11. Christopher Klemek, *The Transatlantic Collapse of Urban Renewal: Postwar Urbanism from New York to Berlin* (Chicago: University of Chicago Press, 2011).

12. Illegal living among countercultural groups occurred elsewhere on a wide scale, most notably the squatting movement in Berlin in the late 1970s and early 1980s. See, for example, Andrej Holm and Armin Kuhn, "Squatting and Urban Renewal: The Interaction of Squatter Movements and Strategies of Urban Restructuring in Berlin," *International Journal of Urban and Regional Research* 35, no. 3 (May 2011): 644–58.

13. The classic texts on the urban crisis include Sugrue, *Origins of the Urban Crisis*; K. Jackson, *Crabgrass Frontier*. On the effects of urban renewal, see Hirsch, *Making the Second Ghetto*;

Robert Caro, *The Power Broker: Robert Moses and the Fall of New York* (New York: Vintage, 1975); Eric Avila, "Revisiting the Urban Interstates: Politics, Policy, and Culture Since World War II," *Journal of Urban History* 50, no. 5 (September 2014): 827–30. For views of the urban crisis and additional analyses of urban renewal in New York, see Zipp, *Manhattan Projects*; Joe Austin, *Taking the Train: How Graffiti Art Became an Urban Crisis in New York City* (New York: Columbia University Press, 2001); Miriam Greenberg, *Branding New York: How a City in Crisis Was Sold to the World* (New York: Routledge, 2008); Martin Shefter, *Political Crisis/Fiscal Crisis: The Collapse and Revival of New York City* (New York: Basic Books, 1985); Jonathan Mahler, *Ladies and Gentlemen, the Bronx Is Burning: 1977, Baseball, Politics, and the Battle for the Soul of a City* (New York: Farrar, Straus and Giroux), 2005.

14. Alexandra Anderson-Spivy, *Anderson and Archer's SoHo: The Essential Guide to Art and Life in Lower Manhattan* (New York: Simon and Schuster, 1979); Abigail R. Esman and Roland Hagenberg, eds., *SoHo: A Guide; A Documentary* (New York: Egret Publications, 1978).

15. Dorothy Seiberling, "SoHo: The Most Exciting Place to Live in the City," *New York Magazine*, May 20, 1974, 52–53.

16. Lloyd, *Neo-Bohemia*, 66; Jerrold Seigel, *Bohemian Paris: Culture, Politics, and the Boundaries of Bourgeois Life, 1830–1930* (New York: Viking, 1986); Mary Gluck, *Popular Bohemia: Modernism and Urban Culture in Nineteenth-Century Paris* (Cambridge, MA: Harvard University Press, 2005); Christine Stansell, *American Moderns: Bohemian New York and the Creation of a New Century* (New York: Metropolitan Books, 2000); Caroline F. Ware, *Greenwich Village, 1920–1930: A Comment on American Civilization in the Post-War Years* (1935; repr., Berkeley: University of California Press, 1994), 20–21; Ross Wetzsteon, *Republic of Dreams: Greenwich Village: The American Bohemia, 1910–1960* (New York: Simon and Schuster, 2002); Currid, "Bohemia as Subculture," 368–82. Other studies of urban bohemians include Daniel Hurewitz, *Bohemian Los Angeles and the Making of Modern Politics* (Berkeley: University of California Press, 2007), and Elizabeth Wilson, *Bohemians: The Glamorous Outcasts* (New Brunswick, NJ: Rutgers University Press, 2000).

17. Richard Florida, *The Rise of the Creative Class . . . and How It's Transforming Working, Leisure, Community, and Everyday Life* (New York: Basic Books, 2002); Ann Markusen and Anne Gadwa, "A White Paper for the Mayors' Institute on City Design, a Leadership Initiative on the National Endowment for the Arts in Partnership with the United States Conference of Mayors and American Architectural Foundation" (National Endowment for the Arts, Washington, DC, 2010).

18. See, for example, Ann Markusen, "Urban Development and the Politics of a Creative Class: Evidence from a Study of Artists," *Environment and Planning A* 38, no. 10 (October 2006): 1921–40; Ian David Moss, "Creative Placemaking Has an Outcomes Problem," May 9, 2012, http://createquity.com/2012/05/creative-placemaking-has-an-outcomes-problem.html. For a summary of critiques of Florida's creative class theory, see Joel Kotkin, "Richard Florida Concedes the Limits of the Creative Class," *Daily Beast* (blog), March 20, 2013, http://www.thedailybeast.com/articles/2013/03/20/richard-florida-concedes-the-limits-of-the-creative-class.html.

Chapter One

1. "Report of Collapse of Building, 466–468 Broadway, February 16, 1966," Box 5, Folder 6, Records of Weiss & Klau Co., MS 687, New-York Historical Society (hereafter cited as *Weiss & Klau*); "Loft Caves in—Six Trapped," *New York Post* (hereafter cited as *NYP*), January 27,

1966, 1, Box 5, Folder 10, *Weiss & Klau*; "Plant Caves In; 11 Hurt; Dig Out Five," *New York Daily News* (hereafter cited as *NYDN*), January 28, 1966, 1, Box 5, Folder 10, *Weiss & Klau*; "Civil War Building Collapse; 12 Hurt," *New York Herald-Tribune* (hereafter cited as *NYH-T*), January 28, 1966, 1, Box 5, Folder 10, *Weiss & Klau*; "2 Are Trapped and 4 Injured; Hundreds Flee," *New York Journal-American*, Box 5, Folder 10, *Weiss & Klau*.

2. "Report of Collapse"; "Civil War Building Collapse."

3. "Report of Collapse."

4. *SoHo–Cast Iron District Designation* (New York City Landmarks Preservation Commission, 1973), 37; "Summary of Minutes of 461 Broadway Corporation," Box 1, Folder 7, *Weiss & Klau*.

5. Although the phrase "SoHo" was not popularly used to describe the area south of Houston Street until the late 1960s and early 1970s, for simplicity's sake I have used the term to refer to the area before that time.

6. Joel Schwartz, *The New York Approach: Robert Moses, Urban Liberals, and the Redevelopment of the Inner City* (Columbus: Ohio State University Press, 1993), 229–38. Chicago experienced similar efforts to replace and upgrade light industry near downtown, as a progrowth coalition of business and government leaders worked to remove printers, garment makers, metalworkers, food processors, and manufacturers in turn-of-the-century loft buildings near downtown. Many of these lofts were transformed into upscale residences and back-office spaces for downtown corporations. See Joel Rast, *Remaking Chicago: The Political Origins of Urban Industrial Change* (DeKalb: Northern Illinois University Press, 1999).

7. Schwartz, *New York Approach*, 234.

8. Joshua B. Freeman, *Working-Class New York: Life and Labor Since World War II* (New York: New Press, distributed by W. W. Norton, 2000), 10, 14–15.

9. Schwartz, *New York Approach*, 251.

10. "Housing Dispute Put Up to Mayor," *NYT*, June 2, 1963, 46.

11. Klemek, *Transatlantic Collapse of Urban Renewal*, 136–39, 145–60.

12. It is worth noting that this resistance to industrial renewal occurred before the city's fiscal crisis, the period when Schwartz found that resistance to job-destroying renewal projects first arose.

13. "SoHo," in Kenneth Jackson, ed., *The Encyclopedia of New York City* (New Haven, CT: Yale University Press, 1995), 1088; *SoHo—Cast Iron Historic District Designation*, 4.

14. *SoHo—Cast Iron Historic District Designation*, 4–5.

15. Ibid., 5.

16. Ibid.

17. Ibid., 5; Charles Lockwood, *Manhattan Moves Uptown: An Illustrated History* (Boston: Houghton Mifflin, 1976), 36.

18. Lockwood, *Manhattan Moves Uptown*, 73, 100, 125.

19. K. Jackson, *Encyclopedia of New York City*, 1088.

20. Lockwood, *Manhattan Moves Uptown*, 133, 162; *SoHo—Cast Iron Historic District Designation*, 6; Bernstein and Shapiro, *Illegal Living*, 4.

21. Timothy Gilfoyle, *City of Eros: New York City, Prostitution, and the Commercialization of Sex, 1790–1920* (New York: W. W. Norton, 1994), 30, 53, 120–24.

22. Chester Rapkin, *The South Houston Industrial Area: A Study of the Economic Significance of Firms, the Physical Quality of Buildings, and the Real Estate Market in an Old Loft Section of Lower Manhattan* (New York: City of New York City Planning Commission-Department of City Planning, 1963), 10–12; K. Jackson, *Encyclopedia of New York City*, 1088; *SoHo—Cast Iron Historic District Designation*, 7.

23. Lockwood, *Manhattan Moves Uptown*, 284–86; Bernstein and Shapiro, *Illegal Living*, 8, 10.

24. Bernstein and Shapiro, *Illegal Living*, 16; K. Jackson, *Encyclopedia of New York City*, 1088; *SoHo—Cast Iron Historic District Designation*, 9.

25. *SoHo—Cast Iron Historic District Designation*, 12, 14.

26. Ibid., 22; K. Jackson, *Encyclopedia of New York City*, 1088.

27. *SoHo—Cast Iron Historic District Designation*, 14, 22.

28. Ibid.

29. Rapkin, *South Houston Industrial Area*, 10–12.

30. Nancy L. Greene, "From Downtown Tenements to Midtown Lofts: The Shifting Geography of an Urban Industry," in Daniel Soyer, ed., *A Coat of Many Colors: Immigration, Globalization, and Reform in New York City's Garment Industry* (New York: Fordham University Press, 2006), 33–36.

31. Rapkin, *South Houston Industrial Area*, 10–12.

32. Louis Meisel, interview with the author, New York, NY, August 8, 2012; Michelle Stone, interview with the author, New York, NY, August 13, 2012.

33. Bernstein and Shapiro, *Illegal Living*, 19–33.

34. "Summary of Minutes of the Weiss & Klau Co.," Box 1, Folder 7; "Born in 1877 . . . A Brief Biography of the Weiss & Klau Co. and Those Who Helped It Grow . . ." (1939), Box 12, Folder 6; "Letter to the IRS Re. The Weiss & Klau Co. Partial Liquidation, Draft (3/9/67)," Box 11, Folder 6, all in *Weiss & Klau*. The company officially took the name Weiss & Klau Co. after a merger with the Napaul Corporation, December 30, 1922. Adjusted sale price derived from Bureau of Labor Statistics CPI Inflation Calculator, May 16, 2015 (http://www.bls.gov/data/inflation_calculator.htm).

35. "Summary of Minutes of the Weiss & Klau Co." Inflation figures from CPI Inflation Calculator, May 16, 2015 (http://www.bls.gov/data/inflation_calculator.htm); "Born in 1877"; "Report of Closing to Title, 462–4 Broadway, Manhattan, New York City, December 30, 1941," Box 4, Folder 13, *Weiss & Klau*.

36. "Summary of Minutes for the 462 Broadway Corporation," Box 1, Folder 7; "The Market Outlook for Oilcloth," Box 9, Folder 5, "Summary of Minutes of the Weiss & Klau Co."; "Summary of Minutes for Standard Coated Products Corporation," Box 1, Folder 7, all in *Weiss & Klau*.

37. "Summary of Minutes of the Weiss & Klau Co."; "Memo Dated 11/12/65 from Weiss & Klau Co. to DeSoto Chemical Coatings of Des Plaines, IL Re. Possible Merger," Box 10, Folder 2, *Weiss & Klau*.

38. Rapkin, *South Houston Industrial Area*, 12–17.

39. Ibid., 17–19.

40. Gail Garfield Schwartz, "Industrial Accommodation in New York City: The Women's and Children's Undergarment Industry" (PhD diss., Columbia University, 1972).

41. Rapkin, *South Houston Industrial Area*, 21–29, 37–39, 101–5.

42. Ibid., 47, 54–56, 117, 121. Inflation statistics calculated with CPI Inflation Calculator, May 16, 2015 (http://www.bls.gov/data/inflation_calculator.htm).

43. Rapkin, *South Houston Industrial Area*, 66–77.

44. Ibid., 66–77, 136–37, 144.

45. Ibid., 93–97, 105–8.

46. "Loft Caves In—Six Trapped"; "Plant Caves In"; "Loft Building Collapse Spurs Plea for Inspections," New York World Telegram & Sun (hereafter cited as NYWT&S), January 27, 1966, 3, Box 5, Folder 10; "Loft Collapse Spurs Cleanup of 'Hell's Acres," [January 1966], Box 5, Folder 10;

"Moerdler Promises to End Corruption," *NYH-T*, February 2, 1966, Box 5, Folder 10; "Collapse of Loft Spurs City Drive," *NYT*, January 29, 1966, 1, Box 5, Folder 10; "Letter to the IRS," all in *Weiss & Klau*.

47. "Weiss & Klau Still Delivering Despite Cave-In at Building," *Home Furnishings Daily*, January 31, 1966, Box 5, Folder 10; "Letter to the IRS"; both in *Weiss & Klau*.

48. "Letter to the IRS"; "Memo of Sale to Breneman, Inc. of Cincinnati 2/26/1966," Box 10, Folder 3, *Weiss & Klau*. Sales data taken from New York City Automated City Register Information System (ACRIS, http://a836-acris.nyc.gov/Scripts/DocSearch.dll/BBL), June 9, 2012, Block 473, Lot 001; "Summary of Minutes of the Weiss & Klau Co."; "Closing Memorandum for Sale of Assets of the Weiss & Klau Co. to American Cyanamid Company, October 2, 1968," Box 11, Folder 2, "Liquidation and Dissolution of 462 Broadway Corporation and Sale of Real Property of 462 Broadway Corporation to Chatham Associates, Inc.," Box 11, Folder 5; all in *Weiss & Klau*.

49. Title I of the Housing Act of 1949 provided federal funding for municipalities to purchase land in areas they deemed "slums." The federal government would pay two-thirds of the cost, with local governments covering the remainder. The property would then be given to private builders to develop in a way the city saw fit.

50. Sugrue, *Origins of Urban Crisis*; Michael Carriere, "Fighting the War against Blight: Columbia University, Morningside Heights, Inc., and Counterinsurgent Urban Renewal," *Journal of Planning History* 10, no. 1 (February 2011): 5–29.

51. "Letter from Henry R. Heald to Robert Moses about Slum Clearance, 12/6/52," "Letter from Chancellor Henry T. Heald to Robert Moses 2/16/1953," "Draft of a Statement to City Hall Dictated by the Office of Mr. Beggs at the Slum Clearance Committee, 3/11/1953," all in Records of the Office of the President/Chancellor; RG 3.0.6, Box 12, Folder 3, New York University Archives, New York University Libraries (hereafter cited as *NYU* Archives).

52. "RE: Washington Square Southeast Project [1953]," "Statement by New York University on Proposed Washington Square Southeast Redevelopment Project, October 8, 1953," Box 12, Folder 3, NYU Archives.

53. "Conference held February 6, 1953, in Chancellor Heald's Office Concerning the Slum Clearance Project in the Washington Square Vicinity," "RE: Washington Square Southeast Project [1953]," Box 12, Folder 3; both in NYU Archives.

54. "Report on Clearance Issued," *Villager*, August 27, 1953; "Planning Washington Square," *NYT*, August 8, 1953; "Washington Square Plans of NYU Hit by Broker," *New York World Telegram & Sun* (hereafter cited as *NYWT&S*), September 2, 1953; "'Village' Rebuilding Opposed," *NYT*, September 3, 1953; "Village Plans" *NYH-T*, August 1953; all in Box 12, Folder 8, NYU Archives.

55. "Statement re. Greenwich Village," "Statement on the Proposed Washington Square Southeast Redevelopment Project, Leonard Mandelbaum, President, Student Council Washington Square College, CPC Hearing, 10/14/53," "Statement of the Proposed Washington Square Southeast Redevelopment Project, David D. Henry, Executive Vice Chancellor, New York University, New York City Planning Commission Hearing, October 14, 1953," all in Box 12, Folder 5, NYU Archives.

56. The Board of Estimate was the governing body that had authority to set the city's budget, as well as other residual powers, made up of the mayor, the five borough presidents, the city council president, and the comptroller. "Board of Estimate," in K. Jackson, *Encyclopedia of New York City*, 122.

57. "Washington Square Plea," *NYH-T,* November 16, 1953; "Washington Sq. Protest," *NYT,* December 16, 1953; "N.Y.U. Head Chides Slum Razing Foes," *NYT,* January 6, 1954; "Washington Sq. Project Plea Planned by N.Y.U.," *NYH-T,* January 6, 1954; "Moses Plan Adopted by NYU," *Villager,* January 7, 1954; "'Village' Project Is Opposed Anew," *NYT,* January 12, 1954; "'Village' Plan Opposed,'" *NYT,* January 14, 1954; "Citizens Union Opposes Project," *Villager,* January 21, 1954; "Washington Sq. Plan Called Costly to City," *NYH-T,* January 11, 1954; "Washington Sq. Project Seen Increasing Jobless," *NYH-T,* January 12, 1954; "Business to Fight Village Project," *NYT,* January 12, 1954; "Washington Square," *NYT,* January 13, 1954; all in Box 12, Folder 8, NYU Archives.

58. "Washington Square," *NYT,* January 13, 1954; "Southeast of the Square," *NYH-T,* January 22, 1954; both in Box 12, Folder 8, NYU Archives.

59. "Okay Wash. Sq. Housing Table, Two Projects," *NYDN,* January 27, 1954; "Washington Sq. Housing Voted," *New York Journal-American,* January 27, 1954; "Washington Sq. OKd," *NYP,* January 27, 1954; "High-Rental Project OKd for the Village," *NYWT&S,* January 27, 1954; "Protests Fail, Board Votes Village Housing," *Villager,* January 28, 1954; "9-Block Project for 'Village' Gets Board's Approval," *NYT,* January 27, 1954; all in Box 12, Folder 8, NYU Archives.

60. "6-Block Project to Rise in Village," *NYT,* July 15, 1957, 21; "Bohemian Flair Fades In Village," *NYT,* December 8, 1957, W1; "Urban Renewal Failure," *NYT,* January 12, 1964, R1; "NYU's Bid for Title I Land Denounced at GVA Meeting," *Village Voice* (hereafter cited as *VV*), April 13, 1960, 1; "NYU Co-op: The Shape of Things to Come," *VV,* January 26, 1961, 1; all in Box 12, Folder 9, NYU Archives; Francis Morrone, *The Architectural Guidebook to New York City* (Salt Lake City, UT: Gibbs Smith, 2002), 80.

61. "Report of Mr. Pitman Regarding the Washington Square Southeast Slum Clearance Project before the Sub-Committee on Small Business, House of Representatives," July 29, 1955, Box 12, Folder 4, NYU Archives; "Probers Air Housing Deal in the Village," *NYWT&S,* April 19, 1955; "Committee Sifts 'Village' Project," *NYT,* April 20, 1955; "Early Decision on Razing Area Here," *Villager,* April 28, 1955; all three in Box 12; Folder 9, NYU Archives; *Handbook of Texas Online,* s.v. "Patman, John William Wright (1893–1976)," by Philip A. Grant Jr., http://www.tshaonline.org/handbook/online/articles/fpa62.

62. "Planners Okay Three Housing Developments," *NYDN,* December 10, 1953; "Okay Wash. Sq. Housing Table, Two Projects," *NYDN,* January 27, 1954; both in Box 12, Folder 8, NYU Archives.

63. K. Jackson, *Encyclopedia of New York City,* 228; City Club of New York, *The Wastelands of New York City: A Preliminary Inquiry into the Nature of Commercial Slum Areas, Their Potential for Housing and Business Redevelopment* (New York: City Club of New York, 1962).

64. City Club of New York, *Wastelands of New York City.*

65. Ibid.

66. "Letter from Mr. I. D. Robbins to Charles D. Moerdler, Commissioner City of New York Department of Buildings," January 28, 1966, City Planning Commission Subject Files, Commissioner William F. R. Ballard, 68–015, Box 1, Folder 10, Municipal Archives of the City of New York; "Report on 1962–3 Urban Renewal Program," City Planning Commission Subject Files, Commissioner H. Goldstone 69–004, Box 26, Folder 2, Municipal Archives of the City of New York; "Is Loft Area Incubator or Slum?" *VV,* April 2, 1964, 5.

67. Rapkin, *South Houston Industrial Area.*

68. Ibid., 3–29, 47–50, 62.

69. Ibid., 39–44, 101–3.

70. Ibid., 5, 75, 283–99.
71. "South Houston Industrial Area: A Report and Program by the New York City Planning Commission," 1, 10–11, Margot Gayle Papers, New-York Historical Society.
72. Ibid., 1, 12.
73. Ibid., 1, 13.
74. Ibid., 15–16.
75. "Housing Dispute Put Up to Mayor;" *NYT*, June 2, 1963, 46.

Chapter Two

1. Stephen Antonakos and Naomi Antonakos, interview with the author, New York, NY, June 26, 2012.
2. Jared Bark, interview with the author, New York, NY, June 26, 2012.
3. Jack Ceglic, interview with the author, East Hampton, NY, August 9, 2012.
4. Samuel Zipp, "The Roots and Routes of Urban Renewal," *Journal of Urban History* 39, no. 3 (May 2013): 366–91.
5. Osman, *Invention of Brownstone Brooklyn*, 10.
6. Elizabeth Currid-Halkett, *The Warhol Economy: How Fashion, Art, and Music Drive New York City* (Princeton, NJ: Princeton University Press, 2007), 4, 7, 74, 92; Stephen and Naomi Antonakos interview.
7. "City Artists Facing New, Lofty Problem," *NYWT&S*, November 14, 1962, 3; Volunteer Lawyers for the Arts, *Housing for Artists: The New York Experience* (New York: Willkie Farr and Gallagher/Volunteer Lawyers for the Arts, 1976), 14–15.
8. S. J. Makielski Jr., *The Politics of Zoning: The New York Experience* (New York: Columbia University Press, 1966).
9. Volunteer Lawyers for the Arts, *Housing for Artists*, 9.
10. Michael Levine, *Artist Housing in South Houston: A Report Presented by the New York City Planning Commission, Prepared by Michael E. Levine (1968–9)* (New York: New York City Planning Commission, 1969), in SoHo Artists Association records, 1963–1972, Archives of American Art, Smithsonian Institution, Washington, DC (hereafter cited as *SAA Records*), Box 1, Folder 9; "Untitled 24 Page History of Artist Housing in SoHo written by Gerhardt Liebmann [1970]," Box 1, Folder 6, SAA Records; Peter Mellman, "SoHo Artists' Bohemia Imperiled," *New York Magazine*, 1970, Box 1, Folder 14, SAA Records; "SoHo Artists Association: A White Paper on the Need to Legitimize Artists' Studio-Residences in the South Houston Area," n.d., Box 1, Folder 4, SAA Records.
11. Serge Guilbaut, *How New York Stole the Idea of Modern Art: Abstract Expressionism, Freedom, and the Cold War*, trans. Arthur Goldhammer (Chicago: University of Chicago Press, 1983), 119; Donna M. Binkiewicz, *Federalizing the Muse: United States Arts Policy and the National Endowment for the Arts, 1965–1980* (Chapel Hill: University of North Carolina Press, 2006), 19–20.
12. Jed Perl, *New Art City: Manhattan at Mid-Century* (New York: Knopf, 2005).
13. Wetzsteon, *Republic of Dreams*.
14. "Artists May Strike to Save Lofts," *NYT*, March 6, 1961, 1; "Portrait of the Loft Generation," *NYT*, January 7, 1962, 207; "Living Big in a Loft," *Life*, March 27, 1970, 61–65.
15. Meisel interview; Naomi and Stephen Antonakos interview; Stone interview.
16. United States Bureau of Labor Statistics, "100 Years of U.S. Consumer Spending: Data for the Nation, New York City, and Boston" (Washington, DC: United States Bureau of Labor

NOTES TO PAGES 49–57   251

Statistics, 2006), March 15, 2010, http://www.bls.gov/opub/uscs/report991.pdf; "'Last Frontier' Homes: Big Rooms, Small Rents in Rundown Lofts, Flats," *NYWT&S*, May 25, 1964; "Artists May Strike to Save Lofts," 1.

17. Hall Winslow, *Artists in Metropolis: An Exploration for Planners* (Brooklyn: Planning Department, School of Architecture, Pratt Institute, 1964), 23–33.

18. Levine, *Artist Housing in South Houston*.

19. Ibid., 20, 22, 24, 27–28.

20. Greg Turpan, interview with the author, East Hampton, NY, June 25, 2012; Barbara Toll, interview with the author, New York, NY, June 20, 2012; Meisel interview.

21. Turpan interview; Mary Heilmann, interview with the author, New York, NY, June 20, 2012.

22. Barbara Haskell, interview with the author, New York, NY, March 14, 2012; Ceglic interview; Naomi and Stephen Antonakos interview.

23. Zukin, *Loft Living*, 96–110; Simpson, *SoHo*, 57–59.

24. Kostelanetz, *SoHo*, 37.

25. Various artist résumés, A.I.R. Gallery Archive, New York University Libraries (hereafter cited as *A.I.R.*), Boxes 6–8; Folders 238, 270, 280, and 293; "A.I.R. Grant Application, 1975–6," New York State Council on the Arts Grant Application Files, 1967–2001, New York State Archives, Albany, New York (hereafter cited as *NYSCA Archives*), 1064–84, Box 1; Tomar Levine, BA City College 1966; Janet Schneider, BA Queens 1972; Sally Auster, MA Columbia 1961; Irene Buszko MA Queens 1972; Rosemary Hamilton, BA Pratt 1966; James David Gruba, MA Queens 1972, "Prince Street Gallery Grant Application Form, 1974–5," 1064–85, Box 474, NYSCA Archives.

26. Kostelanetz, *SoHo*, 114.

27. Meisel interview; Yukie Ohta, interview with the author, New York, NY, June 20, 2012.

28. "Prince Street Gallery Grant Application Form, 1974–5"; various artist résumés, *A.I.R.*; "A.I.R. Grant Application, 1975–6"; Kostelanetz, *SoHo*, 75.

29. Haskell interview; Toll interview; Hirotsugu Aoki, interview with the author, New York, NY, August 13, 2012.

30. Turpan interview; Bark interview.

31. K. Jackson, *Encyclopedia of New York City*, 281; New York State, "About the Mitchell-Lama Housing Program, December 5, 2013, http://www.nyshcr.org/Programs/mitchell-lama.

32. Toll interview.

33. Bernstein and Shapiro, *Illegal Living*, 35–73; Kostelanetz, *SoHo*, 45–54; "George Maciunas: The Phantom Co-oper," *VV*, March 21, 1977, 24.

34. Bernstein and Shapiro, *Illegal Living*, 45–47; Kostelanetz, *SoHo*, 45–54.

35. Bernstein and Shapiro, *Illegal Living*, 45–73.

36. Ibid.

37. Ibid.

38. Ibid.

39. Ibid.

40. "Peter Gee Biography," June 8, 2015, http://www.petergee.com/about.php; Aoki interview; Meisel interview.

41. Meisel interview.

42. Susan Meisel, interview with the author, New York, NY, August 8, 2012.

43. Ceglic interview; Stephen and Naomi Antonakos interview. The practice of "selling of fixtures" was common in SoHo. Residents who rented lofts "sold" the improvements they had

made to the loft (for example, putting in bathrooms, sanding the floors) to the next tenant. This was a means to recapture the capital that they had put into renovations to a space they did not own. However, some residents profited from this arrangement, charging more for their fixtures than they paid for them. Over time, this practice drew the ire of SoHo landlords, who believed they should be the ones profiting from buildings they owned.

44. Turpan interview.

45. Frits de Knegt, interview with the author, New York, NY, March 12, 2013. De Knegt organized the cooperative in 1978.

46. Cornell University Law School Legal Information Institute, "Purchase Money Mortgage," http://topics.law.cornell.edu/wex/purchase_money_mortgage; "Loft Living: Can You Make It on the Urban Frontier?" *Apartment Life,* April 1977, 62–67. Most commonly, a deed was recorded between a buyer and a seller simultaneously with a mortgage from the seller to the buyer. This practice indicates that obtaining capital for investing in SoHo properties from formal sources was difficult due in large part to the still-illegal nature of loft living.

47. Bernstein and Shapiro, *Illegal Living,* 56; Bark interview.

48. Jim Stratton, *Pioneering in the Urban Wilderness* (New York: Urizen Books, 1977), 112.

49. Ibid., 104.

50. Ibid., 125–36, 146–49.

51. Bark interview.

52. Ceglic interview; Aoki interview; Turpan interview.

53. Heilmann interview; Stephan and Naomi Antonakos interview; Turpan interview.

54. "Untitled 24 Page History."

55. "SoHo Artists Association: SoHo Referendum (November, 1970)," Box 1, Folder 3, SAA Records.

56. "Living Big in a Loft."

57. Stephen and Naomi Antonakos interview; Ohta interview.

58. "Visit SoHo in New York [1970–1?]," Box 1, Folder 13, SAA Records.

59. Ibid. Fukui was a relatively successful artist. Max Hutchinson Galleries represented Fukui in the early 1970s, and he showed his work at museums and galleries throughout the country during that time, including the National Museum of Modern Art in Tokyo and the Indianapolis Museum of Art. His works are currently part of collections in the Museum of Modern Art, among other museums; Peter Hastings-Falk, ed., *Who Was Who in American Art, 1564–1975* (Madison, CT: Sound View Press, 1999), 1:2024. Browne exhibited her work at MoMA in 1968, SoHo Artists Festival in 1970, and other galleries nationally throughout the late 1960s and early 1970s. "Browne, Vivian," in ibid., 1:4477.

60. "Hazards of the Arts," *NYH-T,* June 9, 1961, 19; "Visit SoHo in New York."

61. "Visit SoHo in New York"; "Living Big in a Loft."

62. "Landscaped Home Zone for Greenwich Village," *NYH-T,* August 24, 1953; "Report on Clearance Issued," *Villager,* August 27, 1953; Gwendolyn Wright, *Building the Dream: A Social History of Housing in America* (Cambridge, MA: MIT University Press, 1981), 252.

63. "The Lofty Approach to Living," *NYP,* April 11, 1970, 50; "Living Big in a Loft."

64. Stephen and Naomi Antonakos interview.

65. Ibid.; Heilmann interview; Turpan interview.

66. Toll interview.

67. Ibid.; L. Meisel interview.

68. Bark interview.

69. Ohta interview; Turpan interview; Aoki interview.
70. Toll interview.
71. Bark interview.
72. Ibid.

Chapter Three

1. "Lower Manhattan Expressway: An Essential Key to Business Growth and Job Opportunities in Lower Manhattan and New York City (July 1964)," Downtown–Lower Manhattan Association, Inc., Records, 1937–1995, Rockefeller Archives Center, Sleepy Hollow, New York (hereafter cited as *DLMA Records*), Series 2.5, Box 215, Folder 1905.

2. Adam Rome, *The Bulldozer in the Countryside: Suburban Sprawl and the Rise of American Environmentalism* (New York: Cambridge University Press, 2001); Zachary M. Schrag, *The Great Society Subway: A History of the Washington Metro* (Baltimore: Johns Hopkins University Press, 2006), 119–141; Klemek, *Transatlantic Collapse of Urban Renewal*, 133–42; Raymond A. Mohl, "Stop the Road: Freeway Revolts in American Cities," *Journal of Urban History* 30, no. 5 (July 2004): 674–706; Raymond A. Mohl, "Citizen Activism and Freeway Revolts in Memphis and Nashville: The Road to Litigation," *Journal of Urban History* 40, no. 5 (September 2014): 870–93; Eric Avila, "Revisiting the Urban Interstates: Politics, Policy, and Culture Since World War II," *Journal of Urban History* 50, no. 5 (September 2014): 827–30.

3. Gratz, *Battle for Gotham*, 95–119; Anthony Flint, *Wrestling with Moses: How Jane Jacobs Took on Robert Moses and Transformed the American City* (New York: Random House, 2009), 145–78; Owen Gutfreund, "Rebuilding New York in the Auto Age: Robert Moses and His Highways," in *Robert Moses and the Modern City: The Transformation of New York*, ed. Hillary Ballon and Kenneth Jackson (New York: W. W. Norton, 2007); Osman, *Invention of Brownstone Brooklyn*, 228–29, Klemek, *Transatlantic Collapse of Urban Renewal*, 138–39.

4. Mohl, "Citizen Activism."

5. "Report on Annual Meeting March 6, 1963," Series 2.4, Box 196, Folder 1794; "Directors, Downtown–Lower Manhattan Association (2/1/66)," Series 2.1.1, Box 12, Folder 108; "1966 Business Member List" and "Membership Information," Series 2, Box 63, Folder 844, all in DLMA Records. In addition to Chase Manhattan Bank, the DLMA Board of Directors included top executives from the American Stock Exchange, the *Wall Street Journal*, Lehman Brothers, the Continental Insurance Companies, the Guardian Life Insurance Company, Morgan Stanley, the First National City Bank, the American Express Company, Goldman Sachs, Chemical Bank New York Trust Company, the Morgan Guaranty Trust Company of New York, Manufacturers Hanover Trust, Merrill Lynch, AT&T, Khun, Loeb, Marine Midland Grace Trust Company, and the United States Steel Corporation. Although the DLMA included some smaller local companies among its members, it was these major financial institutions that made up the bulk of its membership.

6. "Letter from John B. Goodman, DLMA to Landmarks Preservation Commission," January 9, 1967, Series 2.3, Box 112, Folder 1207, DLMA Records; David Rockefeller, *Memoirs* (New York: Random House, 2002), 387.

7. "One Square Mile of Change," January 7, 1964, Series 2.4, Box 200, Folder 1822, DLMA Records.

8. "Who Will Own New York?" *New York Magazine*, May 13, 1974, Series 2.4, Box 203, Folder 1843, DLMA Records.

9. "Urban Renewal: The Problem of the Central City," address by David Rockefeller at the First Annual Meeting of the San Francisco Planning and Urban Renewal Association, January 24, 1961, Series 2.1.4, Box 39, Folder 589, DLMA Records.

10. Edgar M. Hoover et al., *Anatomy of a Metropolis: The Changing Distribution of People and Jobs within the New York Metropolitan Region* (Cambridge, MA: Harvard University Press, 1959), 237.

11. "Address by David Rockefeller Vice Chairman Board of Directors the Chase Manhattan Bank at the Eastern Mortgage Conference Hotel Commodore, New York May 4, 1959, Redevelopment in Lower Manhattan," Series 2.1.4, Box 39 Folder 578, DLMA Records.

12. Ibid.; "Comprehensive Plan for Land Use, Redevelopment and Traffic Improvements in Lower Manhattan Presented to the City," October 14, 1958, Series 2.4, Box 196, Folder 1780; "Second Report of the Downtown–Lower Manhattan Association," 1964, Series 2.4, Box 197, Folder 1809; both in DLMA Records.

13. "Urban Renewal: Problem of the Central City"; "Downtown–Lower Manhattan Association Progress Report, 1959, Series 2.1.4, Box 39, Folder 581, DLMA Records.

14. K. Jackson, *Encyclopedia of New York City*, 774–75; Caro, *Power Broker*.

15. "Statement of the Downtown–Lower Manhattan Association before the Planning Commission Hearing on the Lower Manhattan Expressway 'Demapping' April 17, 1963," Series 2.3, Box 119, Folder 1253, DLMA Records; "Expressway Plan Goes to O'Dwyer," *NYT*, October 14, 1946, 24; "Start Set on Last 'Loop' Link on Lower Manhattan Expressways," *NYT*, August 20, 1949, 26; Flint, *Wrestling with Moses*, 141.

16. "Statement before Planning Commission"; "Crosstown Links May Start Soon," *NYT*, April 2, 1956, 1; "Accord Advances Downtown Expressway," *NYT*, December 1, 1958, 1; Flint, *Wrestling with Moses*, 139.

17. "Statement by David Rockefeller, Chairman Downtown–Lower Manhattan Association, Inc. at Planning Commission Hearing on Arterial Master Plan, City Hall, NY May 6, 1959," Series 2.4, Box 196, Folder 1780; "Statement of the D.-L. M. A. Concerning the Lower-Manhattan Expressway before Planning Commission Hearing December 9, 1959," Series 2.3, Box 119, Folder 1253; "Bulletin Report on Transportation in Downtown Manhattan May 27, 1960," Series 2.4, Box 196, Folder 1786; all in DLMA Records.

18. "Accord Advances Downtown Expressway"; "Downtown Route Submitted to City," *NYT*, November 13, 1959, Series 2.4, Box 196, Folder 1780, DLMA Records.

19. "Canal St. Expressway Gets Planning Body's Approval," *NYT*, February 4, 1960, 1; "Residents Assail Downtown Route," *NYT*, December 10, 1959, 44; "Crosstown Expressway Project Gains," *NYH-T*, February 4, 1960, Series 2.4, Box 196, Folder 1780, DLMA Records; "Moses Asks City to Double Tenant Relocation Bonus," *NYT*, February 17, 1960, 1; "Cioffi Sees Delays in City Expressway," *NYT*, February 5, 1960, 20; "Canal Street Expressway Facing Long Delay Over Tenant Shift," *NYT*, May 28, 1960, 1; "New Study Voted for Expressway," *NYT* June 24, 1960, 29.

20. "Downtown Road Linking 2 Rivers Is Voted by City," *NYT*, September 16, 1960; "Crosstown Road Deemed Far Off," *NYT*, November 1, 1960, 41; "State Presses City on Starting Lower Manhattan Expressway," *NYT*, December 26, 1960, 1; "City Withholding Expressway Data," *NYT*, January 3, 1961, 46.

21. "Expressway Gets Mayor's Support," *NYT*, February 13, 1961, 29; "Board Expedites City Expressway," *NYT*, April 6, 1962, 37; "Planners Press Crosstown Road," *NYT*, May 4, 1962, 35; "Mayor Clears Plan for Downtown Expressway," *NYT*, April 5, 1962, 1; "Twenty-one Years to Act," *NYT*, April 10, 1962, 40. Because of the delays in the project, its expected costs had quadrupled since 1941 to $100 million.

NOTES TO PAGES 80–83   255

22. "Notes on the Lower Manhattan Expressway," Series 2.3, Box 18, Folder 20, DLMA Records; "Marchers Protest Crosstown Road," *NYT,* August 10, 1962, 8; "New Delay Looms for Expressway," *NYT,* August 17, 1962, 12; "City Puts Off Expressway Action as Pickets March," *NYT,* August 24, 1962, 26; "Wagner Puts Off Expressway Plan," *NYT,* October 20, 1962, 25; "Downtown Group Fights Road Plan," *NYT,* December 5, 1962, 49; "Wagner Opposes Moses and Barnes Over Expressway," *NYT,* April 12, 1963, 1; Flint, *Wrestling with* Moses, 146–51.

23. "Artists, Politicians, People Join Fight for Little Italy," *VV,* August 30, 1962, 1; "Political Powerhouse Kills Broome St. Expressway," *VV,* December 13, 1962, 1.

24. "City Withholding Expressway Data."

25. "Expressway Vote Delayed by City," *NYT,* December 7, 1962, 32; "Wagner Opposes Moses and Barnes"; "Political Powerhouse Kills Broome St. Expressway."

26. Gutfreund, "Rebuilding New York," 93.

27. "Expressway Plan Revived by Moses," *NYT,* April 11, 1963, 35; "Wagner Opposes Moses and Barnes"; "Planners Urged to Revive Downtown Expressway," *NYT,* April 18, 1963, 1; "Statement before Planning Commission Hearing."

28. "$2-Million Lost in 'Death' of Road Here," *NYT,* September 26, 1969, 92.

29. "Executive Committee Minutes, March 2, 1964," Series 2.1.3, Box 18, Folder 207; "Executive Committee Meeting Minutes, June 15, 1964," Series 2.1.3, Box 18, Folder 208; both in DLMA Records; "New Drive Begun for Expressway," *NYT,* March 1, 1964, 64; "Revival Plan Stirs Foes of Expressway," *NYT,* January 31, 1964, 56.

30. "New Drive Begun for Expressway," 64; "Revival Plan Stirs Foes"; "Showdown Near on Expressway to Traverse Lower Manhattan," *NYT,* June 5, 1964, 63.

31. "Association Supports Position of City Planning Commission in Litigation Involving Lower Manhattan Expressway Project June 5, 1964," Series 2.4, Box 196, Folder 1798; "Bulletin Lower Manhattan Expressway Project Kept Alive through Court Decision July 6, 1964," Series 2.4, Box 196, Folder 1799; both in DLMA Records; "Expressway Gets New Lease on Life," *NYT,* July 3 1964, 45; "Expressway Plan Is Revived by City," *NYT,* December 8, 1964, 1; "Statement of the Downtown–Lower Manhattan Association, Inc. before the New York City Board of Estimate at the Hearing in City Hall, December 22, 1964, Presented by John B. Goodman, Vice President," Series 2.3, Box 119, Folder 1253, DLMA Records; "Decision Pending on Expressway," *NYT,* January 24 1965, 71; Flint, *Wrestling with* Moses, 163.

32. "Lindsay Dubious on Expressway," *NYT,* February 20, 1965, 29; "Expressway Plan Faces New Delay," *NYT,* May 14, 1965, 1; "Wagner Orders Building of Manhattan Expressway," *NYT,* May 26, 1965, 1; "Executive Committee Meeting Minutes May 24, 1965," Series 2.1.3, Box 18, Folder 210; "Lower Manhattan Elevated Expressway (November, 1965)," Series 2.4, Box 215, Folder 1907; both in DLMA Records; "Suit Filed to Stop the Expressway," *NYT,* July 23 1965, 32.

33. "Expressway Held Legally Conceived in 2 Court Rulings," *NYT,* November 19, 1965, 41; "Expressway Plan Definitely Out, Price Discloses," *NYT,* March 7, 1966, 1; "Lindsay Removes Moses from Post as Road Planner," *NYT* July 13, 1966, 1.

34. "Downtown Tunnel Studies Instead of an Expressway," *NYT,* January 17, 1966, 1; "4 Lanes Weighed for Tunnel Road," *NYT,* January 23, 1967, 1; "New Plans Prepared for Downtown Expressway," *NYT,* March 28, 1967, 1; "'Villagers' Protest 'Secret' Road Plan," *NYT,* March 15, 1967, 44; "Expressway Plan Assailed in Study," *NYT,* November 14, 1966, 43.

35. "Jane Jacobs Is Arrested at Expressway Hearing," April 11, 1968, 28; "Statement of the Downtown–Lower Manhattan Association, Inc. before the New York State Transportation Department, April 10, 1968," Series 2.3, Box 119, Folder 1253, DLMA Records; "City Expressway Opposed," *NYT,* May 9, 1968, 46.

36. "An Exercise in Chinese Irony," *NYT*, December 1, 1968, D40.

37. "A 'Binuclear' Show for the Bieñal," *NYT*, May 18, 1969, D28; "Artists Assail Downtown Expressway," *NYT*, June 20, 1969, 37. Donald Judd purchased the building at 101 Spring Street for less than $70,000 in 1968; "The Proto-Loft, Reborn," *NYT*, March 23, 2006.

38. Ibid.

39. "Artists Assail Downtown Expressway."

40. "Pollution Study Could Doom Expressway," *VV*, January 9, 1969, 1; "An Aroused Nation Seeks Billions to Dam the Rising Tide of Pollution," *NYT*, January 6, 1969, 74; "Lindsay Warned of Expressway Air Pollution," *VV*, December 19, 1968, 1; "Expressway Plan Viewed as Hazard," *NYT*, January 9, 1969, 95; "Red Light for the Expressway," *NYT*, January 20, 1969, 46; "U.S. Will Sponsor Air Pollution Study of City Road Plan," *NYT*, June 21, 1969, 31; "5 Officials Score Crosstown Route," *NYT*, February 3, 1969, 69; "Sutton Proposes an Alternate to Lower Manhattan Expressway," *NYT*, April 4, 1969, 67; "U.S. Aid Sought in Study for New Expressway," *NYT*, March 28, 1969, 26.

41. "Mayor Drops Plans for Express Roads Across 2 Boroughs," *NYT*, July 17, 1969, 1; "Planners Ratify 2 Lindsay Policy Shifts," *NYT*, August 21, 1969, 9; "$2-Million Lost in 'Death' of Road Here," *NYT*, September 26, 1969, 92; "Demapping Urged for Expressways," *NYT*, December 18, 1968, 93; "Lower Manhattan Road Killed Under State Plans," *NYT*, March 25, 1971, 78. It is worth noting that the Lower Manhattan Expressway came to life one last time thanks to an architectural study published from 1972 to 1974. In 1967 the Ford Foundation commissioned a study of the project by architect Paul Rudolph, eventually published under the title *The Evolving City: Urban Design Proposal by Ulrich Franzen and Paul Rudolph*. The proposal included a series of large residential and commercial towers flanking the expressway route, creating a "gateway" to Manhattan along with A-frame megastructures covering much of the depressed roadway. The plan also included a transit "HUB" connecting the two approaches to the expressway, surface roads, subway lines, and a new monorail-mounted people mover. Ed Rawlings and Jim Walrod, *Paul Rudolph: Lower Manhattan Expressway* (New York: Drawing Center, 2010).

42. "Crosstown Road Deemed Far Off"; "Expressway Opposed," *NYT*, January 13, 1964, 34.

43. "Court Orders City to Decide Quickly on Downtown Road," *NYT*, April 4, 1964, 29; "Moses' Prediction Angers Opponents of Manhattan Expressway," *NYT*, June 28, 1964, 41.

44. "The Lower Manhattan Expressway: An Essential Key to Business Growth and Job Opportunities in Lower Manhattan and New York City (July 1964)," Series 2.4, Box 215, Folder 1907, DLMA Records.

45. "Moses' Prediction Angers Opponents"; "Tenant Sues City on Expressway," *NYT*, June 13, 1965, R1.

46. Ada Louise Huxtable, "Where It Goes Nobody Knows," *NYT*, February 2, 1969, D29; "5 Officials Score Crosstown Route," *NYT*, February 3, 1969, 69.

47. "Loft Decision: What Next?" *SoHo Weekly News* (hereafter cited as *SWN*), January 3, 1980, 5.

48. Dates from *SWN*; Anderson-Spivy, *Anderson and Archer's SoHo*; Esman and Hagenberg, *SoHo*. For galleries for which opening dates were not readily available, the date listed in the table is the first entry for the enterprise in New York phone books.

Chapter Four

1. "Violations Found before Loft Fire," *NYT*, November 22, 1960, 37; "Warning by Cavanagh," *NYT*, 21 February 21, 1961, 41.

NOTES TO PAGES 92–103

2. "No Beatnik Pads in Loft Bldgs.," *NYH-T,* February 27, 1961, 1.
3. Klemek, *Transatlantic Collapse of Urban Renewal,* 131; Zipp, *Manhattan Projects,* 22.
4. "Violations Found before Loft Fire."
5. Rapkin, *South Houston Industrial Area,* 147–50.
6. "Warning by Cavanagh."
7. "Art: The Angry Dwellers," *Newsweek,* May 29, 1961.
8. "Artists Organize to Save Lofts as Studios Despite Fire Hazard," *NYT,* April 6, 1961, 122.
9. "List of ATA A.I.R.s," Artist Tenants Association Records, 1959–1976, Archives of American Art, Smithsonian Institution, Washington, DC (hereafter cited as *ATA Records*), Box 1 Folder 6; "Gahagan, Peter" and "Henry, Robert," in Hastings-Falk, *Who Was Who in Art,* 2: 1230, 1534.
10. "Artists of the City Unite to Save Their Garrets, Seek Public's Aid Against Fire Department," *NYH-T,* May 9, 1961, 25.
11. "City Artists Facing New, Lofty Problem," *NYWT&S,* November 14, 1962, 3; "Portrait of the Loft Generation," *NYT,* January 7, 1962, 207.
12. "A Portrait of the Artist as a Loft-Dweller," *NYP,* March 13, 1961, 63; "Art is Lofty—600 March at City Hall to Save Studios" *NYH-T,* April 4, 1964; "Artist-Tenants Association Press Release" and "Artists Tenants Association Newsletter, December 28, 1962," both Getty Research Institute, Irving Sandler Papers, 2000.M.43, Box 48, Folder 2.
13. "Artists Unite to Save Garrets"; "Eases Stand on Artists Lofts," *NYP,* May 10, 1961, 15; "Art: Angry Dwellers."
14. "Cavanagh Assures Artists on Housing," *NYT,* May 10, 1961, 35. At the meeting, Cavanagh said there had been no mass evictions of artists from Lower Manhattan and that only seven of seventy-one buildings inspected on the west side of Greenwich Village had been ordered vacated.
15. Ibid.; "Portrait of Artist as Loft-Dweller."
16. "Artists and New York Settle Housing Dispute," *Art News* 60, no. 5 (September 1961): 3.
17. "Artists May Strike to Save Lofts," *NYT,* June 3, 1961, 1; "Untitled Timeline of ATA Actions Towards Legalized Artist Housing in SoHo [1964]," Box 1, Folder 6, ATA Records.
18. "Artists Meet with City Officials on Dispute over Loft Studios," *NYT,* August 16, 1961, 35.
19. "Artists Tenants Association Agreement with City, 1961," Box 1, Folder 15, SAA Records.
20. "Strike over Lofts Put Off by Artists as Formula is Set," *NYT,* August 23, 1961, 35; "Artists and New York Settle Housing Dispute."
21. "Artists Say City Breaks Loft Pact," *NYP,* December 1, 1961, 4.
22. "Untitled Timeline of ATA Actions"; "Untitled 24 Page History."
23. "Artists Tenants Association Newsletter, December 28, 1962"; "Artists to Picket in Loft Protest," *NYT,* February 29, 1964, 23.
24. "Mitchell-Lama," in K. Jackson, *Encyclopedia of New York City,* 765.
25. Ibid.; "Art Notes: Fighting City Hall," *NYT,* March 29, 1964, X20.
26. "In the Art Galleries," *NYP,* March 29, 1964, 40.
27. "1,000 Artists March to Protest Zoning Rules on Loft Studios," *NYT,* April 4, 1964, 29; "Art Is Lofty"; "Lofty Debate," *NYDN,* April 4, 1964, 17.
28. "Untitled Timeline of ATA Actions."
29. Volunteer Lawyers for the Arts, *Housing for Artists,* 15–17, B-1[e].
30. Ibid., 15–19, 24–26. Another issue was the amendment's restrictive definition of "artist." In response, a 1968 amendment to article 7-B of the Multiple Dwelling Law (the section covering loft housing) expanded this definition to persons engaged in "the performing or creative arts," allowing filmmakers, musicians, and other fine artists to gain legal access to converted lofts.

31. "Untitled Timeline of ATA"; "Negotiations with the City, Begun after Our April 3 Demonstration Have Collapsed! (7/6/64)" Box 1, Folder 6, ATA Records.

32. "A.T.A. on A.I.R.," May 1967, Box 1, Folder 1, ATA Records.

33. "Message from the Artists Tenants Association, New York City" and "Artist-Tenants Association Statement [1962–3?];" Getty Research Institute, Irving Sandler Papers, 2000.M.43, Box 48, Folder 2.

34. "Victims of the Clean Slate," *Nation,* August 10, 1964, 43.

Chapter Five

1. "The Gal Who Didn't Like Galleries," *NYP Magazine,* February 23, 1970, 5.

2. Paula Cooper, interview with the author, New York, NY, August 14, 2012.

3. "Going to Pieces," *SWN,* January 27, 1977, 17; "Opening of a Large New Gallery," Park Place Gallery Art Research records and the Paula Cooper Gallery Records, 1965–1998, Archives of American Art, Smithsonian Institution, Washington, DC (hereafter cited as *Cooper*), Box 2, Folder 13; "Gal Who Didn't Like Galleries."

4. Cooper interview; "Art Benefit for the Student Mobilization Committee to End the War in Vietnam (Advertisement)," *NYT,* October 20, 1968, D25.

5. Data for 1973 taken from listings in the *SoHo Weekly News*; some 1974 data and all data for 1979 taken from Anderson-Spivy, *Anderson and Archer's SoHo,* and Esman and Hagenberg, *SoHo.*

6. "Art: A Downtown Scene," *NYT,* November 28, 1970, 15; "Art: Highlights of a Downtown Scene," *NYT,* December 11, 1970, 56; "Palley Gallery Opens Downtown in Uptownish Style," *NYT,* March 16, 1970, 52.

7. Perl, *New Art City*; Baruch D. Kirschenbaum, "The Scull Auction and the Scull Film," *Art Journal* 39, no. 1 (Autumn 1979): 50–54. Inflation data calculated using Bureau of Labor Statistics CPI Inflation Calculator, May 16, 2015, http://www.bls.gov/data/inflation_calculator.htm.

8. "Palley Gallery Opens Downtown."

9. "Art Galleries," in K. Jackson, *Encyclopedia of New York City,* 18.

10. Irving Sandler, "Avant-Garde Artists of Greenwich Village," in *Greenwich Village: Culture and Counterculture,* ed. Rick Beard and Leslie Cohen Berlowitz (New Brunswick, NJ: Rutgers University Press, 1993).

11. Grace Glueck, "Up At Eros' Pad," *NYT,* October 23, 1966, X30.

12. Ibid.

13. "Promotional Flyer for Paula Cooper Gallery featuring 'To Experience Art as It Is Evolving,'" *NYT,* December 28, 1969," Box 6, Folder 5, Cooper.

14. Alan Jones and Laura de Coppet, *The Art Dealers: The Powers behind the Scenes Tell How the Art World Really Works* (New York: Clarkson N. Potter, 1984), 144.

15. Helene Zuker Seeman and Alanna Siegfried, *SoHo: A Guide* (New York: Neal-Schuman, 1978) "Palley Gallery Opens Downtown in Uptownish Style," *NYT,* March 16, 1970, 52.

16. "*SoHo Statement,* Vol. 1 No. 1 November 20, 1971," Box 1, Folder 15, SAA Records; Seeman and Siegfried, *SoHo.*

17. De Knegt interview.

18. Ibid.

19. "Leo Castelli Gallery History (ca. 1981)," Leo Castelli Gallery records, circa 1880–2000, bulk 1957–1999, Box 33, Folder 5, Archives of American Art, Smithsonian Institution; "Leo Ca-

stelli Gallery records, circa 1880–2000, bulk 1957–1999," Archives of American Art, http://www.aaa.si.edu/collections/leo-castelli-gallery-records-7351/more.

20. Simpson, *SoHo*, 16; inflation data calculated using Bureau of Labor Statistics CPI Inflation Calculator, June 3, 2015, http://www.bls.gov/data/inflation_calculator.htm.

21. Nancy Hoffman, interview with the author, New York, NY, June 20, 2012; John Canaday, "Art: Surprising Show by Miss Bieser," *NYT*, December 23, 1972, 13.

22. Betty Cunningham, interview with the author, New York, NY, August 10, 2012.

23. L. Meisel interview.

24. Ibid.

25. Hoffman interview.

26. Cunningham interview.

27. "Biography for Forrest Myers, Paula Cooper Gallery, 96 Prince St," Box 3, Folder 14; "Press Release for Chris Wilmarth at Paula Cooper 1 March 1972," Box 1, Folder 24; "Biography for Keith Hollingworth," Box 5, Folder 9; "Chris Wilmarth Biography," Box 6, Folder 22; "Biography of Edwin Ruda," Box 6, Folder 11; "Biography of Harvey Quaytman," Box 5, Folder 5/6; "Biography of Rosemarie Castoro," Box 2, Folder 3; "Resume of David Diao," Box 5, Folder 1; all in Cooper; Cooper interview.

28. Cunningham interview; L. Meisel interview; Hoffman interview.

29. Paula Cooper Ledger Books, Located Between Folders 11 and 12, Cooper; "Paula Cooper, Inc. 1968 Tax Return," Box 5, Folder 16, both in Cooper; inflation data calculated using Bureau of Labor Statistics CPI Inflation Calculator, June 3, 2015, http://www.bls.gov/data/inflation_calculator.htm.

30. Cooper interview.

31. Cooper Ledger Books; "Letter from Paula Cooper to Robin Lynn, New York State Council on the Arts (1972)," Box 3, Folder 18; "Letter from Paula Cooper to Dore Ashton, SVA, (1969)" and "Letter from Paula Cooper to the Lionel & Sylvia Bauman Foundation (1969)," Box 3, Folder 16; all in Cooper.

32. Hoffman interview; Cunningham interview; Jones and de Coppet, *Art Dealers*, 148.

33. Information compiled from André Emmerich Gallery records and André Emmerich Papers, circa 1929–2008. Sales charts in Box 131, Folder 18, and receipts (with addresses) in Boxes 135 and 136, Archives of American Art, Smithsonian Institution.

34. "The Coop Alternative," Box 4, Folder 184, A.I.R.; Seeman and Siegfried, *SoHo*; Anderson and Archer, *SoHo*.

35. "Prince Street Gallery All-Purpose Form, 1975–6," 1064–84, Box 474, NYSCA Archives; inflation data calculated using Bureau of Labor Statistics CPI Inflation Calculator, June 3, 2015, http://www.bls.gov/data/inflation_calculator.htm.

36. "Original Press Release, 55 Mercer Gallery (Reprint of 1969 Document)," "A Toast to 55 Mercer by Joseph Masheck (Ca. 1984)," "Statement of Stephen Rosenthal to Open Public Hearing of the Artworkers' Coalition at SVA, 4/10/69"; all in 55 Mercer Gallery records, 1971–2007, Box 1, Folder 16, Archives of American Art, Smithsonian Institution.

37. "The A.I.R. Gallery," Box 2, Folder 61; "Mission Statement," Box 2, Folder 61; "AIR Proposal, 1972," Box 2, Folder 64; "Bypassing the Gallery System," *Ms. Magazine*, February 1973, 33; in Box 4, Folder 182; all in A.I.R.

38. "Who We Are & What We Do," Box 2, Folder 62; "A.I.R. (1972)," Box 2, Folder 62; "Artists in Residence: The First Five Years," *Womanart*, Winter 1977–78, in Box 4, Folder 181; all in A.I.R.

39. "An Interview with Members of A.I.R.," *Arts Magazine*, December–January 1973, Box 4, Folder 182; "Minutes, November 1973," Box 2, Folder 67; "Proposed Plan for Running A.I.R. Smoothly, December '73–June '74," Box 1, Folder 55; "Gallery Maintenance Guidelines," Box 1, Folder 55; "Count-Down to an Exhibition," Box 1, Folder 55; "Gallery Sitting Policy," Box 1, Folder 55; all in A.I.R.

40. Cooper interview; Hoffman interview; Cunningham interview.

41. "Beyond the Frame," *SWN*, November 8, 1973, 5; "Co-op Galleries: Good Idea, Bad Art, Poor Planning," *SWN*, June 26, 1976, 12; "The Coop Alternative," Box 4, Folder 184, A.I.R.

42. Binkiewicz, *Federalizing the Muse*, 139.

43. Zukin, *Loft Living*, 96–105.

44. All Berr, "New York State Council on the Arts," in *The Encyclopedia of New York State*, ed. Peter Eisenstadt and Laura-Eve Moss (Syracuse, NY: Syracuse University Press, 2005), 1095–96.

45. "SoHo 20 Income and Expenses, 1975–6," 1064–84, Box 535; "First Street Gallery, Budget: 1973–4," 1064–84, Box 216; "SoHo 20 Fiscal Review sheet, 1977–8," 1064–84, Box 639; all in NYSCA Archives.

46. "Artists in Residence: First Five Years"; "Letter from Seymour Knox, Chairman, New York State Council on the Arts to Agnes Denes, AIR Gallery, August 3, 1972," Box 1, Folder 1; "Letter from Eric Larrabee, Executive Director, NYSCA to Barbara Zucker, AIR Gallery, October 10, 1973," Box 1, Folder 1; "Proposed Plan"; "Budgets, September 1977," Box 2, Folder 67; all in A.I.R.

47. RoseLee Goldberg, *Performance: Live Art since 1960* (New York: Harry N. Abrams, 1998), 12, 15.

48. Ibid.

49. "112 Greene Street: An Interview with Alan Saret and Jeffrey Lew," *Avalanche*, Winter 1971, 12.

50. Ibid.; Robyn Brentano and Mark Savitt, *112 Workshop, 112 Greene Street: History, Artists, and Artworks* (New York: New York University Press, 1981), vi–viii.

51. Brentano and Savitt, *112 Workshop*, ix.

52. Ibid., x.

53. "112 Workshop All Purpose Form, 1975–6," "112 Workshop All Purpose Form, 1976–7," and "112 Workshop All Purpose Form, 1977–8," all in 1064–84, Box 639, NYSCA Archives.

54. "There's Dance Downtown, Lofts of It," *SWN*, September 29, 1977, 30.

55. Ibid.

56. Cooper interview; "Dance," *SWN*, March 21, 1974, 19; "A Wing and a Prayer," *SWN*, June 19, 1975, 23; "On Dance," *SWN*, June 13, 1974; "On Dance," *SWN*, October 3, 1974, 17; "Dancing from a Strange and Wondrous Culture," *SWN*, October 21, 1976, 26.

57. Stephen J. Bottoms, *Playing Underground: A Critical History of the 1960's Off-Off-Broadway Movement* (Ann Arbor: University of Michigan Press, 2004).

58. "On Dance," *SWN*, October 24, 1974, 17; "Meredith Monk," *SWN*, April 3, 1975, 29; "A Nice House to Visit," *SWN*, May 22, 1975, 34; "Sylvia Whitman's 'Going,'" *Avalanche*, December 1974, 13; "The Rhythms of Adaptation," *SWN*, May 20, 1976.

59. "Boarder Checkpoint: 23rd Street," *SWN*, October 13, 1977, 24; "Dance's Renaissance Man to Settle in SoHo," *SWN*, June 26, 1976, 16.

60. "Details of Meeting between NYSCA and Byrd Hoffman Foundation, April 29, 1974," and "Byrd Hoffman Foundation Budget Summary 1972–3," 1064–84, Box 91, NYSCA Archives; "Byrd Hoffman Foundation All-Purpose Form, 1979–80," 1064–85, Box 33, NYSCA Archives.

61. "SoHo Ensemble in Review," *SWN*, December 13, 1973, 12; "The Way Chamber Music Should Be," *SWN*, February 2, 1978, 30.

62. "Jazz Lofts," *SWN*, April 11, 1974, 16; "The Cream Rises," *SWN*, October 6, 1977, 30; "I Was Sitting on My Patio One Afternoon and I Hallucinated a Loft Jazz Concert," *SWN*, June 2, 1977, 41.

63. "Jazz Lofts."

64. "'Pertinent and Impertinent by Jay Jacobs, The Art Gallery, December 1969," Box 6, Folder 3, Cooper; Jones and de Coppet, *Art Dealers*, 71.

65. "'Pertinent and Impertinent'"; "Future Shock—It's Present Tense Around Here," *SoHo Statement*, Vol. 1 No. 1 November 20, 1971," Box 1, Folder 15, SAA Records; Jones and de Coppet, *Art Dealers*, 199.

66. "'Pertinent and Impertinent."

67. "Art World Is Big Business," *Villager*, May 10, 1977, Box 2, Folder 6, ATA Records.

68. Cooper interview; Hoffman interview.

69. "SoHo 20, 1976–7 All Purpose Form," 1064–84, Box 535; "Spectrum Gallery, 1973 NYSCA Information Return and Request for Assistance," 1064–84, Box 543; both in NYSCA Archives.

70. "Haleakala Inc (The Kitchen) All Purpose Form, 1978–9" and "Haleakala Inc (The Kitchen) All Purpose Form, 1979–80," 1064–85, Box 88, NYSCA Archives.

71. "Details of Meeting between NYSCA and Byrd Hoffman Foundation, April 29, 1974" and "Byrd Hoffman Foundation Budget Summary 1972–3," 1064–84, Box 91, NYSCA Archives; "Byrd Hoffman Foundation All-Purpose Form, 1979–80," 1064–85, Box 33, NYSCA Archives.

Chapter Six

1. "SoHo Artists Festival Program [1970]," Box 1, Folder 15, SAA Records.

2. "Kids," *VV*, May 14, 1970, 37, Box 1, Folder 14, SAA Records.

3. "SoHo Artist Association [1970]," Box 1, Folder 3, SAA Records.

4. Vincent J. Cannato, *The Ungovernable City: John Lindsay and His Struggle to Save New York* (New York: Basic Books: 2001), 78–91, 155–88, 301–51; K. Jackson, *Encyclopedia of New York City*, 115, 145, 163, 357, 697, 655.

5. Austin, *Taking the Train*, 13.

6. "SoHo Artist Association Member List [1970]," Box 1, Folder 3, SAA Records.

7. "SoHo Artist Association [1970]"; "So-Ho Artist's Association Planning Committee, September 1970, The Planning Philosophy," Box 1, Folder 3, SAA Records.

8. Grace Glueck, "SoHo Is Artists' Last Resort," *NYT*, May 11, 1970, 37.

9. "So-Ho Artist's Association Planning Philosophy"; "SoHo Artists Association: Invitation to a Benefit June 8, 1970 at the Playhouse Center," Box 3, ATA Records. Also included were Timothy Costello, deputy mayor; Percy E. Sutton, deputy mayor; Louis Lefkowitz, New York State attorney general; and Dore Schary, commissioner, Department of Cultural Affairs.

10. "Letter from Doris C. Freedman, Citizens for Artists Housing to Friends of the Group (September, 1970)," Box 1, Folder 1; "Letter from Doris Freedman, Chairman, Citizens for Artist Housing to Donald Elliot, October 8, 1970," Box 1, Folder 1, both SAA Records. Representatives from the political world included August Heckscher, who was a member of the New York State Council on the Arts, administrator of Parks, Recreation and Cultural Affairs, and commissioner of Parks of New York City, as well Mrs. Jacob K. (Mary Ann Boris) Javits, wife of the New York senator.

11. "The Fact Sheet on Artist Housing in SoHo (September, 1970)," Box 1, Folder 3, SAA Records.

12. Ibid.; Peter Mellman, "SoHo Artists' Bohemia Imperiled"; "Untitled 24 Page History."
13. "SoHo Artists Association: SoHo Referendum.
14. Ibid.; "Letter from G. Liebmann to D. Elliot, 11/30/70," Box 1, Folder 1; Letters from Canal Street Business Owners to City Planning Commission, Box 1, Folder 2; both SAA Records; Rapkin, *South Houston Industrial Area*, 192.
15. "Mayor Asks Aid to 'SoHo' Artists," *NYT*, September 24, 1970, 48; Volunteer Lawyers for the Arts, *Housing for Artists*, 23–25; Doris Freedman to Gerhardt Liebmann, June 23, 1971, Box 1, Folder 2, SAA Records.
16. "Application for Artists' Certification," Box 1, Folder 5, SAA Records; Volunteer Lawyers for the Arts, *Housing for Artists*, 25–6; Toll interview; Susan Meisel interview.
17. "The Lofty Approach to Living."
18. Glueck, "SoHo Is Last Resort"; "Costs for 'SoHo' Lofts Are Rising Drastically," *NYT*, July 26, 1970, 200.
19. "Untitled 24 Page History."
20. "SoHo Referendum (November, 1970).".
21. Lawrence Alloway, *10 Downtown, 10 Years* (New York: s.n., 1978).
22. Grace Glueck, "They Create a New Art Scene," *NYT*, May 5, 1974, 179.
23. "Artists' District Plans a Weekend of Shows," *NYT*, May 8, 1970, 27; Notes for Gerhardt Liebmann Speech [undated], Box 1, Folder 4, SAA Records; Mellman, "SoHo Artists' Bohemia Imperiled."
24. "SoHo Last Resort"; Mellman, "SoHo Artists' Bohemia Imperiled."
25. Mellman, "SoHo Artists' Bohemia Imperiled"; Glueck, "They Create New Art Scene."
26. "Untitled 24 Page History."
27. "Visit SoHo in New York [1970–1?]," Box 1, Folder 13, SAA Records.
28. Ibid.
29. "Cornell Visits SoHo (May 2, 1971)" and "Tour of Artist's Studios in 'SoHo' (South of Houston) Area, Submitted by Peter E Meyer Submitted to Cornell Alumni Association of New York," Box 1, Folder 13, SAA Records.
30. Ibid.
31. "Dodging Trucks Was a Part of the $125 Tour," *NYT*, January 26, 1971, 38.
32. Ibid.
33. "Living Big in a Loft."
34. Zukin, *Loft Living*, 60, 62.
35. "SoHo Artists' Bohemia Imperiled"; Zukin, *Loft Living*, 62.
36. "SoHo Scene May Include Pollock Pl." *NYT*, February 7, 1972, 33.
37. "Soho Artists Are Divided on Jackson Pollock Place," *NYT*, February 17, 1972, 30; "'Jackson Pollock Place,' Give My Regards to West Broadway," *VV*, March 23, 1972, 35.
38. Ibid. Members of the Italian community suggested that the street be named after another Italian American, as was the case with LaGuardia Place, the name of West Broadway from Washington Square Park to Houston Street.
39. "A 21-Story Sports Center for SoHo Wins Approval," *NYT*, November 15, 1972, 51.
40. "Artists' Housing Wasting of Westbeth, Strangling of SoHo," *VV*, July 22, 1972, 3.
41. Norman Tyler et al., *Historic Preservation: An Introduction to Its History, Principles, and Practice*, 2nd ed. (New York: W. W. Norton, 2009), 27–50.
42. "Calendar of the Landmarks Preservation Commission of the City of New York" December 9, 1965" and "Letter from Geoffrey Platt Chairman, Landmarks Preservation Commission

to Hon. Herbert Evans, Chairman Housing and Redevelopment Board April 29, 1966," both in Box 8, Folder 1, City Planning Commission Subject Files Commissioner William F. R. Ballard, 68–015, Municipal Archives of the City of New York; "Noted Buildings in Path of Road," *NYT*, July 22, 1965, 33, in Box 8, Folder 2, City Planning Commission Subject Files Commissioner William F. R. Ballard, 68–015, Municipal Archives of the City of New York.

43. Margot Gayle, *Cast-Iron Architecture in New York: A Photographic Survey* (New York: Dover, 1974), v–xviii; "Noted Buildings in Path of Road"; "An Architectural Tour of SoHo's Cast-Iron Heritage," *NYT*, May 5, 1978, C1.

44. Gayle, *Cast-Iron Architecture*, v–xviii; "Noted Buildings in Path of Road"; "Architectural Tour of Cast-Iron Heritage."

45. "Calendar of Landmarks Preservation Commission"; "Letter from Geoffrey Platt"; "Noted Buildings in Path of Road."

46. "Noted Buildings in Path of Road."

47. Huxtable, "Where It Goes, Nobody Knows."

48. "Moses Rebuffed on Expressway," *NYT*, February 11, 1966, 43; "Noted Buildings in Path of Road.".

49. Douglas Martin, "Margot Gayle, Urban Preservationist and Crusader with Style, Dies at 100," *NYT*, September 29, 2009, B6.

50. "Going Out Guide," *NYT*, March 29, 1972, 34; "Going Out Guide," *NYT*, March 1, 1973, 54; "Going Out Guide," *NYT*, June 2, 1973, 18; "New York's Largest Outdoor Museum, Made of Cast Iron," *NYT*, February 23, 1975, XXI; "Preservation Is Pushed," *NYT*, May 26, 1974, 309; Gayle, *Cast-Iron Architecture*.

51. "SoHo to Be Made a Landmark Area," *NYT*, March 22, 1973, 52; "Tramway Project Approved by City," *NYT*, October 5, 1973, 35; "SoHo Made a Historic District,' *NYT*, August 17, 1973, 35; "Good Buildings Have Friends," *NYT*, May 24, 1970, X26; "SoHo Wins Landmark Fight," *VV*, October 11, 1973, 1.

52. "SoHo—Cast Iron Historic District Designation Report," New York City Landmarks Preservation Commission (1973), 1, 8; "SoHo Wins Landmark Fight"; "The SoHo Scene: Guide to Lofts and Galleries South of Houston Street," Box 1, Folder 15, SAA Records.

53. "SoHo to Be Made Landmark Area"; "Tramway Project Approved"; "SoHo Made Historic District"; "Good Buildings Have Friends"; "SoHo Wins Landmark Fight."

54. Louis Meisel interview.

55. Esman and Hagenberg, *SoHo*; Anderson-Spivy, *Anderson and Archer's SoHo*.

56. "Design: A Landmark Loft in SoHo," *NYT*, November 24, 1974, 318.

57. Lees, "Reappraisal of Gentrification."

58. Bark interview.

Chapter Seven

1. "SoHo: The Boom Town of Bohemia," *Town and Country*, September 1977, 123; Esman and Hagenberg, *SoHo*, 74.

2. Zukin, *Loft Living*, 24–27.

3. "Confidential Draft, Industry" [1963–64], Box 17, Folder 9; "Department of City Planning Newsletter June–July 1966, 'Jobs in Transition,'" Box 26, Folder 10; "Jobs in Transition," July 31, 1966, Box 27, Folder 1; all in City Planning Commission Subject Files, Commissioner H. Goldstone 69–004, Municipal Archives of the City of New York; Peter S. Richards and Phil-

lip B. Wallick, *Plan for New York City: A Proposal* (New York: New York City Department of City Planning, 1969), 17; Sugrue, *Origins of the Urban Crisis*, 6.

4. Richards and Wallick, *Plan for New York City*, 17.

5. Levine, *Artist Housing in South Houston*.

6. Ibid., 5–6.

7. Ibid., 6–8.

8. Ibid., 14–16.

9. SoHo's art-related retail businesses did not exist in a vacuum, however, as the neighborhood was located close to New York's Little Italy and Chinatown neighborhoods. Both of these neighborhoods was a vibrant restaurant and shopping district for SoHo artists and early visitors.

10. "Saturday South of Houston," *SWN*, November 8, 1973, 7.

11. "Soho's First Holiday Shopping Guide," *SWN*, December 6, 1973, 1; "A Downtown Frontier of Boutiques and Studios," *NYT*, July 12, 1972, 44; "Art World Is Big Business," *Villager*, May 10, 1977, Box 2, Folder 6, ATA Records.

12. "A Nebulous Art Presence," *Art Rite*, Winter–Spring 1975.

13. "The SoHo Look," *SWN*, April 11, 1974, 21; "SWN Discoveries," *SWN*, October 23, 1975; inflation data calculated using Bureau of Labor Statistics CPI Inflation Calculator, June 3, 2015, http://www.bls.gov/data/inflation_calculator.htm.

14. "Harriet Love," *SWN*, March 18, 1976; "Where'd Ya Get It? SoHo!" *SWN*, January 26, 1978, 14.

15. "Local Color," *SWN*, June 27, 1974, 10; "Local Color," *SWN*, September 12, 1974.

16. Catherine Morris, Klaus Bussmann, and Markus Müller, *Food: An Exhibition by White Columns, New York* (Münster: Westfälisches Landesmuseum für Kunst und Kulturgeschichte, 1999); "Food's Family Fiscal Facts," *Avalanche*, Spring 1972.

17. Ibid.

18. "SoHo Seeks to Preserve a Life-Style," *NYT*, January 25, 1972, 37.

19. "SoHo Grows Up Rich and Chic," *NYT*, October 12, 1975, 184; "SoHo Finds," *SWN*, October 23, 1975.

20. "SoHo Finds"; "At Last a SoHo Café," *SWN*, November 20, 1975; "A Savory Guide to the Town's Best Brunches," *NYT*, March 18, 1977, 56; "One-Upmanship" *SWN*, November 3, 1977, 17.

21. L. Meisel interview; "For the Owners of Chanterelle, Success without Celebrity," *NYT*, April 22, 1987, C1.

22. "Cheap Food in SoHo," *SWN*, August 11, 1977, 12.

23. "SoHo: The Most Exciting Place to Live in the City," *New York Magazine*, May 20, 1974, 52–54.

24. "Lofty Living," *New York Magazine*, May 20, 1974, 54–60; "Arman," in Hastings-Falk, *Who Was Who in Art*, 1:129. The National Museum of Modern Art in Paris, the Museum of Modern Art in New York City, and the Walker Art Center in Minneapolis, among others, currently hold Arman's work; "Board of Directors, African Literacy Art and Development," January 28, 2008, http://www.aladafrica.org/Board-of-Dir.html (site discontinued).

25. "There They Are in Aaron Burr's House in SoHo—Dreaming," *NYT*, March 18, 1976, 63.

26. "SoHo: Boom Town."

27. "Home Style," *SWN*, June 15, 1978, 13.

28. "A Loft that Looks Lived In," *NYT*, November 3, 1976, 61.

29. "Lofty Living"; "Remington, Deborah," in Hastings-Falk, *Who Was Who in Art*, 3:2741.

Remington exhibited paintings at the Whitney Painting Annuals in 1956, 1957, and 1972, as well as in museums in France, the Bykert Galleries in New York, and the Pyramid Galleries in Washington, DC. Several museums, including the Whitney, own her works in their collections, and her work continues to be shown at art museums in the United States and abroad. Inflation figures calculated with CPI Inflation Calculator, May 16, 2015 (http://www.bls.gov/data/inflation_calculator.htm).

30. "Lofty Living"; "Nesbitt, Lowell (Blair)," in Hastings-Falk, *Who Was Who in Art*, 2:2403; Nesbitt exhibited work in biennials in Tokyo, São Paulo, and the Whitney Museum, as well as galleries in Germany, Switzerland, and New York. The National Museum of American Art, the Hirshhorn Museum and Sculpture Garden in Washington, DC, the Aachen Museum in Germany, and several US government agencies hold his works in their collections. Inflation figures calculated with CPI Inflation Calculator, May 16, 2015 (http://www.bls.gov/data/inflation_calculator.htm).

31. "Keeping Aloft," *SWN*, August 8, 1974, 2.
32. "Art Talk: Loft Life," *SWN*, October 10, 1974, 10.
33. "SoHo Loft Expo 1978," *VV*, March 24, 1978, Box 2, Folder 6, ATA Records.
34. Norma Skurka, "Design: Three Years Ago It Was a Toy Factory; Now It's 4,000 Square Feet of Living Room," *NYT*, March 3, 1974, 260; Ceglic interview.
35. Ceglic referred to himself as "the ampersand" in Dean & DeLuca; the trio decided that the store's name sounded better using only two of their surnames. It is also worth noting that Ceglic and Dean were partners in both business and life. The two are the most prominent example in SoHo at the convergence of the phenomena of artist- and gay-led gentrification. The Gay Activist Alliance had a presence in the neighborhood. Its Firehouse on Wooster Street served as a place where gay men (including artists such as Robert Mapplethorpe and Keith Haring) could socialize at weekly dances and special artist speakers' series.
36. Turpan interview.
37. Ibid.
38. "White on White," *SWN*, November 2, 1978, 42; Ceglic interview.
39. Ceglic interview.
40. Ann Barry, "A Lofty Spot for a Food Shop," *NYT*, October 26, 1977, 68.
41. Ibid.
42. Ibid.
43. Ceglic interview.
44. "SoHo Loft Expo 1978."
45. "Useful Ideas for Empty Spaces," *New York Magazine*, April 17, 1978, 62.
46. Turpan interview; Joan Kron and Suzanne Slesin, *High-Tech: The Industrial Style and Source Book for the Home* (New York: Clarkson N. Potter, 1980).
47. Turpan interview.
48. Ibid.
49. Ibid.
50. "Living with Industry," *SWN*, April 13, 1976, 30; Macy's advertisement, *SWN*, August 2, 1979, 2.
51. "Keeping Aloft," *SWN*, May 16, 1974, 3.
52. "A Downtown Frontier of Boutiques and Studios," *NYT*, July 12, 1972, 44; Wendy Perron, "Flu as Fashion and Art as Business," *SWN*, May 18, 1978, 15.
53. "Loft's Labor Lost," *SWN*, May 7, 1980, 5.
54. Cunningham interview.

Chapter Eight

1. "The City's New Loft Plan," *SWN*, August 20, 1980, 6–7; "Loft Leaders Speak Up," *SWN*, September 17, 1980, 6.
2. "Total and Foreign-Born Population New York City, 1970–2000," June 8, 2015, http://www.nyc.gov/html/dcp/pdf/census/1790-2000_nyc_total_foreign_birth.pdf.
3. Jeff Chang, *Can't Stop, Won't Stop: A History of the Hip-Hop Generation* (New York: Picador, 2005), 7–19; Greenberg, *Branding New York*, 133–36, 156–57, 183–91; Shefter, *Political Crisis/Fiscal Crisis*; James E. Goodman, *Blackout* (New York: North Point Press), 2003.
4. "Costs for 'SoHo' Lofts Are Rising Drastically," *NYT*, July 26, 1970; "Loft Living: Can You Make It?"; United States Bureau of Labor Statistics, *100 Years of U.S. Consumer Spending: Data for the Nation, New York City, and Boston* (Washington, DC: United States Bureau of Labor Statistics, 2006).
5. Zukin, *Loft Living*, 10, 142.
6. Data taken from New York City Automated City Register Information System (ACRIS), June 8, 2015, http://a836-acris.nyc.gov/CP/.
7. "When the SoHo Romance Is Over," *SWN*, October 9, 1975, 14.
8. Emanuel Tobier, "Setting the Record Straight on Loft Conversions," *New York Affairs* 6, no. 4 (1981).
9. "Keeping Aloft," *SWN*, December 25, 1975, 11; "SoHo Organizes to Meet City and Disco Threats," *SWN*, January 8, 1976, 6.
10. Kostelanetz, *SoHo*, 43.
11. New York City Department of City Planning, *SoHo/NoHo Occupancy Survey* (New York: New York City Department of City Planning, 1983), 37.
12. "Artist-In-Residence Loft Conversion Can Offer Investment Opportunity," *Real Estate Weekly*, October 13, 1975.
13. Bureau of the Census, *Census of Population, 1950: A Report of the Seventeenth Decennial Census of the United States* (Washington, DC: US Government Print Office, 1952); *1960 Final Report* (Washington, DC: Bureau of the Census, 1961); Bureau of the Census, *1970 Census of Population and Housing: Census Tracts* (Washington, DC: Bureau of the Census, 1971); *1980 Census of Population* (Washington, DC: Bureau of the Census, 1980).
14. Real Estate Board of New York, *Residential Use of Manhattan Loft Buildings: Analysis and Recommendations* (New York: Real Estate Board of New York, September 1975, amended 1976), 1–2.
15. City of New York Department of City Planning and Mayor's Midtown Action Office, *Residential Re-Use of Non-Residential Buildings in Manhattan* (New York: City of New York Department of City Planning, 1976).
16. Tobier, "Setting Record Straight," 35–38.
17. Real Estate Board of New York, *Residential Use of Manhattan Loft Buildings*, 1, 18, 25.
18. Ibid., 1.
19. Ibid., 23–24.
20. City of New York Department of City Planning and Mayor's Midtown Action Office, *Residential Re-Use of Non-Residential Buildings*, 1.
21. Ibid., 8, 31.
22. Ibid., 2.
23. Ibid., 41–47.
24. Ibid.

NOTES TO PAGES 192–202 267

25. Ibid.

26. Ibid., 2, 60–62.

27. "Splendid Architecture," *SWN*, 17 October 1974, 11.

28. Office of Lower Manhattan Development, Office of the Mayor, City of New York, *Lower Manhattan TriBeCa Study Area* (New York: Office of Lower Manhattan Development, 1974).

29. Jim Stratton, "Keeping Aloft," *SWN*, July 11, 1974, 2; Suzanne R. Wasserman, "Washington Market," in K. Jackson, *Encyclopedia of New York City*, 1243.

30. Jim Stratton, "Keeping Aloft," *SWN*, November 7, 1974, 2; Jim Stratton, "Keeping Aloft," *SWN*, October 16, 1975, 13.

31. "Rezoning Sought for Loft Space," *NYT*, October 16, 1975, 43.

32. Ibid.

33. "City Planners Have Bad Ideas for Lofts," *SWN*, November 27, 1975, 8; "SoHo Organizes to Meet City and Disco Threats," January 8, 1976, 6.

34. "Sutton Tours Washington Market," *SWN*, December 5, 1974, 4.; "NoHo Residents Resist Loft Rezoning," *NYT*, November 9, 1975, 26.

35. "NoHo Artists Ask Legalizing of Homes," *NYT*, February 26, 1976, 26.

36. Ibid.

37. "SoHo Loft Plans," *SWN*, March 4, 1976, 11.

38. The ordinance allowed for residential conversions in NoHo and SoHo loft buildings less than 5,000 square feet, except for buildings on a section of Broadway. Previously, loft conversions were only allowed in SoHo buildings less than 3,600 square feet.

39. "Keeping Aloft," *SWN*, May 27, 1976, 6; "Lofts in Tribeca Win Zone Change," *NYT*, June 12, 1976, 15.

40. Real Estate Board of New York, *Residential Use of Manhattan Loft Buildings*, 40; Debra S. Vorsanger, "New York City's J-51 Program: Controversy and Revision," *Fordham Urban Law Journal* 12, no. 1 (1983).

41. Zukin, *Loft Living*, 56–57, 159–62.

42. "Study Finds Banks Reducing Investing in New York Real Estate Because of Drop in Property Values," *NYT*, August 22, 1976, Box 162, Folder 1555, DLMA Records; City of New York Department of City Planning and Mayor's Midtown Action Office, *Residential Re-Use of Non-Residential Buildings in Manhattan*, 9.

43. "Keeping Aloft," *SWN*, November 29, 1973, 3.

44. Property Records for New York County, Block 488, Lot 37, New York City ACRIS, June 8, 2015, http://a836-acris.nyc.gov/CP/.

45. Ibid.; "Trouble on Broome Street," *SWN*, February 12, 1976, 4.

46. Property Records for New York County, Block 193, Lot 36, New York City ACRIS, June 8, 2015, http://a836-acris.nyc.gov/CP/; "The Loftlord Tapes: Behind the First Loft Rent Strike," *VV*, May 15, 1978, 1.

47. "Loftlord Tapes."

48. "Loft Decisions Due This Spring," *SWN*, 19 April 1979, 7.

49. Property Records for New York County, Block 193, Lot 36.

50. Property Records Search for Eliau Lipkis, New York City ACRIS, June 8, 2015, http://a836-acris.nyc.gov/CP/. His properties were located at 64 White Street, 47 Walker Street, and 71–73 Franklin Street in addition to 55 Walker Street.

51. "Showdown on Bond Street," *SWN*, April 23, 1980, 6; Property Records for New York County, Block 529, Lot 10, New York City ACRIS, June 8, 2015, http://a836-acris.nyc.gov/CP/.

52. Property Records for New York County, Block 529, Lot 10.
53. "Who Owns SoHo," *VV*, March 21, 1977, 22–26.
54. Ibid.
55. Property Records for New York County, Block 485, Lot 14; Block 515, Lot 37; Block 501, Lots 8 and 10; and Block 229, Lot 20, New York City ACRIS, June 8, 2015, http://a836-acris.nyc.gov/CP/.
56. "Who Owns SoHo."
57. Ibid.; "Peter Gee"; Property Records for New York County, Block 485, Lot 14; Block 515, Lot 37; Block 501, Lots 8 and 10; and Block 514, Lot 41, New York City ACRIS, June 8, 2015, http://a836-acris.nyc.gov/CP/.
58. "James Yu and His Co-op Crew," *SWN*, May 26, 1977, 4.
59. Ibid.; Property Records for New York County, Block 474, Lot 29, New York City ACRIS, June 8, 2015, http://a836-acris.nyc.gov/CP/.
60. Stone interview; Vincent Hanley interview with the author, New York, NY, March 14, 2013.
61. "The Loft King's Allhart," *SWN*, June 17 1976, 10.
62. Ibid.
63. Ibid.
64. "Stop that Coop," *SWN*, July 15, 1976, 11.
65. Ibid.

Chapter Nine

1. "Loft Tenants Gird for Winter," *SWN*, October 4, 1979, 5, "Loft Decision, What Next?" *SWN*, January 3, 1980, 5.
2. "Loft Decision, What Next?"
3. "Loft Inspections, Why Now?" *SWN*, July 20, 1978, 10.
4. Real Estate Board of New York, *Residential Use of Manhattan Loft Buildings*, 29.
5. Hanley interview.
6. Property Records Search for Harry Macklowe, New York City ACRIS, May 25, 2011, http://a836-acris.nyc.gov/Scripts/DocSearch.dll/BBL (site discontinued). Macklowe's properties included 31–33 E. 28th Street (Midtown), 408 E. 88th Street (Upper East Side), 196 W. 10th Street (Village), 505 Watts Street (Tribeca), 86 Thompson Street (SoHo), 439 E. 75th Street (Upper East Side), 150 Spring Street (SoHo), 355 W. Broadway (SoHo), 86 Thompson Street (SoHo), 55–57 Grand Street (SoHo), 363 Lexington Avenue (Midtown), 42 Broad Street (Financial District), 1143–45 1st Avenue (Upper East Side), 1154–56 1st Avenue (Upper East Side), 305–11 47th Street (Midtown), 272–28 Bleecker Street (Village), 75th Street and 3rd Avenue (Upper East Side), 1079 1st Avenue (Upper East Side), 144 E. 44th Street (Midtown), and 139–41 W. 44th Street (Midtown).
7. "Artists Hold Out in Tribeca," *SWN*, June 7, 1979, 10; Property Records for New York County, Block 212, Lot 56, New York City ACRIS, June 8, 2015, http://a836-acris.nyc.gov/CP/.
8. Ibid.
9. Ibid.
10. "Artists Left Loftless," *SWN*, June 14, 1979, 9; Property Records for New York County, Block 212, Lot 56.
11. Property Records for New York County, Block 529, Lot 1; Block 498 Lot 5; Block 522, Lot 14; Block 530, Lot 1; and Block 532, Lot 20, New York City ACRIS, June 8, 2015, http://a836-acris.nyc.gov/CP/.

12. "Loft Blaze Mystery," *SWN*, February 22, 1979, 4.; Property Records Search for Fine, Martin, Skysound and Don't Tread on Me, New York City ACRIS, June 8, 2015, http://a836-acris.nyc.gov/CP/. Fine's properties included 503–5 E. 73rd Street, 504 E. 84th Street, 521-A E. 85th Street, 315 E. 78th Street, 339 E. 58th Street, 1825–27 Second Avenue, 247 E. 62nd Street, and 161 E. 88th Street (Upper East Side); 56 W. 87th Street and 407–8 Central Park West (Upper West Side); 309 E. 37th Street, 336 E. 50th Street, 426–28 W. 48th Street, and 301–5 E. 37th Street (Midtown); 417 E. 12th Street and 55 and 97–99 St. Marks Place (East Village); 20 W. 15th Street (West Village); and 92 Perry Street and 581–83 Hudson Street (Tribeca).

13. "Loft Blaze Mystery"; "Loft Speculator Wins One," *SWN*, July 19, 1979, 10.

14. Ibid.; "Tale of Two Buildings," *SWN*, April 26, 1979, 5.

15. "Tale of Two Buildings."

16. "Loft Speculator Wins One."

17. Property Records for New York County, Block 498, Lot 7, New York City Automated City ACRIS, June 8, 2015, http://a836-acris.nyc.gov/CP/; "Stalwart in SoHo," *SWN*, August 31, 1978, 17; "Loft Ripoff," *SWN*, March 29, 1979, 6.

18. "Stalwart in SoHo"; "Loft Ripoff," *SWN*, March 29, 1979, 6; "Singer Building Still on Hold," *SWN*, November 1, 1979, 5.

19. New York City Planning Commission, *Lofts: Balancing the Equities* (New York: City Planning Commission, 1981), 27–28.

20. "Loft Ripoff."

21. "City Moves on Illegal Lofts," *SWN*, July 5, 1979, 5.

22. "Singer Building Still on Hold."

23. "Singer Building Owners Appeal," *SWN*, November 29, 1979, 5.

24. "Singer Building: A Zoning War," *SWN*, December 13, 1979, 6–7.

25. Ibid.; "SoHo Squeeze," *SWN*, June 25, 1980, 6.

26. "SoHo Squeeze."

27. "Loft Decision, What Next?"; "Loft Decision Aftermath," *SWN*, January 31, 1980, 5. There was also a question of whether the decision applied to just the lofts in the building—buildings with six or more units rented for residential use before January 1, 1974, the date New York's Emergency Tenant Protection Act went into effect—or to all lofts that were de facto residences. In this latter case, each tenant would likely have to go to court to force his or her landlord into adhering to rent stabilization laws.

28. Hanley interview.

29. Ibid.

30. "Loft Inspections, Why Now?"

31. Untitled advertisement for Manhattan Loft Tenants Association, *SWN*, January 4, 1979, 5.

32. "Loft Dwellers, Digging In," *SWN*, January 25, 1979, 11.

33. "Loft Dwellers Will March," *SWN*, March 1, 1979, 24; "Invasion of the Loft People," *SWN*, March 15, 1979, 6.

34. "Loft Decisions Due This Spring," *SWN*, April 19, 1979, 7; "Loft Tenants Gird for Winter."

35. "How Loft Conversions Imperil Jobs," *SWN*, February 8, 1979, 8; Property Records for New York County, Block 545, Lot 59, New York City ACRIS, June 8, 2015, http://a836-acris.nyc.gov/CP/.

36. "How Loft Conversions Imperil Jobs"; Property Records for New York County, Block 545, Lot 59.

37. "Loft Decision Aftermath"; "Taking Lofts to Albany," *SWN*, February 13, 1980, 4.

38. "Workers, Artists Unite on Lofts," *SWN*, February 27, 1980, 4.

39. "Loft Tenants Lobby Albany," *SWN*, June 4, 1980, 7; "Losing at Loft-Opoly," *SWN*, June 24, 1981, 7; "SoHo Squeeze"; "Up in a Loft without a Net," *SWN*, November 12, 1980, 6; "New Loft Law, How It Happened," *SWN*, November 26, 1980, 8.

40. "The City's New Loft Plan," *SWN*, August 20, 1980, 6–7; "Loft Leaders Speak Up," *SWN*, September 17 1980, 6.

41. "Loft Leaders Speak Up."

42. "The Loft Plan Everybody Hates," *SWN*, January 14, 1981, 5.

43. Michael Goodwin, ed., *New York Comes Back: The Mayoralty of Ed Koch* (New York: powerHouse Books, 2005); Kim Moody, *From Welfare State to Real Estate: Regime Change in New York City from 1974 to the Present* (New York: New Press, 2007).

44. The Garment Center was located at West Thirty-fifth to West Sixty-ninth Streets between Fifth and Sixth Avenues.

45. "Koch Rezoning Nearly Aloft," *SWN*, March 25, 1981, 6; "Lofts Zoned Again," *SWN*, April 22, 1981, 7.

46. "Losing in the Lofts," *SWN*, July 1, 1981, 6; "Loft Conversion Law Gets Mixed Review," *NYT*, March 28 1982, R10.

47. "Loft Conversion Law Gets Mixed Review"; "Bill Signed to Legalize Status of Lofts' Tenants," *NYT*, June 23, 1982, B3.

48. Carl Weisbrod, interview with the author, New York, NY, March 11, 2013.

49. Ibid.

50. Neil Smith, "Toward a Theory of Gentrification: A Back to the City Movement by Capital, not People," *Journal of the American Planning Association* 45, no. 4 (1979): 538–48.

51. "Loft Decision Aftermath"; New York City Planning Commission, *Lofts: Balancing the Equities*, 41; Tobier, "Setting the Record Straight."

Conclusion

1. Toll interview; Heilmann interview; Aoki interview; Penzner interview; Vivian S. Toy, "Co-ops Reap Unexpected Bonanza," *NYT*, January 20, 2008.

2. Kristina Ford, *Housing Policy and the Urban Middle Class* (New Brunswick, NJ: Rutgers University Center for Urban Policy Research, 1978), 10, 19, 26–28, 95–107.

3. "For Tribeca, Delicate Diversity or Wall Street North?" *NYT*, June 13, 1989, B1.

4. "Most Expensive New York City Neighborhoods in Q1 2012," accessed April 24, 2013, http://www.propertyshark.com/Real-Estate-Reports/2012/05/04/most-expensive-nyc-neighborhoods-in-q1-2012/. Prices were $1,592 per square foot in Midtown, $1,424 per square foot in the West Village, $1,399 per square foot in SoHo, and $1,376 per square foot in Tribeca. Weisbrod interview.

5. Corey Kilgannon, "From Metalwork to Luxury Condos: Century-Old SoHo Shop Ends Its Run," *NYT*, May 16, 2008, B3.

6. Michael Idov, "Trump SoHo Is Not an Oxymoron," *NYT*, April 7, 2008, 34, 36–39, 109–10.

7. Christine Haughney, "Suddenly, SoHo Starts to Heed a Law Limiting Lofts to Artists," *NYT*, November 12, 2010, A1.

8. Laura Kusisto, "Push to Count SoHo Artists Stirs Debate," *Wall Street Journal*, July 6, 2012, A15. Interestingly, certified artist and real estate broker Susan Meisel helped raise funds for this study.

9. "NoHo Art," *SWN*, May 4, 1978, 26; "Somewhere West of SoHo . . . ," *SWN*, October 18, 1979, 7.

NOTES TO PAGES 232–36

10. "SoHo Squeeze."

11. "Fall 1980 Newsletter," Box 4, Folder 164; "Who We Are & What We Do," Box 2, Folder 62; "Letter Regarding Affiliate Program with Move to 63 Crosby Street, April 23, 1981," Box 1, Folder 4; "Lease at 63 Crosby Street," Box 2, Folder 63; all in A.I.R.

12. "Space Hits the Roof," *SWN*, April 1, 1981, 1.

13. Ann Fensterstock, *Art on the Block: Tracking the New York Art World from SoHo to the Bowery, Bushwick, and Beyond* (New York: Palgrave Macmillan, 2013); Jenny Schuetz, "Central Agents or Canaries in the Coal Mine? Art Galleries in Neighborhood Change," in *Creative Communities: Art Works in Economic Development*, ed. Michael Rushton (Washington, DC: Brookings Institution Press, 2013).

14. Cooper interview; Hoffman interview; L. Meisel interview; de Knegt interview.

15. Ceglic interview; Louis Meisel interview; Toll interview; Stone interview.

16. Cara Buckley, "Critics of SoHo Proposal Ask, You Call This Improvement?" *NYT*, January 30, 2012, A1.

17. "Artists' Escape to Williamsburg," *SWN*, April 30, 1980, 6.

18. "L.I. City a Mix That Works," *SWN*, July 2, 1980, 6; "Artists Put Down Roots in L.I. City," *NYT*, January 21, 1979, 1.

19. Julie Anne Podmore, "(Re)Reading the 'Loft Living' Habitus in Montreal's Inner City," *International Journal of Urban and Regional Research* 22, no. 2 (June 1998): 283–302; Chris Hamnett and Drew Whitelegg, "Loft Conversion and Gentrification in London: From Industrial to Postindustrial Land Use," *Environment and Planning A* 39 no, 1 (July, 2006): 106–24; Wendy S. Shaw, "Sydney's SoHo Syndrome? Loft Living in the Urbane City," *Cultural Geographies* 13, no. 2 (April 2006): 182–206.

20. Barbara Ballinger, "Space and Style: The Loft Goes Upscale and Suburban," *Realtor*, April 1, 2006, http://realtormag.realtor.org/home-and-design/architecture-coach/article/2006/04/loft-goes-upscale-and-suburban.

21. Even New York City has continued in the SoHo vein beyond NoHo and Tribeca to create DUMBO (Down Under the Manhattan Bridge Overpass) and NoLIta (North of Little Italy). SoHo itself evokes the London neighborhood of Soho, part of that city's West End entertainment district.

22. Elizabeth Currid-Halkett, "Where Do Bohemians Come From," *NYT*, October 16, 2011, SR 12.

Bibliography

Manuscript Collections

ARCHIVES OF AMERICAN ART, SMITHSONIAN INSTITUTION, WASHINGTON, DC

André Emmerich Gallery records and André Emmerich papers, 1929–2008
Artist Tenants Association records, 1959–1976 (ATA Records)
55 Mercer Artists, Inc. records, 1939–2007, bulk, 1970–2007
Jackie Windsor interviews, 1990–1992
Leo Castelli Gallery records, circa 1880–2000, especially 1957–1999
Park Place Gallery Art Research records and Paula Cooper Gallery records, 1965–1998 (Cooper)
Robin Forbes's slides of SoHo, 1976
SoHo Artists Association records, 1963–1972 (SAA Records)
SoHo 20 Gallery records

GETTY RESEARCH INSTITUTE, LOS ANGELES, CA

Irving Sandler Papers

NEW YORK CITY MUNICIPAL ARCHIVES

City Planning Commission Subject Files, Commissioner William F. R. Ballard
City Planning Commission Subject Files, Commissioner James Felt
City Planning Commission Subject Files, Commissioner H. Goldstone
New York City Cultural Council
Office of Cultural Affairs

NEW-YORK HISTORICAL SOCIETY

Margot Gayle Papers, 1959–2005
Shirley Hayes Papers, 1948–2001, especially 1952–1979
Washington Square Park Redevelopment Collection, 1952–1966
Records of the Weiss & Klau, Co., MS 687, 1892–1988 (Weiss & Klau)

NEW YORK STATE ARCHIVES, ALBANY, NEW YORK

New York State Council on the Arts Grant Application Files, 1967–2001 (NYSCA Archives)

NEW YORK UNIVERSITY LIBRARIES

A.I.R. Gallery Archive (A.I.R.)
Judson Memorial Church Archive
Records of the Office of the President/Chancellor New York University (NYU Archives)
Wendy Perron's "Concepts in Performance," SoHo Weekly News

ROCKEFELLER ARCHIVE CENTER, SLEEPY HOLLOW, NEW YORK

Downtown–Lower Manhattan Association, Inc., Records, 1937–1995 (DLMA Records)
Papers of Governor Nelson Rockefeller

GOVERNMENT PUBLICATIONS

City of New York Department of City Planning. *SoHo/NoHo Occupancy Survey.* New York: New York City Department of City Planning, 1983.
City of New York Department of City Planning and Mayor's Midtown Action Office. *Residential Re-Use of Non-Residential Buildings in Manhattan.* New York: City of New York Department of City Planning, 1976.
Levine, Michael. *Artist Housing in South Houston: A Report Presented by the New York City Planning Commission, Prepared by Michael E. Levine (Based on 1968 Field Study).* New York: New York City Planning Commission, 1969.
New York City Department of City Planning. *Lofts: An Information Handbook.* New York: New York City Department of City Planning, February 1979.
New York City Landmarks Preservation Commission. *SoHo–Cast-Iron Historic District Designation Report.* New York: Landmarks Preservation Commission, 1973.
New York City Planning Commission. *Lofts: Balancing the Equities.* New York: City Planning Commission, 1981.
Office of Lower Manhattan Development, Office of the Mayor, City of New York. *Lower Manhattan TriBeCa Study Area.* New York: Office of Lower Manhattan Development, 1974.
Rapkin, Chester. *The South Houston Industrial Area: A Study of the Economic Significance of Firms, the Physical Quality of Buildings, and the Real Estate Market in an Old Loft Section of Lower Manhattan.* New York: City of New York City Planning Commission–Department of City Planning, 1963.
Real Estate Board of New York. *Residential Use of Manhattan Loft Buildings: Analysis and Recommendations.* New York: Real Estate Board of New York, 1975 [amended 1976].
Report of the Mayor's Committee on Cultural Policy. New York: Mayor's Committee on Cultural Policy, 1974.
Richards, Peter S., and Phillip B. Wallick, eds. *Plan for New York City: A Proposal.* New York: New York City Department of City Planning, 1969.

South Houston Industrial Area: A Report and Program by the New York City Planning Commission. New York: New York City Planning Commission, 1963.

United States Bureau of Labor Statistics. *100 Years of U.S. Consumer Spending: Data for the Nation, New York City, and Boston*. Washington, DC: United States Bureau of Labor Statistics, 2006.

Selected Works

Alexiou, Alice Sparberg. *Jane Jacobs: Urban Visionary*. New Brunswick, NJ: Rutgers University Press, 2006.

Alloway, Lawrence. *10 Downtown, 10 Years: 1968, 1969, 1970, 1971, 1972, 1973, 1974, 1975, 1976, 1977*. New York: s.n., 1978.

Anderson-Spivy, Alexandra. *Anderson and Archer's SoHo: The Essential Guide to Art and Life in Lower Manhattan*. New York, Simon and Schuster, 1979.

Austin, Joe. *Taking the Train: How Graffiti Art Became an Urban Crisis in New York City*. New York: Columbia University Press, 2001.

Avila, Eric. "Revisiting the Urban Interstates: Politics, Policy, and Culture Since World War II." *Journal of Urban History* 50, no. 5 (September 2014): 827–30.

Ballon, Hillary, and Kenneth Jackson, eds. *Robert Moses and the Modern City: The Transformation of New York*. New York: W. W. Norton, 2007.

Banes, Sally. *Greenwich Village, 1963: Avant-Garde Performance and the Effervescent Body*. Durham, NC: Duke University Press, 1993.

———. *Subversive Expectations: Performance Art and Paratheater in New York, 1976–85* (Ann Arbor: University of Michigan Press, 1998).

Barton, Michael. "An Exploration of the Importance of the Strategy Used to Identify Gentrification." *Urban Studies*, December 3, 2014. http://usj.sagepub.com/content/early/2014/12/03/0042098014561723.full.pdf+html.

Berg, Peter F. *New York City Politics: Governing Gotham*. New Brunswick, NJ: Rutgers University Press, 2007.

Bernstein, Roslyn, and Shael Shapiro. *Illegal Living: 80 Wooster Street and the Evolution of SoHo*. Vilnius, Lithuania: Jonas Mekas Foundation, 2010.

Binkiewicz, Donna M. *Federalizing the Muse: United States Arts Policy and the National Endowment for the Arts, 1965–1980*. Chapel Hill: University of North Carolina Press, 2006.

Block, René. *New York, Downtown Manhattan, SoHo*. Berlin: Akademie der Künste, 1976.

Blomley, Nicholas. *Unsettling the City: Urban Land and the Politics of Property*. New York: Routledge, 2004.

Brecher, Charles, and Raymond Horton. *Power Failure: New York City Politics and Policy Since 1960*. New York: Oxford University Press, 1993.

Brenner, Neil, and Nik Theodore. *Spaces of Neoliberalism: Urban Restructuring in North America and America and Western Europe*. Malden, MA: Oxford, Blackwell, 2002.

Brentano, Robyn, and Mark Savitt. *112 Workshop, 112 Greene Street: History, Artists, and Artworks*. New York: New York University Press, 1981.

Bryan-Wilson, Julia. *Art Workers: Radical Practice in the Vietnam War Era*. Berkeley: University of California Press, 2009.

Burton, Mary W. "Dwellings and Studios: A Historic Survey of Artists' Quarters in Selected Cities." *Ekistics* 48, no. 288 (May–June 1981): 218–33.

Cameron, Stuart, and Jon Coaffee. "Art, Gentrification and Regeneration—From Artist as Pioneer to Public Arts." *European Journal of Housing Policy* 5, no. 1 (April 2005): 39–58.

Cannato, Vincent J. *The Ungovernable City: John Lindsay and His Struggle to Save New York*. New York: Basic Books, 2001.

Caro, Robert. *The Power Broker: Robert Moses and the Fall of New York*. New York: Vintage, 1975.

Carpenter, Juliet, and Loretta Lees. "Gentrification in New York, London, and Paris: An International Comparison." *International Journal of Urban and Regional Research* 19, no. 2 (March 1995): 286–303.

Carriere, Michael. "Fighting the War against Blight: Columbia University, Morningside Heights, Inc., and Counterinsurgent Urban Renewal." *Journal of Planning History* 10, no. 1 (February 2011): 5–29.

Caulfield, Jon. *City Form and Everyday Life: Toronto's Gentrification and Critical Social Practice*. Toronto: University of Toronto Press, 1994.

Chang, Jeff. *Can't Stop, Won't Stop: A History of the Hip-Hop Generation*. New York: Picador, 2005.

City Club of New York. *The Wastelands of New York City: A Preliminary Inquiry into the Nature of Commercial Slum Areas, Their Potential for Housing and Business Redevelopment*. New York: City Club of New York, 1962.

Clark, Terry Nichols, and Richard Lloyd. "City as an Entertainment Machine." Paper prepared for presentation at the annual meeting of the American Sociological Association, 2000, faui.uchicago.edu/EM3.SS.doc.

Curran, Winifred. "'From the Frying Pan to the Oven': Gentrification and the Experience of Industrial Displacement in Williamsburg, Brooklyn." *Urban Studies* 44, no. 8 (July 2007): 1427–40.

Currid, Elizabeth. "Bohemia as Subculture, 'Bohemia' as Industry: Art, Culture, and Economic Development." *Journal of Planning Literature* 23, no. 4 (May 2009): 368–82.

Currid-Halkett, Elizabeth. *The Warhol Economy: How Fashion, Art, and Music Drive New York City*. Princeton, NJ: Princeton University Press, 2007.

Deutsche, Rosalyn, and Cara Gendel Ryan. "The Fine Art of Gentrification." *October* 31 (Winter 1984): 91–111.

Diamondstein, Barbaralee. *Remaking America: New Uses, Old Spaces*. New York: Crown, 1986.

Douglas, Ann. *Terrible Honesty: Mongrel Manhattan in the 1920s*. New York: Farrar, Straus and Giroux, 1995.

Eisenstadt, Peter, and Laura-Eve Moss, eds. *The Encyclopedia of New York State*. Syracuse, NY: Syracuse University Press, 2005.

Esman, Abigail R., and Roland Hagenberg, eds. *SoHo: A Guide; A Documentary*. New York: Egret, 1985.

Fairbridge, Kingsley C., and Harvey-Jane Kowal. *Loft Living: Recycling Warehouse Space for Residential Use*. Boston: Saturday Review Press, 1976.

Fensterstock, Ann. *Art on the Block: Tracking the New York Art World from SoHo to the Bowery, Bushwick, and Beyond*. New York: Palgrave MacMillan, 2013.

Fitch, Robert. *The Assassination of New York*. New York: Verso, 1993.

Flint, Anthony. *Wrestling with Moses: How Jane Jacobs Took on New York's Master Builder and Transformed the City*. New York: Random House, 2009.

Florida, Richard. *The Rise of the Creative Class . . . and How It's Transforming Working, Leisure, Community, and Everyday Life*. New York: Basic Books, 2002.

Ford, Kristina. *Housing Policy and the Urban Middle Class*. New Brunswick, NJ: Rutgers University Center for Urban Policy Research, 1978.
Freeman, Joshua B. *Working-Class New York: Life and Labor Since World War II*. New York: New Press, 2000. Distributed by W. W. Norton.
Freeman, Lance. *There Goes the Hood: Views of Gentrification from the Ground Up*. Philadelphia: Temple University Press, 2006.
Gayle, Margot. *Cast-Iron Architecture in New York: A Photographic Survey*. New York: Dover, 1974.
Gerhardt Liebmann—Alexander Carlson Gallery, New York. New York: Alexander Carlson Gallery, 1981. Exhibition catalog.
Gilfoyle, Timothy J. *City of Eros: New York City, Prostitution, and the Commercialization of Sex, 1790–1920*. New York: W. W. Norton, 1994.
Glass, Ruth. "Aspects of Change." In *London Aspects of Change*, edited by Ruth Glass et al. London: Center for Urban Studies, 1964.
Gluck, Mary. *Popular Bohemia: Modernism and Urban Culture in Nineteenth-Century Paris*. Cambridge, MA: Harvard University Press, 2005.
Goldberg, RoseLee. *Performance: Live Art since 1960*. New York: Harry N. Abrams, 1998.
Goldstein, Brian. "A City within a City: Community Development and the Struggle over Harlem, 1961–2001." PhD diss., Harvard University, 2013.
Goodman, James E. *Blackout*. New York: North Point Press, 2003.
Goodwin, Michael, ed. *New York Comes Back: The Mayoralty of Ed Koch*. New York: powerHouse Books, 2005.
Gordon, David L. A. *Battery Park City: Politics and Planning on the New York Waterfront*. Amsterdam: Gordon and Breach, 1997.
Gratz, Roberta Brandes. *The Battle for Gotham: New York in the Shadow of Robert Moses and Jane Jacobs*. New York: Nation Books, 2010.
Greenberg, Miriam. *Branding New York: How a City in Crisis Was Sold to the World*. New York: Routledge, 2008.
Greene, Nancy L. "From Downtown Tenements to Midtown Lofts: The Shifting Geography of an Urban Industry." In *A Coat of Many Colors: Immigration, Globalization, and Reform in New York City's Garment Industry*, edited by Daniel Soyer. New York: Fordham University Press, 2006.
Guilbaut, Serge. *How New York Stole the Idea of Modern Art: Abstract Expressionism, Freedom, and the Cold War*. Translated by Arthur Goldhammer. Chicago: University of Chicago Press, 1983.
Hackworth, Jason, and Neil Smith. "The Changing State of Gentrification." *Tijdschrift voor Economische en Sociale Geografie* 92, no. 4 (2002): 464–77.
Hamnett, Chris. "The Blind Men and the Elephant: The Explanation of Gentrification." *Transactions of the Institute of British Geographers*, n.s., 16, no. 2 (1991): 173–89.
———, and Drew Whitelegg. "Loft Conversion and Gentrification in London: From Industrial to Postindustrial Land Use." *Environment and Planning A* 39, no.1 (July 2006):106–24.
Harvey, David. *A Brief History of Neoliberalism*. New York: Oxford University Press, 2005.
———. *The Condition of Postmodernity: An Enquiry into the Origins of Cultural Change*. New York: Blackwell, 1990.
Hastings-Falk, Peter, ed. *Who Was Who in American Art, 1564–1975*. 3 vols. Madison, CT: Sound View Press, 1999.

Heilbrun, James. "Art and Culture as Central Place Functions." *Urban Studies* 29, no. 2 (April 1992): 205–15.
Henderson, A. Scott. *Housing and the Democratic Ideal: The Life and Thought of Charles Abrams*. New York: Columbia University Press, 2000.
Hirsch, Arnold R. *Making the Second Ghetto: Race and Housing in Chicago, 1950–1960*. 1983. Reprint, Chicago: University of Chicago Press, 1998.
Holm, Andrej, and Armin Kuhn. "Squatting and Urban Renewal: The Interaction of Squatter Movements and Strategies of Urban Restructuring in Berlin." *International Journal of Urban and Regional Research* 35, no. 3 (May 2011): 644–58.
Hoover, Edgar M., et al. *Anatomy of a Metropolis: The Changing Distribution of People and Jobs within the New York Metropolitan Region*. Cambridge, MA: Harvard University Press, 1959.
Hudson, James R. "SoHo: A Study of Residential Invasion of a Commercial and Industrial Area." *Urban Affairs Quarterly* 20, no. 1 (1984): 46–63.
———. *The Unanticipated City: Loft Conversions in Lower Manhattan*. Amherst: University of Massachusetts Press, 1987.
Hurewitz, Daniel. *Bohemian Los Angeles and the Making of Modern Politics*. Berkeley: University of California Press, 2007.
Isenberg, Alison. *Downtown America: A History of the Place and the People Who Made It*. Chicago: University of Chicago Press, 2004.
Jackson, Kenneth. *Crabgrass Frontier: The Suburbanization of the United States*. New York: Oxford University Press, 1985.
———, ed., *The Encyclopedia of New York City*. New Haven, CT: Yale University Press, 1995.
Jackson, Peter. "Neighborhood Change in New York: The Loft Conversion Process." *Journal of Economic and Social Geography* 76, no. 3 (1983): 202–15.
Jacobs, Jane. *The Death and Life of Great American Cities*. New York: Random House, 1961.
Jones, Alan, and Laura de Coppet. *The Art Dealers: The Powers behind the Scenes Tell How the Art World Really Works*. New York: Clarkson N. Potter, 1984.
Keegan, Robin, et al. *Creative New York*. New York: Center for an Urban Future, 2005.
Kennedy, Maureen, and Paul Leonard. "Dealing with Neighborhood Change: A Primer on Gentrification and Policy Changes." Discussion paper prepared for the Brookings Institution Center on Urban and Metropolitan Policy, Washington, DC, April 2001.
Klemek, Christopher. *The Transatlantic Collapse of Urban Renewal: Postwar Urbanism from New York to Berlin*. Chicago: University of Chicago Press, 2011.
Kostelanetz, Richard. *SoHo: The Rise and Fall of an Artists' Colony*. New York: Routledge, 2003.
Kotynek, Roy, and John Cohassey. *American Cultural Rebels: Avant-Garde and Bohemian Artists, Writers and Musicians from the 1850s through the 1960s*. Jefferson, NC: McFarland, 2008.
Kron, Joan, and Suzanne Slesin. *High-Tech: The Industrial Style and Source Book for the Home*. New York: Clarkson N. Potter, 1980.
Lassiter, Matthew D. *The Silent Majority: Suburban Politics in the Sunbelt South*. Princeton, NJ: Princeton University Press, 2006.
Lauman, Edward O., and James S. House. "Living Room Styles and Social Attributes: The Patterning of Material Artifacts in a Modern Urban Community." In Edward O. Lauman et al., eds., *The Logic of Social Hierarchies*. Chicago: University of Chicago Press, 1970.
Lees, Loretta. "A Reappraisal of Gentrification: Towards a 'Geography of Gentrification.'" *Progress in Human Geography*, no. 24 (2000): 389–408.
Ley, David. "Artists, Aestheticisation and the Field of Gentrification." *Urban Studies*, no. 12 (November 2003): 2527–44.

———. *The New Middle Class and the Remaking of the Central City*. New York: Oxford University Press, 1996.
Lloyd, Richard. *Neo-Bohemia: Art and Commerce in the Postindustrial City*. Chicago: University of Chicago Press, 2005.
Lockwood, Charles. *Manhattan Moves Uptown: An Illustrated History*. Boston: Houghton Mifflin, 1976.
MacCannell, Dean. *The Tourist: A New Theory of the Leisure Class*. Berkeley: University of California Press, 1976.
Mahler, Jonathan. *Ladies and Gentlemen, the Bronx Is Burning: 1977, Baseball, Politics, and The Battle for the Soul of a City*. New York: Farrar, Straus and Giroux, 2005.
Makielski, S. J. Jr. *The Politics of Zoning: The New York Experience*. New York: Columbia University Press, 1966.
Markusen, Ann. "Urban Development and the Politics of a Creative Class: Evidence from a Study of Artists." *Environment and Planning A* 38, no. 10 (October 2006): 1921–40.
Markusen, Ann, and Anne Gadwa. "A White Paper for the Mayors' Institute on City Design, a Leadership Initiative on the National Endowment for the Arts in Partnership with the United States Conference of Mayors and American Architectural Foundation." White paper, National Endowment for the Arts, Washington, DC, 2010.
McDonough, Yona Zeldis. *Gerhardt Liebmann: A Renaissance Man*. Geneva: Patrick Cramer, 1996.
McFarland, Gerald W. *Inside Greenwich Village: A New York City Neighborhood, 1898–1918*. Amherst: University of Massachusetts Press, 2001.
McNickle, Chris. *To Be Mayor of New York: Ethnic Politics in the City*. New York: Columbia University Press, 1993.
Mele, Christopher. *Selling the Lower East Side: Culture, Real Estate, and Resistance in New York City*. Minneapolis: University of Minnesota Press, 2000.
Mohl, Raymond A. "Citizen Activism and Freeway Revolts in Memphis and Nashville: The Road to Litigation." *Journal of Urban History* 40, no. 5 (September 2014): 870–93.
———. "Stop the Road: Freeway Revolts in American Cities." *Journal of Urban History* 30, no. 5 (July 2004): 674–706.
Mollenkopf, John, and Manuel Castells. *Dual City: Restructuring New York*. New York: Russell Sage Foundation, 1991.
Molotch, Harvey, and Mark Treskon. "Changing Art: SoHo, Chelsea, and the Dynamic Geography of Galleries in New York City." *International Journal of Urban and Regional Research* 33, no. 2 (June 2009): 517–41.
Moody, Kim. *From Welfare State to Real Estate: Regime Change in New York City from 1974 to the Present*. New York: New Press, 2007.
Moore, Alan. "Collectives: Protest, Counter-Culture and Political Postmodernism in New York City Artists' Organizations, 1969–1985." PhD diss., City University of New York, 2000.
Morris, Catherine, Klaus Bussmann, and Markus Müller. *Food: An Exhibition by White Columns, New York*. Münster: Westfälisches Landesmuseum für Kunst und Kulturgeschichte, 1999.
Morrissey, Lee. *The Kitchen Turns Twenty: A Retrospective Anthology*. New York: Kitchen Center for Video, Music, Dance, Performance, Film, and Literature, 1992.
Moss, Ian David. "Creative Placemaking Has an Outcomes Problem." May 9, 2012. http://createquity.com/2012/05/creative-placemaking-has-an-outcomes-problem.html.
Newfield, Jack, and Wayne Barrett. *City for Sale: Ed Koch and the Betrayal of New York*. New York: Harper and Row, 1988.

Nicolaides, Becky. *My Blue Heaven: Life and Politics in the Working-Class Suburbs of Los Angeles, 1920–1935.* Chicago: University of Chicago Press, 2002.

Osman, Suleiman. *The Invention of Brownstone Brooklyn: Gentrification and the Search for Authenticity in Postwar New York.* New York: Oxford University Press, 2011.

Page, Max. *The Creative Destruction of Manhattan.* Chicago: University of Chicago Press, 1999.

Perl, Jed. *New Art City: Manhattan at Mid-Century.* New York: Knopf, 2005.

Petrus, Stephen. "From Gritty to Chic: The Transformation of New York City's SoHo, 1962–1976." *New York History* 84, no. 1 (2003): 50–87.

Phillips, Rhonda. "Artful Business: Using the Arts for Community Economic Development." *Community Development Journal* 39, no. 2 (Spring 2004): 112–22.

Podmore, Julie Anne. "Loft Conversions in a Local Context: The Case of Inner City Montreal." PhD diss., McGill University, 1994.

———. "(Re)Reading the 'Loft Living' *Habitus* in Montreal's Inner City." *International Journal of Urban and Regional Research* 22, no. 2 (June 1998): 283–302.

Rast, Joel. *Remaking Chicago: The Political Origins of Urban Industrial Change.* DeKalb: Northern Illinois University Press, 1999.

Rawlings, Ed, and Jim Walrod. *Paul Rudolph: Lower Manhattan Expressway.* New York: Drawing Center, 2010.

Roberts, Sam, ed. *America's Mayor: John V. Lindsay and the Reinvention of New York.* New York: Columbia University Press, 2010.

Rockefeller, David. *Memoirs.* New York: Random House, 2002.

Rome, Adam. *The Bulldozer in the Countryside: Suburban Sprawl and the Rise of American Environmentalism.* New York: Cambridge University Press, 2001.

Rycroft, Simon. "The Geographies of Swinging London." *Journal of Historical Geography* 28, no. 4 (2002): 566–88.

Sanders, Jay, and J. Hoberman. *Rituals of Rented Island: Object Theater, Loft Performance, and the New Psychodrama—Manhattan, 1970–1980.* New York: Whitney Museum, 2013.

Sandler, Irving. *American Art of the 1960s.* New York: Harper and Row, 1988.

Schrag, Zachary M. *The Great Society Subway: A History of the Washington Metro.* Baltimore: Johns Hopkins University Press, 2006.

Schrank, Sarah. *Art and the City: Civic Imagination and Cultural Authority in Los Angeles.* Berkeley: University of California Press, 2009.

Schuetz, Jenny. "Central Agents or Canaries in the Coal Mine? Art Galleries in Neighborhood Change." In *Creative Communities: Art Works in Economic Development,* edited by Michael Rushton. Washington, DC: Brookings Institution Press, 2013.

Schulman, Bruce J. *From Cotton Belt to Sunbelt: Federal Policy, Economic Development, and the Transformation of the South, 1938–1980.* Oxford: Oxford University Press, 1991.

Schwartz, Gail Garfield. "Industrial Accommodation in New York City: The Women's and Children's Undergarment Industry." PhD diss., Columbia University, 1972.

Schwartz, Joel. *The New York Approach: Robert Moses, Urban Liberals, and the Redevelopment of the Inner City.* Columbus: Ohio State University Press, 1993.

Seeman, Helene Zuker, and Alanna Siegfried. *SoHo: A Guide.* New York: Neal-Schuman, 1978.

Seigel, Jerrold. *Bohemian Paris: Culture, Politics, and the Boundaries of Bourgeois Life, 1830–1930.* New York: Viking, 1986.

Self, Robert O. *American Babylon: Race and the Struggle for Postwar Oakland.* Princeton, NJ: Princeton University Press, 2003.

Shaw, Wendy S. "Sydney's SoHo Syndrome? Loft living in the Urbane City." *Cultural Geographies* 13, no. 2 (April 2006): 182–206.
Shefter, Martin. *Political Crisis/Fiscal Crisis: The Collapse and Revival of New York City*. New York, Basic Books, 1985.
Shelley, Thomas. *Greenwich Village Catholics: St. Joseph's Church and the Evolution of an Urban Faith Community*. Washington, DC: Catholic University of America Press, 2003.
Simpson, Charles P. *SoHo: The Artist in the City*. Chicago: University of Chicago Press, 1981.
Smith, Neil. "Gentrification and the Rent Gap." *Annals of the Association of American Geographers* 77, no. 3 (September 1987): 462–65.
———. "Gentrification and Uneven Development." *Economic Geography* 58, no. 2 (April 1982): 139–55.
———. *The New Urban Frontier: Gentrification and the Revanchist City*. New York: Routledge, 1996.
———. "Toward a Theory of Gentrification: A Back to the City Movement by Capital, not People." *Journal of the American Planning Association* 45, no. 4 (1979): 538–48.
Solnit, Rebecca. *The Hollow City: The Siege of San Francisco and the Crisis of American Urbanism*. New York: Verso, 2000.
Stansell, Christine. *American Moderns: Bohemian New York and the Creation of a New Century*. New York: Metropolitan Books, 2000.
Stratton, Jim. *Pioneering in the Urban Wilderness*. New York: Urizen Books, 1977.
Sugrue, Thomas J. *The Origins of the Urban Crisis: Race and Inequality in Postwar Detroit*. Princeton, NJ: Princeton University Press, 1996.
Taylor, Marvin J., ed. *The Downtown Book: The New York Art Scene, 1974–84*. Princeton, NJ: Princeton University Press, 2006.
Teaford, Jon C. *The Rough Road to Renaissance: Urban Revitalization in America, 1940–1985*. Baltimore: Johns Hopkins University Press, 1990.
———. *The Twentieth-Century American City*. 2nd ed. Baltimore: Johns Hopkins University Press, 1993.
Throsby, David. *Economics and Culture*. New York: Cambridge University Press, 2001.
Tung, Anthony M. *Preserving the World's Great Cities: The Destruction and Renewal of the Historic Metropolis*. New York: Clarkson Potter, 2001.
Tyler, Norman, et al. *Historic Preservation: An Introduction to Its History, Principles, and Practice*. 2nd ed. New York: W. W. Norton, 2009.
Volunteer Lawyers for the Arts. *Housing for Artists: The New York Experience*. New York: Willkie Farr and Gallagher/Volunteer Lawyers for the Arts, 1976.
Ward, David, and Oliver Zunz. *The Landscape of Modernity: New York City, 1900–1940*. Baltimore: Johns Hopkins University Press, 1992.
Ware, Caroline F. *Greenwich Village 1920–1930: A Comment on American Civilization in the Post-War Years*. 1935. Reprint, Berkeley: University of California Press, 1994.
Waxman, Lori. "The Banquet Years: Food, A SoHo Restaurant." *Gastronomica: The Journal of Food and Culture* 8, no. 4 (Fall 2008): 24–33.
Wetzsteon, Ross. *Republic of Dreams: Greenwich Village; The American Bohemia, 1910–1960*. New York: Simon and Schuster, 2002.
Whiting, Cecile. *Pop L.A.: Art and the City in the 1960s*. Berkeley: University of California Press, 2006.
Wilson, Elizabeth. *Bohemians: The Glamorous Outcasts*. New Brunswick, NJ: Rutgers University Press, 2000.

Winslow, Hall. *Artists in Metropolis: An Exploration for Planners.* Brooklyn: Planning Department, School of Architecture, Pratt Institute, 1964.
Wright, Gwendolyn. *Building the Dream: A Social History of Housing in America.* Cambridge, MA: MIT Press, 1981.
Zipp, Samuel. *Manhattan Projects: The Rise and Fall of Urban Renewal in Cold War New York.* New York: Oxford University Press, 2010.
———. "The Roots and Routes of Urban Renewal." *Journal of Urban History* 39, no. 3 (May 2013): 366–91.
Zukin, Sharon. *Loft Living: Culture and Capital in Urban Change.* Baltimore: Johns Hopkins University Press, 1982.
Zurier, Rebecca. *Picturing the City: Urban Vision and the Ashcan School.* Berkeley: University of California Press, 2006.

Index

Page numbers in italic refer to illustrations.

abstract expressionism, 46, 97, 98, 102, 149
African Americans, 16, 136, 225
  employment of, 8, 27, 39, 40, 162, 207
A.I.R. *See* Artist in Residence
A.I.R. Gallery, 21, 52, 53, 89, 120, 121–22, 123, 232
Aldrich, Larry, 138
Aldrich Museum, 138
Allsteel Scale Corporation, 166–67
alternative spaces, 110, 123–24, 125, 127, 131
Alvarez, Luz, 12
American art, 47, 102, 122, 145, 155
American Express Company, 74, 253n5
American Jewish Congress, 146
American Stock Exchange, 74, 253n5
Anatomy of a Metropolis: The Changing Distribution of People and Jobs within the New York Metropolitan Region (Hoover et al.), 75
Anderson, Warren, 224
Anderson and Archer's SoHo (Anderson-Spivy), 155
Andre, Carl, 108
André Emmerich Gallery, 89, 114, 119, 149
Antonakos, Naomi, 42–43, 45, 57, 61, 63, 67
Antonakos, Stephen, 42–43, 49, 51, 57, 67
Aoki, Hirotsugu, 53, 57, 60, 69
architecture, 5, 7, 55, 61, 83, 84, 87, 124–25, 151, 152, 155, 237
  cast-iron, 7, 151, 152, 153, 193, 230
  modernist, 44, 66
  SoHo, 16, 44, 48–49, 51, 152–53, 230
Arman, 169, *171*, 205, 264n24
art festivals, 1, 134, 142–44, *143*, 156
Artforum, 120

Art Gallery, 130
Art Institute of Chicago, 117
Artist in Residence (A.I.R.), 6, 98–101, 103–4, 188
artist(s)
  certification of, 7, 102, 103, 140–41, 212, 220, 224, 232, 270n8
  colony, 20, 40, 49, 70, 122, 124, 169, 181, 185, 230
  gentrification led by, 4, 5, 6, 9–10, 73, 181, 207, 228–29, 265n35
  housing, 56, 94, 96, 97, 103, 104, 105, 136, 138–39, 150, 162, 190, 195, 196, 213, 214, 217, 218
  strikes by, 6, 98–99, 101–2, 136, 196
  tenants, 6, 8, 9, 41, 48, 49, 50, 59, 95–96, 99–100, 101, 112, 135, 169, 182, 183, 198–99, 201, 202, 203, 204, 206, 209, 211, 224, 226, 227–28, 229
Artists Against the Expressway, 84–85, 90
Artists Housing Coalition, 213, 214, 218
Artist Tenants Association (ATA), 48, 49, 95–98, 101, 102–4, 149, 169
  artists' strike, march, and rally organized by, 6, 98–99, 101–2, 103, 136
  formation of, 6, 95
  loft agreement reached with city, 99–101
  SAA as spin-off of, 135
art market, 5, 110, 120, 131
Art News, 98, 99–100
arts
  funding for the, 51, 56, 110, 119, 121, 122–23, 125, 129, 130–31
  patrons of the, 97, 129
art world, 5, 45, 47, 55, 67, 108, 110, 114–15, 120, 121–22, 130, 137
  New York, 52, 93, 97

Association of Commercial Property Owners, 223
Association of the Bar of the City of New York, 86
Astor, John Jacob, 17
Astor Place, 17
Atlanta, 235
AT&T, 74, 253n5
August, Barnett, 86
Austin, 235
avant-garde, 46, 55, 117

Bark, Jared, 43, 53, 58, 60, 68, 69, 157
Barnard College, 52
Barwick, Kent, 196
Bas-Cohen, Rachel, 53
Battery Park City, 75
Baur, John I. H., 138
Bayard, Nicholas, 16
Beach Street, 213
Bearden, Romare, 95, 226
beatniks. *See* bohemians
Belt Parkway, 77
Benkel, Sam, 202
Berne, Michelle, 126
Bernstein, Judith, 53
Bernstein, Roslyn, 23
blacks. *See* African Americans
Blackwell, Linda, 64–65, 65
Blackwell, Tom, 64–65, 65
Blake, Betty, 118
Blake, Peter, 138
Bleckner, Ross, 116–17
Bleecker Street, 90, 192, 215, 268n6
Bloomingdale's, 181, 220
Board of Estimate, New York City, 139, 140, 153, 210, 212, 213–14, 225, 226, 248n56
    Lower Manhattan Expressway and, 79, 80, 81, 82, 83, 86, 87
    Washington Square Southeast and, 33, 34
Board of Standards and Appeals, New York City, 210, 213
    zoning variances and, 150, 192, 204, 206, 212, 213, 214, 215–16, 217, 218, 219, 226
Bobrick, Robert, 99
Boehm, Abraham, 23
Bogardus, James, 152
bohemians, 10, 11, 135, 149, 169
    vs. "beatniks," 92, 93, 96, 98
Bohnen, Blythe, 53
Bond Street, 128, 201
Bontecou, Lee, 112
boutiques, 1, 9, 159, 165, 166, 168, 169, 180, 232, 234, 235
Boutis, Tom, 122
Bowery Gallery, 89, 120, 233

Bowie, David, 173
Bowling Green, 17
Brady, Diamond Jim, 177
Brata Gallery, 111
Brecht, George, 55
Brentano, Robyn, 125
Broadway, 26, 40, 50, 67, 95, 127, 146, 149, 162, 194, 201, 222, 233, 267n38
    building collapse at no. 466–68, 12–14, 29
    clash at no. 561, 216–17
    confrontation at no. 644, 214–16
    during early years of SoHo, 16, 17, 18, 19
    galleries on, 89, 204
    red-light district on, 18
    sale prices for buildings on, 186, 191
Bronx, 14, 77, 184, 194, 222
    South Bronx, 136, 184
Bronx Whitestone Bridge, 77
Brooklyn, 14, 24, 28, 42, 52, 53, 77, 101, 180, 225
    Brooklyn Heights, 151, 231
    "Brownstone Brooklyn," 5, 44
    Brownsville, 136
    Bushwick, 1, 3
    DUMBO, 271n21
    East New York, 136
    Gowanus, 3, 77
    Park Slope, 231
    Williamsburg, 2–3, 234
Brooklyn Academy of Music, 138
Brooklyn-Battery Tunnel, 77
Brooklyn Loft Tenants, 224
Brooklyn-Queens Expressway, 77
Brooks, Conrad, 17
Broome Street, 35, 36, 56, 117, 142, 146, 152, 186, 199, 200, 204, 209
    galleries and alternative spaces on, 89, 122, 203
    Lower Manhattan Expressway and, 71, 76, 78, 80, 81, 84, 85, 86, 87, 90
    sale prices for buildings on, 186
Brown, Trisha, 5, 127
Browne, Vivian, 64, 137, 145, 252n59
brownstones, 5, 18, 44, 66, 112, 141, 234
Buchman & Deisler, 21
Buenos Aires, 235
building codes, 59–60, 82, 92, 212, 224
    commercial, 60, 100
    residential, 45, 211, 226
Burger, Steven, 232
Burgess, Ernest, 75
Burke, Margaret Smith, 188
Burke, Michael, 188
Buszco, Irene, 53
Byers, J. Frederick, 203
Byrd Hoffman Foundation, 89, 127–28, 131, 180

INDEX 285

Cadamatori, Juan, 12
cafés, 1, 10, 168
California, 43, 51, 52, 117, 118, 119
Canaday, John, 115
Canal Street, 17, 18, 19, 23, 35, 67, 78, 81, 87, 95, 107,
    149, 150, 153, 154, 166, 213, 214
  south of, 35, 74, 81, 182, 209, 221
Cape Cod, 96
Carey, Hugh, 223–25
Carson, Deirdre, 217–18
Carter, Jimmy, 122
cast-iron architecture, 7, 13, 15, 19–21, *20, 21*, 23, 51,
    63, 117, 146, 153, 174, 193, 235
  hazards of, 94–95
  preservation and landmark designation of, 7,
    134, 151, 152–53, 230
Cast-Iron Architecture in New York (Gayle), 153
Castoro, Rosemarie, *48*, 117
Cavanagh, Edward F., Jr., 94, 95, 98, 257n14
Cedar Tavern, 47
Ceglic, Jack
  Dean & DeLuca and, 43, 176–78, 179, 233,
    265n35
  loft of, 43, 51, 57, 60, 176, 179
certificates of occupancy, 54, 182, 190–91, 192, 201,
    204, 209, 210, 212, 219, 220, 221–22, 223,
    224, 227
Chamberlain, John, 115
Chamber of Commerce of Greenwich Village, 34
Chambers-Canal Civic Association, 213, 214
Chambers Street, 14, 29, 213, 214
Chase Manhattan Bank, 71, 74, 119, 253n5
Cheese Store, 165, 176
Chelsea Loft Dwellers, 224
Chemical Bank New York Trust Company, 253n5
Chicago, 3, 19, 52, 118, 235, 246n6
Christo, 226
Chryssa, 112
Chrystie Street, 82
Cioffi, Louis A., 79
Citizens for Artist Housing (CAH), 138–39, 140,
    146, 261n10
City Club of New York, 15, 35, 36, 37, 41
City Hall, 17, 18, 82
  march on, 6, 102, 196
City Planning Commission (CPC), 9, 46, 49, 61,
    102, 139–40, 144, 145, 154, 167, 189–90,
    194, 195, 198, 210, 212, 213, 216–17, 218,
    220, 224
  Lower Manhattan Expressway and, 78, 79, 81,
    83, 85
  report on SoHo industry sponsored by, 8, 37,
    38–40, 41, 160–62
  Washington Square Southeast and, 33, 35
City University of New York, 52, 53, 251n25
  Hunter College, 43, 52

Clark, Dave, 234
Close, Chuck, 5
Cohen, Charles, 222
Cold War, 31, 122
Coleman, Ornette, 5, 128, 129, 137
color-field painting, 47
Columbia University, 30, 52
Commercial Building Owners' and Tenants'
    Association of Lower New York, 33
Committee on Lower Manhattan, Inc., 74
communism, 122
community planning boards, 210, 212, 213, 215,
    216, 218, 221
Connecticut, 138, 231
Continental Insurance Companies, 253n5
Cook's Supply Corps, 179
Coon, Lewis, 23
Cooper, Paula, 43, 130, 138, 141, 233
  gallery of, 20, 89, 107–9, 112, 117, 118–19, 126–
    27, 128, 139, 146, 233
cooperatives (co-ops), 53, 54, 61, 122, 191, 203, 204,
    206, 215, 217, 218, 219, 220, 230
  artist, 11, 23, 43, 55, 56–57, 84, 125, 135–36, 137,
    140, 146, 168, 192, 203, 204
  buying lofts through, 42–43, 53, 54–58, 65, 69,
    175, 188, 202, 204
  Fluxhouse, 23, 58, 61, 137
Cooper Union, 52, 55
Cornell, Joseph, 47
Cornell Alumni Club, loft tour organized by,
    145–46
Cosell, Howard, 184
Costello, Timothy, 261n9
Crosby Street, 52, 154, 233
Cross Bronx Expressway, 77
Cross Island Parkway, 7
Cunningham, Betty, gallery of, 89, 115–18, 119,
    121, 181
Cunningham, Merce, 180
Currid-Halkett, Elizabeth, 45

Dada, 55
Dalí, Salvador, 68
dance, 8, 10, 48, 109, 110, 123, 124, 125, 126–28, 129,
    131, 133, 144, 180, 215, 265n35
David, Michael, 202
Dean, Joel, 43, 51, 176, 177, 178, 265n35
Dean & DeLuca, 43, 265n35
  displays at/embrace of loft aesthetic by, 159,
    174, 175–78, 179, 180
  opening and later expansion of, 9, 181, 233
Death and Life of Great American Cities, The
    (Jacobs), 151
Death Wish, 184
deindustrialization, 5
  Lower Manhattan and, 160, 197, 236

deindustrialization (*continued*)
   New York and, 4, 96, 160, 190
   SoHo and, 3, 4, 7, 11, 49–51, 94, 109, 160–65, 236
   Tribeca and, 193–94
de Knegt, Frits, 57–58, 114, 252n45
de Kooning, Willem, 47, 93, 98
DeLaney, Chuck, 225
DeLuca, Giorgio G., 165, 176, 177, 178, 265n35
Denver, 235
Department of Air Resources, New York City, 85
Department of Buildings, New York City, 13, 92, 101, 102, 210, 212, 216, 217, 220
Department of City Planning (DCP), New York City, 188, 189, 191, 192, 215, 216
Department of Health, Education, and Welfare, U.S., 85
Department of Highways, New York City, 82
Department of Housing Preservation and Development, New York City, 219, 224
Department of Parks, Recreation, and Cultural Affairs, New York City, 7, 133, 138, 143, 149, 261n10
department stores, 18, 179–80
De Salvio, Louis, 80
Detroit, 14
Dia:Beacon, 3
Diao, David, 117
Diether, Doris, 216
Diffrient, Niels, 173
Di Suvero, Mark, 118
Downtown–Lower Manhattan Association (DLMA), 71–73, 74–76, 78–79, 81–83, 87, 91, 253n5
Drexler, Arthur, 84
Duchamp, Marcel, 166
Dudley, Edward R., 37
Duker, Samuel, 31–33
Dunkelman, Loretta, 53
Dunn, Douglas, 127
Dvorkin, Jerry, 222
Dwan, Virginia, gallery of, 114

East Side Chamber of Commerce, 86
Edelman, Alexander, 216
Eighty-first Street, 111
Eins, Stefan, 165–66
Eleventh Street, 192
Elliot, Donald, 139, 140
Emergency Tenant Protection Act, 269n27
Emmerich, André, 138, 149
   gallery of, 89, 114, 119
Europe, 10, 114, 145, 149, 152, 176, 230
eviction, 202, 204, 210–11, 212, 213, 214, 219, 220, 221, 226, 257n14
   efforts to prevent, 6, 96, 98, 100, 195, 210, 221–22, 223, 224
   threat of or vulnerability to, 6, 46, 53, 54, 59, 69, 93, 95, 98, 100, 167, 196, 199–200, 201, 208, 209, 211, 221
Evolving City: Urban Design Proposal by Ulrich Franzen and Paul Rudolph, The (Rudolph), 256n41
Ewers, Ken, 137

factories, conversions of, 3, 5, 6, 8, 24, 44, 45, 51, 59, 60, 64, 69, 107, 112, 113, 134, 145, 176
Fanelli, Mike, 107, 116
Federal Bureau of Public Roads, 79
Federal Housing Association, 58
Feigen, Richard, 84, 138
   gallery of, 83–84, 111–12, 115
feminist art, 122
Fernandez, Ann, 145
Fernandez, Steve, 145
55 Mercer Gallery, 89, 120, 121–22, 146
Fifty-ninth Street, south of, 191, 210, 220
Fifty-seventh Street, 78
   galleries on or near, 107, 111, 114
Findlay, Michael, 129
Fine, Martin R., 214–16, 228, 269n12
fires, building inspections prompted by, 6, 92, 94–95, 98, 100
First National City Bank, 253n5
First Street Gallery, 89, 120, 123
Fischbach Gallery, 42
fixture fees, 141, 182, 199, 205–6, 227, 251–52n43
Flavin, Dan, 108, 115
Florida, Richard, 10
Fluxhouse, 23, 55–57, 58, 61, 137
Fluxus, 55
food shops, 165, 168
   See also Dean & DeLuca
Forbes, Robin, *48, 113, 143, 170*
Ford, Gerald, 122
Ford Foundation, 256n41
Foreman, Richard, 52, 180
14 Sculptors, 89, 120, 233
Fortieth Street, 190
Forty-second Street, 22
Fourteenth Street, 14, 107, 189
Fourth Avenue, 111
Fourth Street, 31, 89
France, 107, 265n29
Frankfurter, Alfred M., 98
Franklin Street, 193, 267n50
Freedman, Doris, 138, 146
Freeman, Joshua, 14
freeway revolts, 72–73

INDEX 287

Freidus, Stephen, 188
French & Company, 115
Friedlander, Miriam, 195, 218, 221
Friedman, Alfred S., 87
Friends of Cast Iron Architecture, 7, 153
Fukui, Nobu, 63, 252n59
  loft of, 63–64, *64*, 146
fur industry, 19, 22

Gable, Hortense, 99
Gahagan, James, 48, 49, 96–97, 99, 100
Galdez, Jesus, 222
galleries
  cooperative, 47, 52, 107, 109–10, 111, 119–23, 125, 130–31, 232–33
  for-profit (commercial), 109, 110, 111, 117–19, 120–21, 123, 125, 126–27, 129, 130, 233
  Midtown, 87–88, 107, 111, 114
  SoHo, 8–9, 43, 53, 89–90, 107–31, 158, 159, 165, 167, 168, 203, 204
  uptown, 57, 107, 108, 111–12, 115, 116, 125, 129
garment industry, 6, 16, 22, 162, 166, 216, 217, 223, 225–26, 246n6
Gay Activist Alliance, 265n35
Gayle, Margot, 7, 153, 154
Gee, Peter, 57, 203–4
Geldzahler, Henry, 84
gentrification, 3–4, 243n3
  artist-led, 4, 5, 6, 9–10, 73, 181, 207, 228–29, 265n35
  loft law and, 223, 227–29
  New York City and, 5, 73, 228, 229
  SoHo and, 3, 6, 9–10, 40, 73, 90, 92, 131, 156–57, 183, 203, 206–8, 228, 229
Germans, Wouter, 114
Germany, 107, 119, 265n30
Geyer, Michael, 201–2
Ghent, Manny, 145
Gilded Age, 19
Gilfoyle, Timothy, 18
Girouard, Tina, 125
Glass, Philip, 5, 53, 115, 125
Glass, Ruth, 4, 229, 243n5
Gliedman, Anthony, 224
Glueck, Grace, 112, 144
Goldberg, RoseLee, 124
Goldman, Ira, 195
Goldman Sachs, 74, 253n5
Goldstone, William, 154
Gooden, Caroline, 167
Gottlieb, Harold, 166
Gottlieb, Toby, 166
Gowanus Expressway, 77
Grace, William R., 203
Grand Central Parkway, 77

Grand Central Terminal, 111
Grand Street, 56, 89, 146, 150, 168, 206, 231, 268n6
gray areas, 75, 76
Great Depression, 24
Greece, 42, 107
Greenbaum, Marty, 149
Greenberg, Clement, 98
Greene Street, *20, 21, 28*, 36, 153, 162, 166, 186
  artists' co-ops on, 56, 57, 146
  galleries on, 83–84, 89, 90, 112, 113
  lofts on, 42, 49, 63–64, 124, 146
Green Mountain Gallery, 89, 233
Greitzer, Carol, 83, 222
Guardian Life Insurance Company, 253n5
Guggenheim Foundation, 117
Guggenheim Museum, 47, 121, 138
guidebooks, 109, 155
Gussow, Roy, 234

Hanley, Vincent "Oz," 219–20
Hannan, Tom, 96
happenings, 55, 68, 123
Haring, Keith, 265n35
Harmatz, Harold H., 86
Harris, Suzanne, 125
Hartnett, Thomas J., 92
Harvard University, 75
Haskell, Barbara, 51, 53
Haughwout Building, 146, 153
Heald, Henry T., 31, 33
Heckscher, August, 149, 261n10
Heilmann, Mary, 51, 60–61, 67
Henry, Robert, 96
Hernmark, Helena, 173
Herrman, Augustine, 16
Hewitt, Bob, 108
high-rises, 31, 35, 154
High-Tech: The Industrial Style and Source Book for the Home (Kron and Slesin), 179
Hightower, John, 138
Hill, Norman, 225
Hirshhorn, Joseph H., 129
Hirshhorn Museum and Sculpture Garden, 118, 265n30
historic preservation, 151, 153
  of cast-iron building/SoHo architecture, 83–84, 93, 134, 151–56
Hoboken, 2, 96
Hockney, David, 119
Hoffman, Nancy, gallery of, 89, 115, 116, 117, 119, 121, 130, 233
Hofmann, Hans, 96, 119
Holland Tunnel, 28, 78
Hollingworth, Keith, 117

Horn, Joe, 216, 218–19, 228
Hornick, Sandy, 215, 216, 217, 222
hotels, 17, 18, 19
House and Garden, 64
housing
  artist, 56, 94, 96, 97, 103, 104, 105, 136, 138–39, 150, 162, 190, 195, 196, 213, 214, 217, 218
  developments, 15, 30, 31, 33, 37, 41, 103, 105, 154, 191
  loft, 7, 9, 70, 97, 98, 102, 104, 106, 139, 144, 189, 193, 197–98, 212, 235, 257n30
  projects, 5, 7, 15, 30, 31, 35, 37, 40, 66, 71–72, 74, 81, 84, 114, 207, 218
Housing and Redevelopment Board, 152
Houston Street, 18, 19, 29, 30, 31, 67, 83, 112, 133, 149, 153, 154, 162
  north of, 9, 17, 183
  south of, 1, 3, 16, 39, 40, 43, 46, 92, 101, 108, 110, 141, 246n5, 262n38
  West, 35, 39
how-to guides, 59
Hundred Acres, 53
Husey, Karen, 137
Hutchinson, Max, gallery of, 113, 252n59
Huxtable, Ada Louise, 83, 87, 152–53

IBM, 119
industrial sector
  of New York, 14
  of SoHo, 18, 53, 159, 160, 179
industry
  decline of, 9, 22, 38–39, 49, 57–58, 159, 160–65, 236
  light, 1, 22, 33, 62, 76, 101, 150, 193, 236, 246n6
  SoHo, 15, 22, 30, 81, 83, 160–62, 183
  See also garment industry; paper/textile recycling; warehousing
installation, 5
International Ladies Garment Workers' Union, 225
Interstate Highway Act, 78
Irwin, Robert, 112

J. M. Kaplan Fund, 56
Jackson, Harry, 80–81
Jacobs, Jane, 15, 137, 231
  Death and Life of Great American Cities, The, 151
  Lower Manhattan Expressway and, 15, 72, 80, 81, 82, 83, 90
Jane Street Gallery, 119–20
Javits, Jacob. K., 138
Javits, Mrs. Jacob. K., 138, 261n10
jazz, 5, 9, 125, 128, 137
  lofts, 110, 123, 128–29
Jefferson Market Courthouse, 153
Johns, Jasper, 99, 111, 115, 205
Johnson, Lyndon, 122

Joint Committee to Stop the Lower Manhattan Expressway, 80, 82, 90
Jouchmans, Pierre, 137
J-51 tax-relief program, 191, 192, 197–98, 217, 221, 222, 223, 224
Judd, Donald, 5, 47, 84, 108, 115, 137, 138, 256n37
Judd, Julie, 84, 137, 138
Judson Memorial Church, 47, 96, 101, 124

Kaprow, Allan, 55
Karp, Ivan, 113–14, 149, 196
  gallery of, 53, 112–13, 119, 129
Katz, Alex, 5, 99
Kelly, Ellsworth, 115
Kertess, Klaus, 135
Khun, Loeb, 253n5
Kitchen, 89, 120, 127, 131, 203
Klau, David W., 24
Klau, Nathan, 24
Klein, Jack, 205–6
Klemek, Christopher, 5, 15
Kline, Franz, 119
Koch, Edward, 83
  loft policy and, 197, 211, 217–18, 219, 220, 222, 223, 224, 225–26
Korn, Moses, 12
Kostelanetz, Richard, 52, 188, 244n6
Kramer, Louise, 53
Kron, Joan, 179

Lafayette Street, 219
LaGuardia Place, 43, 90, 107
Lam, Kwong, 168
Lam, Maryann, 168
Lama, Alfred A., 54, 101
LaMountain, Gerard, 80, 87
landlords, 9, 18, 34, 44, 45, 46, 49, 59, 86, 87, 100, 101, 184, 191, 197, 212, 216, 223, 226–27, 233, 234, 252n43
  conflicts with, abuses of, and efforts to evict, tenants, 9, 181, 182–83, 198–207, 209–10, 211, 219, 220–21, 223, 224, 225, 228, 229, 269n27
Landmark Gallery, 89, 122
Landmarks Preservation Commission, 134, 151, 152, 154, 156, 210
Landmarks Preservation Law, 151, 153
Lannan, Patrick, 118, 119
Las Vegas, 235
Latinos, 8, 207
Lefkowitz, Louis, 261n9
LeFrak City, 61, 66
Lehman, Maxwell, 99
Lehman Brothers, 74, 253n5
Lehner, Edward, 223
Leo Castelli Gallery, 89, 112, 114–15, 117

Leslie, Charles, 145
Leslie-Lohman Gallery, 90, 203
Levine, Michael, 139
Levine, Tomar, 53
Lew, Jeffrey, 124, 125
LeWitt, Sol, 108
Lexington Avenue, 192, 268n6
Ley, David, 4
Lichtenstein, Roy, 115, 138, 169, 205
Liebmann, Gerhardt, 141, 143, 150
    loft of, 61–62, 63, 66, 136, 137, 144, 148
Life. See "Living Big in a Loft"
Limited Profit Housing Companies Act, 54
Lincoln Center, 94, 128
Lincoln Savings Bank, 198
Lindsay, John, 29, 133, 136, 138, 139, 140
    Lower Manhattan Expressway and, 82–83, 85, 153
Lipkis, Eli, 182, 200, 201, 267n50
Lippard, Lucy, 108
"Living Big in a Loft," 28, 48, 62, *62*, 64, *64*, 65, *65*, *135*, 137, 148
LoCicero, John, 220
"loft letter." *See* loft, policy/law
Loft Living (Zukin), 4, 51, 122–23, 148, 185, 197
loft(s)
    aesthetic, 9, 44, 61–67, 175–81
    conversion, 9, 56, 59, 103, 104, 137, 140, 174, 188–89, 190–91, 192, 196–99, 202, 210, 211, 212, 216–19, 220, 222–24, 226, 228–29, 234, 235, 267n38
    demand for, 155, 183, 184–98, 199, 200–201, 206, 207, 209
    illegality of converting and living in, 6, 7, 9, 41, 46, 52, 53, 54, 57, 59, 69, 70, 92, 95, 151, 167, 174, 182, 183, 189, 191, 193, 195, 198, 199, 200, 201, 204, 205, 208, 210, 211, 212, 213–14, 216–18, 220, 223, 224, 226–27, 232, 234, 244n12, 252n46
    lifestyle, 159, 169, 174, 180
    policy/law, 9, 98–104, 190, 192–93, 197, 199, 201, 210–29
    renovation, 9, 56, 58–67, 134, 159, 173, 174–75
    riskiness/danger of converting and living in, 6, 8, 15, 30, 43–44, 58–59, 67, 69–70, 94–95, 116–17
    tours of, 61, 143, 144–48, *147*
Lohman, J. Frederic, 203
Lombardi, Felipe Rojas, 176, 177
London, 235, 271n21
Long Island, 28, 53, 76
    Expressway, 66, 77
Lord & Taylor, 18, 19
Louis, Morris, 114
Louis, Murray, 127, 226
Louis K. Meisel Gallery, 68, 89, 116, 118, 168, 233

Low, Charles, 150
Lower Manhattan
    artists in, 48, 95, 97, 98, 100, 196, 221
    deindustrialization in, 160, 197, 236
    See also Lower Manhattan Expressway; Lower Manhattan Loft Tenants
Lower Manhattan Expressway, 8, 41, 70, 71–91, 77, 142–43, 150, 152, 153, 209, 256n41
Lower Manhattan Loft Tenants (LMLT), 220–21, 224, 225
Lower Manhattan Tenants' Association, 181
Lubar, Cindy, 131
Lustington, Max H., 189

Maciunas, George, 23, 55–57, 58, 61, 137
Macklowe, Harry, 213–14, 268n6
Macy's, 179–80
Madison Avenue, 141, 188
    galleries on or near, 107, 111–12, 113, 116, 196
Madison Square, 189
Major Deegan Expressway, 77
Mand, George, 99
Mandel, Joseph, 87, 209
Manhattan
    Battery, 16, 75, 77
    Bowery, 29, 65, 117, 179
    Chelsea, 3, 224–25, 226, 233
    Chinatown, 112, 189, 236, 264n9
    East Village, 52, 214, 269n12
    Financial District, 30, 35, 71, 72, 73, 76, 91, 231, 268n6
    Fur District, 42, 43, 60, 205
    Garment District (Garment Center), 22, 224, 225, 226, 270n44
    Gramercy Park, 54
    Greenwich Village, 41, 43, 83, 95, 96, 98, 101, 135, 149, 151, 153, 154, 166, 189, 213, 225, 236, 257n14
        artists and galleries, 10, 43, 47, 96, 111, 119–20
        industrial renewal in, 30–35
        Middle Income Cooperators of, 7, 15, 71–72
        West Village, 15, 80, 214, 231, 269n12, 270n4
    Harlem, 5
    Little Italy, 189, 236, 264n9, 271n21
    Lower East Side, 118, 136, 184
    Meatpacking District, 3, 117
    Midtown, 14, 22, 26, 35, 43, 47, 74, 96, 111, 189, 205, 214, 222, 224, 225, 268n6, 269n12
        Action Office, 191, 192
        galleries, 87–88, 107, 111, 114
        highways in, 78
        real estate values in, 71, 193, 213, 231, 270n4
        South, 189, 191, 192
    NoHo, 90, 188, 191, 192, 201, 214, 221, 232, 271n21
        loft housing and zoning in, 9, 183, 189, 190,

Manhattan—NoHo (*continued*)
  193, 194, 195, 196, 197, 206, 222, 224, 226, 267n38
 Tribeca, 35, 191, 192, 212–13, 219, 221, 226, 268n6, 269n12, 270n4
  impact of, and parallels with, SoHo, 193, 194, 206, 231, 234, 237, 270n4, 271n21
  loft housing/conversions in, 9, 182, 183, 189, 193–95, 196–97, 200, 206, 214, 224
  as moniker, 194, 235
 Upper East Side, 54, 65, 111, 138, 175, 193, 213, 214, 268n6, 269n12
 Upper West Side, 52, 141, 193, 214, 269n12
 Washington Heights, 54, 221
 See also Lower Manhattan; SoHo
Manhattan Bridge, 78, 271n21
Mankoff, Walter, 225
Manoco, 222
Manufacturers Hanover Trust, 253n5
Mapplethorpe, Robert, 265n35
Marchi, John, 223
Marcus, Norman, 218
Marine Midland Grace Trust Company, 253n5
Markus, Marvin, 219
Marson, Bernard, 216
Mas, Augustin, 12
Masheck, Joseph, 120
Matta-Clark, Gordon, 124, 125, 167
Max Hutchinson Galleries, 113, 252n59
Mayor's Midtown Action Office, 191, 192
Mayor's Slum Clearance Committee, 30
Mayor's Task Force on Loft Conversions, 217–18, 222
McCamy, Arden, 66
Meehan, Richard, 204
Meisel, Louis, 48–49, 52, 196, 233
 gallery of, 68, 89, 116, 118, 168, 233
 loft of, 57, *172*
Meisel, Susan, 141, 270n8
 loft of, 57, 141, *172*
Mercer Street, 26, 31, 36, 127, 153, 161, 204
 galleries on, 89, 90, 120, 121–22, 146
 lofts on, 25, 43, 127
 sale prices for buildings on, 186
Merle, Jean Pierre, 102
Merrill Lynch, 74, 253n5
Messer, Thomas M., 138
Messinger, Ruth, 221
Metropolitan Museum of Art, 53, 84, 97, 115, 121, 138
Metzler, Paul, 215
Miami, 72, 235
Michels, Stanley, 221–22
Michelson, Annette, 188
middle class

appeal of loft living to the, 4, 66, 122–23, 148, 169, 188, 225
 artists and, 4, 10, 51, 69, 137, 237
 SoHo's attraction for the, 11, 17, 52, 53–54, 69, 148, 169, 236, 237
Middle Income Cooperators of Greenwich Village (MICOVE), 7, 15, 37, 40, 71–72, 81, 84, 218
Mihalik, Robert, 173
Milliken, Alexander F., 158, 159
Milne, David, 195
minimalism, 115
minorities, 4, 225
 employment of, 15, 37, 38, 39, 82, 105, 137, 222, 228
Mitchell, Jeff, 137
Mitchell, McNeil, 101, 103
Mitchell-Lama Limited-Profit Housing Companies Law, 54, 101
mixed media, 5, 6, 8, 133
Moerdler, Charles C., 13, 29
Monk, Meredith, 124, 127
Montreal, 234
Morgan Guaranty Trust Company, 253n5
Morgan Stanley, 74, 253n5
Morley, Jeanany, 234
Morris, Robert, 115, 180
Morse, Samuel F. B., 17
mortgages, 54, 101, 198, 202, 215, 232, 252n46
 purchase money, 58
Moses, Robert, 15, 30, 31, 34, 74, 76–77, 81, 86
 Lower Manhattan Expressway and, 71, 72, 77, 78, 79, 81, 82, 83, 86, 87, 153
 Washington Square Southeast and, 15, 30
Moskowitz, Morris, 199–200
Motherwell, Robert, 99
Mott Street, 80
Mulberry Street, 80
Multiple Dwelling Law, 7, 45, 101–3, 136, 140, 190, 201, 212, 221, 257n30
Municipal Art Society, 196
Museum of Modern Art (MoMA), 47, 71, 84, 85, 103, 108, 111, 115, 117, 121, 138, 181, 203, 252n59
Myers, Forrest, 117, 118, 119

Nation, 104
National Endowment for the Arts (NEA), 10, 117, 122
National Endowment for the Humanities, 119, 126
National Historic Preservation Act, 151
National Park Service, 151
National Register of Historic Places, 151
National Trust for Historic Preservation, 151
Nauman, Bruce, 115

INDEX

neoclassicism, 19
Nesbitt, Lowell, 175, 265n30
New Jersey, 2, 28, 76, 118, 119, 131, 162, 215, 217
Newman, Barnett, 47, 84–85
New School for Social Research, 52, 55
New York City
   art scene/art world, 52, 93, 97, 111, 146
   blackout, 1, 184
   council, 83, 102, 195, 211, 212, 218, 221–22, 224, 248n56
   urban crisis of, 4, 7, 136, 184, 236, 238
   See also specific boroughs; departments; streets
New York Daily News, 153
New York Herald-Tribune, 12, 34, 64, 92–93
New York Magazine, 2, 9, 144, 148, 158, 169, *171*, 174–75, 178, 180
New York Post, 12, 141
New York State
   assembly, 223–24
   legislature, 78, 85, 101, 103, 140, 197, 212, 222–23, 224, 226
   supreme court, 86, 209–10, 212, 213–14, 218, 219
New York State Council on the Arts (NYSCA), 119, 123, 125–26, 128, 130–31, 138, 261n10
New York Times, 33, 48, 79, 80, 96, 98, 110, 112, 115, 131, 141, 143, 144, 146, 149, 152, 153, 165, 167–68, 169, 173, 176, 177, 195–96, 198, 233, 234
New York University (NYU), 15, 47, 52, 124, 150, 188
   Washington Square Southeast and, 15, 30–31, 33, 34
Niemeyer, Ulrich, 87, 209–10, 219
Nikolais, Alwin, 127
Ninety-second Street YMCA, 53
Nixon, Richard, 122
Noguchi, Isamu, 93, 98, 234
North America, 10
Norvell, Patricia Ann, 52

Oberlin, Wendy, x
O'Dwyer, Paul, 102
Office of Lower Manhattan Development, 193, 195
Office of Midtown Enforcement, 226
Off-Off Broadway Theater, 127
Ohrenstein, Manfred, 223
Ohta, Yukie, 52, 63, 68
OK Harris Gallery, 89, 112–13, 128, 129
Oldenburg, Claes, 115, 165–66, 226
112 Workshop, 89, 120, 124, 125–26, 167
125th Street, 78
Oppenheim, William, 29

Osman, Suleiman, 5
Otis, Elisha Grave, 20
outer boroughs, 14, 66
   See also specific boroughs

Pagella, Charles, 33
Paley, William S., 203
Palley, Reese, gallery of, 110, 111, 113–14, 115, 145, 146
paper/textile recycling, 6, 23, 25, 37, 49, 57–58, 124, 161, 205, 236
Papp, Joseph, 226
Paris, 10, 46, 51, 179, 264n24
Park, Robert, 75
Park Avenue, 66
Park Place Gallery, 107
Parsons School of Design, 43
Patman, Wright, 34
Paul, Clara, 216
Paul, Samuel, 216
Paula Cooper Gallery, 20, 117, 118, 139, 146, 233
   importance of, 108–9, 112
   opening of, 89, 107–9, 112
   performances at, 119, 126–27, 128
   sales at/purchases from, 118–19
Paxton, Steve, 124
Pei, I. M., 34
Pennsylvania Station, 22
performance art, 5, 8, 9, 55, 109, 110, 119, 122, 123, 124, 125, 126, 177
Performing Garage, 89, 127
Perl, Jed, 47
Perron, Wendy, 180
photorealism, 61, 118
Pikus, Mario, 182
Pikus, Rebecca, 200–1
Pioneering in the Urban Wilderness (Stratton), 59
Pittsburgh, 14, 55
Pleiades and Cloud, 90, 120
Pollock, Jackson, 47, 111
   proposed renaming of West Broadway after, 149–50, 262n38
Poons, Larry, 112
pop art, 57, 110, 112, 138
Porr, Valerie, 175
Port Authority of New York and New Jersey, 78, 118
Porter, Fairfield, 47, 99
Porter, Frank, 118
Pratt Institute, 52, 61, 155, 251n25
Prince Street, 128, 137
   art fair, *143*
   galleries on or near, 20, 52, 53, 83, 89, 90, 107, 108, 110, 113, 116, 120, 146, 173, 233
   lofts on, 5, 42, 51, 56, 57, 64, 84, 145, 146, 203–4

Prince Street (*continued*)
  restaurants and other retail on, 21, 162, 165, 166, 167, 168, 176
  sale prices for buildings on, 186–87, 203
Prince Street Gallery, 52, 53, 89, 120, 233
Progressive Era, 35
Project Studios 1 (P.S. 1), 234
prostitution, 18, 19
Provincetown Painters, 96
Puerto Ricans, 136
  employment of, 27, 39, 40, 82, 162

Quaytman, Harvey, 117
Queens, 14, 66, 77
  Jackson Heights, 54
  Long Island City, 2, 234

Rainer, Yvonne, 5
Raman, Ely, 137
Rapkin, Chester, report on SoHo industry by, 8, 15, 25, 37–39, 40, 41, 72, 81, 82, 137, 139, 159, 160–61
Rauschenberg, Robert, 115, 138, 205, 226
real estate
  development, 23, 57, 97, 149, 184, 192, 197, 198, 202, 203, 207, 221, 236
  investment, 1, 11, 44, 69, 150, 194, 205, 216
  market, 1, 45, 66, 135, 138, 154, 191, 196, 202, 203, 206, 207, 211, 213, 227, 230, 237
  speculation, 1, 54, 150, 183, 191, 192, 193, 196, 199–200, 201–2, 203, 205, 207, 211, 214, 218, 220, 221–22, 228
Real Estate Board of New York, 189, 190, 192, 195
Real Estate Weekly, 188
Realtor, 235
Reese Palley Gallery, 110, 111, 113–14, 115, 145, 146
Regional Plan Association, 78
Regional Plan of New York and Its Environs, 14
Reicher, Mel, 137
Reidy, Peter, 99
Reigenborn, Gary, 131
Reinhardt, Ad, 99
Remington, Debora, 174–75, 265n29
rent
  control, 183, 201, 210, 219
  stabilization, 210, 223, 224, 225, 226, 269n27
  strikes, 9, 182, 183, 198, 201, 204
Rent Guidelines Board, 219
Residential Re-Use of Non-Residential Buildings in Manhattan (DCP and the Mayor's Midtown Office), 191
Residential Use of Manhattan Loft Buildings: Analysis and Recommendations (Real Estate Board of New York), 190
restaurants, 1, 3, 193, 234, 264n9

SoHo, 1, 8, 9, 11, 18, 21, 26, 53, 57, 73, 155, 159, 165, 167–68, 196
  retail, 8, 14, 19, 25, 26, 43, 79, 215, 230, 232
  emergence and thriving of new sector for, 106, 131, 159, 162–68, 174, 178, 179, 180, 181, 232, 233, 264n9
Reuben Gallery, 111
Richard Feigen Gallery, 83–84, 111–12, 115
Richardson, Henry Hobson, 19
Rivers, Larry, 57
Rivers, Sam, 128–29
Robbins, I. D., 36
Rochon, Thomas, 201
Rockefeller, David, Lower Manhattan Expressway and, 71, 72, 73, 74, 75–76, 78–79, 81, 82, 84–85, 91
Rockefeller, Nelson, 77, 85, 123
Roosevelt, Eleanor, 80, 97
Roosevelt Building, 146
Rorimer, James J., 97–98
Rosenfeld, Jay, 137
Rosenquist, James, 114, 115, 226
Rosenthal, Stephen, 120
Ross, John, 218, 223
Rothko, Mark, 47
Rothschild, Amalie, 221
Rousseau, Theodore, Jr., 138
row houses, 17, 234
Rubell, Donald, 116
Rubell, Mera, 116
Ruda, Edwin, 117, 118
Rudolph, Paul, 256n41
Russell, Lillian, 177
Rutgers University Center for Urban Policy Research, 230

Saatchi, Charles, 116
Sanders, David, 179
Sandler, Irving, 102, 111
San Francisco, 3, 72, 96, 235
Saret, Alan, 124
Savitt, Mark, 125
Schary, Dore, 261n9
Schwartz, Joel, 14, 246n12
Scull, Robert, 110–11
Searles, Sidney Z., 86
Serra, Paul, 204
Serra, Richard, 117, 124
Seventy-ninth Street, 111, 116
Seventy-seventh Street, 114
Shapiro, Herbert, 214
Shapiro, Miriam, 222
Shapiro, Shael, 23, 137, 140
Shopsin, William C., 140
Simkhovitch Houses, 35

INDEX

Simpson, Charles R., 51
Singer Building, 146, 216–19
Sixth Avenue, 35, 90, 270n44
Sixty-fourth Street, 114
Sklar, Robert, 188
Slesin, Suzanne, 179
slum(s), 8, 14, 33, 34, 105
    clearance, 5, 7, 8, 11, 30, 31, 34, 35, 90–91, 93, 104, 154, 236
    SoHo as, 15, 35–40, 44, 81–83, 87
    Title I and, 248n49
Small Business Administration, 34
Smith, Neil, 4, 229
SoHo
    early history of, 16–18
    embourgeoisement of, 158–81
    illegality of living in, 5, 6, 41, 44, 45, 46, 53, 54, 55–56, 57, 70, 95, 141, 143, 167, 189, 208, 231, 232, 234, 244n12
    impact of/"SoHo-ization," 2–3, 11, 110, 179–80, 194, 235–37
    landmarking of, 7, 40, 134, 150, 151, 154–56, 205, 230
    as moniker, 3, 110, 235, 237
    tours of, 145–48, *147*, 216–17
SoHo Alliance, 233
SoHo Artists Association (SAA), 46, 61, 64, 135–36, *135*, 137–38, 139, 140, 141, 148, 149, 150, 156, 157, 169, 188, 195, 213, 214
    arts festival organized by, 133, 143–44
    founding of, 7, 133, 135
    goals of, 135
    loft tours organized by, 144–45, 146, 216–17
SoHo Artists Festival, 133, 143–44, 148, 149, 157, 252n59
SoHo Cast-Iron Historic District, 7
SoHo Dance Festival, 126
SoHo Development Corporation, 203
SoHo Ensemble, 128
SoHo Performing Arts Association, 126
SoHo Statement, 129–30
SoHo 20, 89, 120, 121–22, 123
SoHo Weekly News, 122, 126, 127, 128, 137, 165, 166–67, 168, 173, 175, 179, 180, 181, 185, 188, 193, 194, 204, 205, 206, 214, 215, 218, 222, 232, 234
Solomon, Louis H., 34
Sonnabend, Ileana, 42, 114, 126
South Houston Industrial Area
    sale prices for buildings in, 186
    study on, 37, 38, 39, 186
Soviet Union, 94, 122
Sports Palace, proposed construction of, 149, 150
Spring Street, 17, 52, 68, 117, 137, 231, 256n37, 268n6
    galleries on, 89, 90, 128

retail on, 162, 166, 232
    sale prices for buildings on, 187, 203
    squatting, 167, 244n12
Standard Oil, 74
Staten Island, 223
Stella, Frank, 112, 115
Stern, Henry, 195
Stockholm, 235
Stratton, Jim, 59, 137, 180, 193–94
Streep, Meryl, 226
Student Mobilization Committee to End the War in Vietnam, 108
suburbs, 4, 24, 52, 72, 74
    relocation to/suburbanization, 5, 7, 75, 96, 105, 136, 160, 236
    SoHo lofts as rivaling homes in, and appealing to those from, the, 65, 66–67, 148, 156, 175, 237
    suburbanites' visits to SoHo, 130, 144, 167, 168
Sugarman, George, 43
Sutton, Percy E., 84, 195, 261n9
Sydney, 113, 235

Tanager Gallery, 111
Tarr, Bill, 66–67, 148
Tarr, Yvonne, 66–67, 148
Taxi Driver, 184
tenants
    artist, 6, 8, 9, 41, 48, 49, 50, 59, 95–96, 99–100, 101, 112, 135, 169, 182, 183, 198–99, 201, 202, 203, 204, 206, 209, 211, 224, 226, 227–28, 229
    industrial, 45, 49, 50, 59, 104, 182, 183, 189, 194–95, 197, 198, 199, 200, 204, 206, 207, 215, 216, 217, 222, 224, 226, 227
    residential, 80, 182, 183, 193, 195, 199, 200, 201, 221, 228
Ten Downtown, 142–43
Tenth Street, 47, 111, 112, 268n6
Thirty-fourth Street, 22, 78, 189, 190
Thompson Street, 89, 168, 232, 268n6
Thornhill, Ana, 169–70
3 Mercer Store, 165–66
Throgs Neck Bridge, 77
Tierney, Larry, 149
Tiffany & Co., 18, 19
Title I, 30, 31, 248n49
Toll, Barbara, 51, 53, 54, 68, 69, 141
Torregrosa, Manuel, 12
Town and Country, 173
Triborough Bridge, 77
Triborough Bridge and Tunnel Authority, 34, 78, 82, 86–87
Trump, Donald, 231

Turpan, Greg, 50–51, 53, 57, 60, 61, 67, 68–69, 176
  Turpan Sanders and, 178–79, 181
Twelfth Street, 43, 269n12
Twenty-ninth Street, 42, 43
Twenty-seventh Street, 191
Twombly, Cy, 115

Udell, Nathan, 201
undergarment industry, 26
Union Square, 17
United Federation of Teachers, 136
United Hatters, Cap, and Millinery Workers' Union, 15, 37, 218, 223
United States, 5, 10, 42, 46–47, 52, 72, 94, 118, 151, 176, 235, 265n29
  gentrification in, 4, 228
  Midwest, 7, 160
  Northeast, 7
  Sun Belt, 7
  women artists in, 120–21
United States Steel Corporation, 253n5
urban crisis, 4, 5, 7, 93, 134, 184, 236, 237, 238
urban development, 16, 30, 34, 38, 75
  artist-led, 3, 7, 11, 91, 94, 104–6, 238
  loft conversions as, 15, 132, 133, 134, 196, 198, 207, 227–28
  SoHo as model for, 1, 3, 11, 234, 238
urban renewal
  opponents of/resistance to, 15–16, 39–40, 80, 83, 90, 91, 231
  slum clearance, 5, 7, 8, 11, 30, 31, 34, 35, 90–91, 93, 104, 154, 236
  SoHo and, 3, 4, 7–8, 13–14, 15, 16–17, 32, 35, 37, 39–40, 44, 70, 72–73, 81, 85, 90–91, 93–94, 104, 105, 137, 156, 189, 207, 236–37
  Washington Square Southeast and, 31, 34, 40, 44

Van Buren, Richard, 124
video art, 5, 122, 131
Vietnam War, 43, 108
Villager, 130, 165
Village Voice, 43, 133, 150, 178, 200, 202, 203–4, 215
Viola Farber Dance Company, 215
Volunteer Lawyers for the Arts, 102–3, 139, 140–41

Wagner, Robert, 15, 40
  loft policy and, 6, 98, 99, 100
  Lower Manhattan Expressway and, 79–80, 81, 82
Wagner, Robert F., Jr., 216–17, 218
Walker Art Center, 118, 264n24
Walker Street, 90, 201, 267n50
  rent strike at no. 55, 182, 200–201
Wall Street, 82, 91, 150, 154, 231, 237
Wall Street Journal, 74, 253n5
Ward Nasse Gallery, 89, 120
warehousing, 6, 13, 19, 22, 24, 26, 234, 236
Warhol, Andy, 47, 115, 169, 226
Warren Street, 192
Washington Square Neighbors, 34
Washington Square Park, 15, 30, 34, 262n38
Washington Square Southeast, 15, 32–35, 39, 40, 44, 66
Washington Square Village, 30, 34, 35
Wastelands of New York City, The (City Club of New York), 35–37, 36
Weber, John, 89, 114, 130
Weigand, Ingrid, 188
Weigand, Robert, 62, 62, 137, 140, 141–42, 146, 148
Weisbrod, Carl, 226–27, 231
Weiss & Klau Company, 12–14, 22–30, 116, 247n34
Weissman, Ira, 216, 217
West, Ehrlich, 199–200
West, Scarlet, 199–200
West Broadway, 25, 26, 29, 31, 35, 51, 67, 68, 139, 150, 154, 162, 204
  clash at no. 260, 212–13
  effort to rename, 149–50, 262n38
  galleries at no. 420, 8, 57, 88, 89, 114, 115, 130, 149, 233
  galleries on, 8, 57, 88, 89, 90, 112, 113, 114, 115, 128, 130, 146, 149, 233
  lofts at no. 451, 61, 64, 135–36, 137, 145, 146
  lofts on or near, 42, 43, 49, 51, 56, 57, 61, 64, 127, 135–36, 137, 145, 146, 169, 175, 231
  restaurants and retail on, 162, 166, 168
  sale prices for buildings on, 187, 203
Westbroadway/Alternative Space, 90, 120
Westchester, 52, 130, 148, 225, 231
Westerfield, Ron, 64, 102
West Side Highway, 78
white flight, 5, 75, 105, 136
White Street, 90, 267n50
Whitney Museum of American Art, 53, 84, 111, 117, 118, 138, 265n30
Wiener, Sam, 64, 145
Williams, Susan Lewis, 52
Williamsburg Bridge, 78
Wilmarth, Chris, 117, 118
Wilson, Ann, 128
Wilson, Robert, 128
Wines, James, 49
With Heritage so Rich (National Trust for Historic Preservation), 151
women, 22, 26, 27, 129, 146, 166
  artists, 89, 120–21

INDEX

Woodward Foundation, 119
Wooster Street, 153, 166, 206, 265n35
   galleries on, 21, 89, 90, 233
   lofts at no. 80, 23, 43, 52, 56, 58, 137
   lofts on, 23, 43, 52, 56, 58, 137
   sale prices for buildings on, 187, 188–89, 203
World House Gallery, 107
World's Columbian Exposition, 19
World's Fair (1964), 52, 81
World War I, 13, 22
World War II, 1, 5, 13, 14, 24, 42, 46, 47, 54, 110
Wright, Frank Lloyd, 47

Yagoda, David, 206
Yang, Hanford, 155

Yehuda, Yehuda Ben, 57
Young, LaMonte, 55
Yu, James, 204

zoning, 46, 92, 95, 103, 135, 150, 190, 192, 194, 196–97, 202, 204, 206, 212, 214, 215, 217–19, 222–26, 231, 232
   artists' efforts to change legislation on, 7, 93–94, 101–2, 135, 138, 139–40, 141–42, 143, 150, 195, 196, 221
Zukin, Sharon, *Loft Living*, 4, 51, 122–23, 148, 185, 197

HISTORICAL STUDIES OF URBAN AMERICA

Edited by Lilia Fernández, Timothy J. Gilfoyle, and Amanda I. Seligman
James R. Grossman, Editor Emeritus

Series titles, continued from front matter

Aaron Shkuda, *The Lofts of SoHo: Gentrification, Art, and Industry in New York, 1950–1980*

Mark Krasovic, *The Newark Frontier: Community Action in the Great Society*

Ansley T. Erickson, *Making the Unequal Metropolis: School Desegregation and Its Limits*

Andrew L. Slap and Frank Towers, eds., *Confederate Cities: The Urban South during the Civil War Era*

Evan Friss, *The Cycling City: Bicycles and Urban America in the 1890s*

Ocean Howell, *Making the Mission: Planning and Ethnicity in San Francisco*

Benjamin Looker, *A Nation of Neighborhoods: Imagining Cities, Communities, and Democracy in Postwar America*

Nancy H. Kwak, *A World of Homeowners: American Power and the Politics of Housing Aid*

Andrew R. Highsmith, *Demolition Means Progress: Flint, Michigan, and the Fate of the American Metropolis*

Lila Corwin Berman, *Metropolitan Jews: Politics, Race, and Religion in Postwar Detroit*

Gillian O'Brien, *Blood Runs Green: The Murder that Transfixed Gilded Age Chicago*

Marta Gutman, *A City for Children: Women, Architecture, and the Charitable Landscapes of Oakland, 1850–1950*

N. D. B. Connolly. *A World More Concrete: Real Estate and the Remaking of Jim Crow South Florida*

Cindy R. Lobel, *Urban Appetites: Food and Culture in Nineteenth-Century New York*

Jeffrey Helgeson, *Crucibles of Black Empowerment: Chicago's Neighborhood Politics from the New Deal to Harold Washington*

Christopher Lowen Agee, *The Streets of San Francisco: Policing and the Creation of a Cosmopolitan Liberal Politics, 1950–1972*

Camilo José Vergara, *Harlem: The Unmaking of a Ghetto*

Sarah Jo Peterson, *Planning the Home Front: Building Bombers and Communities at Willow Run*

Lawrence J. Vale, *Purging the Poorest: Public Housing and the Design Politics of Twice-Cleared Communities*

Lilia Fernández, *Brown in the Windy City: Mexicans and Puerto Ricans in Postwar Chicago*

A complete list of series titles is available on the University of Chicago Press website.

www.ingramcontent.com/pod-product-compliance
Lightning Source LLC
Chambersburg PA
CBHW022039290426
44109CB00014B/907